JOHN BENSON'S

ROTISSERIE®

BASEBALL

A to Z

**DIAMOND
LIBRARY**

Executive Editor: Bill Gray—Associate Editors: Alan Boodman and Marc Bowman

Library of Congress Cataloging-in-Publication Data
Benson, John
Rotisserie Baseball A to Z.
1. Baseball -- United States -- History
2. Baseball -- United States -- Records
I. Title

ISBN 1-880876-35-3

For information address: Diamond Library.

Published by Diamond Library, a division of Diamond Analytics Corporation, 28 Sugarloaf Drive, Wilton, Connecticut, 06897. Telephone 203-834-0812.

PRINTED IN THE UNITED STATES OF AMERICA

Cover design by Option One with graphics by Rob Pawlak and Joe Palys

Rotisserie League Baseball is a registered trademark of The Rotisserie League Baseball Association, Inc. For information contact R.L.B.A. at 370 Seventh Avenue, Suite 312, New York, New York 10001. Telephone 212-629-4036.

Statistics are provided by STATS, Inc., 7366 N. Lincoln Avenue., Lincolnwood, Illinois 60646-1708. Telephone 708-676-3322.

This book is dedicated to the memory of my father,

Purnell Handy Benson

1913-1992

He put a baseball in my hands when I was just old enough to walk.

He played catch with me.

He showed me how to oil a glove, and how to keep my eye on the ball.

Contributing Writers

Alan Boodman
Marc Bowman
Lary Bump
Pete DeCoursey
Jon Dunkle
Greg Gajus
Bill Gilbert
Peter Graves
Bill Gray
Bob Hazlewood
Dic Humphrey
Mark Leitner
Fred Matos
Bart Pachino
Peter Pascarelli
John Perrotto
Adam Stein
Rob Wood

Acknowledgments

This book is a team effort reflecting many hours, days, and weeks of effort from a number of bright, competent, and dedicated people. The writers on the preceding page are the core of this team. Without them, there wouldn't be any book. One of the difficult aspects of producing a volume like this one, is that I have so little time to say "thank you" and to offer well-earned words of praise while the work is being assembled. The writers who called me during October and November know only too well that I was always pressed for time. So to these people especially, I now say: Thanks, guys. I really appreciate you, and value your work beyond anything I could write here.

The production crew that transformed these words and numbers into this useful volume, that you hold in your hands, were all essential members of the team: Carmelita Benson, James Benson, Jo Ann Dugdale, Steve Lunsford, and Joe Palys. My wife Carmelita deserves more profound thanks than I could possibly verbalize, because she not only carried a huge burden of the work but also tolerated my presence in our home during all the crises and pressures that accompanied this project.

Thanks to John Dewan for his special attention on the statistics. And last but not least, I want to highlight the efforts of Bill Gray for keeping me motivated and for helping at every stage from beginning to end, and to Alan Boodman and Marc Bowman for their superior editorial skills.

John

INTRODUCTION

The purpose of this book is to provide a single reference source where baseball fans can quickly find a capsule profile and 1993 outlook for just about every baseball player.

The book is intended especially for competitors in Rotisserie leagues and related contests to pick the best players at the beginning of the baseball season. These readers should find the book useful year-round, as a desktop guide to answer the inevitable question, "Who is this guy?"

In writing an introduction, especially for a new book, it is difficult to draw the line between what is common knowledge, and what needs to be explained. Considering that some readers may need more background information than others, I am dividing the introduction into three parts.

1. For people who never heard of Rotisserie League Baseball:

A Rotisserie league is an organized competition to see who can pick the best players at the beginning of each baseball season. The winner is decided by adding up actual player statistics after the season ends. There are various forms of these "pick-your-player" contests which have soared in popularity since the mid 1980's. Some are true Rotisserie. Some are not. They are all captivating fun for the people who get into them.

The ingenious rules and scorekeeping methods, codified and published by Glen Waggoner, Robert Sklar, Dan Okrent, and their colleagues in the original Rotisserie League, elevated the boyhood argument, "I can pick a better team than you can," to a level that now surpasses chess, bridge, poker, and horse racing, for excitement, strategic elegance and tactical complexity -- and fun. The emergence of the personal computer as a home appliance came at exactly the right time to feed the appetite for information that naturally resulted from these games.

The new games require new literature. There are two basic categories of writing for Rotisserie competitors: permanent advice on how to play the game, and annual analyses of the baseball player population. Some books, including Waggoner's official Rotisserie League Baseball, include both comprehensive information on how to play the game, and annual updates on players and their values.

2. For people who haven't seen my work before:

I have written, and will continue to write, both types of books for Rotisserie competitors: annual previews and permanent advice. For five years now, I have been producing a book called The Rotisserie Baseball Annual, a serious and exhaustive effort reflecting hard work from many good writers and analysts. I won't be modest, except to say that it would be impossible for any one person to produce such a book. The same writers who contributed to this A to Z book also work on the Annual, and there are many other contributors. Critics are fairly unanimous that it's the most useful annual for people who take their Rotisserie competition seriously.

The meat of the Annual is a detailed discussion of every position on every major league baseball team -- who's playing first base for Los Angeles, for example; last year we discussed the strengths and weaknesses of the Dodgers' Eric Karros, Todd Benzinger, and Kal Daniels as candidates to fill the void created by the departure of Eddie Murray. The Rotisserie Baseball Annual is that kind of book -- team by team, position by position, this player versus that player at each position, with predictions for the coming year. The annual also includes forecast statistics for every player -- the same as presented here, except that the Annual comes out later and has somewhat more up-to-date information.

The first few editions of the Annual also included lots of permanent advice, too. We never tried to explain Rotisserie to beginners; that book isn't for beginners. But we did include a great deal of writing on strategy and tactics. The permanent material grew to the point where it deserved to become a separate book, and it did. Two books, in fact.

In 1993 there are two new volumes filled with permanent advice, strategy, and tactics: Rotisserie Baseball Playing for Fun, and Rotisserie Baseball Playing for Blood. As the titles imply, one is more concerned with the basics of the game, getting organized, and fundamental strategies, and the other is more concerned with clobbering your opponents. There is a shamelessly commercial presentation of all these titles on page 256 of this book, so I won't go into them here. But if you have torn out page 256 already, the phone numbers you want are 800-292-6338 and 203-834-0812.

In addition to writing these books and contributing to several others, I write a couple of newspaper columns, publish my own Baseball Monthly, and do a number of other writing projects, but I am digressing. What you need to know about my work is that I spend 365 days a year studying baseball, talking about baseball with both insiders and outsiders, and writing about it.

My professional passion is predicting the full-season performance of individual baseball players. I use every possible source of information to get little insights. I talk to players, coaches, managers, GM's and other front office people, sabermetricians, and innumerable fans and amateur analysts. This book is the latest result of that ongoing work.

3. About this "A to Z" book:

THE PLAYERS

The players in this book have been selected because they should, or could, be considered for Rotisserie leagues or similar player selection contests. Obviously, we go beyond the basic Opening Day rosters. We include veteran minor leaguers who might be called up as injury replacements in midseason, and long-term prospects who are growing toward major league careers. We include some very young players for leagues that have farm systems, reserve rosters, and Ultra rules.

The inclusion of a player is not a recommendation. Many players are included just to give a warning label. Very often in midseason, a minor leaguer comes up and suddenly appears in a box score. Without a good reference library, it is too easy to make bad choices based on brief appearances. Midseason replacement selections can be especially difficult. You have to make hasty decisions to grab good players before other people do. You may be looking at a catcher who just hit two home runs in a week, or a shortstop who just got three hits and stole a couple of bases. People call me and ask, "Who is this guy? Shall I grab him quick, before somebody else does?" Now you can look him up and see quickly if he's a prospect or a suspect.

Among the hitter population, just about every conceivable player is included. It would amaze me if more than two or three players reach the major leagues in 1993 without first appearing in this book -- and those few would all be marginal players you don't want, anyway. Even for 1994-1995, just about every potential major league regular is in here.

In the case of pitchers, we have been just a bit less exhaustive when going into the low minors. Don't get me wrong -- the minor league pitcher listings are extensive. Everyone I like is in here, and a hundred or so minor leaguers whom I don't like. After the expansion draft, it was my intention to list every player picked by the Rockies and Marlins; but soon I found myself looking at names of A-ball pitchers who weren't nearly as good as many A-ball pitchers who weren't selected. Once you get below Class AA pitching, everyone's future is just a speculation, anyway. If I had tried to include every pitcher with a chance at the majors this year, the book would have taken forever to complete. And second, we would be giving you too many names not worth knowing. For your minor league selections, I strongly recommend -- and practice for my own purposes -- a heavy emphasis on hitters, not pitchers, anyway. Think about Todd Van Poppel and Roger Salkeld if you want to know why.

Finally, you will find a few players -- just a few -- who have retired already. I think somebody during the spring of 1993 might be curious what happened to Gary Carter or Brian Downing, for example, so I have listed them along with a few similar cases so that such questions can be answered.

1992 STATISTICS

This isn't a "stat" book. We have deliberately limited the presentation of 1992 statistics, to include only those records that might be relevant when considering a player for 1993. If a 32-year-old catcher hit .198 with one home run in the Pacific Coast League last year, it is sufficient just to say in his profile, "He can't hit."

Limiting the book to relevant, helpful statistics gives an appearance that may seem odd, at first. We are all accustomed to seeing books with exactly the same format and presentation for every player. My simple objective is to give a capsule summary for every player. When words alone will suffice, I leave out the numbers. Similarly, many stat lines based on just a few games have been omitted because they are meaningless.

For people who want statistics, I recommend you go directly to the source: STATS, Inc. They publish three outstanding statistical volumes every year; and the books come out so early, that you can begin enjoying them even before the memory of the World Series begins to fade, certainly long before the first snowfall here in New England. STATS offers other books including the HarperCollins Scouting Report (for which I cover the Mets and Yankees). And STATS provides numerous other useful products and services, including an on-line stat service, fax reports tailored for your individual Rotisserie/fantasy roster, and Bill James Fantasy Baseball, just for example. STATS has a close association with Bill James and gives you direct access to his high quality work. I urge you to call STATS at 708-676-3322 and ask for information. You will be glad you did. STATS has become a vital part of the baseball scene in America; they have scouts and scorers covering every game. Simply stated, they provide more information and better information faster than any other baseball data service. Take advantage.

1993 PROJECTIONS

On the subject of projections, every reader will want an introduction. There are three types of 1993 projections in this book: Base Case, High Range, and Low Range. The idea is to show a range of possibilities that are all conceivable within a fairly normal season. All three lines are based on actual points of reference within each players's career, or points of reference from other players with similar careers. These points of reference vary, depending on the player's age, background, and experience. For all players, however, the probabilities are consistent. There is an implicit estimate that the player's actual performance has a 16% chance of being lower than the Low Range, and a 16% chance of being higher than the High Range, for that statistic. Thus my confidence in the numbers is this: I am 68% confident that a player's performance in each category will be somewhere between within the High and Low Range.

The genesis of this high/low presentation is illuminating. Often people have called and asked me about a specific forecast statistic. For example: "You have a .277 batting average forecast for Joe Bimbleman; do you feel very confident that he is safe to reach .277?" The answer, if you think about it, has to be: "No. The .277 average is a 50/50 proposition, precisely. I believe that player has a 50% chance of reaching .27700 and a 50% chance of falling short. The .277 is my median expectation, exactly at the 50/50 point. I am completely neutral in my opinion as to whether the player will meet that expectation or fall short. If you ask me if he is likely to hit .278, I will say no. If you ask me if he will probably exceed .276, I will say yes. But at .277, it's 50/50."

The follow-up question, quite naturally, is something like: "Well then, what batting average do you feel confident he will achieve?" And I will answer something like: "I have 70% confidence that Bimbleman will achieve at least a .260 average. I am 90% confident he will achieve at least .250." The farther away from the Base Case we go, the more certain I can be about a player's chance to perform above or below a stated level. The implicit statements are these: I am 84% confident that the player will achieve or surpass the Low Range, and 84% confident that he will fall short of the High Range.

To visualize the thinking behind the forecasts, you need to visualize a bell curve distribution. If you took statistics in college, or if you simply have no interest, you can skip the next four paragraphs.

A player's likely performance in the coming season is not just one number. There is a range of possibilities. To visualize a range of numbers, ask yourself the question: "If this player got six separate chances to play through the 1993 season, what kinds of outcomes would occur in those ten seasons? If you look at the player and see that, over the past six years, his home run output per year has been 26, 21, 25, 29, 27, 25, and that he has an established role with regular playing time, and that he is healthy and not too old, then your answer would be something like: "This player is likely to hit about 25 home runs. In a strong year, he could hit 28 or 30, and in a soft year he might hit only 20 or 22. It would be an unusual outcome if he hit 19 or fewer home runs, and it would be an unusual year if he hit more than 30.

Or you might say: "The Base Case prediction for this player is 25 home runs for 1993. There is an 84% probability that he will produce at least 21 home runs, and an 84% probability that he will not exceed 29 home runs. The Low Range is 21, and the High Range is 29." This book presents thinking along those lines. It tells you not only the most likely "Base Case" for each stat, but also it tells you the ranges about which I feel confident.

The Low Range projection is not a "worst case scenario." The worst case for every player is that he gets injured in spring training and misses the entire season. "Low Range" actually assumes the player stays fairly healthy, but has a bad year. If he played six years, the Low Range would be the worst performance among those six outcomes. Most players are not as consistent as the reliable home run hitter used in the above example. Just look at anyone with six years experience, category by category, and you will see what I mean.

These ranges enable you to see instantly which players I regard as "blue chip" or "known quantity" and which are "risky" or "high potential but unproven" type of players. The method is to treat each player as an individual. There is no set formula or recipe to take past performance and change it into a forecast for every player, although we do begin with a defined mathematical profile of each player. Statisticians will recognize the traces of standard deviations in our stated probabilities, but the end result is not a mathematical exercise. We don't use a formula for the Base Base, and we don't use a formula for the high and low range.

If Yankees pitching coach Mark Connor tells me that Russ Springer will get two or three saves in 1993, I will very likely write down two or three saves as the Springer Base Case for 1993, even though Springer has zero saves in his pro career. If I consider how Connor raved about Springer's fastball ("We had him up to 95 MPH") and Springer's ability to bounce back day after day ("He's got that kind of arm"), and if I reflect on the failures of John Habyan and Rich Monteleone during September 1992, then I can begin to see three saves pretty clearly, even when there is no track record.

With any new method, there is a certain amount of experimentation involved. No one has ever done high range and low range forecasts for baseball statistics, to the best of my knowledge. But we have to begin somewhere. Our 1989 Rotisserie Baseball Annual was the first book that had any kind of forecast stats. In each succeeding Annual, we got a little better at forecasting accurately (you learn from mistakes). But at the same time, most readers were thrilled with the accuracy of the 1989 forecasts. I hope readers will react as favorably to this first attempt at high range and low range; and yet I know it will be another learning experience. We may find that readers want a tighter range with a lower probability, or we may find that readers want a wider range with a higher probability.

In stating High Range and Low Range, each stat category is treated separately. If the High Range is 29 home runs, that means that once in six years, that player will reach 29 HR or more. If the High Range is a .300 batting average, that means once in six years, that player will hit .300 or higher. The High Range line, showing the 29 HR and the .300 BA, does not mean that player has one chance in six of hitting .300 AND producing 29 home runs this year. Achieving High Range in every category may be a hundred-to-one chance.

Stat categories have tradeoffs. Usually batting average and stolen bases will rise and fall together, as will home runs and runs batted in. But very often a player will hit more home runs while batting for a lower average, or steal more bases while driving in fewer runs. Tradeoffs are affected by external factors, such as where the player appears in the batting order. Leadoff is good for BA and SB. Cleanup is good for HR and RBI.

For this reason, we do not give dollar values for High Range and Low Range. We do not expect that High Range can be reached in every category. It makes more sense to read the stat columns vertically, within each category, than to read them horizontally and look for a dollar value at the far right.

SELECTION OF CASES

While we developed a Base Case, High Range, and Low Range for every player, we do not show all three cases for all players. The reason is simple: many of the cases are simply not useful. For hundreds of players, the Low Range is zero games in the major league. For hundreds more, the Base Case is zero at bats.

If you see that a player has no Low Range stat line for 1993, that means the Low Range is zero or worthless. If there is no Base Case shown, that also means the Base Case was zero or worthless.

Finally, there are no High Range and Low Range projections for pitchers. If I wrote down the numbers for which I feel 84% confident that a pitcher will be over or under, you wouldn't find them useful. Pitchers are highly unpredictable. "Blue chip" pitchers and "high risk" pitchers are described verbally in their profiles.

DOLLAR VALUES

All values are based on standard Rotisserie rules and categories. Runs and strikeouts are shown in the stat projections for information purposes only; they are not figured into the values.

1992 dollar values are simple allocations of total available money ($260 per team) to all available players -- 23 players per team, 12 teams per league for AL, 10 teams per league for NL -- based on 1992 statistics in the eight standard categories (BA, HR, RBI, SB, W, SV, ERA, and BPI). The total number of players valued at $1 or more is 276 players for the AL, and 230 players for the NL, plus a small number of players who are all worth $1, rounded.

1993 dollar values are similar allocations of available money ($260 per team) to the 1993 player population -- in this case 12 teams each for AL and 12 teams for NL, 23 players per team. The 1993 stats are the 1993 Base Case projections for the eight standard categories for each player.

Valuation methods are explained in exquisite detail in the book, Rotisserie Baseball Playing for Blood (see page 256). One basic point: money is allocated 65% for hitting and 35% for pitching, because that's how intelligent players actually allocate their money in real auctions.

Another basic point: dollar values are not recommended bids. Bidding is a whole separate subject. In a new league where all money and all players are available, you should bid consistently lower than calculated value (about 80% to 85% for star hitters and ace relievers, as low as 35% for unestablished starting pitchers and unknown scrubs). That's the concept of optimal bidding, and again, it's explained in Rotisserie Baseball Playing for Blood. For a league where many players are being retained at low salaries, creating an auction with lots of money and very few good players, you might need to bid 130% to 150% of calculated value to get your fair share of available talent. That's the concept of draft inflation, also explained in Rotisserie Baseball Playing for Blood.

A zero and a minus sign do not have the same meaning. Many players have negative dollar values. My method includes a threshold or minimum production level for a player to be worth $0. The "no performance" player (e.g. a hitter who gets zero at bats, or a pitcher who never pitches) would be worth about minus three dollars using this method. To avoid penalizing players who simply haven't yet reached the major leagues, I have just shown a simple minus sign (-) for all players with net negative values. Just keep in mind that a $0 value is better than a "-" value. A player valued at zero is very close to being valuable; a player with a minus - is not as close.

The presence or absence of a Base Case, Low Range, or High Range projection often depends on dollar values. When the player's Base Case is a negative value, we often do not bother to show a Low Range. And when the Base Case is a deep negative (or the Base Case for playing time is a complete zero) we often do not show the Base Case, either. Finally, if the player has less than a 16% chance of even appearing in the major leagues in 1993, we don't show any projection whatsoever. For those players where the only case shown is the High Range, be careful not to assume that's what the player will do, if he gets to the major leagues; it is a 16% probable outcome in each individual stat category.

AGES, POSITIONS, AND TEAMS

Players' ages are stated as of April 1, 1993. Most people will be reading this book most intensely in March 1993, so it tells you how old the player is/was at that time.

Positions tell where the player is expected to appear most in 1993. Various Rotisserie Leagues and other fantasy leagues have all kinds of rules about which players qualify at which positions. Position eligibilities are available every year, just before draft day, from the Rotisserie League Baseball Association, of which everyone should be a member. Call the number or write to the address on the copyright page. It is my wish that no one should use this A to Z book to argue that a player does or does not qualify at any particular position. If you catch someone doing that, show them this paragraph.

Teams are listed solely for the purpose of helping you know which player is which. Most teams are those with whom the player ended the 1992 season. Many players have been updated since then -- notably the Rockies and Marlins. But there were 150 free agents in November 1992, so much of the player population was simply unaffiliated when we wrote this book. Pay attention to the news for team changes and other updates.

THE IMPORTANCE OF CONTEXT

Rotisserie baseball is a game of context. Winners are people who can maintain the broadest perspective. Losers are people who rely extensively on one source, or who become over-fascinated with one particular fact or opinion. Victory depends on finding subtle patterns in disconnected bits of information. Those who can look at the same question from several different points of view, and develop a synergistic approach, will always do the best.

To succeed in any competition, especially an information competition, it is vital that you have many sources and work to stay current. I recommend *USA TODAY Baseball Weekly*, *The Sporting News*, and *Baseball America*. The daily *USA TODAY* is essential, but don't ignore your local daily, especially if it has a good sports department.

My work involves helping Rotisserie competitors with news analysis to keep their context current. The Benson Baseball Monthly is devoted to highlighting changes in the major league playing scene -- especially those changes involving marginal players who don't get much attention in the conventional media. We keep track of who's coming and who's going, who's hot and who's not. The same writers who work on this A to Z book and on the Rotisserie Annual also contribute to the Monthly. And we have lots of technical essays, too. Sometimes I think of calling it "The New England Journal of Rotisserie Science," but it's more than that. So let's just say "The Monthly." Look at page 256 if you're interested.

Finally, you can always call me and chat baseball. Review your roster, your retentions, your auction strategy, trades, rules, baseball news, injuries, anything that crosses your mind. I used to provide this service for free, but in 1990 I answered 20,000 baseball questions that took time away from supporting my family; so in 1991 I started charging $1.99 per minute, to separate the serious calls from the whimsical, and to make sure that enough of my time gets devoted to paying the mortgage.

The number is 1-900-773-7526 (that spells 900-PRE-PLAN). I am there from 1 PM to 11 PM Eastern time every day, year round, except that I often go to baseball games. Not to worry -- if I'm out you get a free message saying when I'll be back. Most of the time, it goes, "ring, ring ... Hello, this is John."

I hope you enjoy the book.

John Benson
December, 1992

ABARE, BILL - Blue Jays IF - BL - Age 24
Young infielders who produce double-digit home runs are not all future stars. Abare was released in 1992.

ABNER, SHAWN - White Sox OF- BR - Age 26
1992 was his best season since 1987. Now playing for his third organization in three years. Has a long swing that could be improved with further help from hitting coach Walt Hrniak. Defensively talented in center field. A former number one pick overall (1984). Could still become valuable.

	AB	R	HR	RBI	SB	BA	$
1992 Chicago AL	208	21	1	16	1	.279	1
1993 Low Range	150	12	0	10	0	.220	
1993 Base Case	283	31	3	26	2	.255	2
1993 High Range	407	49	5	43	4	.285	

AFENIR, TROY - Reds C- BR - Age 29
In four visits to the major leagues, Afenir has amassed only 79 career at bats. If he comes up again in 1993, it will be for insurance purposes, sitting on the bench. Base Case is zero at bats. Look elsewhere.

ALDRETE, MIKE - Indians OF/1B - BL - Age 32
Veteran Mike Aldrete has a number of other players ahead of him in the Indians outfield and first base depth charts. A six-season major leaguer, Aldrete hit .325 for the Giants in 1987. He was last up with Cleveland in 1991. Now he's a career minor leaguer. Base Case is zero at bats.

	AB	R	HR	RBI	SB	BA	$
1992 Col. Sp. AAA	463	69	8	84	1	.322	
1993 High Range	171	19	1	18	1	.257	

ALDRETE, RICH - Cardinals OF - BL - Age 28
Mike's younger brother. Aldrete peaked in 1988 when he was a California League all star. In 1992 he got 88 at bats at Arkansas and Louisville combined, and was unimpressive. He's at the end of the line.

ALEXANDER, MANNY - Orioles SS - BR - Age 22
Slick-fielding and with explosive speed (92 SB in two years). With the trades of Juan Bell and Ricky Gutierrez to NL teams, Baltimore has identified Alexander as Cal Ripken's heir. Alexander made an Offerman-like number of errors in 1992, but is still a superb defensive prospect. Just needs to get on base.

	AB	R	HR	RBI	SB	BA	$
1992 Hagerstown AA	499	70	2	41	43	.259	
1992 Rochester AAA	24	3	0	3	2	.292	
1992 Baltimore AL	5	1	0	0	0	.200	-
1993 Base Case	222	23	0	15	10	.230	1
1993 High Range	327	37	1	25	20	.259	

ALICEA, LUIS - Cardinals 2B - BB - Age 27
Just when it seemed like he had fallen off the face of the earth, he re-established himself as a semi-regular in 1992. He showed surprising power, hitting 11 triples for the Cardinals in only 265 at bats. Now that Alicea has finally learned how to hit a little, he's too old to be a prospect. His future is in utility work, and he won't help you much in any category.

	AB	H	HR	RBI	SB	BA	$
1992 Louisville AAA	71	11	0	6	0	.282	
1992 St. Louis NL	265	26	2	32	2	.245	2
1993 Low Range	172	15	1	15	1	.203	
1993 Base Case	273	26	2	27	3	.243	1
1993 High Range	392	41	3	45	5	.273	

ALLANSON, ANDY - Unsigned C - BR - Age 31
Got just 25 at bats in 1992. Hasn't been valuable since 1988.

ALLRED, BEAU - Indians OF - BL - Age 27
The Indians keep their old players in Colorado Springs and their young players in Cleveland. Allred isn't likely to make it back. If he does, he will hit about .240 with one home run per 40 at bats.

ALOMAR, ROBERTO - Blue Jays 2B - BB - Age 25
Before Alomar, the last guy to get 50 steals and 40 doubles in a season was Lou Brock. And the last guy before Brock was Ty Cobb. And Alomar is getting better. Think Hall of Fame, and you get the idea.

	AB	R	HR	RBI	SB	BA	$
1992 Toronto AL	571	105	8	76	49	.310	39
1993 Low Range	506	85	9	55	29	.277	
1993 Base Case	537	100	12	68	51	.305	42
1993 High Range	634	129	17	89	73	.332	

ALOMAR, SANDY - Indians C - BR - Age 26
1992 was another injury plagued year for Sandy Alomar. Once good enough to be regarded as the key player traded for Joe Carter, now he's just Roberto's older brother. Catchers who get hurt a lot early in their careers are not safe picks, unless their name is Fisk.

	AB	R	HR	RBI	SB	BA	$
1992 Cleveland AL	299	22	2	26	3	.251	2
1993 Low Range	214	15	2	15	1	.216	
1993 Base Case	359	27	4	29	4	.257	5
1993 High Range	429	35	6	40	6	.287	

ALOU, MOISES - Expos OF - BR - Age 26
After missing all of 1991 because of shoulder surgery, Alou came back to establish himself as a potential star in his rookie season of 1992. Being the son of the manager carried no weight, though, in the stretch drive. His father, Felipe, decided to go with Ivan Calderon in left field once he recovered from shoulder surgery of his own. Alou should play regularly from now on, maybe even at first base. More likely, Alou will play LF while Calderon sits or plays 1B.

	AB	R	HR	RBI	SB	BA	$
1992 Montreal NL	341	53	9	56	16	.282	16
1993 Low Range	252	35	6	34	7	.238	
1993 Base Case	423	59	11	62	20	.269	19
1993 High Range	517	82	16	86	31	.300	

AMARAL, RICH - Mariners SS/2B - BR - Age 31
Stole 54 bases in 1988 and 57 in 1989, then fell to 20 in 1990. Amaral is a former Cubs farmhand who became a six-year minor league free agent after three full seasons of double-A ball. He was recalled from Calgary when Omar Vizquel went on the DL and was brought back when rosters expanded in September. His on base percentage exceeded .400 each year from 1989 to 1991 and he can steal bases. Amaral won the PCL batting crown in 1991, with a .346 BA. If he were five years younger, he would be a great prospect. In a Rotisserie league he is still one of those little assets you need to know: an MI who won't hurt your BA.

	AB	R	HR	RBI	SB	BA	$
1992 Calgary AAA	403	79	0	21	53	.318	
1992 Seattle AL	100	9	1	7	4	.240	0
1993 Low Range	55	5	0	3	1	.207	
1993 Base Case	153	16	1	11	6	.248	1
1993 High Range	290	34	2	23	17	.277	

AMARO, RUBEN - Phillies OF - BB - Age 28

Amaro, as most everyone knows, got his opportunity about 10 minutes into the 1992 season when Lenny Dykstra got his wrist fractured. Amaro hit well for about two weeks and spent most of the year battling it out with the Mendoza line. Another elderly prospect with good PCL credentials (led the league in runs and doubles in 1991) Amaro can get playing time if somebody gets hurt. On a team with four healthy outfielders, he'll sit on the bench and wait. Amaro is a good $1 speculation for speed, but after 1992 he looks like a regular player on paper, and will be overvalued in most leagues.

	AB	R	HR	RBI	SB	BA	$
1992 Philadelphia NL	374	43	7	34	11	.219	5
1992 Scranton AAA	68	8	1	10	2	.294	
1993 Low Range	175	18	2	14	3	.207	
1993 Base Case	277	31	5	25	7	.227	1
1993 High Range	328	41	7	34	12	.256	

ANDERSON, BRADY - Orioles OF - BL - Age 29

Anderson's 1992 year was a surprise to everyone. He's had hot streaks before but he always fizzled. In 1992 he stayed hot long enough to have a good year, although he hit just .246 after July and .223 in September/October. Smart owners have already traded him away. He has reached a new, higher level, but that plateau is far below the stats we saw in 1992.

	AB	R	HR	RBI	SB	BA	$
1992 Baltimore AL	623	100	21	80	53	.271	39
1993 Low Range	329	44	7	28	14	.209	
1993 Base Case	578	86	15	57	42	.249	24
1993 High Range	620	101	19	69	55	.279	

ANDERSON, DAVE - Dodgers IF - BR - Age 32

One non-statistical indication that a player is at the end of his career: he returns to the team that had him when he was young and productive. Even if Anderson gets 200 at bats (highly unlikely) he won't be worth a roster spot, certainly not on draft day.

ANDERSON, GARRET - Angels OF - BL - Age 20

Anderson was promoted from A to AA at the All-Star break. Anderson was placed on the Angels' Arizona "Fall League" team, indicating their interest in his future. He will reach the majors in 1994.

	AB	R	HR	RBI	SB	BA	$
1992 Palm Springs A	322	46	1	62	1	.323	
1992 Midland AA	146	16	2	19	2	.274	

ANDREWS, SHANE - Expos 3B - BR - Age 21

A first round pick in 1990, Andrews is a high-power, high-strikeout type of hitter. He's been in the South Atlantic League (one of the weaker "A" leagues) for two years. While he whiffs frequently and fails to hit for average, Montreal executives keep talking about the huge potential. Why don't minor league teams have hitting instructors, anyway? Andrews led his league in HR despite the problems. Two years away.

	AB	R	HR	RBI	SB	BA	$
1992 Albany A	453	76	25	87	8	.230	

ANTHONY, ERIC - Astros OF - BL - Age 25

Finally had the kind of season the Astros were hoping for after he led three different minor leagues in home runs in his first three full seasons. The big improvement came from cutting down on his strikeouts, with a smarter "two strike" approach at the plate. GM Bill Wood concluded Anthony had a "thinking" problem and sent Anthony back down for the third time in 1991. A .336 BA for Tucson showed that Anthony had finally addressed the mental aspects. Many people don't realize how young he is, because 1993 will be the fifth year he appears for Houston. Still can't hit lefties; might platoon some in 1993.

	AB	R	HR	RBI	SB	BA	$
1992 Houston NL	440	45	19	80	5	.239	15
1993 Low Range	311	33	12	45	2	.206	
1993 Base Case	506	59	24	85	6	.247	16
1993 High Range	552	71	31	102	9	.277	

ARIAS, ALEX - Marlins SS - BR - Age 25

A good fielder who has twice led his league in just about every defensive category. For Florida he will be just a backup and defensive replacement, behind Walt Weiss.

	AB	R	HR	RBI	SB	BA	$
1992 Iowa AAA	409	52	5	40	14	.279	
1992 Chicago NL	99	14	0	7	0	.293	-
1993 Base Case	135	18	1	10	1	.245	-
1993 High Range	254	29	2	20	3	.286	

ASHLEY, BILLY - Dodgers OF - BR - Age 22

Ashley is a 6'7" raw power prospect who needs more time in the minors. His 24 HR led the Texas League. During his September call-up he demonstrated that he is not ready to play major league defense, often looking pathetic. Strikes out too much.

	AB	R	HR	RBI	SB	BA	$
1992 San Antonio AA	380	60	24	66	13	.279	
1992 Albuquerque AAA	95	11	2	10	1	.211	
1992 Los Angeles NL	95	6	2	6	0	.221	-
1993 Base Case	68	7	1	7	1	.233	-
1993 High Range	243	26	6	27	4	.262	

AUSMUS, BRAD - Rockies C - BR - Age 23

Regarded by many as the top defensive catcher in the expansion draft, Ausmus is a great all-around athlete and very smart. He's one of those rare catchers who steals bases. Hit .301 in A-ball but needs work on offense. If he reaches the majors in 1993, he will hit about .225 without power. Look for him in September.

AZOCAR, OSCAR - Padres OF/1B - BL - Age 28

Free swinger? Azocar got only two walks in his first 214 major league at bats. He was not the answer to San Diego's left field woes and got released. It's extremely doubtful that he will have a major league career at this point. 1993 Base Case: zero at bats.

	AB	R	HR	RBI	SB	BA	$
1992 San Diego NL	168	15	0	8	1	.190	-

BAAR, BRYAN - Dodgers C - BR - Age 24

In four minor league seasons in hitters' ballparks, he's produced a .244 career average with moderate power stats. Not a threat to Mike Piazza.

BACKMAN, WALLY - Phillies IF - BL - Age 33

For a guy who's generally available every winter, Wally has managed to land on his feet with unusual regularity. Backman won't be back in Philly, but might turn up with a club who could use a decent left-handed hitting middle infielder. Or he might not.

	AB	R	HR	RBI	SB	BA	$
1992 Philadelphia NL	48	6	0	6	1	.271	-
1993 Base Case	57	5	0	4	1	.240	-
1993 High Range	155	18	1	11	3	.280	

BAERGA, CARLOS - Indians 2B - BB - Age 24

Baerga is an emerging superstar ranked second only to Roberto Alomar among AL second basemen. He is an outstanding talent who strives for excellence. Baerga can improve on his already outstanding numbers, and contending for the batting title is genuinely possible. Peak ability? He hit .333 in July and .346 in September/October. When he's in a slump, he hits .280.

	AB	R	HR	RBI	SB	BA	$
1992 Cleveland AL	657	92	20	105	10	.312	33
1993 Low Range	501	64	16	78	5	.280	
1993 Base Case	601	85	24	108	9	.308	37
1993 High Range	652	101	31	124	14	.330	

BAEZ, KEVIN - Mets SS - BR - Age 26

Baez isn't the Mets' shortstop of the future. He has proven he can't hit any sort of pitching at any level. He has a gun for an arm, but won't end up in the majors in 1993 unless there's desperation somewhere.

	AB	R	HR	RBI	SB	BA	$
1992 Tidewater AAA	352	30	2	33	1	.236	
1992 New York NL	13	0	0	0	0	.154	-
1993 Base Case	50	10	0	7	1	.220	-
1993 High Range	218	16	1	17	1	.235	

BAGWELL, JEFF - Astros 1B - BR - Age 24

1991 NL Rookie-of-the-year finished strong to put up better power numbers than in 1991. Struggled through most of the season with batting average in the .240's before going back to old unorthodox, uppercut hitting style. Didn't miss a game in 1992. Could be a consistent .300-20-100 hitter for the next ten years if he cuts down on his strikeouts.

	AB	R	HR	RBI	SB	BA	$
1992 Houston NL	586	87	18	96	10	.273	24
1993 Low Range	500	68	14	76	5	.260	
1993 Base Case	570	85	19	100	9	.288	28
1993 High Range	591	97	24	110	13	.320	

BAILEY, MARK - Giants C - BB - Age 31

Hasn't had 65 at bats in a major league season since 1986. Look elsewhere.

BAINES, HAROLD - Athletics DH/OF - BL - Age 34

Career DH due to terrible knees, Baines slipped a notch last season. A line drive hitter, he no longer has the speed to convert gap hits into extra bases.

	AB	R	HR	RBI	SB	BA	$
1992 Oakland AL	478	58	16	76	1	.253	11
1993 Low Range	414	48	11	58	1	.214	
1993 Base Case	463	59	16	75	1	.255	12
1993 High Range	550	77	23	98	2	.285	

BALBONI, STEVE - Rangers DH - BR - Age 36

The leading HR hitter in the American Association in 1992, Balboni is a symbol of what AAA baseball is becoming: a mix of so-so prospects and former major leaguers. Balboni's arrangement with the Rangers allows for his immediate release in the event any major league team wishes to sign him. In two years, no team has even inquired about him.

	AB	R	HR	RBI	SB	BA	$
1992 Okla. City AAA	454	75	30	104	0	.251	

BARBARA, DON - Angels 1B - BL - Age 24

Barbara is a contender for the Angels first base job, a position that can be wide open if Lee Stevens continues to be overmatched at the plate, and no trades or free agents address the situation. Barbara can hit for a good average with a little power. More power will come as he matures. Base Case is zero at bats, but the upside is worth a look.

	AB	R	HR	RBI	SB	BA	$
1992 Edmonton AAA	396	70	4	63	9	.298	
1993 High Range	204	22	3	29	2	.272	

BARBERIE, BRET - Marlins 2B - BB - Age 25

The Expos moved Tim Wallach off third and installed Barberie there at the start of last season. When Felipe Alou replaced Tom Runnells as manager in late May, he gave third base back to Wallach. Barberie struggled and ended up back in the minors. He has good potential but must find a position.

	AB	R	HR	RBI	SB	BA	$
1992 Indianapolis AAA	43	4	3	8	0	.395	
1992 Montreal NL	285	26	1	24	9	.232	2
1993 Low Range	298	25	1	22	8	.225	
1993 Base Case	364	34	3	31	13	.254	3
1993 High Range	504	51	9	49	20	.284	

BARFIELD, JESSE - Yankees OF - BR - Age 33

Absolutely plagued by injuries. Fell in his home sauna and burned/broke his wrist last year. Still immensely talented. Rumored to be headed for Japan. Now if the body parts can just hang together ...

	AB	R	HR	RBI	SB	BA	$
1992 New York AL	95	8	2	7	1	.137	-
1993 Low Range	125	13	3	13	0	.181	
1993 Base Case	304	34	10	36	2	.229	2
1993 High Range	458	56	19	62	4	.250	

BARNES, SKEETER - Tigers OF/IF - BR - Age 36

Sparky Anderson keeps giving older minor leaguers a shot late in their career. Barnes was the beneficiary in 1992. Expect a decline, especially with Trammell back.

	AB	R	HR	RBI	SB	BA	$
1992 Detroit AL	165	27	3	25	3	.273	4
1993 Low Range	90	13	1	11	1	.232	
1993 Base Case	174	28	3	24	3	.264	3
1993 High Range	283	51	6	44	7	.295	

BARRETT, TOM - Red Sox 2B - BB - Age 32

Good speed and defense during a long minor league career. Surfaced briefly with Phillies in 1988-1989, and got three at bats with Boston in 1992, but he's not a factor for 1993.

BASS, KEVIN - Mets OF - BB - Age 33

Bass was acquired when the Mets ran out of outfielders after the All-Star break, and staged a minor comeback. The Mets released him anyway. Among the older, unsigned, oft-injured players, Bass is one of the best speculations for 1993, if he just gets a roster spot.

	AB	R	HR	RBI	SB	BA	$
1992 Two Teams	402	40	9	39	14	.269	14
1993 Low Range	220	20	4	17	3	.236	
1993 Base Case	403	41	9	36	9	.259	11
1993 High Range	507	56	14	51	16	.299	

BATISTE, KIM - Phillies SS - BR - Age 24

Batiste is in jeopardy of being the odd man out. Mariano Duncan will play every day somewhere, Juan Bell is a perennial prospect due to come around, and Joe Millette didn't commit 13 errors in a quarter of a season, as Batiste did when he was handed the Phillies' shortstop job. So-so work habits.

	AB	R	HR	RBI	SB	BA	$
1992 Philadelphia NL	136	9	1	10	0	.206	-
1992 Scranton AAA	269	30	2	29	6	.260	
1993 Base Case	75	7	0	5	1	.213	-
1993 High Range	311	23	3	26	5	.248	

BATTLE, HOWARD - Blue Jays 3B - BR - Age 21

Toronto's fourth-round pick in '90, Battle has a strong arm. Home run hitters are rare in the FSL.

	AB	R	HR	RBI	SB	BA	$
1992 Dunedin A	520	76	17	85	6	.254	

BEAMON, TREY - Pirates OF - BL - Age 18

One of the Pirates' two second-round picks in last June's draft, Beamon started off in the Gulf Coast Rookie League then moved up to short-season Class A New York-Penn League where he held his own against older players. He made that kind of progress despite signing late and suffering a hamstring injury.

	AB	R	HR	RBI	SB	BA	$
1992 Bradenton R	39	9	1	6	0	.308	
1992 Welland A	69	15	3	9	4	.290	

BECKER, RICH - Twins OF - BB - Age 21

Part of a cadre of Minnesota OF prospects making it easier to trade Midre Cummings. Becker, the Twins' third-round pick in '90, is a terrific defensive asset. Led California League outfielders with 17 assists. Good gap power, walks frequently but strikes out too much. With a hot first half he could get a callup in 1993, and will likely appear in September if he just makes good progress.

	AB	R	HR	RBI	SB	BA	$
1992 Visalia A	506	118	15	82	29	.316	

BELCHER, KEVIN - Rangers OF - BR - Age 25

In 1992, Belcher spent his third year at AA, and, although his power numbers improved, his overall performance did not. His status as a prospect is slipping and 1993 will be a crucial year for him. He will probably start at AAA. The departure of Kevin Reimer didn't hurt Belcher's chances.

	AB	R	HR	RBI	SB	BA	$
1992 Tulsa AA	381	55	18	60	6	.244	
1993 Base Case	129	16	5	18	1	.227	-
1993 High Range	251	33	11	40	4	.249	

BELL, DEREK - Blue Jays OF - BR - Age 24

One of my favorite picks to soar in value in 1993. Bell hit .346 for AAA Syracuse in 1991. If he had spent the 1992 season in the minors, instead of sitting with an injured wrist in Toronto, he would be the odds-on most-hyped rookie since Gregg Jefferies, and people would be bidding $30 for him. Because he had a miserable 1992 campaign, you can get him for much less.

	AB	R	HR	RBI	SB	BA	$
1992 Toronto AL	161	23	2	15	7	.242	2
1993 Low Range	217	29	3	23	6	.238	
1993 Base Case	375	55	8	46	17	.270	15
1993 High Range	526	85	13	73	33	.301	

BELL, GEORGE - White Sox DH/OF - BR - Age 33

Bell has averaged over 25 home runs and 100 RBI the last nine years, including a peak of 47 HR, but in the expansion draft, no one wanted him. Known for his bad attitude and dislike for DH duty. Led the league in grounding into double plays. Despite the mediocre BA in 1992, he is a career .282 hitter and should help you in that category.

	AB	R	HR	RBI	SB	BA	$
1992 Chicago AL	627	74	25	112	5	.255	20
1993 Low Range	495	51	17	74	2	.229	
1993 Base Case	585	67	25	101	3	.260	21
1993 High Range	620	78	31	114	5	.290	

BELL, JAY - Pirates SS - BR - Age 27

Though his home run total dropped almost in half, he continued to show he is one of the game's finest young shortstops. He has good gap power and is an outstanding hit-and-run man, and a master of the sacrifice bunt. And yet, late last season, there was discussion about dropping Bell down in the order where he can concentrate more on power. If that happens, it will help his Rotisserie value.

	AB	R	HR	RBI	SB	BA	$
1992 Pittsburgh NL	632	87	9	55	7	.264	13
1993 Low Range	512	65	7	44	3	.234	
1993 Base Case	582	81	9	58	6	.266	14
1993 High Range	624	95	12	71	9	.297	

BELL, JUAN - Phillies 2B/SS - BB - Age 25

George's little brother has the tools to become a premier defensive shortstop, and has shown flashes of offensive competence over the years (hit .300 at AAA Albuquerque in 1988), but he is rapidly making the transition from prospect to suspect. Only 25 years old, Bell is now in his third different organization. Though still showing little sign he will ever be a useful offensive player, he could emerge from spring training with the Phillies' shortstop job.

	AB	R	HR	RBI	SB	BA	$
1992 Philadelphia NL	147	12	1	8	5	.204	-
1992 Rochester AAA	138	21	2	14	2	.196	
1993 Low Range	151	15	1	10	3	.188	
1993 Base Case	256	28	2	20	7	.228	0
1993 High Range	427	49	5	39	16	.257	

BELL, MIKE - Braves 1B/OF - BL - Age 24

Fair hitter, but he's in an organization overloaded with outfielders and first basemen. Most likely his future role is helping other prospects develop, by playing alongside them in the minors. Hit .254 with nine home runs last year.

BELLE, ALBERT - Indians OF/DH - BR - Age 26

Slugger Albert Belle had an outstanding year in '92, establishing himself as one of the premier power hitters in the game. Belle needs to be "into" the game because he hits much better when he's playing the outfield than when he's the DH. If you see Reggie Jefferson or someone else taking over the DH chores, look for Belle to produce at the higher range of his abilities. Somebody is likely to hit 50 home runs in 1993, with the pitching ranks depleted by expansion; Belle is high on my list of candidates.

	AB	R	HR	RBI	SB	BA	$
1992 Cleveland AL	585	81	34	112	8	.260	26
1993 Low Range	486	62	22	82	4	.237	
1993 Base Case	576	81	33	113	8	.269	29
1993 High Range	600	93	45	125	12	.300	

BELLIARD, RAFAEL - Braves SS - BR - Age 31

Belliard returned to a much more normal .211 average in 1992. Expect more of the same as his playing time shrinks. Good defensive play by Jeff Blauser would leave Belliard with a very small role on the team.

	AB	R	HR	RBI	SB	BA	$
1992 Atlanta NL	285	20	0	14	0	.211	-
1993 Low Range	153	10	0	7	0	.179	
1993 Base Case	226	15	0	12	0	.208	-
1993 High Range	286	22	0	17	0	.242	

BELTRE, ESTEBAN - White Sox SS - BR - Age 26

Once considered the heir to Ozzie Guillen, Beltre long ago proved that he was never going to be a hitter. He was disappointing in his role as emergency replacement, and his slick defense is not a Rotisserie asset.

	AB	R	HR	RBI	SB	BA	$
1992 Chicago AL	110	21	1	10	1	.191	-
1992 Vancouver AAA	161	17	0	16	4	.267	
1993 Base Case	111	15	1	8	2	.205	-
1993 High Range	209	30	1	18	4	.243	

BENAVIDES, FREDDIE - Rockies SS - BR - Age 26

A second round draft pick in 1987, Benavides filled in at shortstop for Barry Larkin during his fairly frequent injuries and also appeared occasionally at second base in 1993. Good glove / weak bat, will play regularly for the Rockies.

	AB	R	HR	RBI	SB	BA	$
1992 Cincinnati NL	173	14	1	17	0	.231	-
1993 Low Range	220	16	1	19	1	.208	
1993 Base Case	355	26	2	25	3	.222	0
1993 High Range	501	40	3	40	4	.252	

BENITEZ, YAMIL - Expos OF - BR - Age 20

Benitez shows good power and speed with the ability to hit for average. He was regarded as a star in the Class A New York-Penn League. He struggled, though, when moved up to full-season Class A club.

	AB	R	HR	RBI	SB	BA	$
1992 Jamestown A	157	24	3	23	17	.274	
1992 Albany A	79	6	1	6	0	.165	

BENJAMIN, MIKE - Giants SS - BR - Age 27

Perennial back-up shortstop, Benjamin deserves his good field, no-hit reputation. Minor league career average of .241 over parts of six seasons. When Royce Clayton is ready, Benjamin's career is about done; amazingly, the Giants protected Benjamin just to make sure the transition to Clayton goes smoothly.

	AB	R	HR	RBI	SB	BA	$
1992 San Francisco NL	75	4	1	3	1	.173	-
1992 Phoenix AAA	108	15	0	17	3	.306	
1993 Base Case	69	7	1	4	1	.181	-
1993 High Range	228	25	3	15	5	.218	

BENZINGER, TODD - Dodgers 1B/OF - BB - Age 30

Benzinger was insurance for the Daniels-at-First experiment which failed in April. After Karros blossomed, Benzinger's role was reduced to pinch hitting and an occasional outfield start. His on-base percentage below .300 and only 15 walks in 293 at-bats are very weak for a non-slugger.

	AB	R	HR	RBI	SB	BA	$
1992 Los Angeles NL	293	24	4	31	2	.239	2
1993 Low Range	88	7	1	8	0	.199	
1993 Base Case	193	17	3	20	2	.240	0
1993 High Range	271	26	5	32	3	.269	

BERGMAN, DAVE - Tigers 1B/DH - BL - Age 39

Bergman was once a classic, safe $1 pick. No longer. Steer clear.

	AB	R	HR	RBI	SB	BA	$
1992 Detroit AL	181	17	1	10	1	.232	-
1993 Low Range	87	7	0	4	0	.192	
1993 Base Case	207	19	1	11	1	.230	-
1993 High Range	255	26	2	16	1	.261	

BERROA, GERONIMO - Reds OF - BR - Age 28

Signed as a minor league free agent, Berroa earned a return to the majors with a big year in AAA Nashville. Given an opportunity, Berroa would make an offensive contribution but is not likely to get that opportunity in Cincinnati. Classic proof that once a player is labeled as an ex-prospect, that label doesn't change.

	AB	R	HR	RBI	SB	BA	$
1992 Nashville AAA	461	73	22	88	8	.328	
1992 Cincinnati NL	15	2	0	0	0	.267	-
1993 Base Case	101	12	2	12	1	.273	1
1993 High Range	267	36	7	35	2	.304	

BERRY, SEAN - Expos 3B - BR - Age 27

Quietly, the Expos picked up this prospect last August, trading pitchers Chris Haney and Bill Sampen for him and minor-league pitcher Archie Corbin. Berry can hit and is versatile. He is the type of player who could get 400-450 at bats while playing a variety of positions. He played shortstop in Arizona Fall League. The departure of Bret Barberie helps Berry's chances for more playing time.

	AB	R	HR	RBI	SB	BA	$
1992 Omaha AAA	439	61	21	77	6	.287	
1992 Montreal NL	57	5	1	4	2	.333	1
1993 Low Range	122	14	2	13	1	.227	
1993 Base Case	399	46	8	52	8	.258	8
1993 High Range	505	60	12	63	10	.288	

BERRYHILL, DAMON - Braves C - BB - Age 29

May have found his niche as a backup catcher with power off the bench. An excellent pick for your second catcher.

	AB	R	HR	RBI	SB	BA	$
1992 Atlanta NL	307	21	10	43	0	.228	4
1993 Low Range	230	18	3	25	0	.219	
1993 Base Case	275	24	7	34	1	.233	1
1993 High Range	414	30	13	61	0	.259	

BICHETTE, DANTE - Rockies OF - BR - Age 29

A horrendous second-half slump eroded his average but still left him at a career-high level, probably a fluke. With Colorado he will easily get back up to double-digit home runs, but will run less than he did in 1992.

	AB	R	HR	RBI	SB	BA	$
1992 Milwaukee AL	387	37	5	41	18	.287	16
1993 Low Range	370	38	8	42	6	.214	
1993 Base Case	445	50	11	58	8	.254	16
1993 High Range	510	58	20	75	18	.280	

BIGGIO, CRAIG - Astros 2B - BR - Age 27

Made unprecedented conversion from all-star catcher to all-star second baseman. Played every game in 1992. If you can't get Sandberg or DeShields, Biggio is your man. His value is enhanced significantly if runs (96) and walks (94) count in your league. Biggio had a higher OBA in 1992 than Sandberg and DeShields. Steals were up from 19 in 1991 to 38 in 1992 with less wear and tear on his legs. Four solid years without any significant injuries make him a very safe bet.

	AB	R	HR	RBI	SB	BA	$
1992 Houston NL	613	96	6	39	38	.277	25
1993 Low Range	499	68	3	28	18	.248	
1993 Base Case	589	88	5	38	36	.275	23
1993 High Range	604	99	6	45	47	.306	

BILARDELLO, DANN - Padres C - BR - Age 33

Hasn't had over 80 at bats in a season since 1986. Career BA is .204. Look elsewhere.

BLANKENSHIP, LANCE - Athletics 2B/OF/3B - BR - Age 29

Just a 29 year-old utility man, Blankenship has never been able to earn a starting job. Last season was his most productive offensive year.

	AB	R	HR	RBI	SB	BA	$
1992 Oakland AL	349	59	3	34	21	.241	10
1993 Low Range	185	31	2	15	6	.195	
1993 Base Case	291	54	3	27	15	.236	6
1993 High Range	401	81	5	43	28	.265	

BLAUSER, JEFF - Braves IF - BR - Age 27

Blauser had an amazing second half to make up for a down first half. The result was a season almost identical to his 1989-1991 seasons, with slightly more power. Blauser was steadier in the field, which bodes well for increased playing time in 1993.

	AB	R	HR	RBI	SB	BA	$
1992 Atlanta NL	343	61	14	46	5	.262	12
1993 Low Range	334	58	10	36	3	.248	
1993 Base Case	456	87	16	57	6	.275	17
1993 High Range	546	99	23	77	10	.306	

BLOSSER, GREG - Red Sox OF - BL - Age 21

Boston's top pick in 1989. His power increase can be partly attributed to shorter dimensions at New Britain's Beehive Field; still it's a very tough park, and Blosser's performance made the record books. Should appear in Boston by September.

	AB	R	HR	RBI	SB	BA	$
1992 Pawtucket AAA	0	1	0	0	0	--	
1992 New Britain AA	434	59	22	71	0	.242	
1993 Base Case	150	15	4	19	1	.222	-
1993 High Range	308	33	10	44	2	.251	

BLOWERS, MIKE - Mariners IF - BR - Age 27

Formerly a serious prospect in the Expos organization, Blowers had his best chance with the Yankees when they really needed a third baseman, in late 1990, but he hit just .188 and was shaky in the field.

	AB	R	HR	RBI	SB	BA	$
1992 Seattle AL	73	7	1	2	0	.192	-
1993 Base Case	50	5	1	4	0	.213	-
1993 High Range	309	34	6	28	0	.246	

BOGGS, WADE - Red Sox 3B - BL - Age 34

Great hitters rarely decline as quickly as Boggs did in 1992. A .259 BA was so far off Boggs' career average (.338) you must search for a reason. The contract hassle was one negative factor. My theory is that he simply stopped enjoying the game in Boston. Boggs' 1992 home batting average was 109 points lower than his career BA at Fenway; his road batting average in 1992 was just 14 points off the career mark. Whatever the problem, it sure wasn't defensive positioning or some new trick from the pitchers.

	AB	R	HR	RBI	SB	BA	$
1992 Boston AL	514	62	7	50	1	.259	7
1993 Low Range	444	57	4	37	0	.272	
1993 Base Case	523	73	5	51	1	.300	17
1993 High Range	624	96	8	69	1	.330	

BOLICK, FRANK - Mariners 3B - BB - Age 26

Bolick is a career .284 hitter in six minor league seasons. It took him that long to reach Triple-A. At least he's still making progress. The 1993 Base Case is zero at bats.

	AB	R	HR	RBI	SB	BA	$
1993 High Range	157	15	4	18	0	.265	

BONDS, BARRY - Pirates OF - BL - Age 28

Bonds further established himself as the best all-around player in 1992. He reached the 30/30 club for the second straight year. He also carried the Pirates over the final six weeks to their third straight National League East championship, despite being constantly pitched around. He then hit the free agent market with unprecedented expectations, all reasonable.

	AB	R	HR	RBI	SB	BA	$
1992 Pittsburgh NL	473	109	34	103	39	.311	49
1993 Low Range	454	85	22	84	22	.262	
1993 Base Case	505	104	30	108	40	.290	44
1993 High Range	570	129	40	129	57	.322	

BONILLA, BOBBY - Mets OF - BB - Age 30

The 1992 Mets were a team that crumbled under the weight of injuries and expectations as well as the nearly constant stream of fan and media abuse. Nobody felt the weight more or was deemed more responsible for all of it than Bobby Bonilla, but there actually were a few positives in his season: He had more homers than in 1991, despite playing in 29 fewer games and having 139 fewer AB. His .16 RBI per AB in 1992 is almost exactly his career average, and he did it this time in an offense that had no leadoff hitter, a .223 batter in the 3-slot, and Dick Schofield hitting second.

	AB	R	HR	RBI	SB	BA	$
1992 New York NL	438	62	19	70	4	.249	15
1993 Low Range	390	55	12	56	2	.231	
1993 Base Case	487	76	19	81	3	.262	17
1993 High Range	608	104	29	108	6	.292	

BOOKER, ROD - Astros IF - BL - Age 34

In the majors from 1987 to 1991. He didn't hit more than .226 any year after 1989. Booker was at AAA Tucson in 1992.

BOONE, BRET - Mariners 2B - BR - Age 23

Boone's present claim to fame is being the first third-generation player in the major leagues -- father Bob and grandfather Ray were also major leaguers. His future claim is likely that of All-Star. He hit .255 with 19 home runs at AA Jacksonville in 1991.Then he improved in 1992 at AAA Calgary, which is friendly to hitters. The Mariners called him up for a trial in September and stopped his season one at bat short of losing his rookie status for 1993. One of Boone's good qualities for 1993 is that his weak-looking stats from the callup period will make him much less expensive than he would have been after hitting .300 for a month.

	AB	R	HR	RBI	SB	BA	$
1992 Calgary AAA	439	73	13	73	17	.314	
1992 Seattle AL	129	15	4	15	1	.194	-
1993 Low Range	225	26	4	24	2	.208	
1993 Base Case	404	52	9	51	7	.249	8
1993 High Range	524	74	15	74	12	.279	

BORDERS, PAT - Blue Jays C - BR - Age 29

Just a platoon catcher, Borders inflated his value by hitting .286 with 15 home runs in 1990. Now his price is lower, although his likely value is as high as it ever was.

	AB	R	HR	RBI	SB	BA	$
1992 Toronto AL	480	47	13	53	1	.242	7
1993 Low Range	290	24	6	30	1	.204	
1993 Base Case	406	38	11	50	1	.244	6
1993 High Range	484	49	16	67	2	.274	

BORDICK, MIKE - Athletics 2B/SS - BR - Age 27

Undrafted out of college, Bordick was on the verge of becoming a career minor leaguer in 1992. He had never hit more than .270, but was leading the AL in hitting in June, with a .352 average. Also managed to hit over .280 in the second half, indicating he has reached a new level, but the big picture is that he just had a peak year. Can also play a fine shortstop. Helped by departure of Walt Weiss.

	AB	R	HR	RBI	SB	BA	$
1992 Oakland AL	504	62	3	48	12	.300	17
1993 Low Range	231	23	1	18	3	.215	
1993 Base Case	410	45	2	42	10	.260	8
1993 High Range	495	60	2	52	15	.286	

BOSTON, DARYL - Mets OF - BL - Age 30

This .249 hitter was once again one of the Mets' few bright spots. He consistently displays better power and more speed than anyone expects. Boston looks like a lock to be in the 20/20 club if he could ever become a full-time player, which he can't. He's also considered to be the best overall defensive outfielder the Mets have, at least among those who began 1992 in the big leagues.

	AB	R	HR	RBI	SB	BA	$
1992 New York NL	289	37	11	35	12	.249	11
1993 Low Range	221	27	5	23	6	.213	
1993 Base Case	269	36	8	33	12	.254	9
1993 High Range	327	48	12	45	20	.285	

BOURNIGAL, RAFAEL - Dodgers SS - BR - Age 26

After starting the season as a 25-year-old player-coach in Class A, Bournigal became the regular SS at AAA Albuquerque, hit .324 and made only 9 errors. As a result, he has a slim chance to move into a utility role in L.A. Base Case is zero at bats.

	AB	R	HR	RBI	SB	BA	$
1992 Albuquerque AAA	395	47	0	34	5	.324	
1992 Los Angeles NL	20	1	0	0	0	.150	-
1993 High Range	230	20	0	11	1	.272	

BRADLEY, SCOTT - Mets C - BL - Age 33

Got just six at bats with two major league teams in 1992. Now near the end of his career.

BRAGGS, GLENN - Japan OF - BR - Age 30

A one time minor league sensation (with batting averages like .390 and .360) Braggs never fulfilled his promise and settled into a backup role. For the second straight year, his season was cut short by injuries. Off season surgery repaired cartilage damage to his right knee. Now gone to Japan.

BRANSON, JEFF - Reds IF - BR - Age 26

A 1988 Olympian and second round draft pick, Branson was making almost no progress as a hitter until 1992. Recalled three different times from Nashville, Jeff made his mark as a pinch-hitter, with a .382 PH average and 10 RBI. He got 93% of his at bats against righty pitchers. Branson's career is now in jeopardy, due to an injury suffered in a collision turning a double play in September.

	AB	R	HR	RBI	SB	BA	$
1992 Nashville AAA	123	18	4	12	0	.325	
1992 Cincinnati NL	115	12	0	15	0	.296	1
1993 Base Case	230	21	1	26	2	.253	1
1993 High Range	319	32	2	41	3	.283	

BREAM, SID - Braves 1B - BL - Age 32

1992's performance was almost exactly what was expected and is about what you should expect again. If he plays full-time, he'll have better power numbers but lose some BA points. The Bream/Hunter platoon has been one big reason for back-to-back championships so the Braves aren't likely to break up this team.

	AB	R	HR	RBI	SB	BA	$
1992 Atlanta NL	372	30	10	61	6	.261	12
1993 Low Range	265	21	7	39	3	.229	
1993 Base Case	388	34	13	66	8	.260	13
1993 High Range	460	45	18	87	13	.290	

BRETT, GEORGE - Royals DH - BL - Age 39

Brett was considering retirement after reaching the 3000-hit milestone. Well past his prime, he could still contribute. Probably won't play at all unless he can play well. If he is around, try to get him after his May 15th birthday - he always warms up when the weather does.

	AB	R	HR	RBI	SB	BA	$
1992 Kansas City AL	592	55	7	61	8	.285	16
1993 Low Range	303	27	3	31	3	.246	
1993 Base Case	484	47	5	58	7	.273	13
1993 High Range	592	63	8	80	12	.304	

BREWER, ROD - Cardinals 1B/OF - BL - Age 27

He was one of the most improved players in baseball last season. He went from being a good-field, no-hit first baseman with a limited future into a productive offensive player with a shot at major league time.

	AB	R	HR	RBI	SB	BA	$
1992 Louisville AAA	423	57	18	86	0	.288	
1992 St. Louis NL	103	11	0	10	0	.301	0
1993 Base Case	202	21	2	22	1	.244	0
1993 High Range	346	39	4	42	3	.274	

BRILEY, GREG - Mariners OF - BL - Age 27

Briley had a tremendous rookie year in 1989 batting .266 with 13 HR, 52 RBI and 11 SB. He went downhill over the next couple of years but appeared to be bouncing back before being hurt. Briley is a good role-player but not an everyday starter.

	AB	R	HR	RBI	SB	AVG	$
1992 Seattle AL	200	18	5	12	9	.275	6
1993 Low Range	152	12	2	10	4	.231	
1993 Base Case	264	24	5	21	12	.262	8
1993 High Range	384	38	9	34	24	.292	

BRITO, BERNARDO - Twins DH - BR - Age 29

1992 was Brito's fourth year in AAA where he has put up some decent numbers. Considering the young prospects ahead of him, his best shot may be with another organization. He is very much in danger of becoming a career minor leaguer. Base Case is zero at bats.

	AB	R	HR	RBI	SB	BA	$
1992 Portland AAA	564	80	26	96	0	.270	
1992 Minnesota AL	14	1	0	2	0	.143	-
1993 High Range	254	29	5	33	0	.269	

BROGNA, RICO - Tigers 1B - BL - Age 22

Brogna was a bright prospect two years ago, but his progress stalled in 1991, and Fielder's dominance at first base means Rico won't get much opportunity in the majors for a while, or he'll be traded. Keep your eye on him because he does have the potential to be a power hitting 1B. Detroit's No. 1 pick in '88 out of high school, where he also was a quarterback. Played some OF in Double-A in '91. A better-than-average defensive 1B, one positive factor when comparisons are made between Brogna and Fielder.

	AB	R	HR	RBI	SB	BA	$
1992 Toledo AAA	387	45	10	58	1	.261	
1992 Detroit AL	26	3	1	3	0	.192	-
1993 Base Case	233	24	5	27	1	.231	0
1993 High Range	351	40	9	46	2	.260	

BROOKS, HUBIE - Angels OF - BR - Age 36

Brooks had some decent years in the National League, and the Angels were hoping to get another good year from him. Now California will play more rookies and younger players in '93. At age 36, Brooks is near the end of his career.

	AB	R	HR	RBI	SB	BA	$
1992 California AL	306	28	8	36	3	.216	2
1993 Low Range	214	18	4	23	1	.198	
1993 Base Case	345	33	9	43	2	.239	4
1993 High Range	495	51	15	71	4	.269	

BROSIUS, SCOTT - Athletics 2B/OF/3B - BR - Age 26

Entering last season Brosius was ready for a regular major league job, but he split a mediocre year between the majors and Triple-A. Once hit 23 home runs at Double- A. With Carney Lansford's retirement, Brosius was discussed as a candidate for the third base job in 1993.

	AB	R	HR	RBI	SB	BA	$
1992 Oakland AL	87	13	4	13	3	.218	1
1992 Tacoma AAA	236	29	9	31	8	.237	
1993 Low Range	124	15	3	14	2	.203	
1993 Base Case	269	37	9	36	6	.244	6
1993 High Range	402	60	16	61	14	.274	

BROWN, JARVIS - Twins OF - BR - Age 26

The fastest man in a slow organization, Brown is a speedy outfielder whose role is pinch running and some occasional outfield. Brown led his league in runs scored every year from 1988-1990, and stole as many as 72 bases in a season, but that didn't get him a major league job. Now he is a backup player who at best will provide a few stolen bases.

	AB	R	HR	RBI	SB	BA	$
1992 Portland AAA	224	25	2	16	17	.250	
1992 Minnesota AL	15	8	0	0	2	.067	-
1993 Base Case	189	27	2	18	9	.248	3
1993 High Range	319	50	4	36	22	.278	

BROWNE, JERRY - Athletics 3B - BB - Age 27

Released by Cleveland after 1991, Browne became a key utility player and pinch hitter for Oakland last season. He was another player considered a possible successor to Carney Lansford at the end of 1992.

	AB	R	HR	RBI	SB	BA	$
1992 Oakland AL	324	43	3	40	3	.287	8
1993 Low Range	277	35	2	31	2	.245	
1993 Base Case	304	42	3	40	4	.272	7
1993 High Range	383	58	5	57	7	.303	

BRUETT, J.T. - Twins OF - BL - Age 25

Like Jarvis Brown, Bruett is a speedy outfielder whose role is pinch running and occasional outfield defensive support.

	AB	R	HR	RBI	SB	BA	$
1992 Portland AAA	280	41	0	17	29	.250	
1992 Minnesota AL	76	7	0	2	6	.250	1
1993 Base Case	209	22	0	12	11	.235	1
1993 High Range	302	34	0	20	22	.264	

BRUMFIELD, JACOB - Reds OF - BR - Age 27

Despite hitting .336 in 1990 and leading the American Association in SB in 1991, Brumfield was let go by the Royals. He made a big impression on the Reds during spring training 1992 and just missed the final cut. He did well enough at Nashville to get a midseason callup and could be a useful reserve in 1993.

	AB	R	HR	RBI	SB	BA	$
1992 Nashville AAA	208	32	5	19	22	.284	
1992 Cincinnati NL	15	6	0	2	6	.133	-
1993 Base Case	127	17	2	12	7	.245	2
1993 High Range	334	46	5	38	25	.274	

BRUMLEY, MIKE - Red Sox IF/OF - BB - Age 27

If the Red Sox had one more outfield injury in 1992, Brumley could have become a major league regular. He got just one at bat, as it turned out. Back in 1991, he got 118 AB in a utility role.

	AB	R	HR	RBI	SB	BA	$
1992 Pawtucket AAA	365	50	4	41	14	.263	
1993 Base Case	61	7	0	5	2	.229	-
1993 High Range	207	26	3	21	13	.245	

BRUNANSKY, TOM - Red Sox OF - BR - Age 32

Bruno was the leading boomer on the Sox with just 15 HR in 1992. He can do that for the next couple of years but makes too much money to generate such average numbers. He got released.

	AB	R	HR	RBI	SB	BA	$
1992 Boston AL	458	47	15	74	2	.266	13
1993 Low Range	189	18	4	27	0	.205	
1993 Base Case	308	33	9	51	1	.246	5
1993 High Range	482	56	16	88	2	.276	

BUECHELE, STEVE - Cubs 3B - BR - Age 31

Had shown good power until his trade to the Cubs last year, after which he hit just one homer in 239 AB. He was American Association MVP in 1985, despite a mid-season promotion. Has never hit for high average or stolen many bases. He is an exceptional defensive player which assures him playing time.

	AB	R	HR	RBI	SB	BA	$
1992 Two Teams NL	524	52	9	64	1	.261	11
1993 Low Range	388	36	9	43	1	.203	
1993 Base Case	483	49	14	63	1	.244	8
1993 High Range	517	57	17	76	2	.274	

BUFORD, DAMON - Orioles OF - BR - Age 22

Buford is a speedy base-stealing outfielder who needs at least another year in the minors. He was promoted from AA to AAA ball, where he then stole 21 bases in a month.

	AB	R	HR	RBI	SB	BA	$
1992 Hagerstown AA	373	53	1	30	41	.239	
1992 Rochester AAA	155	29	1	12	23	.284	

BUHNER, JAY - Mariners OF - BR - Age 28

Buhner was a slugging Yankee prospect who finally emerged in 1991. Buhner said that disagreements with former manager Jim Lefebvre hurt his performance. Last year, under Bill Plummer, Buhner had 140 more AB, but hit two fewer homers, drove in only two more runs and knocked a point off his average. Buhner has great raw power and a rocket arm.

	AB	R	HR	RBI	SB	BA	$
1992 Seattle AL	543	69	25	79	0	.243	13
1993 Low Range	390	46	14	47	0	.208	
1993 Base Case	509	66	23	71	0	.249	13
1993 High Range	552	79	29	86	0	.279	

BULLETT, SCOTT - Pirates OF - BL - Age 24

Good speed, fair power. Not likely to appear in 1993, but if he does, expect a few stolen bases and one or two homers in a hundred at bats. Got a peek at AAA Buffalo last year (went four for ten) after doing this at Double-A:

	AB	R	HR	RBI	SB	BA	$
1992 Carolina AA	518	60	8	45	29	.270	

BULLOCK, ERIC - Expos OF/1B - BL - Age 33

Speedy leadoff man who has never hit major-league pitching and is a career AAA player. How long has he been around? He's been involved in trades with Clay Christenson, Tommy Herr, Tom Nieto and Shane Rawley.

	AB	R	HR	RBI	SB	BA	$
1992 Indianapolis AAA	305	50	5	40	21	.305	
1992 Montreal NL	5	0	0	0	0	.000	-
1993 Base Case	50	4	0	4	2	.220	-
1993 High Range	247	28	2	28	11	.291	

BURKS, ELLIS - Red Sox OF - BR - Age 28

Burks' injuries are puzzling. Burks can always be a high value with a healthy season, but he may well have peaked already. A trade to another team might revive him; certainly wouldn't hurt. Would I take a chance on Burks? A qualified yes. If you need to take chances, Burks offers high potential; but if you are rounding out a contending roster, paying "expected value" for Burks could be your mistake of the year.

	AB	R	HR	RBI	SB	BA	$
1992 Boston AL	235	35	8	30	5	.255	6
1993 Low Range	310	42	8	34	4	.215	
1993 Base Case	472	70	16	60	10	.256	15
1993 High Range	527	86	22	76	16	.286	

BURNITZ, JEROMY - Mets OF - BR - Age 23

Burnitz showed more speed than power at Tidewater last year, but he's got the power - 31 homers at AA Williamsport in 1991, a neutral park in a pitcher's league. Jeromy is a great all-around athlete who has improved his defense and is learning to cut down his swing when behind in the count.

	AB	R	HR	RBI	SB	BA	$
1992 Tidewater AAA	445	56	8	40	30	.243	
1993 Base Case	150	23	4	23	9	.223	2
1993 High Range	301	39	10	36	11	.249	

BUSH, RANDY - Twins OF/1B - BL - Age 34

Bush's roles are just pinch hitting, some DH, and occasional outfield, and will be the same even if he signs with another team.

	AB	R	HR	RBI	SB	BA	$
1992 Minnesota AL	182	14	2	22	1	.214	-
1993 Low Range	87	6	1	9	0	.194	
1993 Base Case	198	15	2	24	1	.234	-
1993 High Range	254	21	3	35	2	.263	

BUTLER, BRETT - Dodgers OF - BL - Age 35

Even at age 35, Butler has stayed injury-free and consistently produced averages over .290 and SB totals in the high 30's. His great second half in 1992 suggests that no precipitous decline is on the immediate horizon. His batting eye and bunting ability should keep his on-base percentage high (and therefore maintain a good SB total) even if the average starts to slip.

	AB	R	HR	RBI	SB	BA	$
1992 Los Angeles NL	553	86	3	39	41	.309	30
1993 Low Range	398	58	2	26	18	.262	
1993 Base Case	497	79	3	37	34	.290	26
1993 High Range	610	107	5	52	45	.322	

CABRERA, FRANCISCO - Braves C/1B - BR - Age 26

A good hitter who still needs a place to play. Didn't have a good year at Richmond; still a powerful hitter. He won't play much for the Braves.

	AB	R	HR	RBI	SB	BA	$
1992 Richmond AAA	301	30	9	35	0	.272	
1992 Atlanta NL	10	2	2	3	0	.300	-
1993 Low Range	64	8	2	7	0	.237	
1993 Base Case	137	19	4	18	0	.268	2
1993 High Range	328	50	12	49	1	.299	

CALDERON, IVAN - Expos OF/1B - BR - Age 31

Calderon was slowed by shoulder surgery last season and had one of the worst seasons of his career. He was exposed in the expansion draft and will not be given preference over Moises Alou in 1993, like he was late last year. Calderon is worth more in the National League: "You know I love fastballs. You know how many fastballs I see with these guys [Grissom and Deshields] on base when I come up?" A big smile answers that question.

	AB	R	HR	RBI	SB	BA	$
1992 Montreal NL	170	19	3	24	1	.265	3
1993 Low Range	229	23	5	28	3	.235	
1993 Base Case	377	41	10	52	7	.267	11
1993 High Range	552	68	19	87	15	.298	

CAMERON, STANTON - Orioles 1B - BL - Age 23

Cameron appears to be the best power prospect in the Baltimore organization. Expected to play at the AA or AAA level in 1992. Needs to reduce his strikeouts (121 in 409 at-bats).

	AB	R	HR	RBI	SB	BA	$
1992 Frederick A	409	76	29	92	2	.247	

CAMINITI, KEN - Astros 3B - BB - Age 29

Entered his fourth full season in 1992 as the Astros' third-baseman with a lifetime batting average of .247. He beat that by 47 points. His previous best was .255 in 1989. The big difference was an improvement in hitting left-handed, from .213 in 1991 to .289 in 1992. He missed some time with a separated shoulder and cites that time as the turning point. When he came back after the injury, he started hitting the ball where it was pitched rather than trying to pull everything.

	AB	R	HR	RBI	SB	BA	$
1992 Houston NL	506	68	13	62	10	.294	21
1993 Low Range	452	53	9	48	4	.241	
1993 Base Case	501	64	12	62	8	.263	18
1993 High Range	533	75	15	74	12	.298	

CAMPANIS, JIM - Mariners C - BR - Age 25

Missed his chance to become a third-generation big-leaguer when he suffered a broken left wrist. His career figures to be longer than Gramps' and Dad's combined (120 games), because he has thrown out better than 50 per cent of opponents' base-stealers in each of the last two seasons. For the first time in his four pro years, he failed to reach double figures in HR in '92. Expect a September callup.

	AB	R	HR	RBI	SB	BA	$
1992 Jacksonville AA	286	30	5	29	2	.262	
1993 Base Case	55	4	1	5	1	.234	0
1993 High Range	151	13	3	16	2	.258	

CANALE, GEORGE - Indians 1B - BL - Age 27

Played for the elderly Colorado Springs team in 1992. Not likely to make it back. Got 73 major league at bats in 1989-1991, hitting .164.

CANDAELE, CASEY - Astros IF/OF - BB - Age 32

Consummate utilityman played six positions in 1992, but lost the starting second-base job due to the successful conversion of Craig Biggio. Always popular with fans because of his hustle and off-the-wall personality, he should have a few more years as a major league utility player.

	AB	R	HR	RBI	SB	BA	$
1992 Houston NL	320	19	1	18	7	.213	-
1993 Low Range	143	9	0	8	2	.189	
1993 Base Case	207	14	0	13	5	.229	-
1993 High Range	299	22	1	22	11	.258	

CANGELOSI, JOHN - Rangers OF - BB - Age 30

Held the AL rookie record for stolen bases, before Pat Listach that is. Surfaced briefly with Texas in 1992, but hasn't hit over .220 since 1988. Look elsewhere, unless you need one SB desperately and see Cangelosi surface again somewhere in 1993.

CANSECO, JOSE - Rangers OF- BR - Age 28

Shoulder problems forced him onto the disabled list and into the DH role frequently in 1992, and there is a lingering suspicion of his desire to play hard. He seemed genuinely happy to be in Texas after the trade, however, and the gentle crowds in Arlington should be a balm to his ego. The park should also produce more HR for him than the spacious Oakland Coliseum. Canseco's best basestealing days are behind him, as he was caught stealing more often than he succeeded in 1992. Very likely to be overvalued in 1993.

	AB	R	HR	RBI	SB	BA	$
1992 Two Teams AL	439	74	26	87	6	.244	17
1993 Low Range	299	44	13	52	4	.239	
1993 Base Case	421	69	23	84	8	.256	19
1993 High Range	574	103	37	122	16	.286	

CANSECO, OZZIE - Cardinals OF - BR - Age 28

After an ill-fated 1991 in Japan, Jose's twin brother resurfaced with a big 1992 season in Class AAA. The Cardinals wanted to take a long look at him last September but a shoulder injury prevented that. Though he will never match his brother's accomplishments, he could wind up as a major leaguer after all.

	AB	R	HR	RBI	SB	BA	$
1992 Louisville AAA	308	53	22	57	1	.266	
1992 St. Louis NL	29	7	0	3	0	.276	-
1993 Base Case	122	16	4	12	2	.237	0
1993 High Range	265	39	9	31	5	.267	

CAPRA, NICK - Phillies OF/3B - BR - Age 35
Surfaced with the Rangers and Royals during the 1980's. Led the American Association in runs scored in 1989. Played at AAA Nashville and AAA Scranton in 1992, getting a combined 34 stolen bases, but he isn't likely to do anything in the major leagues in 1993.

CARABALLO, RAMON - Braves 2B/SS - BB - Age 23
Caraballo hits enough to make Mark Lemke sweat, but he's at least a year away as his glove isn't quite ready yet. May get a September call-up, will get a longer look in 1994. Can steal lots of bases and won't hurt your BA. Had back surgery during the off season, so look before you leap.

	AB	R	HR	RBI	SB	BA	$
1992 Greenville AA	93	15	1	8	10	.312	
1992 Richmond AAA	405	42	2	40	19	.281	
1993 Base Case	45	6	0	3	2	.222	-
1993 High Range	135	17	1	10	7	.239	

CARMONA, GREG - Cardinals SS - BB - Age 24
Gets to everything with his glove, gets to nothing with his bat. Look elsewhere.

CARR, CHUCK - Marlins OF - BB - Age 24
He blossomed into a hitter in Class AAA last season and became a prospect. Though he struggled in a September trial with the Cardinals last season, and was left exposed in the draft, his stock has risen. The Cards had seven good outfielders. Carr has great speed and is a significant stolen base threat but must continue to hit if he is going to stay in the majors. The Marlins drafted four center fielders, if you want another vote of no confidence for Carr.

	AB	R	H	RBI	SB	BA	$
1992 Louisville AAA	377	68	3	28	53	.308	
1992 St. Louis NL	64	8	0	3	10	.219	1
1993 Low Range	278	33	1	14	22	.208	
1993 Base Case	356	40	2	20	30	.230	12
1993 High Range	504	60	3	36	40	.249	

CARREON, MARK - Tigers OF - BR - Age 29
He should bounce back from the injuries, but the wear and tear of being a full time player in Detroit, rather than a "supersub" with the Mets, raises the concern that he might perform best only when he can come off the bench. He hit ten home runs in 188 at bats as a PH/sub with the Mets, and ten home runs in almost twice as many at bats as a semi-regular with the Tigers in a much friendlier stadium. Always been a great pinch hitter.

	AB	R	HR	RBI	SB	BA	$
1992 Detroit AL	336	34	10	41	3	.232	4
1993 Low Range	174	16	4	19	1	.195	
1993 Base Case	307	31	8	38	3	.235	3
1993 High Range	365	41	12	52	4	.264	

CARTER, GARY - Retired - BR - Age 38
Retired. He returned to Montreal for a final season and was an emotional leader as the Expos challenged the Pirates in the NL East until the final week. He retired after an outstanding 19-year playing career and will remain with the Expos as a broadcaster.

	AB	R	HR	RBI	SB	BA	$
1992 Montreal NL	285	24	5	29	0	.218	0

CARTER, JOE - Blue Jays OF - BR - Age 33

Everyone knows about the home runs and runs batted in, but many people haven't noticed that Carter steals 10 or 20 bases every year. Likely to be showing his age more in 1993.

	AB	R	HR	RBI	SB	BA	$
1992 Toronto AL	622	97	34	119	12	.264	29
1993 Low Range	512	72	22	85	7	.228	
1993 Base Case	590	91	32	114	11	.260	28
1993 High Range	637	108	40	131	21	.290	

CARTER, STEVE - Reds OF - BL - Age 28

Appeared with the Pirates briefly in 1989-1990 and was at one time one of Pittsburgh's brightest prospects. No longer. He could help you just a little in every category but most likely won't appear anywhere in 1993.

CASILLAS, ADAM - Royals OF - BL - Age 27

Good singles hitter, but little power and no speed. Your basic Triple-A extension of the major league bench.

	AB	R	HR	RBI	SB	BA	$
1992 Memphis AA	168	25	2	23	1	.327	
1992 Omaha AAA	362	41	0	27	3	.307	
1993 Base Case	50	7	0	4	0	.244	-
1993 High Range	198	17	0	17	1	.265	

CASTELLANO, PEDRO - Rockies 3B - BR - Age 23

Plucked from the Cubs system; he's a fair glove, weak bat. Won't do anything noteworthy in 1993.

CASTILLA, VINNY - Rockies SS - BR - Age 25

The bad news for Castilla is that Freddie Benavides is most likely to have the shortstop job on Opening Day. The good news is that Benavides can't hit. Castilla has a chance to be a very good $1 pickup.

	AB	R	HR	RBI	SB	BA	$
1992 Richmond AAA	449	49	7	44	1	.252	
1992 Atlanta NL	16	1	0	1	0	.250	-
1993 Low Range	67	7	1	5	1	.196	
1993 Base Case	198	22	2	18	4	.237	0
1993 High Range	336	41	4	35	10	.266	

CASTILLO, BRAULIO - Rockies OF - BR - Age 24

Castillo was once a hot prospect in the Dodgers' organization, showing both speed and power at times, but then he had a bad year in 1990, which, combined with some off-the-field problems, led to his arrival with the Phillies. Braulio thus far has done nothing in the majors, and not a whole lot at AAA. As the fourth outfielder on an expansion team, his playing opportunities are suddenly very good.

	AB	R	HR	RBI	SB	BA	$
1992 Philadelphia NL	76	12	2	7	1	.197	-
1992 Scranton AAA	386	59	13	47	8	.246	
1993 Low Range	259	36	4	25	7	.208	
1993 Base Case	319	41	6	30	10	.237	4
1993 High Range	411	50	10	44	15	.267	

CEDENO, ANDUJAR - Astros SS - BR - Age 23

Once the brightest prospect in the Astros' organization, Cedeno was a major disappointment in 1992 right from the start of spring training. He regressed in every respect over the winter: hitting, fielding, power and concentration, and he never seemed to get it back. He may spend 1993 in the minors if the team acquires a shortstop to shore up a glaring weakness. The main thing he has in his favor is his youth, but if he doesn't cut down his wild looping swing and continues to play tentative defense, he will not play regularly in the majors. That's the bad news. The good news is that he presents a rare wealth of talent, has already achieved some major league hitting success at a young age (9 HR in 251 AB in 1991), and he should be dirt cheap on draft day 1993. Great speculation, arguably the best speculative pick of the year.

	AB	R	HR	RBI	SB	BA	$
1992 Tucson AAA	280	27	6	56	6	.293	
1992 Houston NL	220	15	2	13	2	.173	-
1993 Low Range	242	24	6	22	3	.203	
1993 Base Case	408	45	12	42	9	.244	9
1993 High Range	525	63	19	62	16	.274	

CERONE, RICK - Expos C - BR - Age 38

His career appeared to end when the Expos released him in July and no one picked him up. However, with catching in such woefully short supply, Cerone could find a job again in 1993 if he so desires. He can still play a little as a third-stringer.

	AB	R	HR	RBI	SB	BA	$
1992 Montreal NL	63	10	1	7	1	.270	0
1993 High Range	168	29	3	21	1	.264	

CHAMBERLAIN, WES - Phillies OF - BR - Age 26

Chamberlain began 1992 as the Opening Day left fielder, but rapidly played his way first to the bench, and then to Scranton by early May. An attitude change, combined with a .331 average and injuries to Dale Murphy, Lenny Dykstra, and Tom Marsh hastened his recall. Still possesses the talent he had going into 1992, has revised his outlook, and if he comes out and plays the way he did upon his return to the Vet (.285 average/.452 slugging), he'll be in the lineup all year.

	AB	R	HR	RBI	SB	BA	$
1992 Philadelphia NL	275	26	9	41	4	.258	8
1992 Scranton AAA	127	16	4	26	6	.331	
1993 Low Range	327	28	8	45	5	.228	
1993 Base Case	403	38	12	64	10	.259	14
1993 High Range	557	57	21	97	19	.290	

CHRISTOPHERSON, ERIC - Giants C - BR - Age 23

San Francisco's No. 1 pick in '90, out of San Diego State U. He's the latest in the line of Giants catching hopefuls. A good defensive catcher who hasn't proven he can hit.

	AB	R	HR	RBI	SB	BA	$
1992 Shreveport AA	270	36	6	34	1	.252	

CIANFROCCO, ARCHI - Expos 3B/1B - BR - Age 26

After a good start, Cianfrocco had trouble making the jump from Class AA to the majors in 1992. He wound up in AAA and was conspicuously absent from the September callups. Early in the summer, just before he got dropped lower in the batting order, but before he got removed, Cianfrocco told me that he had definitely noticed pitchers making adjustments to him, and were pitching him differently than they had during spring training and his early success in April-May. My opinion is that he is not a big talent, but just had a big spring training with a team that needed a first baseman at the time.

	AB	R	HR	RBI	SB	BA	$
1992 Indianapolis AAA	59	12	4	16	1	.305	
1992 Montreal NL	232	25	6	30	3	.241	4
1993 Base Case	181	19	3	21	2	.243	1
1993 High Range	293	34	7	39	4	.273	

CLARK, DAVE - Pirates OF - BL - Age 30

Clark gave the Pirates some big hits off the bench while shuttling between Pittsburgh and Class AAA Buffalo in 1992. The tag of future superstar applied to Clark while he was coming up through the Cleveland farm system is long gone. However, he's still a competent extra man. Base Case is zero at bats.

	AB	R	HR	RBI	SB	BA	$
1992 Buffalo AAA	253	43	11	56	6	.304	
1992 Pittsburgh NL	33	3	2	7	0	.212	-
1993 High Range	206	21	6	28	1	.247	

CLARK, JACK - Red Sox DH - BR - Age 37

Like the energizer bunny, he keeps owing and owing and owing. Went bankrupt in '92 off the field and on.

	AB	R	HR	RBI	SB	BA	$
1992 Boston AL	257	32	5	33	1	.210	-
1993 Low Range	125	14	2	14	0	.177	
1993 Base Case	321	40	7	42	1	.217	-
1993 High Range	500	69	20	75	2	.249	

CLARK, JERALD - Rockies OF - BR - Age 29

Clark was not assured of playing time if he stayed in San Diego, but with The Rockies he gets a fresh start, a high altitude, and a ballpark well-suited to his flyball swing from the right side.

	AB	R	HR	RBI	SB	BA	$
1992 San Diego NL	496	45	12	58	3	.242	9
1993 Low Range	365	25	8	40	2	.220	
1993 Base Case	504	50	15	77	3	.247	12
1993 High Range	549	59	22	90	4	.277	

CLARK, PHIL - Tigers OF - BR - Age 24

He's not ready for the majors yet, but keep your eye on him in Toledo this year; he is not too deep on the depth charts and could chip in a couple of home runs and a harmless batting average. He is Jerald's younger brother.

	AB	R	HR	RBI	SB	BA	$
1992 Toledo AAA	271	29	10	39	4	.280	
1992 Detroit AL	54	3	1	5	1	.407	1
1993 Base Case	95	10	2	13	2	.248	2
1993 High Range	177	22	2	22	3	.291	

CLARK, WILL - Giants 1B - BL - Age 29

One of the best pure hitters in the game today, Clark has hit .295, .301, and .300 the past three seasons. Partial power outage last year attributable to nobody to protect him in the batting order. And if you don't believe in batting order protection for number three hitters, remember that Roger Maris in 1961 was a pathetic hitter, with no production except a lot of walks, in the many games when Mickey Mantle was not batting behind him; with Mantle he was the biggest terror of the last 30 years -- same player, same year, different results.

	AB	R	HR	RBI	SB	BA	$
1992 San Francisco NL	513	69	16	73	12	.300	26
1993 Low Range	491	66	15	74	6	.280	
1993 Base Case	560	84	22	101	11	.299	33
1993 High Range	596	98	29	114	17	.321	

CLAYTON, ROYCE - Giants SS - BR - Age 23

Named minor league player of the year in 1991. Was San Francisco's Opening Day shortstop last year. However, when he inevitably struggled with the bat, Clayton was sent to Phoenix in mid-year where he continued to struggle. Often unfairly compared to a young Barry Larkin; a better comparison would be a young Mariano Duncan. Needs to shorten his big swing before he can become a good major league hitter.

	AB	R	HR	RBI	SB	BA	$
1992 San Francisco NL	321	31	4	24	8	.224	2
1992 Phoenix AAA	192	30	3	18	15	.240	
1993 Low Range	307	33	2	25	6	.200	
1993 Base Case	414	49	4	40	14	.240	6
1993 High Range	579	75	7	63	26	.269	

CLYBURN, DANNY - Pirates OF - BR - Age 19

He was not highly regarded as a high school senior last year in Lancaster, S.C. However, the Pirates used their first of two second-round picks to get him in the draft and he proved to be a steal. Though still raw, he showed major-league tools in the Gulf Coast League.

	AB	R	HR	RBI	SB	BA	$
1992 Bradenton R	149	26	4	25	7	.342	

COACHMAN, PETE - Angels 2B - BR - Age 31

Coachman had a good callup with the Angels in 1990, but hasn't attracted much favorable attention since then. Not likely to be a factor in the majors in 1993. He played with five teams at three different minor league levels in 1992. Here's what he did at Phoenix and Edmonton in the PCL:

	AB	R	HR	RBI	SB	BA	$
1992 Two Teams AAA	209	35	4	28	8	.239	

COCHRANE, DAVE - Mariners C/3B/OF - BB - Age 30

His versatility -- he's played 3B, SS, 1B, LF, CF, RF, and C -- will keep him in the majors, but after playing parts of the last five years in the majors, he is obviously going nowhere fast.

	AB	R	HR	RBI	SB	BA	$
1992 Seattle AL	152	10	2	12	1	.250	0
1993 Low Range	80	6	1	9	0	.240	
1993 Base Case	154	10	2	12	1	.251	0
1993 High Range	290	21	5	26	3	.280	

COLBERT, CRAIG - Giants C - BR - Age 28

Rookie just barely in the majors in 1992. Not enough power to be a major league regular.

	AB	R	HR	RBI	SB	BA	$
1992 San Francisco NL	126	10	1	16	1	.230	-
1992 Phoenix AAA	140	16	1	12	0	.321	
1993 Base Case	130	13	1	14	1	.239	-
1993 High Range	203	22	2	24	2	.269	

COLBRUNN, GREG - Expos 1B - BR - Age 23

Considered one of the game's brightest catching prospects, major elbow surgery in 1991 ended his days behind the plate. However, Colbrunn bounced back and has re-established himself as a decent hitting prospect as a first baseman, and he's still very young. Great upward potential.

	AB	R	HR	RBI	SB	BA	$
1992 Indianapolis AAA	216	32	11	48	1	.306	
1992 Montreal NL	168	12	2	18	3	.268	2
1993 Low Range	226	21	4	24	2	.239	
1993 Base Case	380	39	9	47	5	.271	11
1993 High Range	442	49	13	62	8	.302	

COLE, ALEX - Rockies OF - BL - Age 27

The playing time question is finally resolved. Cole should play 150 games for Colorado. Two notes: (1) Cole is a notorious slow starter; with a long history of second half streaks. You may want to let someone else carry him in April-May. And (2) Cole has a trick shoulder that gets injured easily but heals quickly. In 1992 In Cleveland, which was playing its 38th straight season without a title, he was only the fifth outfielder. He was traded to the Pirates on July 3 and proceeded to play right field and bat leadoff against right-handed pitchers for a team that won its third straight division title. A disturbing trend is developing, though, he has stolen only 43 bases the past two seasons after stealing 40 in 63 games as a rookie in 1990.

	AB	R	HR	RBI	SB	BA	$
1992 Cleveland AL	97	11	0	5	9	.206	
1992 Pittsburgh NL	205	33	0	10	7	.278	4
1993 Low Range	276	39	0	12	13	.240	
1993 Base Case	506	72	0	26	38	.272	15
1993 High Range	535	90	0	31	52	.303	

COLE, STU - Royals IF - BR - Age 27

Hit .236 at AA Memphis and .195 at AAA Omaha in 1992. No value for 1993.

COLEMAN, VINCE - Mets OF - BB - Age 31

Coleman has managed barely 500 at bats in two years in a Mets' uniform. He has done OK with his limited appearances, hitting .264 with 82 runs and 61 steals, but he's unreliable. Good pick if you need to take chances, because he will sell for about half of his potential value (as he should -- just look at the 1992 actual value, versus the 1993 likely value); a bad pick if you have a winning roster and just want to pay fair value for a quantity of stolen bases. If you want to invest in a big speed asset, it's better to get younger players.

	AB	R	HR	RBI	SB	BA	$
1992 New York NL	229	37	2	21	24	.275	12
1993 Low Range	345	51	2	27	20	.244	
1993 Base Case	459	74	4	42	48	.276	26
1993 High Range	566	100	6	59	71	.306	

COLES, DARNELL- Blue Jays OF/IF - BR - Age 30

A strong start at Nashville (.580 Slg%) and Chris Sabo's injuries earned Darnell Coles a return to the majors. Coles was on a hot streak when a severely sprained ankle ended his season. While not a prospect at age 30, Coles could definitely contribute offensively if given the opportunity.

	AB	R	HR	RBI	SB	BA	$
1992 Nashville AAA	81	19	6	16	1	.296	
1992 Cincinnati NL	141	16	3	18	1	.312	4
1993 Low Range	90	9	1	11	0	.208	
1993 Base Case	182	21	4	23	1	.241	1
1993 High Range	283	35	7	41	3	.271	

COLON, CRIS - Rangers SS - BB - Age 24
Colon (no relation) got an extended look as a September call-up from AA Tulsa. Although he is primarily regarded as a glove man, he did hit over .300 at two different minor league stops in 1991 and hit very well in winter ball following that season. For 1993, however, he is unlikely to contribute offensively.

	AB	R	HR	RBI	SB	BA	$
1992 Texas AL	36	5	0	1	0	.167	-
1992 Tulsa AA	374	30	1	42	7	.251	
1993 Base Case	88	9	0	6	1	.200	-
1993 High Range	254	30	3	27	5	.251	

CONINE, JEFF - Marlins 1B/OF - BR - Age 26
Conine will play somewhere for Florida. Most likely first base, if not 1B then left field. The variables after the draft were whether the Marlins get a free agent for either position, and how Monty Fariss looks. Conine had good power numbers at AAA Omaha in 1992, proving his wrist injuries had healed after wrecking his 1991 season. Put up numbers similar to Frank Thomas for Memphis (AA) in 1990. With KC he would have been a great $2 sleeper in many leagues; now he's no secret anywhere.

	AB	R	HR	RBI	SB	BA	$
1992 Omaha AAA	397	69	20	72	4	.302	
1992 Kansas City AL	91	10	0	9	0	.253	-
1993 Low Range	320	38	11	43	5	.255	
1993 Base Case	415	52	14	73	8	.280	14
1993 High Range	507	75	20	88	9	.295	

COOLBAUGH, SCOTT - Padres 3B - BR - Age 26
Coolbaugh was a genuine prospect with the Rangers, but failed to hit for average in any season; and Dean Palmer jumped over him. The BA problem still plagues him (.199 last year at AAA Las Vegas, where just about everybody hits .300). Even if he comes back up, you don't want him, unless you need one home run desperately and don't care about your batting average.

COOPER, GARY - Astros 3B/OF/1B - BR - Age 28
Just a career minor leaguer, but a good one. With a few lucky breaks he could get some major league time in 1993. Hit over .300 with fair power both of the last two years at AAA Tucson.

COOPER, SCOTT - Red Sox 1B/3B - BL - Age 25
Is there life in Boston after Wade Boggs? Sure. Cooper is no star, but he can play. Has better power than what he showed in 1992.

	AB	R	HR	RBI	SB	BA	$
1992 Boston AL	337	34	5	33	1	.276	6
1993 Low Range	322	33	5	25	1	.246	
1993 Base Case	510	57	10	47	2	.273	12
1993 High Range	548	67	13	57	3	.304	

CORA, JOEY - White Sox 2B/SS - BB - Age 27
Cora was acquired by the White Sox from the Padres primarily for his baserunning abilities and as a defensive replacement. Cora hit .310 at Las Vegas in 1989. Hit .174 at New Comiskey last season.

	AB	R	HR	RBI	SB	BA	$
1992 Chicago AL	122	27	0	9	10	.246	3
1993 Low Range	56	11	0	4	3	.205	
1993 Base Case	177	39	0	13	15	.246	4
1993 High Range	304	74	0	26	34	.276	

CORDERO, WILFREDO - Expos SS - BR - Age 21

As he has matured into a hitter, he has been compared to Cal Ripken. More likely he can become the player Andujar Cedeno has been cracked up to be, minus the iron glove. Cordero's odds-on to be the greatest shortstop the Expos have ever had. Still eligible for '93 Rookie of the Year.

	AB	R	HR	RBI	SB	BA	$
1992 Indianapolis AAA	204	32	6	27	6	.314	
1992 Montreal NL	126	17	2	8	0	.302	2
1993 Low Range	166	20	2	14	1	.234	
1993 Base Case	327	43	6	33	5	.266	7
1993 High Range	456	65	10	53	9	.297	

CORDOVA, MARTY - Twins OF - BR - Age 23

Cordova is a highly regarded prospect who tore up the Class A California League in '92 winning the MVP award. Injuries in the past two years have slowed his progress. He's a few years away from the Metrodome, but if he does well at AA/AAA he can win a September callup. And if the Twins have to look deep in their system during the summer, they will promote Cordova ahead of some older farmhands.

	AB	R	HR	RBI	SB	BA	$
1992 Visalia A	513	103	28	131	13	.341	
1993 Base Case	60	7	2	9	0	.240	-
1993 High Range	300	39	11	35	1	.277	

COSTO, TIM - Reds 1B - BR - Age 24

Acquired from Cleveland after the Reggie Jefferson waiver snafu, Costo led the Southern League in homers. He will need to cut down his strikeouts to make the jump to the majors (128 K's in 424 AB's at Chattanooga). Think Pete Incaviglia.

	AB	R	HR	RBI	SB	BA	$
1992 Chattanooga AA	424	63	28	71	4	.241	
1992 Cincinnati NL	36	3	0	2	0	.222	-
1993 Low Range	54	6	1	5	0	.199	
1993 Base Case	125	14	2	14	1	.239	-
1993 High Range	308	38	7	40	3	.269	

COTTO, HENRY - Mariners OF - BR - Age 32

Cotto is one of the most successful base stealers in major league history. His 23 of 25 performance raised his career rate to 84.4%. A good fielder and has a little bit of pop in his bat (the Kingdome helps).

	AB	R	HR	RBI	SB	BA	$
1992 Seattle AL	294	42	5	27	23	.259	12
1993 Low Range	172	23	2	13	9	.229	
1993 Base Case	286	43	4	25	24	.260	11
1993 High Range	367	60	6	36	39	.290	

CRON, CHRIS - White Sox 1B - BR - Age 29

Will only see playing time in the event of an injury to Frank Thomas.

	AB	R	HR	RBI	SB	BA	$
1992 Chicago AL	10	0	0	0	0	.000	-
1992 Vancouver AAA	500	76	16	81	12	.278	
1993 High Range	254	29	5	31	3	.244	

CRUZ, IVAN - Tigers 1B - BL - Age 24

Cruz and Rico Brogna have been racing for the right to move Cecil Fielder to DH. Negatives: Brogna is a better fielder, nearly two years younger and in '90 had the same kind of season that Cruz did last year.

	AB	R	HR	RBI	SB	BA	$
1992 London AA	524	71	14	104	1	.275	

CUMMINGS, MIDRE - Pirates OF - BB - Age 21

The key player from the deal that sent 20-game winner John Smiley to the Twins last March. He showed a good bat from both sides of the plate and above-average speed, though his work ethic was questioned.

	AB	R	HR	RBI	SB	BA	$
1992 Salem A	420	55	14	75	23	.305	

CURTIS, CHAD - Angels OF - BR - Age 24

The departure of Junior Felix helps Curtis. He's a dirty-uniform, Lenny Dykstra-type ballplayer. He batted everywhere from second to sixth in the order, with many at-bats in the third hole. Curtis was caught stealing 18 times, a figure that should decrease in '93 because he knows the league better. Stolen bases and BA should increase in '93.

	AB	R	HR	RBI	SB	BA	$
1992 California AL	441	59	10	46	43	.259	25
1993 Low Range	411	54	7	38	25	.235	
1993 Base Case	542	79	12	59	54	.267	32
1993 High Range	592	94	16	73	71	.298	

CUYLER, MILT - Tigers OF - BB - Age 24

Expect Cuyler to rebound from his 1992 injury, with a season similar to 1991. His speed is tremendous and his SB output should rise steadily over the next couple of years.

	AB	R	HR	RBI	SB	BA	$
1992 Detroit AL	291	39	3	28	8	.241	4
1993 Low Range	237	29	2	20	4	.203	
1993 Base Case	403	54	4	39	20	.249	10
1993 High Range	556	81	7	61	40	.273	

If you have to choose between power and speed -- and it often turns out that you have to make that choice -- you've got to go with speed."

-- Sparky Anderson

DANIELS, KAL - Cubs OF - BL - Age 29

Knee injuries and surgeries have ruined what looked to be a promising career. He hit .296 with 27 HR, and 94 RBI in 1990, but has fallen off sharply since. Got released by the Cubs. Could do well as a DH.

	AB	R	HR	RBI	SB	BA	$
1992 Two Teams NL	212	21	6	25	0	.241	2
1993 Low Range	207	19	5	21	1	.210	
1993 Base Case	415	41	12	49	2	.251	8
1993 High Range	554	60	19	74	3	.281	

DASCENZO, DOUG - Cubs OF - BB - Age 28

Did not commit an error while in the major leagues during 1988, 1989, 1990, or the first half of 1991. He's an outstanding fielder, who hits righties better than lefties. After three full years in the majors, Dascenzo is at best a 4th OF, pinch hitter, pinch runner, and defensive replacement.

	AB	R	HR	RBI	SB	BA	$
1992 Chicago NL	376	37	0	20	6	.255	3
1993 Low Range	221	21	0	15	3	.232	
1993 Base Case	327	35	1	26	8	.264	5
1993 High Range	423	49	1	38	14	.294	

DAUGHERTY, JACK - Rangers OF/1B - BB - Age 32

The past season was likely the end of the line for Daugherty, as he was dropped from the 40-man roster following the season's end. With no speed, power or defense, Daugherty's only asset was the ability to hit for average. Consecutive sub-.220 seasons raise big doubts for 1993.

	AB	R	HR	RBI	SB	BA	$
1992 Texas AL	127	13	0	9	2	.205	-
1992 Okla. City AAA	18	3	0	2	0	.278	
1993 Base Case	125	12	1	9	1	.200	-
1993 High Range	202	23	1	21	2	.244	

DAULTON, DARREN - Phillies C - BL - Age 31

After a career full of injury setbacks, Daulton in 1992 broke through with the best offensive year by a National League catcher in nearly a decade. The left-handed hitter has also matured as an excellent handler of pitchers.

	AB	R	HR	RBI	SB	BA	$
1992 Philadelphia NL	485	80	27	109	11	.270	29
1993 Low Range	374	48	9	47	3	.208	
1993 Base Case	436	61	13	64	6	.249	11
1993 High Range	478	73	17	78	9	.279	

DAVIDSON, MARK - Unsigned OF - BR - Age 32

Just a career minor leaguer at this point. Hit .190 in 85 games with the Astros in 1991.

	AB	R	HR	RBI	SB	BA	$
1992 Colo Springs AAA	309	57	6	44	2	.282	

DAVIS, ALVIN - Japan 1B - BL - Age 32

At mid-season Davis went to Japan hoping to re-find his power stroke. He won't likely come back without it.

	AB	R	HR	RBI	SB	BA	$
1992 California AL	104	5	0	16	0	.250	0
1993 High Range	380	44	12	62	0	.277	

DAVIS, BUTCH - Blue Jays OF - BR - Age 34

Minor leagues all the way. Got one at bat with the Dodgers in 1991, six with the Orioles in 1989.

	AB	R	HR	RBI	SB	BA	$
1992 Syracuse AAA	550	67	9	74	19	.280	

DAVIS, CHILI - Twins DH/OF - BB - Age 33

After having a career year in '91, Davis returned to a more normal range. Nobody had a right to be disappointed. It was a fine year in Davis' career book, although some shallow analysts mentioned the "collapse of Chili Davis" as a reason for the Twins' downfall. Hardly.

	AB	R	HR	RBI	SB	BA	$
1992 Minnesota AL	444	63	12	66	4	.288	16
1993 Low Range	390	52	9	50	2	.229	
1993 Base Case	415	61	12	62	4	.260	13
1993 High Range	558	90	20	92	7	.290	

DAVIS, DOUG - Rangers C - BR - Age 30

No bat. Too old. Don't bother.

	AB	R	HR	RBI	SB	BA	$
1992 Texas AL	1	0	0	0	0	1.000	-
1992 Okla. City AAA	194	20	4	25	0	.186	
1993 Base Case	76	4	1	8	0	.216	-
1993 High Range	231	23	2	26	0	.258	

DAVIS, ERIC - Dodgers OF - BR - Age 30

Obviously, Davis' career has suffered a major decline during the past few seasons. Since 1988, he has played fewer games each year than the preceding year (135, 131, 127, 89 and 76). He had surgery on three different joints in September and in prior years had two knee surgeries, a lacerated kidney and a disc problem in his neck. At 31, only his speed and fielding ability remain. Davis' physical talents can no longer overcome the fundamental problems with his hitched swing. The incentive-laden contract can't hurt.

	AB	R	HR	RBI	SB	BA	$
1992 Los Angeles NL	267	21	5	32	19	.228	9
1993 Low Range	266	27	8	34	10	.201	
1993 Base Case	394	43	14	58	25	.242	16
1993 High Range	494	60	21	82	40	.272	

DAVIS, GLENN - Orioles 1B/DH - BR - Age 32

Davis missed 57 games in '92 due to nagging injuries. The Orioles are running out of patience, but Davis is signed for big money through '93. Davis still has big home run potential, but he needs to be 100% healthy. Hasn't had 400 at bats since 1989.

	AB	R	HR	RBI	SB	BA	$
1992 Baltimore AL	398	46	13	48	1	.276	11
1993 Low Range	422	43	10	49	1	.220	
1993 Base Case	489	55	15	67	1	.252	11
1993 High Range	539	66	20	82	2	.282	

DAVIS, RUSSELL - Yankees 3B - BR - Age 23

Could this guy be the reason the Yankees gave up Charlie Hayes? Not for 1993. Davis was New York's 29th pick in 1988. He raised his average 67 points in his second year in the Eastern League in 1992. He was voted both the league's best batting prospect and its best defensive 3B in the Baseball America poll.

	AB	R	HR	RBI	SB	BA	$
1992 Albany AA	492	77	22	71	3	.285	

DAWSON, ANDRE - Cubs OF - BR - Age 38

Dawson is on the downside of a Hall of Fame career. He's had problems with his knees, which cut into his playing time, for several years now. Dawson is not as good as his stats appear; he's been helped by playing in Wrigley Field and his RBI totals are high only because he refuses to take a walk. He can't run well anymore and is prone to slumps, but when he's hot, he's in a zone alone.

	AB	R	HR	RBI	SB	BA	$
1992 Chicago NL	542	60	22	90	6	.277	24
1993 Low Range	412	41	13	57	3	,245	
1993 Base Case	505	55	20	82	6	.272	21
1993 High Range	595	71	28	103	11	.303	

DECKER, STEVE - Marlins C - BR - Age 27

Will finally get the right job at the right time. Florida will be a low-pressure environment just right to bring out the best in the elderly puppies like Decker. Followed up a disastrous 1991 season (when he was handed the Giants' starting catching job prematurely) with a solid year at Triple-A last season. Decker, still young enough to begin a good career, is back on track.

	AB	R	HR	RBI	SB	BA	$
1992 San Francisco NL	43	3	0	1	0	.163	-
1992 Phoenix AAA	450	50	8	74	2	.282	
1993 Low Range	226	19	5	23	0	.228	
1993 Base Case	388	36	9	44	1	.247	6
1993 High Range	464	44	15	70	2	.270	

DEER, ROB - Tigers OF - BR - Age 32

Deer is paid to swing hard and hit homers. He always has a terrible BA, but 25-30 homers is always a reasonable expectation.

	AB	R	HR	RBI	SB	BA	$
1992 Detroit AL	393	66	32	64	4	.247	17
1993 Low Range	332	52	16	46	2	.183	
1993 Base Case	372	64	23	60	4	.223	9
1993 High Range	479	90	35	86	7	.252	

DELAROSA, JUAN - Blue Jays OF - BR - Age 24

In his second season in Double-A, he raised his average 114 points. He plays CF well and has a strong arm, so he won't have to hit as much in the majors. Needs to improve his strike zone judgment.

	AB	R	HR	RBI	SB	BA	$
1992 Knoxville AA	508	68	12	53	16	.329	
1993 Base Case	50	4	0	4	1	.230	-
1993 High Range	288	25	3	25	4	.258	

DELGADO, CARLOS - Blue Jays C - BL - Age 20

Florida State League MVP, and HR and RBI champ. The league home run champ in 1991 had only 14 jacks. Needs work on defense. Do not expect an early callup to the majors; the Blue Jays know better.

	AB	R	HR	RBI	SB	BA	$
1992 Dunedin A	485	83	30	100	2	.324	

DEMPSEY, RICK - Unsigned C - BR - Age 43

Dempsey was on a sort of "taxi squad" last year. Soon to be 43, he will likely retire for good. Don't look, even if he surfaces somewhere during spring training.

	AB	R	HR	RBI	SB	BA	$
1992 Baltimore AL	9	2	0	0	0	.111	-

DeSHIELDS, DELINO - Expos 2B - BL - Age 24

When Felipe Alou took over as Expos' manager in late May last season, DeShields responded and reestablished himself as one of the game's most exciting young players. He also raised his average against lefthanded pitching from .217 to .316. Strained rib cage slowed him in season's final weeks. Wears his socks abnormally high, in honor of the old Negro leagues.

	AB	R	HR	RBI	SB	BA	$
1992 Montreal NL	530	82	7	56	46	.292	32
1993 Low Range	507	69	6	50	25	.251	
1993 Base Case	547	82	9	63	44	.278	31
1993 High Range	552	91	11	72	55	.309	

DESTRADE, ORESTES - Japan 1B - BL - Age 30

Destrade possesses no speed and isn't much of a contact hitter, but you've got to respect someone who's won three consecutive home run titles, even if it's in a league where Jack Howell can hit 38 of them. The Marlins were acting interested after the expansion draft.

	AB	R	HR	RBI	SB	BA	$
1992 Japan	448	87	41	87	---	.266	

DEVAREZ, CESAR - Orioles C - BR - Age 23

Good defensive catcher, but not a factor for 1993.

	AB	R	HR	RBI	SB	BA	$
1992 Hagerstown AA	319	20	2	32	2	.226	

DEVEREAUX, MIKE - Orioles OF - BR - Age 29

Devereaux had a tremendous career-best year in '92 that will be very difficult to match. Most of his RBI were from batting second in the order behind the hot-hitting Brady Anderson.

	AB	R	HR	RBI	SB	BA	$
1992 Baltimore AL	653	76	24	107	10	.276	26
1993 Low Range	502	51	13	73	7	,232	
1993 Base Case	600	67	19	101	13	.264	23
1993 High Range	642	78	25	115	20	.295	

DIAZ, ALEX - Brewers OF - BB - Age 24

Unlike most minor leaguers, Diaz's SB totals haven't diminished as he's risen higher.

	AB	R	HR	RBI	SB	BA	$
1992 Denver AAA	455	67	1	41	42	.268	
1992 Milwaukee AL	9	5	0	1	3	.111	-
1993 Base Case	100	11	0	6	6	.220	1
1993 High Range	202	24	0	13	13	.249	

DIAZ, MARIO - Rangers IF - BR - Age 32

Strictly a fill-in. You can do better, and so can most major league teams.

	AB	R	HR	RBI	SB	BA	$
1992 Texas AL	31	2	0	1	0	.226	-
1992 Okla. City AAA	167	24	3	20	1	.335	
1993 High Range	100	8	0	8	0	.260	
1993 High Range	205	24	1	23	0	.268	

DiSARCINA, GARY - Angels 2B/SS - BR - Age 25

DiSarcina took over shortstop when Dick Schofield was traded to the Mets. He did a very good job, and his hitting should improve in '93.

	AB	R	HR	RBI	SB	BA	$
1992 California AL	518	48	3	42	9	.247	6
1993 Low Range	420	39	2	34	4	.210	
1993 Base Case	531	54	3	49	8	.251	6
1993 High Range	558	62	3	59	11	.281	

DISTEFANO, BENNY - Astros OF - BL - Age 31
Long-time Pirates farmhand, appeared in Pittsburgh 1988-1989. Near finished now.

	AB	R	HR	RBI	SB	BA	$
1992 Houston NL	60	4	0	7	0	.233	-

DONNELS, CHRIS - Marlins 3B - BL - Age 26
Chris had yet another good AAA year in 1992, and now has a clear shot, with nobody except Gary Scott in the Florida long-range plans after the expansion draft. Donnels' weaknesses are his lack of defensive reliability and limited power. The key variable is what Scott does; if Scott hits, Donnels sits.

	AB	R	HR	RBI	SB	BA	$
1992 Tidewater AAA	279	35	5	32	12	.301	-
1992 New York NL	121	8	0	6	1	.174	
1993 Low Range	250	34	4	39	6	.211	
1993 Base Case	325	46	6	50	9	.243	3
1993 High Range	455	60	9	72	16	.277	

DORAN, BILL - Reds 2B - BB - Age 34
Despite relatively good health, Doran had his worst year since 1989. Getting on base (.342 OBA) is his only positive, power, range, speed, injury history and age are his negatives. End of the line.

	AB	R	HR	RBI	SB	BA	$
1992 Cincinnati NL	387	48	8	47	7	.235	7
1993 Low Range	293	32	5	30	3	.203	
1993 Base Case	320	39	6	38	6	.244	5
1993 High Range	497	66	12	67	12	.274	

DORSETT, BRIAN - Pirates 1B/C - BR - Age 31
Good AAA performer but has failed to hit in repeated major league trials.

	AB	R	HR	RBI	SB	BA	$
1992 Buffalo AAA	492	69	21	102	1	.289	
1993 High Range	125	8	3	12	0	.238	

DOWNING, BRIAN - Rangers DH - BR - Age 42
Retired at the end of the 1992 season. Could still DH a little more if he wanted to.

	AB	R	HR	RBI	SB	BA	$
1992 Texas AL	320	53	10	39	1	.278	

DOZIER, D.J. - Padres OF - BR - Age 27
D.J. has many of the raw materials required to be a successful baseball player, but he has not so far been able to refine skills which would separate him from the pack of major-league wannabes. Mastering the strike zone has been difficult for him, and it's unlikely that D.J. will progress until he does that.

	AB	R	HR	RBI	SB	BA	$
1992 Tidewater AAA	197	32	7	25	6	.234	
1992 New York NL	47	4	0	2	4	.191	-
1993 Base Case	60	5	1	6	2	.220	
1993 High Range	169	22	3	17	9	.268	

DUCEY, ROB - Angels IF/OF - BL - Age 27

Ducey came over from Toronto in a mid-season trade. He split most of 1988-91 between Toronto and AAA. He hit only .188 in '92 but he's a better hitter than that. Has left a long trail of sparkling minor league stats, just never got a chance in the majors.

	AB	R	HR	RBI	SB	BA	$
1992 Two Teams AL	80	7	0	2	2	.188	-
1993 Low Range	55	6	0	4	1	.199	
1993 Base Case	168	22	1	15	5	.240	0
1993 High Range	410	58	3	42	16	.270	

DUNCAN, MARIANO - Phillies IF/OF - BR - Age 30

If you look closely, you'll notice that Mariano's 1992 season wasn't quite as good as it seemed. He was considered to be an offensive plus because of a decent batting average, moderate power, 40 doubles, and 23 steals with only 3 times caught. With all that, there's still no way that a player with a .292 on base percentage should be hitting anywhere near the middle of a batting order. Lack of plate discipline alone makes him an ineffective hitter, but here you have it. Shawon Dunston puts up similar numbers to Mariano's '92 season every year, and the Cubs still don't have a clue where to put him. Signed as a free agent prior to the 1992 season, Duncan was a versatile acquisition who played left, second, short and third while knocking in 50 runs and placing among league leaders in doubles.

	AB	R	HR	RBI	SB	BA	$
1992 Philadelphia NL	574	71	8	50	23	.267	19
1993 Low Range	258	29	3	18	6	.229	
1993 Base Case	464	56	6	37	19	.260	13
1993 High Range	572	76	9	52	32	.290	

DUNSTON, SHAWON - Cubs SS - BR - Age 30

The first player selected in the 1982 player draft has been on again, off again for much of his career. He has the best throwing arm in baseball, but has never lived up to expectations over a full season. Back surgery for disc injuries cut short his 1992 season

	AB	R	HR	RBI	SB	BA	$
1992 Chicago NL	73	8	0	2	2	.315	0
1993 Low Range	127	13	3	12	2	.229	
1993 Base Case	503	55	13	53	16	.260	16
1993 High Range	552	66	17	67	25	.290	

DYKSTRA, LENNY - Phillies OF - BL - Age 30

Lenny has only managed to play one season's worth of games in the past two years, but over that time has batted right around .300, scored 100 runs, and stolen 54 bases. Dykstra also draws walks and covers as much area as anybody in center field. He's Brett Butler with a little more power and a lot less durability. Injuries have crippled this outstanding player in the last two years when the Phillies are 41 games under .500 with him on the sidelines. Dykstra is a proven .300 hitter, stolen-base threat and superb centerfielder when healthy, but a very high risk to go with his high value.

	AB	R	HR	RBI	SB	BA	$
1992 Philadelphia NL	345	53	6	39	30	.301	22
1993 Low Range	334	49	5	31	16	.264	
1993 Base Case	515	83	10	56	40	.292	32
1993 High Range	566	101	13	70	55	.321	

EASLEY, DAMION - Angels 3B - BR - Age 23

At the end of 1992, Easley looked very much like the Angels' third baseman of the future, with Gary Gaetti assuming a new role as backup at third and first. Easley is a base-stealing Whitey Herzog-type ballplayer. Easley could also play 2B if the Angels want Gonzales in as a regular.

	AB	R	HR	RBI	SB	BA	$
1992 Edmonton AAA	429	61	3	44	26	.289	
1992 California AL	151	14	1	12	9	.258	3
1993 Low Range	154	13	1	9	5	.206	
1993 Base Case	385	35	2	26	20	.247	8
1993 High Range	509	51	3	40	35	.277	

EDMONDS, JIM - Angels OF - BL - Age 22

Good average, fair power. Needs work on defense, but he could reach the majors this year, as the Angels focus on their younger players.

	AB	R	HR	RBI	SB	BA	$
1992 Midland AA	246	42	8	32	3	.313	
1992 Edmonton AAA	194	37	6	36	3	.299	
1993 Base Case	75	9	1	8	1	.240	0
1993 High Range	226	30	3	28	4	.266	

EISENREICH, JIM - Royals OF - BL - Age 33

Best years behind him; Tourette's syndrome cost him his better years. A fourth OF at best, he'll be challenged for playing time by Koslofski and Gwynn and whoever else is around in 1993. Never had much power, his BA is fading and his speed has peaked. Eisenreich's a substitute whose value could disappear in a flash.

	AB	R	HR	RBI	SB	BA	$
1992 Kansas City AL	353	31	2	28	11	.269	8
1993 Low Range	117	9	0	8	2	.233	
1993 Base Case	303	26	1	22	9	.265	6
1993 High Range	364	34	2	31	15	.295	

ELSTER, KEVIN - Mets SS - BR - Age 28

The reconstructed shoulder that Elster got in 1991 lasted him only through the offseason. Even in spring training 1992 there was no question that Kevin could not even begin to consider playing shortstop. He was forcing throws that were obviously feeble, prompting the acquisition of Kevin's American League twin, Dick Schofield. Going into 1993, Elster still faces extensive rehabilitation and stands a chance of producing nothing this season. Added to all this, he needs to find a team willing to take a chance on him, obviously not the Mets who acquired Tony Fernandez as soon as the year ended.

	AB	R	HR	RBI	SB	BA	$
1992 New York NL	18	0	0	0	0	.222	-
1993 Low Range	54	5	1	5	0	.186	
1993 Base Case	263	25	5	26	1	.226	-
1993 High Range	400	41	9	45	3	.255	

ESASKY, NICK - Braves 1B - BR - Age 33

Comeback attempt is a good human interest story, but that's all.

	AB	R	HR	RBI	SB	BA	$
1992 Richmond AAA	108	12	5	14	1	.278	

ESCOBAR, JOSE - Unsigned SS/2B - BR - Age 32
Appeared with the Indians briefly in 1991, but really he's just a hanger-on now, helping younger people learn how to play. There is also a John Escobar who played at AA Reading in the Phillies system last year; he can't hit, either.

ESPINOZA, ALVARO - Indians SS - BR - Age 31
He's a step higher than Escobar, but that's about all. Espinoza had some productive years with the Yankees. If he latches on with another major league team and plays regularly, he might hit .250 with 30 RBI and 3 homers in a full season.

	AB	R	HR	RBI	SB	BA	$
1992 Col. Sp. AAA	483	64	9	79	2	.300	

ESPY, CECIL - Reds OF - BB - Age 30
After getting seven hits and driving in eight runs in first eight pinch-hit at bats, Espy did little else offensively in 1992. He showed enough speed and defense the rest of the season to remain a useful reserve outfielder. He finished second in the AL in steals with the Rangers in 1989, but that seems like a long time ago.

	AB	R	HR	RBI	SB	BA	$
1992 Pittsburgh NL	194	21	1	20	6	.258	3
1993 Low Range	174	17	1	15	3	.226	
1993 Base Case	207	22	1	21	6	.258	3
1993 High Range	309	37	2	36	13	.288	

EUSEBIO, TONY - Astros C - BR - Age 25
Failed in brief trial with Astros in 1991. Spent entire 1992 season at AA Jackson where he made the All-Star team. A marginal prospect.

	AB	R	HR	RBI	SB	BA	$
1992 Jackson AA	339	33	5	44	1	.307	
1993 High Range	50	4	0	6	0	.200	

EVANS, DWIGHT - Orioles OF/DH - BR - Age 41
Cut during spring training 1992. I may have been the last writer to talk to him before he got the news.

EVERETT, CARL - Marlins OF - BB - Age 23
Only the Yankees' bizarre strategy in the expansion draft allowed them to lose a low-paid veteran at a skill position (Charlie Hayes) and then also lose their young hope for an impact center fielder for the late 1990's. Everett isn't likely to appear in the majors in 1993, because the Marlins have two CF's ahead of him -- Chuck Carr and Jesus Tavarez.

	AB	R	HR	RBI	SB	BA	$
1992 Ft Lauderdale A	183	30	2	9	11	.230	
1992 Prince William A	22	7	4	9	1	.318	

FARIES, PAUL - Padres 2B/3B - BR - Age 28
A definite candidate for the 2B job at San Diego, Faries could provide a much-needed speed boost to the lineup. His .293 average at high-average Las Vegas is hardly spectacular but, coupled with the 28 steals, it projects to decent production. Until Stillwell was signed, Faries had a chance to make the squad in the spring of 1992. San Diego had a number of middle infield prospects at Vegas and Faries was moved from his natural position to 3B to enhance his prospects as a UIF and to give Gardner the opportunity at 2B. A platoon with LHH Jeff Gardner is a possibility.

	AB	R	HR	RBI	SB	BA	$
1992 Las Vegas AAA	457	77	1	40	28	.293	
1992 San Diego NL	11	3	0	1	0	.455	-
1993 Base Case	118	11	0	10	3	.230	-
1993 High Range	315	44	1	32	19	.249	

FARISS, MONTY - Marlins 2B/OF - BR - Age 25

Although given a chance in spring training, Fariss was unable to claim a regular job with the Rangers in 1992. Having failed several tests in the infield, his future now appears to be in LF, where his throwing weakness is less visible. He was a #1 pick and still young. The Marlins drafted him with the idea that he could fill in until their top pick, Nigel Wilson, is ready. If you get Fariss and observe Wilson having a big year in the minors, move Monty before its too late.

	AB	R	HR	RBI	SB	BA	$
1992 Texas AL	166	13	3	21	0	.217	-
1992 Okla. City AAA	187	28	9	38	5	.299	
1993 Low Range	225	20	4	30	1	.230	
1993 Base Case	389	42	5	45	3	.240	2
1993 High Range	529	63	8	69	5	.266	

FARRELL, JON - Pirates OF - BR - Age 21

Pittsburgh's No. 1 pick in '91, out of junior college. Drafted as a C-OF, but moved to CF last season. His disappointing '92 season ended early because of an injury.

	AB	R	HR	RBI	SB	BA	$
1992 Augusta A	320	44	8	48	8	.222	

FELDER, KENNY - Brewers OF - BL - Age 22

See if you can convince the other owners in your league that this guy is that same little Felder that the Brewers had a couple years ago, a banjo hitter with great speed. Then draft this one into your minor league system. He's a big, strong power hitting outfielder from Florida State (ex-QB for the Seminoles), the Brewers' #1 pick in the 1992 draft. Several years away, but he may be the Brewers' best power prospect.

	AB	R	HR	RBI	SB	BA	$
1992 Helena R	276	58	15	48	11	.217	

FELDER, MIKE - Giants OF - BB - Age 30

Felder spent six frustrating years in the Milwaukee organization before finding his game in the faster National League. Strictly a part-timer, and fading for the second time. Giants will emphasize youth more in 1993.

	AB	R	HR	RBI	SB	BA	$
1992 San Francisco NL	322	44	4	23	14	.286	11
1993 Low Range	180	24	2	10	5	.232	
1993 Base Case	277	40	4	19	12	.264	7
1993 High Range	315	50	6	24	20	.295	

FELIX, JUNIOR - Marlins OF - BB - Age 25

Whitey Herzog said that the Angels could not be a winner with Felix in center. His defense is poor, and he has a reputation as a malcontent. Furthermore, it's been written that he's really over 30 years old. The Marlins don't want him to play center, and they don't care if he's 30. He will play right field until Darrell Whitmore is ready (which won't be soon) or until they get a big free agent for RF (which isn't likely), or until Felix pops a calf muscle (which is fairly likely).

	AB	R	HR	RBI	SB	BA	$
1992 California AL	509	63	9	72	8	.246	10
1993 Low Range	324	36	4	37	3	.204	
1993 Base Case	504	60	9	68	8	.245	9
1993 High Range	517	69	11	78	11	.275	

FERMIN, FELIX - Indians SS - BR - Age 29

At $800,000 per year, Fermin was the highest paid Indian in '92. As a result, throughout most of '92 the Indians were shopping Fermin around to cut their payroll to a bare-bones minimum. However, Mark Lewis proved to be an erratic shortstop at a young age, so Fermin got playing time and may be retained through '93. Fermin is a contact-type singles hitter.

	AB	R	HR	RBI	SB	BA	$
1992 Cleveland AL	215	27	0	13	0	.270	1
1993 Low Range	102	12	0	9	0	.212	
1993 Base Case	245	31	0	24	0	.253	0
1993 High Range	350	48	0	39	0	.283	

FERNANDEZ, JOSE - Cardinals C - BL - Age 25

Even in the minors, he's just a defensive backup. Look elsewhere.

	AB	R	HR	RBI	SB	BA	$
1992 Arkansas AA	116	7	1	8	0	.155	
1992 Louisville AAA	38	1	1	3	0	.079	

FERNANDEZ, TONY - Mets SS - BB - Age 30

The Mets listened when the Padres publicly stated their desire to trade their 30-year-old shortstop. Fernandez started the season as part of a group of four hitters at the top of the Padres' lineup who each hit over .300 through the All-Star break. He faded miserably in July and August and needed a .300 September to finish at .275. He could be an effective player but has lost some range and speed (caught stealing in 50% of his 40 attempts). Manager Jeff Torborg loves speed and will send Fernandez running frequently anyway.

	AB	R	HR	RBI	SB	BA	$
1992 Padres NL	622	84	4	37	20	.275	17
1993 Low Range	390	45	3	32	7	.235	
1993 Base Case	509	64	5	48	15	.266	14
1993 High Range	612	84	7	66	25	.297	

FIELDER, CECIL - Tigers 1B - BR - Age 29

Failing to hit over 40 homers for the first time in your career is not exactly a catastrophe. As long as Fielder is in Tiger Stadium, he'll drive in a ton of runs and lose enough balls in the seats to keep you very happy. Somebody is likely to hit 50 home runs somewhere in 1993, feasting on the depleted pitching. Who more likely than Cecil?

	AB	R	HR	RBI	SB	BA	$
1992 Detroit AL	594	80	35	124	0	.244	20
1993 Low Range	507	64	35	90	0	.209	
1993 Base Case	557	78	45	119	0	.250	28
1993 High Range	600	92	53	131	0	.280	

FIGUEROA, BIEN - Cardinals - SS - Age 29

He has no power, no speed and is not an offensive factor. In fact, he has hit three home runs in seven professional seasons. At best, he will be a defensive replacement in the majors.

	AB	R	HR	RBI	SB	BA	$
1992 Louisville AAA	319	44	1	23	2	.285	
1992 St. Louis NL	11	1	0	4	0	.182	-
1993 High Range	205	18	0	19	2	.239	

FINLEY, STEVE - Astros OF - BL - Age 28

If you like to see your players' names in the box scores every day, you can't beat Steve Finley. Played in 159 games in 1991 and all 162 in 1992. His challenge in 1992 was to show that his outstanding 1991 season was not a fluke. He improved in essentially every category, with the biggest improvement in stolen bases (44 vs. 34). He was a model of consistency all season. Continued to hit lefthanded pitching well (.279). His outstanding defense will keep him in the lineup against all kinds of pitching.

	AB	R	HR	RBI	SB	BA	$
1992 Houston NL	607	84	5	55	44	.292	31
1993 Low Range	499	66	4	41	22	.254	
1993 Base Case	574	84	5	55	42	.281	29
1993 High Range	610	98	7	67	56	.312	

FISK, CARLTON - White Sox C - BR - Age 45

Fisk is literally on his last legs. He will try to stay around long enough to pass Bob Boone in games caught. He is 25 short. Was injured most of the early part of the season in 1992

	AB	R	HR	RBI	SB	BA	$
1992 Chicago AL	188	12	3	21	3	.229	1
1993 Low Range	55	3	1	5	0	.189	
1993 Base Case	244	16	4	27	1	.229	-
1993 High Range	409	29	8	52	2	.258	

FITZGERALD, MIKE - Angels C - BR - Age 32

Veteran catcher, has been in the majors for nine years with a career .235 BA. His role is backup.

	AB	R	HR	RBI	SB	BA	$
1992 California AL	189	19	6	17	2	.212	0
1993 Low Range	54	5	1	4	0	.180	
1993 Base Case	120	9	2	10	1	.211	-
1993 High Range	302	33	10	31	4	.249	

FLAHERTY, JOHN - Red Sox C - BR - Age 25

In the second half he went to the plate just 24 times for the Sox. He is unlikely to be a big factor, as Pena will be the top guy. The departure of Wedge helps a little.

	AB	R	HR	RBI	SB	BA	$
1992 Pawtucket AAA	104	11	0	7	0	.250	
1992 Boston AL	66	3	0	2	0	.197	-
1993 Base Case	164	11	1	12	0	.216	-
1993 High Range	304	22	2	26	0	.248	

FLETCHER, DARRIN - Expos C - BL - Age 26

Fletcher has carried the reputation of good-hit, no-field catcher. However, he has yet to hit in the majors and was hampered by severe bronchitis last season. Was Big Ten Player of the Year in 1987 at Illinois and finished third in NCAA Division I with a .497 batting average.

	AB	R	HR	RBI	SB	BA	$
1992 Indianapolis AAA	51	2	1	9	0	.255	
1992 Montreal NL	222	13	2	26	0	.243	1
1993 Low Range	260	14	2	26	0	.203	
1993 Base Case	321	19	3	38	0	.243	1
1993 High Range	430	28	5	57	0	.273	

FLETCHER, SCOTT - Brewers 2B - BR - Age 34

An uncharacteristically good offensive year, with lots of playing time made possible by the disability of Bill Spiers, the evaporation of Jim Gantner's skills, and the lack of any appreciable middle-infield talent on the farm. Fletcher is a free agent; if he ends up elsewhere, remember that he is unlikely to attempt 27 steals for any manager other than Phil Garner. Still may be helpful as a third middle infielder.

	AB	R	HR	RBI	SB	BA	$
1992 Milwaukee AL	386	53	3	51	17	.275	1
1993 Low Range	159	20	1	19	2	.211	
1993 Base Case	263	36	2	37	5	.252	4
1993 High Range	391	59	4	63	11	.282	

FLORA, KEVIN - Angels 2B - BR - Age 23

Flora swiped 40 bases in '91 at Class AA Midland, but only 9 last year as he was playing with an injured ankle that finally put him on the DL. He may need another half-year in AAA, before going anywhere.

	AB	R	HR	RBI	SB	BA	$
1992 Edmonton AAA	170	35	3	19	9	.324	
1993 Base Case	100	10	1	8	4	.250	-
1993 High Range	300	50	5	30	20	.270	

FLOYD, CLIFF - Expos OF - BL - Age 20

Though 6-foot-4, 220-pound, he plays a decent center field. Floyd's value as a hitter draws comparison to such talents as Willie McCovey and Dave Parker. He set a Class A South Atlantic League record and led all pro leagues with 16 triples last season for Albany and also had SAL highs in total bases (261), RBI (97) and extra base hits (56) while finishing second in hits (157), third in slugging (.505) and fifth in batting (.304).

	AB	R	HR	RBI	SB	BA	$
1992 Albany A	516	83	16	97	32	.304	
1992 West Palm Bch A	4	0	0	1	0	.000	

FOLEY, TOM - Unsigned IF - BL - Age 33

Foley's value has always been that he is a rare lefthanded batter who can play all four infield positions. However, he has hit under .230 in each of the past four seasons and was released at the end of the 1992 season after batting just .174.

	AB	R	HR	RBI	SB	BA	$
1992 Montreal NL	115	7	0	5	3	.174	-
1993 High Range	181	12	0	9	5	.241	

FORDYCE, BROOK - Mets C - BR - Age 22
Brook is the next Mets' catching prospect, and will be the one who pushes Charlie O'Brien out the door.

	AB	R	HR	RBI	SB	BA	$
1992 Binghampton AA	425	59	11	61	1	.278	
1993 High Range	150	15	3	21	0	.250	

FOX, ERIC - Athletics LF - BB - Age 29
Signed to a minor league contract in 1989 after being released by Seattle, Fox entered last season as a 29 year-old career minor leaguer who had never played in a major league game. Very limited future.

	AB	R	HR	RBI	SB	BA	$
1992 Oakland AL	143	24	3	13	3	.238	1
1992 Tacoma AAA	121	16	1	7	5	.198	
1993 Base Case	83	12	1	8	2	.239	0
1993 High Range	228	35	4	24	6	.269	

FRANCO, JULIO - Rangers DH - BR - Age 31
Missed most of 1992 with patella bursitis (bruised and inflamed knee). The condition surfaced in spring training and never subsided. His status for 1993 is uncertain. He may not even be able to start the season, but may be one of the best DH's while qualifying at MI in many leagues. Watch him carefully in spring training.

	AB	R	HR	RBI	SB	BA	$
1992 Texas AL	107	19	2	8	1	.234	-
1993 Low Range	103	17	2	12	1	.234	
1993 Base Case	284	50	5	38	3	.266	6
1993 High Range	504	98	11	76	7	.297	

FRYE, JEFF - Rangers 2B - BR - Age 26
The Rangers brought him up when Franco couldn't play. He hadn't been considered much of a prospect, but he performed adequately. Frye is capable of hitting for a decent average, but has no power and didn't run much, although he was a good minor league basestealer.

	AB	R	HR	RBI	SB	BA	$
1992 Texas AL	199	24	1	12	1	.256	0
1992 Okla. City AAA	337	64	2	28	11	.300	
1993 Low Range	140	15	0	6	1	.220	
1993 Base Case	313	40	1	25	5	.263	4
1993 High Range	467	65	3	43	11	.294	

FRYMAN, TRAVIS - Tigers 3B/SS - BR - Age 23
He's just now beginning to reach his potential. Last year, Fryman became one of the top five offensive shortstops with 20 homers and 96 RBI. He should bring his BA close to .270-280 and show a bit more longball as he matures this year. He even stole 8 bases.

	AB	R	HR	RBI	SB	BA	$
1992 Detroit AL	659	87	20	96	8	.266	21
1993 Low Range	504	59	15	73	4	.228	
1993 Base Case	604	78	22	101	8	.270	21
1993 High Range	662	94	29	118	12	.290	

GAETTI, GARY - Angels 3B - BR - Age 34

Gaetti's offensive production continues to slip, and his role in '93 will be backup at first and third, and some DH. If it wasn't for his large contract, he would be traded or released.

	AB	R	HR	RBI	SB	BA	$
1992 California AL	456	41	12	48	3	.226	4
1993 Low Range	327	28	8	32	1	,186	
1993 Base Case	389	37	12	45	2	.226	3
1993 High Range	581	60	21	76	4	.255	

GAGNE, GREG - Twins SS - BR - Age 31

A model of consistency for years, although at a low value.

	AB	R	HR	RBI	SB	BA	$
1992 Minnesota AL	439	53	7	39	6	.246	6
1993 Low Range	339	37	4	24	3	.202	
1993 Base Case	404	49	6	34	6	.243	4
1993 High Range	465	62	8	44	9	.273	

GAINER, JAY - Padres 1B - BL - Age 26

Gainer was the Texas League All Star 1B and a legitimate power prospect. His rise is blocked by Guillermo Velasquez and Fred McGriff.

	AB	R	HR	RBI	SB	BA	$
1992 Wichita AA	376	57	23	67	4	.261	
1993 High Range	124	15	5	17	1	.233	

GALARRAGA, ANDRES - Rockies 1B - BR - Age 31

Being reunited with Don Baylor is a big plus. During spring training 1992, Baylor had Galarraga hitting line drives to right center consistently, just like he did in his big seasons during the late 1980's. Then Galarraga broke his wrist in the second game of the season and never made the contributions expected. Once a promising young star; the big downside is that history tells us expansion teams give up on veterans and make changes without thinking twice, and Galarraga isn't making too much money.

	AB	R	HR	RBI	SB	BA	$
1992 Louisville AAA	34	3	2	3	1	.176	8
1992 St. Louis NL	325	38	10	39	5	.243	
1993 Low Range	123	15	2	15	1	.231	
1993 Base Case	321	42	8	44	3	.262	7
1993 High Range	503	73	14	78	6	.293	

GALLAGHER, DAVE - Mets OF - BR - Age 32

Gallagher was getting the lion's share of the playing time last April, during Vince Coleman's initial DL stint. But then he fractured a hand, missed a month and a half, and spent the rest of the year pinch-hitting and playing late-inning D, which is really about all you'd want him to do anyway. Manager Jeff Torborg is a big fan of Gallagher, which helps.

	AB	R	HR	RBI	SB	BA	$
1992 New York NL	175	20	1	21	4	.240	1
1993 Low Range	90	9	0	9	1	.199	
1993 Base Case	196	22	1	24	4	.240	0
1993 High Range	254	32	2	35	6	.270	

GALLEGO, MIKE - Yankees IF - BR - Age 32

After six years of puny hitting, Gallego suddenly popped 12 home runs in 1991. Last year he was held back by injury, and time is not on his side in 1993.

	AB	R	HR	RBI	SB	BA	$
1992 New York AL	173	24	3	14	0	.254	1
1993 Low Range	186	23	3	13	1	.199	
1993 Base Case	284	39	5	23	3	.240	1
1993 High Range	403	61	8	37	6	.270	

GANT, RON - Braves OF - BR - Age 28

NL pitchers decided not to let Gant beat them in 1992. He saw a steady stream of breaking balls down and unhittable fastballs away. He chased a lot of them. Still in his prime, and will still be a big part of a good hitting lineup. Even in a down year, Gant still ran often and successfully -- 32 SB in 42 tries. Gant's average should climb a little as he regains his power for 1993. Gant can reach MVP territory in any year.

	AB	R	HR	RBI	SB	BA	$
1992 Atlanta NL	544	74	17	80	32	.259	28
1993 Low Range	500	63	20	66	17	.212	
1993 Base Case	530	74	27	82	29	.253	27
1993 High Range	574	88	34	97	40	.283	

GANTNER, JIM - Brewers 2B - BL - Age 39

This season proved that Gantner's career has gone past the common end of the line. If he does come back, he'll do little for your team.

	AB	R	HR	RBI	SB	BA	$
1992 Milwaukee AL	256	22	1	18	6	.246	2
1993 Low Range	131	9	1	9	2	.214	
1993 Base Case	241	19	1	19	6	.255	3
1993 High Range	355	31	3	32	12	.285	

GARCIA, CARLOS - Pirates SS/3B/2B - BR - Age 25

With Lind gone, Garcia jumps in value. Garcia spent his third straight season at Class AAA last year. He was in Buffalo because of a logjam on the major league level, not because he can't play in the big leagues. He played primarily second base during his major league stint in 1992, a telling sign for the future. Pittsburgh will fit him in at one of the three infield skill positions. He can hit, run, and field.

	AB	R	HR	RBI	SB	BA	$
1992 Buffalo AAA	426	73	13	70	21	.303	
1992 Pittsburgh NL	39	4	0	4	0	.205	-
1993 Low Range	228	28	2	24	5	,214	
1993 Base Case	409	55	6	50	15	.255	9
1993 High Range	505	74	10	74	24	.285	

GARCIA, CHEO - Twins 3B - BB - Age 24

Good prospect, on a team that needs help at third base. In the majors he is ready now to hit for fair average and show good speed.

	AB	R	HR	RBI	SB	BA	$
1992 Orlando AA	488	54	4	44	32	.258	
1992 Portland AAA	6	0	0	0	0	.333	
1993 Base Case	77	7	0	6	4	.238	-
1993 High Range	303	35	2	26	15	.255	

GARDNER, JEFF - Padres SS/2B - BL - Age 29

Gardner got the 2B job at Vegas over Paul Faries and outhit his rival, boasting a .400 average in the second half. Gardner was the Vegas MVP. A Faries/Gardner platoon seems a natural at 2B. Gardner does not have Faries' speed but has a better eye (67 walks to 40).

	AB	R	HR	RBI	SB	BA	$
1992 Las Vegas AAA	439	82	1	51	7	.335	
1992 San Diego NL	19	0	0	0	0	.105	-
1993 Base Case	225	24	1	22	3	.250	-
1993 High Range	207	19	0	18	4	.270	

GATES, BRENT - Athletics 2B - BB - Age 23

First round draft pick in 1991, Gates could always hit. Last season he set a Class-A California League record by hitting in 35 consecutive games. Probably two years away from majors.

	AB	R	HR	RBI	SB	BA	$
1992 Modesto A	505	94	10	88	9	.321	

GEDMAN, RICH - Cardinals C - BL - Age 33

When Junior Ortiz was a backup catcher with the Pittsburgh Pirates, his teammates affectionately wore T-shirts that read: "Junior can't hit. Junior can't run. Junior can't throw. Why is Junior here?" That could apply to Gedman. Though he is one of the game's good people, he hasn't been a productive player for five years. Manager Joe Torre likes him, and he can still pop an occasional home run.

	AB	R	HR	RBI	SB	BA	$
1992 St. Louis NL	105	5	1	8	0	.219	-
1993 Base Case	55	3	0	4	0	.220	-
1993 High Range	186	10	2	16	0	.248	

GEREN, BOB - Red Sox C - BR - Age 31

His minor league roomie told me Geren never could hit a slider. Amazingly, it took major league pitchers a year to figure that out, even in the breaking ball league. Might surface during 1993, but not worth grabbing.

	AB	R	HR	RBI	SB	BA	$
1992 Winter Haven A	23	3	1	2	0	.304	
1992 Pawtucket AAA	213	28	9	25	0	.207	

GIANELLI, RAY - Blue Jays 3B/1B - BL - Age 27

Surfaced with the Blue Jays in 1991, but now he's just a AAA extension of the major league bench.

	AB	R	HR	RBI	SB	BA	$
1992 Syracuse AAA	249	23	5	22	2	.229	

GIBRALTER, STEVE - Reds OF - BR - Age 20

A 6th round draft choice in 1990, Gibralter led the Reds Cedar Rapids farm team in average, homers, RBI, and doubles. A gifted athlete who can run, field, hit, and throw. Voted the Midwest League MVP. Good long term pick, but not a factor for 1993.

	AB	R	HR	RBI	SB	BA	$
1992 Cedar Rapids A	529	92	19	99	12	.306	

GIL, BENJI - Rangers SS -BR - Age 20

Gil is the Rangers' best long-term offensive prospect. As he matures, he should display both speed and power; if he can handle the shortstop position defensively, he'll be one of the more valuable middle infielders when he arrives. It is unlikely that he will play in the majors in 1993, but 1994 is not out of the question.

	AB	R	HR	RBI	SB	BA	$
1992 Gastonia A	482	75	9	55	26	.274	
1993 High Range	125	11	0	9	2	.220	

GILBERT, SHAWN - Twins SS - BR - Age 28

Chances for major league play in 1993 are slim; hasn't yet had a ML at bat. May appear if injuries are rampant, and give you one SB; otherwise not worth a look.

	AB	R	HR	RBI	SB	BA	$
1992 Portland AAA	444	60	3	52	31	.245	

GILKEY, BERNARD - Cardinals OF - BR - Age 26

After a disappointing rookie season, Gilkey came back with a good year in 1992. With good power and speed, he figures to be a dependable player for many years. Playing for the Cardinals is the culmination of a lifetime dream; he was born and raised in St. Louis. One downside note: his big 1990 season was followed with an off year in 1991.

	AB	R	HR	RBI	SB	BA	$
1992 St. Louis NL	384	56	7	43	18	.302	19
1993 Low Range	272	37	4	23	8	.247	
1993 Base Case	424	63	8	42	20	.274	17
1993 High Range	528	86	11	59	33	.305	

GIRARDI, JOE - Rockies C - BR - Age 28

He is an outstanding defensive catcher and has been one of the toughest catchers to run against during his career. Girardi showed some (8-10 HR) power in the minors but has never had a multi-homer year in the majors. Mile High Stadium raises the possibilities for 1993.

	AB	R	HR	RBI	SB	BA	$
1992 Chicago NL	270	19	1	12	0	.270	1
1993 Low Range	293	18	2	22	0	.237	
1993 Base Case	364	26	3	30	0	.269	4
1993 High Range	484	40	8	46	0	.299	

GLADDEN, DAN - Tigers OF - BR - Age 35

Gladden had big skills now on the wane. He made Rob Wood's danger list a year ago. He's aging, hurt frequently, and his contribution as a base stealer is virtually gone.

	AB	R	HR	RBI	SB	BA	$
1992 Detroit AL	417	57	7	42	4	.254	6
1993 Low Range	307	38	4	27	2	.208	
1993 Base Case	375	50	6	39	4	.249	5
1993 High Range	505	75	10	60	7	.279	

GLANVILLE, DOUG - Cubs OF - BR - Age 22

Chicago's No. 1 draft pick in '91, out of the U. of Pennsylvania. A smooth-striding CF. Signed somewhat late in '91, played only 36 games. The question is whether he will hit enough to get his speed and defense to the majors.

	AB	R	HR	RBI	SB	BA	$
1992 Winston-Salem A	485	72	4	36	32	.258	

GOFF, JERRY - Expos C/3B/OF - BL - Age 28

He has bounced around for years without sticking in the major leagues; is versatile and his biggest value is that he bats left-handed and can catch. Three at bats and three strikeouts in the majors last year.

	AB	R	HR	RBI	SB	BA	$
1992 Indianapolis AAA	314	37	14	39	0	.239	
1992 Montreal NL	3	0	0	0	0	.000	-
1993 High Range	124	13	2	13	0	.229	

GOMEZ, LEO - Orioles 3B - BR - Age 26

The hard working Leo Gomez proved himself in 1992. He started off strong but slowed down in the second half. He's still improving and could have his career-best year in '93.

	AB	R	HR	RBI	SB	BA	$
1992 Baltimore AL	468	62	17	64	2	.265	13
1993 Low Range	384	42	11	45	1	.228	
1993 Base Case	503	60	18	69	2	.259	14
1993 High Range	558	74	24	85	3	.289	

GONZALES, RENE - Angels IF - BR - Age 31

After a winter of weight training, Gonzales had a surprisingly good career year in '92 that was curtailed by a broken left forearm. He showed surprising power in '92. Gonzales may have lost the third base job to Damion Easley and second to Luis Sojo leaving him to be an all-purpose utility man.

	AB	R	HR	RBI	SB	BA	$
1992 California AL	329	47	7	38	7	.277	9
1993 Low Range	112	13	1	9	2	.198	
1993 Base Case	280	36	4	26	7	.239	3
1993 High Range	313	45	5	34	11	.269	

GONZALEZ, JOSE - Angels OF - BR - Age 28

Jose Gonzalez is a utility outfielder. He spent six years in the Dodgers organization with some major league playing time. The Angels were his fourth organization in two years, and they released him on July 30.

	AB	R	HR	RBI	SB	BA	$
1992 Edmonton AAA	90	16	2	14	9	.322	
1992 California AL	55	4	0	2	0	.182	-
1992 Base Case	111	12	1	7	2	.212	
1993 High Range	85	5	1	7	1	.247	

GONZALEZ, JUAN - Rangers OF - BR - Age 23

Gonzalez won the AL home run title at the tender age of 22. The power part of his game has arrived; the question is whether, and to what extent, he will improve in the other areas. He has the speed to steal bases, but has not developed any technique yet. He also draws very few walks for a power hitter and strikes out frequently. But remember that age.

	AB	R	HR	RBI	SB	BA	$
1992 Texas AL	584	77	43	109	0	.260	26
1993 Low Range	515	64	33	85	0	.226	
1993 Base Case	577	78	46	110	0	.258	28
1993 High Range	596	89	50	121	0	.288	

GONZALEZ, LUIS - Astros OF - BL - Age 25

Demonstrated in 1992 that he could hit lefthanded pitching, which should elevate him to a full-time role. Came close to matching solid 1991 rookie year after a terrible start that sent him down to Triple-A Tucson to get straightened out. Not likely to be a superstar but should be a solid everyday player with his best years in front of him.

	AB	R	HR	RBI	SB	BA	$
1992 Tucson AAA	44	11	1	9	4	.432	
1992 Houston NL	387	40	10	55	7	.243	10
1993 Low Range	390	41	8	47	5	.213	
1993 Base Case	473	52	11	63	9	.254	12
1993 High Range	503	64	15	78	14	.284	

GOODWIN, TOM - Dodgers OF - BL - Age 24

As an outfielder and as a pinch-runner, Goodwin is impressive, but as a hitter, he has appeared overmatched. Goodwin will probably stick as a fifth outfielder and could provide some SB. Barring an injury to Butler, we cannot forecast a very big role; but if anyone gets hurt, Goodwin could become a regular instantly. A year later, the Websters and Benzingers are all a year closer to retirement, while Goodwin and his peers are all a year closer to big league productivity. The time is right in 1993.

	AB	R	HR	RBI	SB	BA	$
1992 Albuquerque AAA	319	48	2	28	27	.301	
1992 Los Angeles NL	73	15	0	3	7	.233	0
1993 Low Range	154	20	0	8	6	.206	
1993 Base Case	273	42	0	18	20	.247	6
1993 High Range	403	64	1	28	34	.277	

GRACE, MARK - Cubs 1B - BL - Age 28

The top Cubs 1B prospect pushed Leon Durham and Rafael Palmeiro out of the organization. Grace was The Sporting News rookie of the year in 1988. He finished in the top 10 in batting average in four of his five major league seasons. He has reached base 200 times in all five of his seasons.

	AB	R	HR	RBI	SB	BA	$
1992 Chicago NL	603	72	9	79	6	.307	23
1993 Low Range	500	52	6	56	3	,273	
1993 Base Case	590	67	10	76	6	.301	25
1993 High Range	617	77	15	89	9	.327	

GREBECK, CRAIG - White Sox IF - BR - Age 28

Aggressive ballplayer who can play second, short, or third. Spent end of season on disabled list with a broken foot. If Guillen does not recover from his injury, Grebeck will see much playing time at short.

	AB	R	HR	RBI	SB	BA	$
1992 Chicago AL	287	24	3	35	0	.268	4
1993 Low Range	127	10	1	15	0	.231	
1993 Base Case	230	20	3	31	0	.263	3
1993 High Range	308	29	4	48	1	.294	

GREEN, GARY - Reds SS - BR - Age 31

Your typical ex-prospect, Green has surfaced in the major leagues five times, with three different organizations, never getting more than 88 at bats in a season. Career .222 hitter.

	AB	R	HR	RBI	SB	BA	$
1992 Cincinnati NL	12	3	0	0	0	.333	-
1993 Base Case	52	3	0	3	0	.207	-
1993 High Range	205	14	2	14	1	.245	

GREEN, SHAWN - Blue Jays OF - BL - Age 20

Toronto's No. 1 pick in the '91 draft. Even though he was the 16th player chosen, Green held out throughout the '91 season and received the second-highest bonus ($700,000), behind only Brien Taylor. He had a very good '92 season for a 19-year-old playing in a tough league. Not much power, but good speed and strike-zone judgment.

	AB	R	HR	RBI	SB	BA	$
1992 Dunedin A	417	44	1	49	22	.273	

GREENE, WILLIE - Reds 3B - BR - Age 21

The Reds top minor league prospect, Greene has already been traded twice in major league deals (the Zane Smith deal and the Dave Martinez/John Wetteland trade). A tremendous season in Cedar Rapids and Chattanooga (27 HR and 106 RBI combined) put Greene into the Reds' 1993 plans. A position change (2B or outfield) is being considered to get Greene into the lineup in 1993, if he doesn't replace Sabo at third.

	AB	R	HR	RBI	SB	BA	$
1992 Cedar Rapids A	120	26	12	40	2	.283	0
1992 Chattanooga AA	349	47	15	66	8	.278	
1992 Cincinnati NL	93	10	2	13	2	.269	
1993 Low Range	186	18	4	21	1	.215	
1993 Base Case	366	40	9	48	4	.256	8
1993 High Range	495	59	15	74	7	.287	

GREENWELL, MIKE - Red Sox OF - BL - Age 29

Greenwell will turn 30 in July. He's spent a large portion of his career on the DL and his performance has tailed off noticeably since 1988. You can hope for a rebound, or trade him now. I recommend the latter. Fenway has granted some good numbers to Greenwell. If he goes elsewhere in 1993, he'll likely tail off another 7%-10% across the board.

	AB	R	HR	RBI	SB	BA	$
1992 Boston AL	180	16	2	18	2	.233	0
1993 Low Range	216	26	3	28	1	.238	
1993 Base Case	466	61	9	70	5	.270	14
1993 High Range	564	81	14	93	9	.301	

GREGG, TOMMY - Reds OF/1B - BL - Age 29

Good pinch hitter and backup. The one time he was given a regular job (1989) he immediately broke a leg and never made it back into the lineup.

	AB	R	HR	RBI	SB	BA	$
1992 Atlanta NL	19	1	1	1	1	.263	-
1993 Base Case	75	7	1	7	1	.269	
1993 High Range	282	28	6	30	6	.300	

GRIFFEY, KEN - Mariners OF - BL - Age 23

He has hit .300 with at least 20 homers in each of his three full seasons, and has knocked in 100 runs, despite the Mariners poor offense, in consecutive seasons. Offers the best combination of high potential and minimal risk of any player for 1993. He probably has the best "Low Range" in this book. And he might hit .360 on the far upside.

	AB	R	HR	RBI	SB	BA	$
1992 Seattle AL	565	83	27	103	10	.308	32
1993 Low Range	505	68	18	79	9	.287	
1993 Base Case	590	88	27	108	16	.316	43
1993 High Range	607	99	33	118	24	.338	

GRIFFIN, ALFREDO - Toronto SS - BB - Age 36
That telltale sign of a career-end: gone back to where it all started. Not what you need for 1993.

	AB	R	HR	RBI	SB	BA	$
1992 Toronto AL	150	21	0	10	3	.233	-
1993 Base Case	154	22	0	10	3	.233	-
1993 High Range	205	32	0	16	6	.263	

GRISSOM, MARQUIS - Expos OF - BR - Age 25
He is rapidly emerging as one of the game's best all-around players. He has led the NL in stolen bases each of the past two seasons and his power and defense are improving rapidly. He understands the team concept as he comes from a family of 16 children.

	AB	R	HR	RBI	SB	BA	$
1992 Montreal NL	653	99	14	66	78	.276	48
1993 Low Range	507	69	8	47	36	.250	
1993 Base Case	607	91	12	65	71	.277	43
1993 High Range	657	108	16	79	84	.308	

GROTEWOLD, JEFF - Phillies C/1B - BL - Age 27
Just another ex-prospect. Twice he hit 15 home runs, but never above the AA level.

	AB	R	HR	RBI	SB	BA	$
1992 Scranton AAA	51	8	1	8	0	.294	
1992 Philadelphia NL	65	7	3	5	0	.200	-
1993 High Range	195	23	4	23	1	.247	

GRUBER, KELLY - Blue Jays 3B - BR - Age 31
After a player has been injured two consecutive years, he becomes more of a speculation and less of an asset. Gruber's value peaked in 1988-1990. Unless you need to take chances, he is not worth what most people will pay for him in 1993. Should still be worth more this year than he was last year.

	AB	R	HR	RBI	SB	BA	$
1992 Toronto AL	446	42	11	43	7	.229	6
1993 Low Range	338	28	6	35	4	.211	
1993 Base Case	458	42	10	55	8	.252	10
1993 High Range	556	56	14	75	14	.282	

GUERRERO, JUAN - Astros IF - BR - Age 26
Rule Five draft acquisition spent essentially all year on the Astros' bench. A fair hitting prospect based on a .334-19-94 season at AA Shreveport in 1991. Did his best defensive work at shortstop, but does not project as an everyday major league shortstop.

	AB	R	HR	RBI	SB	BA	$
1992 Houston NL	125	8	1	14	1	.200	-
1993 Base Case	238	25	4	29	2	.234	1
1993 High Range	415	47	8	58	5	.274	

GUERRERO, PEDRO - Cardinals 1B - BR - Age 36
Shoulder and neck problems limited him to 43 games last season and he was generally ineffective. Age and injuries have taken their toll. Hit .255 in 55 AB at Louisville.

	AB	R	HR	RBI	SB	BA	$
1992 St. Louis NL	146	10	1	16	2	.219	-
1993 Low Range	96	7	2	12	0	.236	
1993 Base Case	261	21	6	37	1	.268	6
1993 High Range	457	41	12	73	3	.299	

GUILLEN, OZZIE - White Sox SS - BL - Age 29

Recovering from major reconstructive knee surgery. Was progressing well at the end of the season and should be OK for spring training. In the past, was most valuable for his stolen bases.

	AB	R	HR	RBI	SB	BA	$
1992 Chicago AL	40	5	0	7	1	.200	-
1993 Low Range	254	29	0	22	4	.213	
1993 Base Case	511	63	1	52	13	,254	9
1993 High Range	593	81	1	69	21	.284	

GULAN, MIKE - Cardinals 3B - BR - Age 22

Gulan was the Cardinals' second round pick in last June's draft and made an immediate professional impact. Though he faced weak competition as a collegian, he easily made the adjustment to the pros.

	AB	R	HR	RBI	SB	BA	$
1992 Hamilton A	242	33	7	36	11	.273	

GUTIERREZ, RICKY - Padres SS - BR - Age 22

Along with pitcher Erik Schullstrum, Gutierrez was acquired by the Padres in the late-season deal for Craig Lefferts. He is most likely to battle for the starting job at SS (or share it with Craig Shipley) now that Fernandez is dealt. Gutierrez hit over .300 in Rochester during the first few months of the season but faded. Despite an excellent fielding reputation, he was not considered the Baltimore organization's best SS candidate and played a great deal at 2B to accomodate current Philiies' prospect Juan Bell and the O's SS-of-the-future, Manny Alexander.

	AB	R	HR	RBI	SB	BA	$
1992 Rochester AAA	431	54	0	41	14	.253	
1993 Base Case	249	28	0	19	7	.231	1
1993 High Range	400	39	0	27	10	.250	

GWYNN, CHRIS - Royals OF - BL - Age 28

Repeated injury prevented Gwynn from ever getting a fair trial. With another chance he'll prove to be a valuable platoon player. Could reach 10 HR with part-time play. Limited opportunities with the Dodgers kept his numbers down - could be a fine $1 speculation.

	AB	R	HR	RBI	SB	BA	$
1992 Kansas City AL	84	10	1	7	0	.286	0
1993 Base Case	172	20	2	14	0	.266	1
1993 High Range	292	38	8	30	0	.297	

GWYNN, TONY - Padres OF - BL - Age 32

Gwynn has become a single-category player; his .317 average was his only Rotisserie contribution. He missed the last 26 games with a sprained left knee and has been rapidly losing speed, while gaining weight. Since 1989 (when he had 41 steals) his SB totals have fallen faster than mortgage rates (17, 8 and 3 the last three seasons). In fact, Gwynn was caught stealing 6 times in his 9 attempts. An intensive, off-season exercise program would be a positive indicator for 1993; Gwynn has become a doughboy.

	AB	R	HR	RBI	SB	BA	$
1992 San Diego NL	520	77	6	41	3	.317	17
1993 Low Range	394	51	4	44	3	.287	
1993 Base Case	524	74	7	68	7	.315	26
1993 High Range	604	94	10	87	12	.336	

HALE, CHIP - Twins 2B - BL - Age 28
Looked like he had the Twins' 2B job in 1990, but manager Kelly changed his mind at the last minute. Hale is still a credible prospect, obviously on the old side.

	AB	R	HR	RBI	SB	BA	$
1992 Portland AAA	474	77	1	53	3	.285	
1993 Base Case	30	2	0	2	0	.233	-
1993 High Range	267	22	2	18	2	.252	

HALL, BILLY - Padres 2B - BB - Age 24
Hall is a very fast, 5'9" dynamo who led the California League in batting and SB. A 17th-round draft pick in 1991 from Wichita State, Hall is a potential leadoff hitter for San Diego but is probably two years away. Second base is an organizational strength.

	AB	R	HR	RBI	SB	BA	$
1992 High Desert A	495	92	2	39	49	.356	

HALL, MEL - Japan OF - BL - Age 32
For years, Hall said that he could play every day, but people looked at his .151 career BA against lefty pitchers and guessed he was wrong. When Hall finally did get to play, he showed it was the stat-watchers who were wrong. For two years he clobbered lefty and righty pitchers alike. The only problem was that he then wanted $3 million, which had already been given to Danny Tartabull.

	AB	R	HR	RBI	SB	BA	$
1992 New York AL	583	67	15	81	4	.280	18

HAMILTON, DARRYL - Brewers OF - BL - Age 28
The quintessential Phil Garner player: good defense, excellent speed, no power. Hamilton is now established as a near-.300 hitter who can deliver 30 to 40 steals, and there is still room for improvement. Hamilton is certain to play, and as long as Garner is manager he will run often. Usually underrated.

	AB	R	HR	RBI	SB	BA	$
1992 Milwaukee AL	470	67	5	62	41	.298	30
1993 Low Range	359	48	5	41	18	.262	
1993 Base Case	466	68	7	62	37	.290	29
1993 High Range	532	85	10	79	53	.322	

HAMILTON, JEFF - Dodgers 3B - BR - Age 29
After being the Dodgers' regular 3B in the late 1980s, Hamilton has seen his career go down the tubes due to a succession of injuries. Hamilton posted decent stats at Albuquerque over 159 at-bats, but suffered a season-ending elbow injury after which the Dodgers released him. If healthy, Hamilton could be productive but the chances are extremely remote. He has not had a full season since 1989.

	AB	R	HR	RBI	SB	BA	$
1992 Albuquerque AAA	159	21	5	30	0	.302	

HAMMONDS, JEFFREY - Orioles OF - BL - Age 22
The fourth player selected in the June, 1992 draft, Hammonds spent the summer as the star center fielder of the U.S. Olympic team. He did not play professionally in 1992. Most scouts considered Hammonds the best amateur player in the U.S. and believe he would have been drafted No. 1 if his contract demands were more reasonable. The Birds expect Hammonds to progress quickly and it is not out of the question for him to make an appearance in the majors in late 1993. Hammonds is a right-handed, Devon White-type with outstanding defensive skills and 15-20 HR power. Hit .315 for the Olympians in 1992.

HANEY, TODD - Expos 2B - BR - Age 27
Hit .339 at Calgary in 1990. He has proven to be a high average hitter in Class AAA but has little power and only average speed. He isn't considered good enough to take the next step, though he did make his major-league debut at the end of 1992. He was outrighted back to the minors at the end of the season.

	AB	R	HR	RBI	SB	BA	$
1992 Indianapolis AAA	200	30	6	33	1	.265	
1992 Montreal NL	10	0	0	1	0	.300	-
1993 High Range	204	27	1	23	5	.277	

HANSEN, DAVE - Dodgers 3B - BL - Age 24
Hansen was given 341 at-bats to prove himself in 1992 and he failed. With Jody Reed at second base, Hansen will once again be pressed by the Harris/Sharperson platoon at 3B. Hansen's average will improve if he is given some unbroken time to develop, but he will never be big in the SB and HR departments.

	AB	R	HR	RBI	SB	BA	$
1992 Los Angeles NL	341	30	6	22	0	.214	-
1993 Low Range	314	26	4	28	0	.203	
1993 Base Case	376	33	5	39	1	.244	2
1993 High Range	537	53	10	62	2	.274	

HANSEN, TERREL - Mets 1B/OF - BR - Age 26
Was recalled by the Mets in mid-season, but never got into a game. Hansen is too slow for outfield duty, and has hit only 24 homers in the past two seasons, which is less than you might want from a first baseman.

	AB	R	HR	RBI	SB	BA	$
1992 Tidewater AAA	395	43	12	47	4	.248	
1993 Base Case	30	3	0	4	0	.200	
1993 High Range	282	30	9	35	3	.258	

HARE, SHAWN - Tigers OF - BL - Age 26
Another bright prospect who can hit for average and should develop power as he matures.

	AB	R	HR	RBI	SB	BA	$
1992 Toledo AAA	203	31	5	34	6	.330	
1992 Detroit AL	26	0	0	5	0	.115	-
1993 Base Case	105	10	1	13	2	.231	-
1993 High Range	227	24	3	31	5	.260	

HARPER, BRIAN - Twins C - BR - Age 33
Harper is one of a small number of good hitting catchers. He has hit around .300 for the past three years, but some decline in '93 would not be surprising as age advances.

	AB	R	HR	RBI	SB	BA	$
1992 Minnesota AL	502	58	9	73	0	.307	17
1993 Low Range	395	40	6	48	0	.273	
1993 Base Case	447	50	9	64	0	.301	18
1993 High Range	512	63	12	82	0	.323	

HARRIS, DONALD - Rangers OF - BR - Age 25
After failing to make the Dallas Cowboys' roster, he returned to baseball, but the news may not be much better there. After three years at AA, Harris has yet to hit well and has walked an average of once in every 23 AB. This year will be a make or break for the former #1 draft pick.

	AB	R	HR	RBI	SB	BA	$
1992 Texas AL	33	3	0	1	1	.182	-
1992 Tulsa AA	303	39	11	39	4	.254	
1993 Base Case	121	10	2	11	2	.223	-
1993 High Range	309	28	5	33	6	.252	

HARRIS, LENNY - Dodgers 3B - BL - Age 28

After several successful seasons as part of the "Har-person" platoon, Harris tailed off in 1992 along with a dozen other Dodgers. Although his average remained high, Harris had only 11 extra-base hits and made a whopping 27 errors. His weak performance opened the door for Jody Reed. Harris can still be an excellent utility player, however, and he is young. With his abilities, you can't write him off yet.

	AB	R	HR	RBI	SB	BA	$
1992 Los Angeles NL	347	28	0	30	19	.271	11
1993 Low Range	205	15	0	16	6	.238	
1993 Base Case	306	24	1	30	16	.269	9
1993 High Range	497	43	1	54	33	.300	

HASELMAN, BILL - Mariners C - BR - Age 26

M's picked him up on waivers. He showed power and speed at Triple-A in 1991 and showed even more power last year. He is not a good defensive catcher, which led Seattle to try him in the OF to get his bat into the line-up. Like Hector Villanueva, if he hits enough, someone will let him play.

	AB	R	HR	RBI	SB	BA	$
1992 Two Teams AAA	302	49	19	53	3	.255	
1992 Seattle AL	19	1	0	0	0	.263	-
1993 High Range	206	12	0	14	0	.247	

HATCHER, BILLY - Red Sox OF - BR - Age 32

Hatcher's major value has been his speed. With the lead-foot BoSox, he stole only 4 bases. He can still run, but is at the age when he'll pop a string or pull something and miss games.

	AB	R	HR	RBI	SB	BA	$
1992 Two Teams	409	47	3	33	4	.249	1
1993 Low Range	113	12	1	8	1	.201	
1993 Base Case	298	33	2	24	5	.242	1
1993 High Range	458	55	3	42	11	.272	

HAYES, CHARLIE - Rockies 3B - BR - Age 27

When Hayes was drafted, GM Gene Michael blushed visibly. Hayes is a good solid player now in his prime. His power will be worth more in the homer-scarce NL.

	AB	R	HR	RBI	SB	BA	$
1992 New York AL	509	52	18	66	3	.257	13
1993 Low Range	413	37	10	48	1	.228	
1993 Base Case	526	55	18	69	2	.262	14
1993 High Range	560	66	22	83	3	.290	

HAYES, VON - Unsigned OF - BL - Age 34

Hayes was released in August as the Angels went to a "changing of the guard" movement. The Angels were looking to Hayes for RBI but he wasn't producing. No other team picked him during the summer.

	AB	R	HR	RBI	SB	BA	$
1992 California AL	307	35	4	29	11	.225	4
1993 Base Case	200	20	2	20	7	.200	-
1993 High Range	335	40	8	40	14	.251	

HEATH, MIKE - Athletics C - BR - Age 38

Too many physical problems. Somebody get a fork.

	AB	R	HR	RBI	SB	BA	$
1992 Tacoma AAA	234	17	2	22	1	.209	

HEFFERNAN, BERT - Mariners C - BL - Age 28

With David Valle getting old, Heffernan will get more than 11 at bats in 1993 if he just stays healthy and stays in the organization.

	AB	R	HR	RBI	SB	BA	$
1992 Jacksonville AA	196	16	2	23	4	.286	
1992 Calgary AAA	46	8	1	4	1	.304	
1992 Seattle AL	11	0	0	1	0	.091	-
1993 Base Case	77	6	0	6	0	.230	-
1993 High Range	208	22	1	22	2	.261	

HELFAND, ERIC - Athletics C - BL - Age 24

The guy drafted by Florida and then traded back, for Walt Weiss. A .270 career hitter in three low minor league seasons, with fair power. Hit just .228 after midyear promotion to AA Huntsville in 1992.

HEMOND, SCOTT - White Sox IF/C - BR - Age 27

Acquired late in the season after the Oakland Athletics put him on waivers. Played six different positions in 25 games. Spent first half of season on disabled list with a rib injury.

	AB	R	HR	RBI	SB	BA	$
1992 Chicago AL	40	8	0	2	1	.225	-
1993 Base Case	50	9	0	5	2	.230	
1993 High Range	159	27	0	14	4	.249	

HENDERSON, DAVE - Athletics OF - BR - Age 34

34 year-old center fielder, Henderson missed almost entire season with a bad hamstring. Very difficult to come back after missing a full season.

	AB	R	HR	RBI	SB	BA	$
1992 Oakland AL	63	1	0	2	0	.143	-
1993 Low Range	188	21	4	22	0	.198	
1993 Base Case	303	36	8	41	1	.239	4
1993 High Range	426	56	14	66	2	.269	

HENDERSON, RICKEY - Athletics OF - BR - Age 34

One of the greatest talents in the game today, Rickey did not play with his accustomed fire last year due to nagging injuries and perennial contract blues. In an "off year", Henderson still stole 48 bases, just behind the league lead. The greatest unknown about Henderson is how much he will be limited by his accumulation of leg injuries.

	AB	R	HR	RBI	SB	BA	$
1992 Oakland AL	396	77	15	46	48	.283	32
1993 Low Range	324	56	10	33	23	.257	
1993 Base Case	419	80	16	49	49	.285	34
1993 High Range	558	117	26	75	75	.316	

HERNANDEZ, CARLOS - Dodgers C - BR - Age 25

Hernandez did not get much playing time despite the disappointing year from Scioscia. With Piazza's defensive development, Hernandez has been passed as Scioscia's heir apparent. Hernandez is a free-swinging slasher, reminiscent of Tony Pena. Ultimately, I think he will hit for a high average. He will platoon or rotate with Piazza. At age 25, he is still a good prospect. His arm is good enough to be a javelin champion.

	AB	R	HR	RBI	SB	BA	$
1992 Los Angeles NL	173	11	3	17	0	.260	1
1993 Low Range	205	16	2	19	0	.238	
1993 Base Case	264	23	4	28	1	.270	5
1993 High Range	307	29	6	37	1	.300	

HERNANDEZ, CESAR - Reds OF - BR - Age 26

Signed as a six year minor league free agent, Hernandez put together a solid year at Nashville and impressed the Reds with his defensive abilities. In line for a 5th outfielder role in 1993.

	AB	R	HR	RBI	SB	BA	$
1992 Chattanooga AA	328	50	3	27	12	.277	
1992 Cincinnati NL	51	6	0	4	3	.275	0
1993 Base Case	110	14	1	7	3	.262	0
1993 High Range	275	37	2	21	9	.292	

HERNANDEZ, JOSE M - Indians SS - BR - Age 19

Needs more minor league experience to solidify his hitting, but he could appear during 1993 if he gets off to a hot start and Cleveland needs help. Be careful which Jose Hernandez you are drafting. There is another shortstop Jose Hernandez who came up through the Rangers organization. Jose M is the better prospect, although they are both capable of reaching the major leagues in 1993.

	AB	R	HR	RBI	SB	BA	$
1992 Canton AA	404	56	3	46	7	.255	
1993 Base Case	30	3	0	3	1	.233	-
1993 High Range	285	27	1	29	4	.288	

HIATT, PHIL - Royals 3B/OF - BR - Age 23

One of few remaining good hitters on Royals farm. Being tried in OF since Gregg Jefferies blocks his path at 3B. Hiatt showed a lot more muscle in 1992 than he had before. If he makes it he must cut down on the strikeouts, and draw more walks without losing the power. Hiatt walked 25 times with 159 Ks in 487 Memphis AB in 1992. He's a distant prospect at best, but is among the best in the weak Royals farm system.

	AB	R	HR	RBI	SB	BA	$
1992 Memphis AA	487	71	27	83	5	.244	
1992 Omaha AAA	14	3	2	4	1	.214	
1993 Base Case	35	3	1	4	0	.190	-
1993 High Range	120	13	3	15	1	.212	

HILL, DONNIE - Twins 2B/SS - BB - Age 32

Peaked in 1986 with .285-3-48 and 9 SB. Now hardly worth a look.

	AB	R	HR	RBI	SB	BA	$
1992 Minnesota AL	51	7	0	2	0	.294	-
1993 Base Case	50	5	0	4	0	.239	-
1993 High Range	259	33	3	27	2	.270	

HILL, GLENALLEN - Indians OF - BR - Age 28

Hill had some clutch hits in '92, but he could still lose playing time as the Indians have a glut of OF/DH types, and Hill is beyond the rookie/prospect stage. He may end up with another team.

	AB	R	HR	RBI	SB	BA	$
1992 Cleveland AL	369	38	18	49	9	.241	12
1993 Low Range	355	34	14	42	6	.201	
1993 Base Case	402	43	20	55	11	.242	13
1993 High Range	503	59	30	77	20	.272	

HOCKING, DENNY - Twins SS - BB - Age 22

Although Hocking spent '92 at Class A Visalia, he's worth watching because he's a hard hitting shortstop who steals bases, a rarity. He's an excellent candidate for a long-range minor league draft pick.

	AB	R	HR	RBI	SB	BA	$
1992 Visalia A	550	117	7	81	38	.331	

HOILES, CHRIS - Orioles C - BR - Age 28

Hoiles was on his way to a 30+ home run season when his right wrist was broken by a pitched ball causing him to miss six weeks. At year end, a second operation was performed when it was discovered that things had not healed completely. The outlook for '93 is for Hoiles to resume his power hitting.

	AB	R	HR	RBI	SB	BA	$
1992 Baltimore AL	310	49	20	40	0	.274	12
1993 Low Range	389	51	14	41	0	.231	
1993 Base Case	404	58	18	49	0	.262	12
1993 High Range	483	77	26	67	0	.292	

HOLBERT, AARON - Cardinals SS - BR - Age 20

St. Louis' first round pick in 1990. Look for him in 1994-1995. Stole 62 bases at "A" Savannah in 1992.

HOLBERT, RAY - Padres SS - BR - Age 22

Spent four years at R and A-ball, but now he's on the move. Expect a full year in the minors in 1993. But in 1994 look for a .250 average and 15-20 stolen bases from an exciting rookie.

	AB	R	HR	RBI	SB	BA	$
1992 Wichita AA	304	46	2	23	26	.283	

HOLLINS, DAVE - Phillies 3B/1B - BB - Age 26

Hollins had hit 11 homers in 265 at bats in the majors prior to 1992, so the power was not a surprise. A steal as a Rule Five draft pick out of the San Diego system, the switch-hitting Hollins established himself as an emerging young star by showing big-time power from both sides of the plate. HBP 19 times.

	AB	R	HR	RBI	SB	BA	$
1992 Philadelphia NL	586	104	27	93	9	.270	27
1993 Low Range	504	85	21	74	4	.248	
1993 Base Case	587	109	30	100	8	.275	29
1993 High Range	596	121	36	109	12	.306	

HORN, SAM - Orioles DH/1B - BL - Age 29

Normally a platoon player, Horn became the forgotten man during the stretch drive as Randy Milligan and Glenn Davis got almost all of the playing time at DH. The Orioles signing a free agent slugger would reduce Horn's playing time even more. Not assured of anything for 1993.

	AB	R	HR	RBI	SB	BA	$
1992 Baltimore AL	162	13	5	19	0	.235	1
1993 Low Range	174	13	4	18	0	.194	
1993 Base Case	248	20	8	29	0	.235	1
1993 High Range	341	30	13	46	0	.264	

HOSEY, STEVE - Giants OF - BR - Age 23

Hosey was the Giants' top draft pick in 1989. In four minor league seasons, Hosey has averaged 14 home runs and 18 SB. Called up in August, Hosey was not given much of a look last season. Solid tools. Should benefit from the pending youth movement.

	AB	R	HR	RBI	SB	BA	$
1992 San Francisco NL	56	6	1	6	1	.250	-
1992 Phoenix AAA	462	64	10	65	15	.286	
1993 Low Range	189	23	3	21	3	.204	
1993 Base Case	258	35	7	33	7	.244	5
1993 High Range	408	61	15	60	14	.274	

HOUSIE, WAYNE - Red Sox OF - BB - Age 27

Appeared with the Red Sox briefly in 1991, but now he's just a career .252 hitter with fair speed, after seven years in the minor leagues.

	AB	R	HR	RBI	SB	BA	$
1992 Pawtucket AAA	456	53	2	28	20	.221	

HOUSTON, TYLER - Braves C - BL - Age 22

The top hitter picked in June 1989 (ahead of Frank Thomas). So far he's been a bust. And with Javy Lopez around, getting back on track wouldn't be enough to reach the majors.

HOWARD, CHRIS - Mariners C - BR - Age 27

Not to be confused with White Sox farm pitcher Chris Howard who was at Vancouver in 1992. The catcher is a typical low-average, fair-power type of backstop, not likely to be a factor in 1993.

	AB	R	HR	RBI	SB	BA	$
1992 Calgary AAA	319	29	8	45	3	.238	

HOWARD, DAVID - Royals SS/2B - BB - Age 26

A typical good field/no hit kind of shortstop that a bad fielding team like the Royals needs to glue its defense together. Of no value for Rotisserie purposes, though, and he'll hurt you with a low BA, no power, little speed. Hasn't yet proved capable of hitting AAA pitching. Don't get stuck with him.

	AB	R	HR	RBI	SB	BA	$
1992 Baseball City A	9	3	0	0	0	.444	
1992 Omaha AAA	68	5	0	5	1	.118	
1992 Kansas City AL	219	19	1	18	3	.224	-
1993 Low Range	105	8	0	7	1	.184	
1993 Base Case	309	28	2	27	4	.224	-
1993 High Range	443	44	3	43	8	.253	

HOWARD, THOMAS - Indians OF - BB - Age 28

Howard had a reasonably good season with Cleveland after coming over in a trade with San Diego. He's a contact-type singles hitter who can steal a dozen bases or more. And although he hasn't yet done it in the majors, he could hit .300 any year. His playing time may diminish in '93 because of a "domino effect" if Reggie Jefferson takes over the DH spot forcing Albert Belle to play left field.

	AB	R	HR	RBI	SB	BA	$
1992 Cleveland AL	358	36	2	32	15	.277	11
1993 Low Range	246	22	2	20	7	.247	
1993 Base Case	322	32	3	31	14	.274	10
1993 High Range	420	46	4	46	25	.305	

HOWELL, JACK - Unsigned 3B - BL - Age 31

Howell was once on track to be the Angels third baseman of the future, but was unfortunately traded to San Diego in 1991, where he became lost in their swamp of borderline major-league infielders, and he figured his odds were better overseas. Which they were: his 30 homers and .331 average both led the league.

	AB	R	HR	RBI	SB	BA	$
1992 Japan	321	55	30	69	---	.331	

HOWELL, PAT - Twins OF - BB - Age 24

Given a chance to play center field for a team that really needed a CF and leadoff hitter, he had one exciting game for the Mets and then faded rapidly.

	AB	R	HR	RBI	SB	BA	$
1992 Tidewater AAA	405	46	1	22	21	.244	
1992 New York NL	75	9	0	1	4	.187	-
1993 High Range	215	20	0	10	15	.242	

HOWIE, MARK - Reds 1B/2B - BR - Age 30

Howie had an awesome year in '91 at AA Midland in the Angels organization but is a career minor leaguer.

	AB	R	HR	RBI	SB	BA	$
1992 Nashville AAA	346	35	4	42	4	.246	-

HOWITT, DANN - Mariners 1B/OF - BL - Age 29

Appeared as an emergency sub with the Athletics every year from 1989-1992; but even with their decimated outfield last year, they didn't find Howitt very useful. The situation is no rosier in Seattle.

	AB	R	HR	RBI	SB	BA	$
1992 Tacoma AAA	140	25	1	27	5	.293	
1992 Calgary AAA	178	29	6	33	4	.303	
1992 Two Teams AL	85	7	2	10	1	.188	-
1993 High Range	203	24	5	27	2	.250	

HRBEK, KENT - Twins 1B - BL - Age 32

Injuries cut back on Hrbek's playing time in '92, and they are one factor behind Hrbek's worst year. He underwent shoulder surgery near the end of the season.

	AB	R	HR	RBI	SB	BA	$
1992 Minnesota AL	394	52	15	58	5	.244	10
1993 Low Range	375	41	11	45	2	.232	
1993 Base Case	402	49	14	56	4	.264	13
1993 High Range	538	72	23	84	8	.295	

HUBBARD, TRENT - Astros 2B - BR - Age 28

Seven-year minor leaguer had best season in 1992 to emerge as a candidate for a major league utility position. Has played every position including catcher. Averaged 32 stolen bases for seven years and gained team MVP honors in first three seasons. Has never appeared in the majors.

	AB	R	HR	RBI	SB	BA	$
1992 Tucson AAA	420	69	2	33	34	.310	-
1993 High Range	200	28	1	12	15	.240	

HUDLER, REX - Cardinals OF/IF -BR - Age 32

He is a good guy to have on a club with his intensity and ability to play anywhere in the infield or outfield. However, his offensive numbers keep slipping and he may not be in the majors much longer. He was a standout wide receiver in high school and nearly wound up accepting a scholarship to Notre Dame.

	AB	R	HR	RBI	SB	BA	$
1992 St. Louis NL	98	17	3	5	2	.245	0
1993 Low Range	110	15	2	7	1	.204	
1993 Base Case	209	32	5	15	4	.245	2
1993 High Range	307	52	8	25	9	.275	

HUFF, MIKE - White Sox OF - BR - Age 29

Former Dodger prospect. Huff was acquired from Cleveland in late 1991. Speedy outfielder, can be valuable if given a platoon role, and if he stays healthy.

	AB	R	HR	RBI	SB	BA	$
1992 Chicago AL	115	13	0	8	1	.209	-
1993 Low Range	122	13	0	7	1	.194	
1993 Base Case	186	21	0	13	2	.234	-
1993 High Range	319	40	0	25	4	.263	

HUGHES, KEITH - Reds OF - BL - Age 29

Career minor leaguer, last up with the Mets in 1990. Career major league average is .208.

HULETT, TIM - Orioles 3B/2B - BR - Age 33

Although Hulett is a utility infielder, he qualifies only at 3B under the Rotisserie 20-game eligibility rules. Like many utility men, he doesn't give you much offensively. Age is another negative factor.

	AB	R	HR	RBI	SB	BA	$
1992 Baltimore AL	142	11	2	21	0	.289	2
1993 Low Range	73	5	1	8	0	.214	
1993 Base Case	173	13	2	23	0	.255	1
1993 High Range	299	25	5	46	0	.285	

HULSE, DAVID - Rangers OF - BL - Age 25

A speedy defensive whiz, Hulse had never played an inning above Class A before 1992, he was a bright spot for the Rangers at the plate and in the field. There is doubt as to whether Hulse is capable of hitting well , but his 1992 performance was encouraging. He stole 44 bases (in 51 attempts) in Class A in 1991.

	AB	R	HR	RBI	SB	BA	$
1992 Texas AL	92	14	0	2	3	.304	1
1992 Okla. City AAA	30	7	0	3	2	.233	
1992 Tulsa AA	354	40	3	20	17	.285	
1993 Low Range	72	7	0	3	2	.228	
1993 Base Case	271	28	1	13	11	.259	4
1993 High Range	320	37	2	17	18	.289	

HUMPHREYS, MIKE - Yankees OF - BR - Age 25
Good talent, but the Yankees outfield has been more crowded than a New York subway during rush hour.

	AB	R	HR	RBI	SB	BA	$
1992 Columbus AAA	408	83	6	46	37	.282	
1993 Base Case	88	11	1	7	4	.259	1
1993 High Range	222	30	3	21	16	.289	

HUNDLEY, TODD - Mets C - BB - Age 23
Hundley's a fine receiver who throws well, but it's going to take a while for the batting average to become respectable. There is big upward possibility for those who need to take chances. He could turn into a .250 hitter with good power any time; just don't count on it.

	AB	R	HR	RBI	SB	BA	$
1992 New York NL	358	32	7	32	3	.209	1
1993 Low Range	324	27	5	26	2	.198	
1993 Base Case	401	37	7	38	5	.228	1
1993 High Range	476	49	10	51	8	.257	

HUNTER, BRIAN - Braves 1B - BR - Age 25
Locked into platoon role with Sid Bream. The pair combined for 24 HR and 102 RBI in 1992. Hunter will get the short end of the platoon since he hits righthanded. With a full-time job, his BA would drop and his power numbers would double. That won't happen with the 1993 Braves, though.

	AB	R	HR	RBI	SB	BA	$
1992 Atlanta NL	238	34	14	41	1	.239	8
1993 Low Range	309	40	15	46	1	.199	
1993 Base Case	340	49	20	59	1	.239	10
1993 High Range	406	64	29	78	2	.269	

HURST, JODY - Tigers OF - BR - Age 26
Gives definition to the term "borderline prospect." He's right on the edge in every aspect: speed, power, average, defense, and age. My prognosis is no major league time in 1993.

	AB	R	HR	RBI	SB	BA	$
1992 Toledo AAA	145	16	3	17	4	.186	
1992 London AA	269	48	11	52	17	.316	

HUSKEY, BUTCH - Mets - 3B - BR - Age 21
Huskey is a good long-range prospect with outstanding power and a clear chance to rise rapidly. The AA third baseman (Chris Butterfield) is nothing special, and the AAA third baseman (Chris Donnels) is now out of the way. The odds of Huskey reaching the majors this year are not good, though.

	AB	R	HR	RBI	SB	BA	$
1992 St. Lucie A	493	65	18	75	7	.254	

HUSON, JEFF - Rangers SS/2B - BL - Age 28
Had his best season in 1992, establishing career highs in doubles, triples, homers and steals. He should continue to have value as an infield backup, or perhaps even a platoon 2B, but is unlikely to regain a full-time starting job. He's one of the better choices to round out your infield for $3 at the end of the draft.

	AB	R	HR	RBI	SB	BA	$
1992 Texas AL	318	49	4	24	18	.261	10
1993 Low Range	251	31	2	19	7	.203	
1993 Base Case	332	45	3	30	15	.244	6
1993 High Range	429	64	5	44	25	.274	

HYZDU, ADAM - Giants OF - BR - Age 21
First round pick in 1990. Good speed/power combination, still maturing. Hit .278 with 9 home runs and 10 SB for "A" San Jose in 1992. Too many strikeouts, but he's improving.

INCAVIGLIA, PETE - Astros OF - BR - Age 28
Salvaged major league career with productive 1992 season. Lost weight during the off-season and worked hard in spring training to make the squad. Exceeded career average by 22 points in 1992 by cutting strikeouts. Can stay around if he stays in shape; but the playing time in Houston is a question.

	AB	R	HR	RBI	SB	BA	$
1992 Houston NL	341	31	11	44	2	.266	10
1993 Low Range	153	13	4	16	1	.205	
1993 Base Case	238	23	8	30	2	.246	3
1993 High Range	368	38	14	52	3	.276	

INGRAM, RICCARDO - Tigers OF - BR - Age 26
About the same as Jody Hurst. There are lots of them in the minor leagues; very few reach the majors.

	AB	R	HR	RBI	SB	BA	$
1992 Toledo AAA	410	45	8	41	8	.251	

> "You've got a hundred more kids than
> you have a place for on your ballclub."
>
> -- Earl Weaver

JACKSON, BO - White Sox DH - BR - Age 30

For box office purposes, he might actually appear during 1993. He was actually hitting well, on paper, during spring training 1992. But you don't want him in 1993, new hip or old.

	AB	R	HR	RBI	SB	BA	$
1993 Base Case	50	2	1	4	0	.221	-
1993 High Range	155	10	4	15	0	.250	

JACKSON, CHUCK - Rangers OF - BR - Age 30

Jackson worked out at catcher in the instructional league in the offseason in an attempt to return to the majors for the first time since 1988 with Houston. A longshot at best.

	AB	R	HR	RBI	SB	BA	$
1992 Okla. City AAA	457	66	10	54	3	.260	
1993 Base Case	60	6	1	5	0	.217	-
1993 High Range	120	13	2	12	1	.225	

JACKSON, DARRIN - Padres OF - BR - Age 29

Jackson appears to be settling in as a predictable, mid-.200s, 15-20 HR type. With Gwynn, Sheffield and McGriff batting in front of him, Jackson should have produced more than 70 RBI. His glove is steady enough to keep him in CF every day. Jackson was one of three Padres to strike out more than 95 times in 1992. He improved to steal 14 bases in 17 attempts in 1992 after just five thefts in 1991 and this total could increase under the aggressive Riggleman approach.

	AB	R	HR	RBI	SB	BA	$
1992 Padres NL	587	72	17	70	14	.249	18
1993 Low Range	415	45	12	45	6	.204	
1993 Base Case	532	63	19	67	12	.245	15
1993 High Range	603	79	26	84	20	.275	

JACKSON, JEFF - Phillies OF - BR - Age 21

Jackson is quite an athlete, but has many a mile to go before he becomes any kind of baseball player. The .242 average he posted at Clearwater was his highest in four professional seasons. Like most athletes, he's got the speed (stole 29 bases in 1991), but unfortunately not much else to build on at this point. Fourth pick overall in the first round in 1989.

	AB	R	HR	RBI	SB	BA	$
1992 Clearwater A	297	35	6	36	6	.242	
1992 Reading AA	108	12	0	6	9	.185	

JACOBY, BROOK - Indians 3B/1B - BR - Age 33

Veteran Jacoby was signed by the Indians as a free agent after his release by Oakland following a very poor '91 season. He was signed as insurance in case of problems with rookie third baseman Jim Thome or first baseman Reggie Jefferson. It was a wise move because both had injuries, and Jacoby found some of his lost skills. With a renewed focus on Thome and Jefferson, and an overall youth movement, look for Jacoby's playing time to decrease in 1993.

	AB	R	HR	RBI	SB	BA	$
1992 Cleveland AL	291	30	4	36	0	.261	4
1993 Low Range	129	11	1	13	0	.211	
1993 Base Case	222	21	3	25	0	.252	1
1993 High Range	406	42	6	53	0	.282	

JAHA, JOHN - Brewers 1B - BR - Age 26

Went through a pattern of being injured in even-numbered years, 1986-1990. With that behind him, the former 14th-round draft choice blossomed into a major leaguer in '92, his first season above Double-A. Was not caught stealing in the majors.

	AB	R	HR	RBI	SB	BA	$
1992 Denver AAA	274	61	18	69	6	.321	
1992 Milwaukee AL	133	17	2	10	10	.226	3
1993 Low Range	155	19	3	19	3	.212	
1993 Base Case	218	29	6	31	7	.253	6
1993 High Range	319	47	11	52	13	.283	

JAMES, CHRIS - Giants OF - BR - Age 30

Journeyman outfielder with occasional power. The Giants' move toward youth won't help him. Had one of the biggest Rotisserie days ever, with 11 RBI in one game in 1991.

	AB	R	HR	RBI	SB	BA	$
1992 San Francisco NL	248	25	5	32	2	.242	3
1993 Low Range	250	23	4	28	1	.201	
1993 Base Case	257	26	5	33	2	.242	2
1993 High Range	339	38	8	50	4	.272	

JAMES, DION - Yankees OF - BL - Age 30

Career looked finished in 1991, but he resurfaced with the Yankees in 1992. Still a career .282 hitter, so he's safe as a fill-in, but definitely not valuable.

	AB	R	HR	RBI	SB	BA	$
1992 New York AL	145	24	3	17	1	.262	2
1993 Base Case	55	5	1	5	1	.251	-
1993 High Range	227	41	6	30	2	.283	

JAVIER, STAN - Phillies OF - BB - Age 27

Javier's reached the point where he's about as good as he's going to get. Stan came up very young (broke in at age 18), but has used up the development phase of his career without managing to develop much. A pickup from the Dodgers when the Phillies were out of outfielders due to injuries, Javier is a switch-hitter who hit nearly 100 points better from the left side and who is valuable largely as a defensive replacement and spot starter.

	AB	R	HR	RBI	SB	BA	$
1992 Two Teams NL	334	42	1	29	18	.249	8
1993 Low Range	156	19	0	12	4	.213	
1993 Base Case	218	29	0	20	10	.254	4
1993 High Range	372	55	1	38	24	.284	

JEFFERIES, GREGG - Royals IF - BB - Age 25

Jefferies has been one of my favorite players for years, because he reached the major leagues so early and was "disappointing" only because of a fantastically huge build-up (BBA minor league player of the year two consecutive years). For comparison, he's the same age as Tino Martinez. Which one would you rather have? Now Jefferies is clearly a budding superstar with batting champion potential. Could hit .300 every year with 50 extra base hits. Will be Royals' best hitter for the next few years, batting third. Good speed, moderate power. Royals are willing to overlook questionable defense to let him play everyday. One of the few Royals hitters you can count on to get better - he's just 25 and already has 600+ major league games under his belt.

	AB	R	HR	RBI	SB	BA	$
1992 Kansas City AL	604	66	10	75	19	.285	23
1993 Low Range	497	50	11	58	12	.262	
1993 Base Case	587	65	16	80	24	.290	31
1993 High Range	614	74	21	93	34	.333	

JEFFERSON, REGGIE - Indians 1B - BB - Age 24

Jefferson was the top prospect in the Cincinnati organization, coming to the Indians in '91 via a trade forced when the Reds found themselves in a trade-or-lose waiver snafu. He was slated to start '92 as the Indians first baseman but came down with an injury. The newly acquired Paul Sorrento then locked up first base when he hit very well, and Jefferson was sent to AAA. He hit like Lou Gehrig after being called up in September. With Sorrento at first against RHP, Jefferson's '93 role will likely be DH, with Albert Belle moving to left field. Jefferson is ripe to have an outstanding season in '93.

	AB	R	HR	RBI	SB	BA	$
1992 Col. Sp. AAA	218	49	11	44	1	.312	
1992 Cleveland AL	89	8	1	6	0	.337	2
1993 Low Range	255	29	3	27	0	.253	
1993 Base Case	308	39	5	38	1	.280	8
1993 High Range	493	69	10	70	2	.311	

JENNINGS, DOUG - Orioles OF - BL - Age 28

Just a journeyman. Jennings appeared with Oakland every year from 1988-1991 but hit only .193 in total. There are too many other players just like him, and a year younger.

	AB	R	HR	RBI	SB	BA	$
1992 Rochester AAA	396	70	14	76	11	.275	
1993 Base Case	50	5	1	5	1	.230	-
1993 High Range	189	20	4	19	3	.263	

JENSEN, MARCUS - Giants C - BB - Age 20

Great athlete, he can also pitch. Unspectacular at "A" Clinton in 1992, but it's still early.

	AB	R	HR	RBI	SB	BA	$
1992 Clinton A	264	35	4	33	4	.239	

JETER, DEREK - Yankees SS - BR - Age 19

How far is it from high school to the Gulf Coast rookie league? Oh, about 270 points. Jeter hit .471 for Central High in Kalamazoo, Michigan, and then did the following in the GCL. Still, he was the top high school pick of 1992 and has about six years to improve.

	AB	R	HR	RBI	SB	BA	$
1992 Tampa R	173	19	3	25	2	.202	

JETER, SHAWN - White Sox OF - BL- Age 27

Drafted by Toronto in 1985. Part of the trade for Cory Snyder. Played first base and outfield in Toronto organization. Could see playing time in right this season. Fits well with ChiSox running game.

	AB	R	HR	RBI	SB	BA	$
1992 Chicago AL	18	1	0	0	0	.111	-
1992 Vancouver AAA	379	61	2	34	26	.301	
1993 Base Case	86	11	1	8	3	.234	-
1993 High Range	223	30	3	24	10	.264	

JOHNS, KEITH - Cardinals SS - BR - Age 21

Just a so-so hitter, he is an outstanding defensive shortstop. Some scouts say his fielding is good enough to play in the majors now.

	AB	R	HR	RBI	SB	BA	$
1992 Hamilton A	275	36	1	28	15	.284	-

JOHNSON, CHARLES - Marlins C - BR - Age 21

A star with the Miami Hurricanes, Johnson was a disappointment as a hitter for Team USA, but his defense is already very credible. Johnson signed with Florida with the understanding that he would finish his degree at Miami during the winter and then report to spring training. He's on the 40-man roster. He was the Marlins' first round pick in June 1992.

JOHNSON, HOWARD - Mets OF/3B - BB - Age 32

First base is the only place he should play, but that won't happen for at least another year. A player with speed is often wasted at first base, but HoJo's still-good legs are of no use to him defensively anyway (and neither is any other part of his body). Offensively, a fourth trip to the 30/30 club isn't out of the question. 1992 was his first truly bad season, but HoJo played hurt for quite a while before giving up the ghost.

	AB	R	HR	RBI	SB	BA	$
1992 New York NL	350	48	7	43	22	.223	11
1993 Low Range	406	51	15	54	14	.202	
1993 Base Case	466	64	21	73	26	.243	21
1993 High Range	540	81	30	93	39	.273	

JOHNSON, LANCE - White Sox OF - BL - Age 29

Everyday centerfielder. His speed makes him a good defensive player. Mostly a singles hitter. Improved stolen base percentage significantly this past season.

	AB	R	HR	RBI	SB	BA	$
1992 Chicago AL	567	67	3	47	41	.279	26
1993 Low Range	444	52	2	34	22	.258	
1993 Base Case	563	72	3	50	45	.285	30
1993 High Range	589	83	4	60	58	.317	

JONES, CHIPPER - Braves SS - BB - Age 21

Jones reversed a bad start at Durham with great numbers at Greenville. He's a little over-aggressive at the plate and shows just enough glove; his bat is good enough for the majors already. Expect a September call-up for 1993, if not midseason, and a chance at regular play by 1994. Rated by many as the best minor leaguer anywhere.

	AB	R	HR	RBI	SB	BA	$
1992 Durham A	264	43	4	31	10	.277	
1992 Greenville AA	266	43	9	42	14	.346	
1993 Low Range	45	5	1	6	1	.234	
1993 Base Case	206	22	5	20	4	.266	5
1993 High Range	408	47	10	44	10	.297	

JONES, CHRIS - Rockies OF - BR - Age 27

Just a fill-in, if he gets to play at all. Base Case is under 100 at bats with a .240 BA, no value.

	AB	R	HR	RBI	SB	BA	$
1992 Tuscon AAA	170	25	3	28	7	.324	
1992 Houston NL	63	7	1	4	3	.190	-
1993 High Range	235	32	4	26	8	.253	

JONES, RON - Giants OF - BL - Age 28

The Phillies' former can't-miss prospect. There is nobody younger with better major league production on a per-at-bat basis: .272 career average, 13 HR and 40 RBI in 239 at bats. Ah, but those aching knees.

	AB	R	HR	RBI	SB	BA	$
1992 Shreveport AA	198	20	4	25	3	.242	-

JONES, TIM - Cardinals SS/2B - BL - Age 30

His value lies in the fact that he is a left-handed hitter who can play any position, even pitch or catch in an emergency. He does not stay in the major leagues because of his bat.

	AB	R	HR	RBI	SB	BA	$
1992 St. Louis NL	145	9	0	3	5	.200	-
1993 Low Range	54	3	0	2	1	.178	
1993 Base Case	126	8	0	6	3	.218	-
1993 High Range	229	17	0	12	8	.250	

JONES, TRACY - Reds OF - BR - Age 32

Good speed/power combination who never got to play full time. Peaked in 1987 with the Reds (.290, 10 homers, 31 steals). Now just a fill-in, but a good midseason pickup if injuries to others somehow create an opportunity.

	AB	R	HR	RBI	SB	BA	$
1992 Vancouver AAA	219	30	1	23	4	.283	

JORDAN, BRIAN - Cardinals OF - BR - Age 26

After getting off to a hot start with the Cardinals last season, Jordan abandoned his two-sport career and stuck with baseball. Then he struggled, wound up back in Class AAA; stayed there after hurting his shoulder and missed September. At spring training 1992 he was the consensus most improved player in Florida, having changed from a raw-talent body into someone who knows how to play.

	AB	R	HR	RBI	SB	BA	$
1992 Louisville AAA	155	23	4	16	13	.290	
1992 St. Louis NL	193	17	5	22	7	.207	2
1993 Low Range	280	27	5	28	7	.186	
1993 Base Case	344	37	7	40	13	.226	5
1993 High Range	433	51	14	63	26	.270	

JORDAN, RICKY - Phillies 1B - BR - Age 27

Jordan has never developed the power that some expected based on his rookie season (11 HR in less than half a season), but it looks like he'll be a consistent .285-range line drive hitter. A broken jaw and John Kruk's big season limited Jordan's playing time in 1992. He remains an undiscplined hitter who walked only 5 times in 276 at bats. A little mental adjustment could boost his performance dramatically.

	AB	R	HR	RBI	SB	BA	$
1992 Scranton AAA	19	1	0	2	0	.263	
1992 Philadelphia NL	276	33	4	34	3	.304	9
1993 Low Range	285	32	5	31	2	.263	
1993 Base Case	340	41	7	43	4	.291	12
1993 High Range	521	70	14	75	9	.319	

JORGENSEN, TERRY - Twins 3B/1B - BR - Age 26

Jorgensen is a first and third baseman who couldn't beat out Scott Leius as part of a 3B platoon. Although his normal position is third base, he filled in at first base when Kent Hrbek was injured. He may get another chance at third if SS Greg Gagne leaves via the free agent route and Leius moves over to short. Base Case is under 100 at bats with a .260 average and no value.

	AB	R	HR	RBI	SB	BA	$
1992 Portland AAA	505	78	14	71	2	.295	
1992 Minnesota AL	58	5	0	5	1	.310	0
1993 High Range	281	32	4	32	1	.304	

JOSE, FELIX - Cardinals OF - BB - Age 27

One of the best physical specimens in the game, he just looks like a player. With above-average power and speed, his potential is unlimited, though his home run total in 1992 was a slight disappointment.

	AB	R	HR	RBI	SB	BA	$
1992 St. Louis NL	509	62	14	75	28	.295	30
1993 Low Range	502	58	11	65	17	.260	
1993 Base Case	552	71	15	83	31	.288	33
1993 High Range	571	80	19	94	41	.320	

JOYNER, WALLY - Royals 1B - BL - Age 30

The Royals pushed aside their best prospect (Jeff Conine) to sign Joyner to a multi-year contract. Had worst full season in 1992, should rebound somewhat. Will hit fourth or fifth in 1993, so his RBI totals will be safe. Expect his BA to return to .280+ level, but don't count on double-digit SB every year.

	AB	R	HR	RBI	SB	BA	$
1992 Kansas City AL	572	66	9	66	11	.269	15
1993 Low Range	514	64	13	78	4	.250	
1993 Base Case	565	77	18	99	8	.277	24
1993 High Range	593	89	23	111	12	.308	

JUSTICE, DAVID - Braves OF - BL - Age 26

A better hitter than he showed in 1992, was often pitched around by NL hurlers wishing instead to face Sid Bream or Brian Hunter with runners aboard. Justice still shows remarkable patience at the plate. Rising walk totals (79 in 1992) are an indication of a hitter getting better. On the other hand, Justice's baserunning is going the other direction; a nagging leg injury kept him from running effectively; he's probably seen his last double-digit SB season (1990, 11 steals).

	AB	R	HR	RBI	SB	BA	$
1992 Atlanta NL	484	78	21	72	2	.256	17
1993 Low Range	399	60	15	53	1	.229	
1993 Base Case	495	82	24	77	2	.260	17
1993 High Range	557	101	32	95	3	.291	

KARKOVICE, RON - White Sox C - BR - Age 29

One of the strongest arms in the majors. Karkovice developed into a decent hitter quickly after a horrendous beginning (.174 in 1988). He's been a consistent .240 hitter with decent power, ever since. It's just taking people a while to catch on.

	AB	R	HR	RBI	SB	BA	$
1992 Chicago AL	342	39	13	50	10	.237	10
1993 Low Range	259	27	6	32	2	.206	
1993 Base Case	406	47	11	58	6	.247	9
1993 High Range	466	59	16	75	9	.277	

KARROS, ERIC - Dodgers 1B - BR - Age 25

Karros' Rookie-of-the-Year season makes it hard to remember that Lasorda was toying with Kal Daniels and Todd Benzinger at 1B in the spring of 1992. Obviously, Karros was one of the few L.A. bright spots in a dismal 1992 season. He appears to be a fixture at 1B for the foreseeable future and should reduce his strikeouts and increase his BA in 1993. The power numbers are legitimate.

	AB	R	HR	RBI	SB	BA	$
1992 Los Angeles NL	545	63	20	88	2	.257	18
1993 Low Range	497	57	13	70	1	.234	
1993 Base Case	547	69	18	90	2	.266	18
1993 High Range	584	81	23	103	4	.296	

KELLY, MIKE - Braves OF - BR - Age 22

Number one 1991 Braves draft pick. Excellent power and speed despite low average and striking out in bunches (161 K in 471 AB). When he gets the whiffs under control he'll be a force. Has been compared to Barry Bonds, who also came out of Arizona State and had a low batting average in his first major league season. Kelly covers ground in the OF like Bonds, but has a strong enough arm to play CF.

	AB	R	HR	RBI	SB	BA	$
1992 Greenville AA	471	83	25	71	22	.229	

KELLY, PAT - Yankees 2B - BR - Age 25

Although impaired by injuries and a crowded middle infield in 1992, Kelly managed to produce a little value in both speed and power categories. He's one of the Yankees' best natural athletes.

	AB	R	HR	RBI	SB	BA	$
1992 New York AL	318	38	7	27	8	.226	4
1993 Low Range	286	35	4	24	6	.207	
1993 Base Case	349	47	6	34	13	.248	8
1993 High Range	441	66	9	50	23	.278	

KELLY, ROBERTO - Reds OF - BR - Age 28

In the National League he will see more fastballs and be asked to run more on the bases. Also, his home runs will be worth more in NL stat leagues. Look for a surge in value. One of my favorites for 1993. He's a sleeping giant, both in "real" baseball and even more for Rotisserie leagues.

	AB	R	HR	RBI	SB	BA	$
1992 New York AL	580	81	10	66	28	.272	23
1993 Low Range	452	63	13	52	22	.252	
1993 Base Case	520	80	18	70	41	.279	33
1993 High Range	621	105	26	92	58	.310	

KENDALL, JASON - Pirates C - BR - Age 18

Short of catching prospects, the Pirates made the son of former major-league catcher Fred Kendall their top pick in last year's draft. He showed solid defensive skills but lacked power. Had a 44-game hitting streak in high school; tied the national scholastic record.

	AB	R	HR	RBI	SB	BA	$
1992 Bradenton R	111	7	0	10	2	.252	

KENT, JEFF - Mets 2B - BR - Age 25

The Mets may turn out to win the David Cone trade after all. Kent was one-half of the Blue Jays payment for Cone, and is the Mets second baseman of the immediate future. His talents are all-around power for a middle infielder, above-average speed (25 steals in 1991), and adequate defense still improving. The Mets will give him PT and won't bury him at the bottom of the batting order; they want Kent to look good.

	AB	R	HR	RBI	SB	BA	$
1992 Toronto AL	192	36	8	35	2	.240	
1992 New York NL	113	16	3	15	0	.239	0
1993 Low Range	295	42	7	38	4	.199	
1993 Base Case	384	60	11	57	8	.239	8
1993 High Range	509	88	18	85	15	.269	

KING, JEFF - Pirates IF - BR - Age 28

Some July 4 fireworks, psychological style, turned King's 1992 season around. On July 4, the top pick in the 1986 draft was hitting just .185 and the Pirates sent him to Class AAA Buffalo. Pirates General Manager Ted Simmons said King was demoted because he was in a "coma". The wake-up call worked. King returned 10 days later, right after Steve Buechele was traded to the Cubs, and put a stranglehold on the third base job.

	AB	R	HR	RBI	SB	BA	$
1992 Buffalo AAA	29	6	2	5	1	.345	
1992 Pittsburgh NL	480	56	14	65	4	.231	9
1993 Low Range	229	26	5	27	2	.196	
1993 Base Case	411	51	11	57	4	.236	6
1993 High Range	510	69	16	79	8	.265	

KINGERY, MIKE - Athletics OF - BL - Age 32

Hit .280 with speed and power for the Mariners in 1987, but never clicked again after that. As an emergency fill-in he's an OK .250 hitter.

	AB	R	HR	RBI	SB	BA	$
1992 Oakland AL	28	3	0	1	0	.107	-
1993 Base Case	40	4	0	4	0	.245	-
1993 High Range	242	31	3	24	5	.263	

KIRBY, WAYNE - Indians OF - BL - Age 29

Kirby is a speedy contact-hitting outfielder who hits well in the minors but has flopped in the majors. The Dodgers gave up on him, and he was then signed by Cleveland. He is running out of chances. Base Case is 50 at bats with a .250 average, no value unless he gets a job as a pinch runner.

	AB	R	HR	RBI	SB	BA	$
1992 Col. Sp. AAA	470	101	11	74	51	.345	
1993 Cleveland AL	18	9	1	1	0	.167	-
1993 High Range	206	34	4	20	11	.289	

KLESKO, RYAN - Braves 1B - BL - Age 21

Disregard Klesko's 0-for-14 in the majors last year. Pay more attention to 48 minor league HR over the last three years. Klesko will eventually replace Sid Bream and produce slightly better power. Klesko isn't a great prospect, but he'll do just fine when he arrives in Atlanta for good in 1994.

	AB	R	HR	RBI	SB	BA	$
1992 Richmond AAA	418	63	17	59	3	.251	
1992 Atlanta NL	14	0	0	1	0	.000	-
1993 Base Case	103	11	3	13	0	.224	-
1993 High Range	334	37	10	42	1	.253	

KMAK, JOE - Brewers C - BR - Age 29

Just had his best year ever, almost certainly too late. Base Case is zero at bats. Brewers have enough catchers already. With another team he could be a #3 backstop but still with no value.

	AB	R	HR	RBI	SB	BA	$
1992 Denver AAA	225	27	3	31	6	.311	-

KNOBLAUCH, CHUCK - Twins 2B - BR - Age 24

With his consistency in '92, Knoblauch proved that he was not a "one-year wonder" as some rookies-of-the-year prove to be. Knoblauch is still young enough to be improving, and you know I love speed.

	AB	R	HR	RBI	SB	BA	$
1992 Minnesota AL	600	104	2	56	34	.297	27
1993 Low Range	491	74	1	42	16	.265	
1993 Base Case	581	96	2	58	30	.292	27
1993 High Range	609	111	3	69	41	.314	

KNORR, RANDY - Blue Jays C - BR - Age 24

Good hitter. Just a question of playing time.

	AB	R	HR	RBI	SB	BA	$
1992 Syracuse AAA	228	27	11	27	1	.272	
1992 Toronto AL	19	1	1	2	0	.263	-
1993 Base Case	63	4	1	6	0	.236	-
1993 High Range	203	15	3	23	1	.266	

KOMMINSK, BRAD - White Sox OF - BR - Age 31

The perpetual prospect. Coulda been a contenduh. Now he's just a .218 career hitter in cameo appearances spread over eight major league seasons.

	AB	R	HR	RBI	SB	BA	$
1992 Vancouver AAA	415	72	10	68	9	.275	

KOSLOFSKI, KEVIN - Royals OF - BL - Age 26

Spent six years in Rookie and Class A before rapidly percolating to the top of the farm system. Good speed, good defense, spark-plug kind of player. Was slated for a platoon role with KC or Omaha, depending on who else is available.

	AB	R	HR	RBI	SB	BA	$
1992 Omaha AAA	280	29	4	32	8	.311	
1992 Kansas City AL	133	20	3	13	2	.248	1
1993 Low Range	126	14	1	12	1	.232	
1993 Base Case	271	33	4	30	3	.264	5
1993 High Range	397	54	7	50	7	.294	

KREMERS, JIMMY - Expos C/1B - BL - Age 27

Spent 1992 at AAA Indianapolis, hitting .215 with two home runs. Look elsewhere.

KREUTER, CHAD - Tigers C - BB - Age 28

He'll play when Tettleton needs a rest. Will contribute a homer or two, not much else.

	AB	R	HR	RBI	SB	BA	$
1992 Detroit AL	190	22	2	16	0	.253	0
1993 Low Range	180	18	2	13	0	.189	
1993 Base Case	242	27	3	20	0	.230	0
1993 High Range	318	39	5	30	0	.259	

KRUK, JOHN - Phillies 1B/OF - BL - Age 32

Kruk really shouldn't be playing the outfield anymore, but may find himself there if the Phillies choose to have Ricky Jordan in the lineup more. Although he hit 21 homers in 1991, Kruk is an opposite-field singles and doubles hitter who's not likely to produce many homers unless he drops 30 or 40 points off his average. Until injuries wore him down, Kruk was in the hunt for a 1992 batting title. His power has been sporadic but there are no more natural, albeit unconventional, hitters in baseball.

	AB	R	HR	RBI	SB	BA	$
1992 Philadelphia NL	507	86	10	70	3	.323	23
1993 Low Range	447	68	9	56	2	.273	
1993 Base Case	510	85	13	74	4	.301	24
1993 High Range	530	97	17	86	5	.323	

KUNKEL, JEFF - Reds SS/OF - BR - Age 31

One of several middle-age free agents signed by the Reds in November. No clear future. Base Case is 50 at bats with a .225 average, no value.

	AB	R	HR	RBI	SB	BA	$
1992 Chicago NL	29	0	0	1	0	.138	-
1993 High Range	242	22	3	21	1	.247	

LAKE, STEVE - Phillies C - BR - Age 36

Lake has managed to hang around forever because he throws extemely well (or at least he used to), and he can hit lefties a little. 1992 was possibly his curtain call; base case is 40 at bats with a .230 average.

	AB	R	HR	RBI	SB	BA	$
1992 Philadelphia NL	53	3	1	2	0	.245	-
1993 High Range	173	11	4	10	0	.275	

LAKER, TIM - Expos C - BR - Age 23

Called up from Class AA at Expos manager Felipe Alou's request in August. Known primarily for his defense, he was solid behind the plate in the majors but did not do anything at bat. Laker has some power but will stick in the big leagues because of his defense. Base Case is 50 at bats with a .210 average.

	AB	R	HR	RBI	SB	BA	$
1992 Harrisburg AA	409	55	15	68	3	.242	
1992 Montreal NL	46	8	0	4	1	.217	-
1993 High Range	165	20	2	20	1	.240	

LAMPKIN, TOM - Padres C - BL - Age 29

Career .204 hitter. Look elsewhere. Base case is 50 at bats and, oh, about a .204 BA.

	AB	R	HR	RBI	SB	BA	$
1992 San Diego NL	17	3	0	0	2	.235	-

LANDRUM, CEDRIC - Brewers OF - BL - Age 29

Landrum has a place in Rotisserie science as the best example of why you should not project stolen bases on a per-at-bat basis. In 1991 with the Cubs, he got 27 steals in 86 AB. Over a full season with 550 at bats, that would project to a season total of 173 SB. The lesson is that you have to back out pinch running stats when you want to analyze a hitter. (The "Cedric Landrum" principle.) Won't play in the majors in 1993 unless he gets lucky. If he does appear, hope he gets work as ... right, a pinch runner.

	AB	R	HR	RBI	SB	BA	$
1992 Iowa AAA	20	4	0	0	1	.300	
1992 Denver AAA	144	20	1	19	15	.313	

LANE, BRIAN - Reds 3B - BR - Age 23

The acquisition of Willie Greene put a wet blanket on Lane's career with Cincinnati. He wouldn't be a big value, anyway.

	AB	R	HR	RBI	SB	BA	$
1992 Chatanooga AA	142	21	3	23	3	.282	
1992 Nashville AAA	67	8	3	8	0	.239	

LANKFORD, RAY - Cardinals OF - BL - Age 25

Lankford was one of my favorite picks for 1992. A true five-tool player, he blossomed into a star last year. He has good power, speed and hits for a high average. He strikes out a bit too much, but his other skills more than compensate. An outstanding athlete, he rushed for 1,000 yards as a junior college running back.

	AB	R	HR	RBI	SB	BA	$
1992 St. Louis NL	598	87	20	86	42	.293	41
1993 Low Range	435	59	12	59	21	.260	
1993 Base Case	535	80	19	85	42	.288	38
1993 High Range	601	98	26	102	59	.320	

LANSFORD, CARNEY - Retired - BR- Age 36

Comeback player of the year after missing 1991 season due to major knee injury (snowmobile accident), Lansford had a decent offensive year. Announced his retirement last October.

	AB	R	HR	RBI	SB	BA	$
1992 Oakland AL	496	65	7	75	7	.262	9

LANSING, MIKE - Expos SS - BR - Age 24

After being purchased from independent Miami of the Class A Florida State League, Lansing blossomed in the Expos' organization. Does not have great tools but has good baseball savvy. Scouts are split on whether he will be a starting shortstop or utilityman in the majors. I think the latter.

	AB	R	HR	RBI	SB	BA	$
1992 Harrisburg AA	483	66	6	54	46	.280	

LARKIN, BARRY - Reds SS - BR - Age 28

The best shortstop in baseball and in the prime of his career. The last shortstop to hit .300 for 4 straight years was Harvey Kuenn. The MVP if he stays healthy for a full year (the Reds won the World Series the only year Larkin was healthy for an entire season).

	AB	R	HR	RBI	SB	BA	$
1992 Cincinnati NL	533	76	12	78	15	.304	26
1993 Low Range	488	62	10	63	8	.272	
1993 Base Case	542	76	14	81	15	.300	29
1993 High Range	592	91	18	97	23	.322	

LARKIN, GENE - Twins 1B/OF - BB - Age 30

Although Larkin could get at least 300 at-bats in past years, his playing time will decrease as the Twins give time to promising rookies such as David McCarty, and more time to Pedro Munoz. At most, Larkin gives you a decent average and a few RBI.

	AB	R	HR	RBI	SB	BA	$
1992 Minnesota AL	337	38	6	42	7	.246	6
1993 Low Range	152	13	2	15	2	,203	
1993 Base Case	257	29	4	34	6	.243	4
1993 High Range	322	34	5	42	9	.273	

LAVALLIERE, MIKE - Pirates C - BL - Age 32

Appeared to be a player in decline in 1992. LaValliere has no power and may be the slowest player in the game. He must hit for a high average and be a good defensive catcher to be a productive player. He slipped in both areas last year. We give him the benefit of the doubt, because of injuries.

	AB	R	HR	RBI	SB	BA	$
1992 Pittsburgh NL	293	22	2	29	0	.256	2
1993 Low Range	228	14	1	20	0	.232	
1993 Base Case	265	18	2	27	0	.264	3
1993 High Range	378	29	3	44	0	.294	

LEE, DEREK - White Sox OF - BL - Age 26

Hit .325 at Birmingham in 1991, but hasn't been a star in the PCL. It would take at least two lucky breaks to get him to the majors in 1993.

	AB	R	HR	RBI	SB	BA	$
1992 Vancouver AAA	381	58	7	50	17	.273	

LEE, MANUEL - Blue Jays SS - BB - Age 27

Given a chance to play, Lee is a steady and solid contributor, though he will never have a high value. People who got him for $1 or $2 last year were all perfectly happy with the results.

	AB	R	HR	RBI	SB	BA	$
1992 Toronto AL	396	49	3	39	6	.263	7
1993 Low Range	286	32	1	23	2	.227	
1993 Base Case	366	44	2	34	5	.258	5
1993 High Range	503	67	3	53	9	.288	

LEE, TERRY - Twins 1B - BR - Age 31

Hit over .300 at A, AA, and AAA on his way up the Reds' ladder, but got only 25 at bats with Cincinnati in 1990-1991 combined. Base Case is zero at bats for 1993.

	AB	R	HR	RBI	SB	BA	$
1992 Col. Springs AAA	71	10	0	11	0	.254	
1992 Portland AAA	296	58	6	45	8	.291	

LEIUS, SCOTT - Twins 3B/SS - BR - Age 27

Leius got more playing time in '92 because of an injury to his platoon partner. As a result, he saw more RHP, against which he hit .223. In 1993 he may platoon again, or he may take over SS if Greg Gagne signs with another team. If he plays regularly, he will see more right handers again causing his BA to stay low.

	AB	R	HR	RBI	SB	BA	$
1992 Minnesota AL	409	50	2	35	6	.249	4
1993 Low Range	255	27	1	18	2	.196	
1993 Base Case	352	41	1	29	4	.236	0
1993 High Range	404	52	2	38	7	.266	

LEMKE, MARK - Braves 2B - BB - Age 27

Just can't quite make that big step forward to claim second base permanently. He played full-time but couldn't contribute much offense. His power increased and Lemke showed good plate discipline (50 walks were second on the team).

	AB	R	HR	RBI	SB	BA	$
1992 Atlanta NL	427	38	6	26	0	.227	0
1993 Low Range	267	25	3	16	1	.188	
1993 Base Case	355	37	6	25	1	.229	
1993 High Range	421	48	8	34	2	.258	

LENNON, PATRICK - Mariners OF - BR - Age 24

Lennon got a brief taste of the majors in 1991 and 1992. He missed most of last year with an injury. In 1991, he batted .329 with 15 HR, 74 RBI, and 12 SB. He is still a top prospect.

	AB	R	HR	RBI	SB	BA	$
1992 Calgary AAA	48	8	1	9	4	.354	
1993 Base Case	223	34	5	33	10	.253	5
1993 High Range	435	62	11	61	24	.283	

LEONARD, MARK - Giants OF - BL - Age 28

Long time minor leaguer with a major league bat. Giants have been egregiously slow in getting him playing time, but it's not yet too late.

	AB	R	HR	RBI	SB	BA	$
1992 San Francisco NL	128	13	4	16	0	.234	0
1992 Phoenix AAA	139	17	5	25	1	.338	
1993 Low Range	83	9	2	9	0	.203	
1993 Base Case	279	33	8	34	1	.244	3
1993 High Range	408	52	14	57	1	.274	

LEVIS, JESSE - Indians C - BL - Age 24

Levis got major league playing time as a result of injuries to Sandy Alomar and Joel Skinner. He is a good hitting prospect, but it's highly unlikely he can dislodge Sandy Alomar.

	AB	R	HR	RBI	SB	BA	$
1992 Col. Sp. AAA	253	39	6	44	1	.364	
1992 Cleveland AL	43	2	1	3	0	.279	-
1993 Low Range	73	6	1	7	0	.261	
1993 Base Case	188	18	3	20	1	.289	4
1993 High Range	314	33	7	38	2	.320	

LEWIS, DARREN - Giants OF - BR - Age 25

Fomerly with Oakland. Great defensive center fielder with good speed. Right field, fly ball hitter. Has a noticeable dip in his swing, causing his bat to slow through the hitting zone. One little adjustment could produce a big change in results.

	AB	R	HR	RBI	SB	BA	$
1992 San Francisco NL	320	38	1	18	28	.231	9
1992 Phoenix AAA	158	22	0	6	9	.228	
1993 Low Range	273	34	1	19	12	.209	
1993 Base Case	368	50	2	30	26	.250	11
1993 High Range	506	76	3	47	45	.280	

LEWIS, MARK - Indians SS/2B - BR - Age 23

Lewis is a young and improving shortstop who had some good streaks in '92, including 11 games when he went 17-for-36 or .472. His season RBI total of 30 is very disappointing but it should improve in '93. Comparison to young Robin Yount are becoming less frequent, but I still see him as one of the best break-out possibilities for 1993. He is certain to improve, at least a little, maybe a lot.

	AB	R	HR	RBI	SB	BA	$
1992 Cleveland AL	413	44	5	30	4	.264	6
1993 Low Range	398	42	4	36	4	.237	
1993 Base Case	501	58	7	52	8	.269	13
1993 High Range	569	72	9	67	13	.300	

LEYRITZ, JIM - Yankees C/3B - BR - Age 29

Held back by misunderstandings with the New York front office during his formative years, Leyritz has recovered to become a decent utility player. Can handle left field OK too.

	AB	R	HR	RBI	SB	BA	$
1992 New York AL	144	17	7	26	0	.257	3
1993 Low Range	64	6	1	6	0	.202	
1993 Base Case	176	19	4	18	1	.243	0
1993 High Range	307	37	7	36	2	.273	

LIEBERTHAL, MIKE - Phillies C - BR - Age 21

No. 1 pick in 1990. For the revolving door in the pitching staffs of the Phillies farm, Lieberthal was a source of stability. The Phillies have been criticized for making this smallish catcher one of the top players drafted but he has held his own. Will spend 1993 at AAA, unless something weird happens.

	AB	R	HR	RBI	SB	BA	$
1992 Reading AA	309	30	2	37	4	.286	
1992 Scranton AAA	45	4	0	4	0	.200	
1993 High Range	125	10	1	12	1	.260	

LIND, JOSE - Royals 2B - BR - Age 28

Never a big offensive threat, he had his worst season in 1992. He spent the season hitting weak grounders and pop ups. Again he was without peer defensively and won his first Gold Glove.

	AB	R	HR	RBI	SB	BA	$
1992 Pittsburgh NL	468	38	0	39	3	.235	0
1993 Low Range	374	28	1	26	1	.205	
1993 Base Case	402	33	1	32	2	.246	1
1993 High Range	513	46	1	47	3	.276	

LINDEMAN, JIM - Phillies OF - BR - Age 31

Lindeman is a former first-round pick who's never been able to carve himself a spot in a lineup, but has emerged as a capable pinch-hitter with the Phillies. He'll never get close to 200 at-bats in a season again. If you ever feel bad about a trade caused by over-emphasis on spring training, remember when the Cardinals traded away Andy Van Slyke, mainly because Jim Lindeman had a big spring training in 1987.

	AB	R	HR	RBI	SB	BA	$
1992 Scranton AAA	53	5	0	8	0	.302	
1992 Philadelphia NL	39	6	1	6	0	.256	-
1993 Base Case	60	9	2	8	0	.256	-
1993 High Range	198	24	6	24	0	.287	

LINDSEY, DOUG - Phillies C - BR - Age 25

Will never hit enough to be a major league asset. Career .220 BA after six minor league seasons.

	AB	R	HR	RBI	SB	BA	$
1992 Scranton AAA	274	28	4	27	0	.208	

LIRIANO, NELSON - Rockies 2B - BB - Age 28

Veteran Nelson Liriano has spent all or part of five years in the majors with a career BA of .255. That's about the best you can expect if he surfaces in Colorado.

	AB	R	HR	RBI	SB	BA	$
1992 Col. Sp. AAA	362	73	5	51	20	.304	
1993 Low Range	97	11	0	7	3	.206	
1993 Base Case	126	17	1	10	4	.238	1
1993 High Range	235	31	1	18	6	.247	

LISTACH, PAT - Brewers 2B/SS - BR - Age 25

What a surprising season! Although his minor league numbers gave no indication that Listach was a legitimate big-leaguer, he showed only one significant weakness: a tendency to chase bad pitches. In 1993, Listach is unlikely to repeat his statistics, as pitchers and defenses are wiser now; but probably he will improve as a player.

	AB	R	HR	RBI	SB	BA	$
1992 Milwaukee AL	579	93	1	47	54	.290	33
1993 Low Range	453	66	1	32	22	.236	
1993 Base Case	503	80	1	41	40	.268	21
1993 High Range	598	105	2	56	57	.299	

LITTON, GREG - Giants IF/OF - BR - Age 28

28 year-old career backup. Career .230 hitter. Has decent power, with 10 HR in 614 AB. But of course he will never get a full season now.

	AB	R	HR	RBI	SB	BA	$
1992 San Francisco NL	140	9	4	15	0	.229	0
1992 Phoenix AAA	85	14	4	19	0	.306	
1993 Base Case	121	8	3	13	0	.229	-
1993 High Range	207	15	5	25	0	.258	

LIVINGSTONE, SCOTT - Tigers 3B - BL - Age 27

Sparky Anderson's nominee for most-improved Tiger of 1992. Had a very hot September (.342) and could still turn into a high-average singles/doubles hitter. The return of Alan Trammell would be a negative for Livingstone's playing time.

	AB	R	HR	RBI	SB	BA	$
1992 Detroit AL	354	43	4	46	1	.282	8
1993 Low Range	329	36	4	39	0	.256	
1993 Base Case	339	41	5	47	1	.283	9
1993 High Range	404	54	7	63	1	.315	

LOFTON, KENNY - Indians OF - BL - Age 25

Lofton played for two months with a broken hamate bone in his hand -- the same bone that caused Jose Canseco to miss almost an entire season. Lofton may be the fastest man in the major leagues; raw speed enabled him to steal bases. He will be even better once he learns more about pitchers' moves and base stealing strategies.

	AB	R	HR	RBI	SB	BA	$
1992 Cleveland AL	576	96	5	42	66	.285	38
1993 Low Range	503	77	3	36	32	.262	
1993 Base Case	566	95	4	48	58	.290	36
1993 High Range	616	114	6	59	74	.322	

LONGMIRE, TONY - Phillies OF - BL - Age 24

Good offense, but no place to play unless several people move out of the way. Career .269 hitter in six minor league seasons. Base Case is 50 at bats and a .230 BA.

LOPEZ, JAVIER - Braves C - BR - Age 22

One of the top two or three minor league catchers of 1992, on everybody's list. Has moderate power and hits for good average. Has a major league arm already. If the Braves think he's ready on Opening Day, he will be in the lineup, but the most likely case is that he starts the year at AAA Richmond.

	AB	R	HR	RBI	SB	BA	$
1992 Greenville AA	442	64	16	60	7	.321	

1992 Atlanta NL	16	3	0	2	0	.375	-
1993 Low Range	130	14	2	12	0	.256	
1993 Base Case	231	26	4	22	1	.284	5
1993 High Range	423	55	10	50	3	.315	

LOPEZ, LUIS - Padres 2B/SS - BB - Age 22

At Las Vegas, .233 is a very low average, and there isn't any speed or power. Figure another year at AAA. Base Case for 1993 is 40 at bats and a .200 BA.

	AB	R	HR	RBI	SB	BA	$
1992 Las Vegas AAA	395	44	1	31	6	.233	

LOPEZ, LUIS - Indians C/IF - BR - Age 28

A great conversation piece on the subject of why Dodgers' farm batting averages don't mean anything. Lopez hit .353 at Albuquerque in 1990 to lead the PCL, when he was still young enough to be a prospect, and Los Angeles let him go. If he appears in 1993, he could get 40 AB as a pinch hitter.

	AB	R	HR	RBI	SB	BA	$
1992 Canton/Ak. AA	82	4	0	7	1	.256	

LOVULLO, TOREY - Angels 2B - BB - Age 27

Sparky Anderson's most famous hyperbole: "The best prospect I've ever seen; will play second base every day." Has a fair shot at a job in Anaheim. Base Case is 170 AB with a .271 average.

	AB	R	HR	RBI	SB	BA	$
1992 Columbus AAA	468	69	19	89	9	.295	

LUZINSKI, RYAN - Dodgers C - BR - Age 19

Son of Greg Luzinski. Hit .251 in Rookie league. Too early to get excited, but the Dodgers will give every opportunity, because they paid a big bonus to get him.

LYDEN, MITCH - Mets C - BR - Age 28

Just below the bottom of the major league depth charts of the Yankees, Tigers, and then the Mets. Has 56 minor league home runs in the last three years, so he's worth a look if he surfaces somewhere.

	AB	R	HR	RBI	SB	BA	$
1992 Tidewater AAA	299	34	14	52	1	.258	

LYDY, SCOTT - Athletics OF - BR - Age 24

After three mediocre minor league seasons, Lydy is now a certified prospect. By vastly improving his strike zone judgment, Lydy was able to hit .395 at Single-A and .305 at Double-A. Scheduled to spend 1993 in the minors. Watch for big stats at AAA Tacoma before you get excited.

	AB	R	HR	RBI	SB	BA	$
1992 Huntsville AA	387	64	9	65	16	.305	
1992 Reno A	124	29	2	27	9	.395	

LYONS, BARRY - Astros C/1B - BR - Age 32

Has had bad luck with Gary Carter showing up, every time Lyons thinks he has a major league backup job nailed down. Now it's probabably too late. Weak hitter anyway (career .236 BA).

	AB	R	HR	RBI	SB	BA	$
1992 Tucson AAA	277	32	4	45	1	.300	

LYONS, STEVE - Red Sox IF/OF - BL - Age 32

"Psycho" to his friends. Staged a minor comeback in 1991, but now has no value. Base Case is zero at bats for 1993.

MAAS, KEVIN - Yankees DH/1B - BL - Age 28

Hit ten home runs faster than any other rookie in history (in 1990) but since then, pitchers won't throw him a fastball when they fall behind in the count. Maas has been unable to make the adjustment to look for the breaking ball and adjust to the fastball. His HR/AB ratio has been half what it was in 1990, making him just another so-so power hitter.

	AB	R	HR	RBI	SB	BA	$
1992 New York AL	286	35	11	35	3	.248	6
1993 Low Range	208	24	6	24	1	.209	
1993 Base Case	305	39	10	40	3	.250	6
1993 High Range	446	63	18	67	6	.280	

MACFARLANE, MIKE - Royals C - BR - Age 28

Macfarlane did at an early age what most catchers do later in their careers -- abandon BA for pure power. Macfarlane tries to pull everything and stands almost on top of the plate to do it - had 15 HBP in 1992 and has led the Royals in HBP for three straight years. Macfarlane is thus an easy out most of the time, but he'll hit a mistake pitch a long way. His value is strictly in his power hitting; he's an abyssmal baserunner and his BA will hurt most teams.

	AB	R	HR	RBI	SB	BA	$
1992 Kansas City AL	402	51	17	48	1	.234	7
1993 Low Range	248	29	7	17	0	.200	
1993 Base Case	353	46	13	44	1	.241	5
1993 High Range	407	58	18	58	1	.271	

MACK, SHANE - Twins OF - BR - Age 29

Although Mack had another outstanding season, Manager Tom Kelly said that he has a "high ceiling" meaning that Mack has the talent to improve on his current record. Mack could improve in all of his offensive categories making him awesome, both in "real" baseball and in Rotisserie.

	AB	R	HR	RBI	SB	BA	$
1992 Minnesota AL	600	101	16	75	26	.315	35
1993 Low Range	507	77	13	63	14	.284	
1993 Base Case	578	96	18	83	25	.313	39
1993 High Range	614	112	24	97	34	.340	

MACLIN, LONNIE - Cardinals OF - BL - Age 26

Spent four years at Rookie /A levels but now is finally moving up fast. Unfortunately for Maclin, the Cardinals have too many outfielders. He will need a lucky break, or the Cards will have to suffer multiple injuries, for Maclin to be a major leaguer in 1993.

	AB	R	HR	RBI	SB	BA	$
1992 Louisville AAA	290	29	1	38	4	.324	
1993 Base Case	50	4	0	5	0	.260	-
1993 High Range	133	10	0	13	1	.280	

MAGADAN, DAVE - Mets 3B/1B - BL - Age 30

Magadan is a slow singles/doubles hitter, with a very good eye. He gets on base a lot, and could win a batting title with a career year in the right circumstances. But the Mets went ahead and signed Eddie Murray, and Magadan wound up at third, and at the end of 1992 he found the Mets didn't want him there either.

	AB	R	HR	RBI	SB	BA	$
1992 New York NL	321	33	3	28	1	.283	6
1993 Low Range	177	17	2	14	0	.248	
1993 Base Case	254	26	3	23	1	.275	4
1993 High Range	328	37	5	34	1	.306	

MAGALLANES, EVER - White Sox 2B/SS - BL - Age 27

If the White Sox didn't need Magallanes in 1992 with every shortstop hurt, they sure won't need Magallenes in the majors in 1993. Base Case is zero at bats.

	AB	R	HR	RBI	SB	BA	$
1992 Vancouver AAA	243	32	3	23	2	.230	

MAKSUDIAN, MIKE - Twins C - BL - Age 26

Never showed power before 1992, and only hit for high average occasionally. If he gets to the major leagues at all, he will be one of the weaker-hitting first basemen. Base Case is zero at bats.

	AB	R	HR	RBI	SB	BA	$
1992 Syracuse AAA	339	38	13	58	4	.280	
1992 Toronto AL	3	0	0	0	0	.000	-
1993 High Range	125	15	2	18	1	.260	

MALDONADO, CANDY - Blue Jays OF - BR - Age 32

Derek Bell's broken wrist made Maldonado a regular player, when he might have rotted on the bench in 1992. He made the most of his opportunity but still isn't assured of anything for 1993. Numbers in 1992 were remarkably similar to John Olerud's, but they are moving in opposite directions.

	AB	R	HR	RBI	SB	BA	$
1992 Toronto AL	489	64	20	66	2	.272	16
1993 Low Range	214	27	6	25	1	.210	
1993 Base Case	401	55	14	55	2	.251	9
1993 High Range	507	77	22	78	4	.281	

MANTO, JEFF - Braves 3B/1B - BR - Age 28

Had his best chances with Cleveland in 1990-1991, but couldn't hit (.216 career BA in the majors). Still a useful Triple-A worker, it is unlikely the Braves can use him in 1993. Base Case is 50 at bats and a .240 average.

	AB	R	HR	RBI	SB	BA	$
1992 Richmond AAA	450	65	13	68	1	.291	
1993 High Range	201	21	5	23	2	.265	

MANWARING, KIRT - Giants C - BR - Age 27

He just keeps hanging on to the catching job. Manwaring has few tangible skills, but the Giants really like him. Another example of the dearth of credible catchers.

	AB	R	HR	RBI	SB	BA	$
1992 San Francisco NL	349	24	4	26	2	.244	2
1993 Low Range	136	9	2	8	1	.196	
1993 Base Case	285	20	4	20	2	.236	2
1993 High Range	344	26	6	28	3	.265	

MARSH, TOM - Phillies OF - BR - Age 27

Marsh is a decent enough defensive outfielder who doesn't do anything at the plate to suggest that he could hold a job in the majors.

	AB	R	HR	RBI	SB	BA	$
1992 Scranton AAA	158	26	8	25	5	.241	
1992 Philadelphia NL	125	7	2	16	0	.200	-
1993 Base Case	71	6	1	8	1	.218	-
1993 High Range	191	16	3	25	2	.250	

MARSHALL, MIKE - Japan 1B/OF - BR - Age 33

Guess what? Marshall managed to get hurt in Japan too. In a land where the work ethic is more important than just about anything, it's hard to believe that Marshall would be a real popular player.

	AB	R	HR	RBI	SB	BA	$
1992 Japan	223	23	9	26	---	.247	

MARTIN, AL - Pirates OF - BL - Age 25

The Pirates felt they had a steal when they signed Martin as a six-year free agent after the Braves failed to place him on the 40-man roster following the 1991 season. Showing outstanding power and speed, Martin did nothing to prove the Pirates wrong in 1992. At the end of 1992 when Barry Bonds looked gone by the free agent route, Martin was being discussed as a credible platoon possibility for left field.

	AB	R	HR	RBI	SB	BA	$
1992 Buffalo AAA	420	85	20	59	20	.305	
1992 Pittsburgh NL	12	1	0	2	0	.167	-
1993 Base Case	225	29	3	25	8	.229	2
1993 High Range	326	46	6	42	15	.258	

MARTIN, NORBERTO - White Sox 2B/SS - BB - Age 26

Converted to shortstop to play alongside Esteban Beltre. Has the talents to play on the major league level, but he's been at Vancouver for three years now with no big progress visible.

	AB	R	HR	RBI	SB	BA	$
1992 Vancouver AAA	497	72	0	29	29	.288	

MARTINEZ, CARLOS - Indians 1B/DH - BR - Age 27

Martinez had a good year with the White Sox in '89 after which he slumped and lost his position to Frank Thomas and was released. Picked up by Cleveland on a minor league contract, he earned another shot with his good minor league record. The Indians first and third positions are very competitive, and the Tribe is likely to give substantial playing time to promising rookies.

	AB	R	HR	RBI	SB	BA	$
1992 Col. Sp. AAA	32	7	0	5	1	.313	
1992 Cleveland AL	228	23	5	35	1	.263	4
1993 Low Range	286	26	5	35	1	.232	
1993 Base Case	301	30	7	43	1	.264	7
1993 High Range	433	48	11	71	3	.295	

MARTINEZ, CARMELO - Japan 1B/OF - BR - Age 32

Could still hit a little in the majors if he came back, maybe three homers in 100 at bats. (I said "a little.")

MARTINEZ, CHITO - Orioles OF - BL - Age 27

Going into the winter meetings, Chito was slated to be the lefty-hitting platooner in right field for 1993. After a promising rookie season in '91, Martinez lost playing time to Joe Orsulak in 1992. Consequently, he had difficulty finding the hitting stroke he displayed in '91. Even platooning, Martinez can hit 20 homers and drive in 70 runs.

	AB	R	HR	RBI	SB	BA	$
1992 Baltimore AL	198	26	5	25	0	.268	3
1993 Low Range	258	27	6	30	1	.231	
1993 Base Case	295	34	9	40	2	.263	7
1993 High Range	408	52	15	62	3	.294	

MARTINEZ, DAVE - Reds OF - BL - Age 28

Martinez was a mild disappointment for the Reds, with his worst offensive year since 1988. His defensive skills were important to the Reds, allowing them to move the very raw Reggie Sanders to LF. Free agency may finally allow him to escape the platoon role he has been trapped in for most of his career.

	AB	R	HR	RBI	SB	BA	$
1992 Cincinnati NL	393	47	3	31	12	.254	8
1993 Low Range	274	29	4	18	5	.235	
1993 Base Case	351	41	6	27	10	.267	9
1993 High Range	455	58	10	40	18	.298	

MARTINEZ, DOMINGO - Blue Jays 1B - BR - Age 25

Nothing more to prove at Triple-A, where he's been hitting with authority for two full years. The only problem is where he could fit in the major leagues. Platooning John Olerud isn't very likely for 1993, but sitting him down against the occasional tough lefty is a viable possibility, if Martinez fits on the roster.

	AB	R	HR	RBI	SB	BA	$
1992 Syracuse AAA	438	55	21	62	6	.274	
1992 Toronto AL	8	2	1	3	0	.625	0
1993 Base Case	121	11	3	14	1	.244	1
1993 High Range	222	31	6	32	2	.290	

MARTINEZ, EDGAR - Mariners 3B - BR - Age 30

Martinez continued to blossom as he led the major leagues in batting average last year. His power and average were to be expected, but his steals were a surprise. Entering 1992, he had only three steals in his three year career. His BA jump came at the expense of walks which fell from 84 to 54, keeping his OBP the same as in 1991. Martinez missed most of September with a bad shoulder.

	AB	R	HR	RBI	SB	BA	$
1992 Seattle AL	528	100	18	73	14	.343	34
1993 Low Range	446	67	10	51	7	.284	
1993 Base Case	511	84	15	68	12	.313	29
1993 High Range	582	106	21	86	20	.336	

MARTINEZ, TINO - Mariners 1B - BL - Age 25

After disappointing trials in 1990 and 1991, Tino Martinez finally showed the major leagues why he was USA TODAY Minor League Player of the Year in 1990 and PCL MVP in 1991. As he plays on a more regular basis, his batting average should improve, which will in turn increase his RBI. Martinez hit 9 HR in only 200 AB after the break.

	AB	R	HR	RBI	SB	BA	$
1992 Seattle AL	460	53	16	66	2	.257	12
1993 Low Range	423	44	13	52	1	.226	
1993 Base Case	493	56	19	71	1	.257	14
1993 High Range	557	69	25	89	2	.288	

MARZANO, JOHN - Red Sox C - BR - Age 30

Just a backup catcher. No value in a stat league.

	AB	R	HR	RBI	SB	BA	$
1992 Boston AL	50	4	0	1	0	.080	-
1993 Base Case	101	10	1	8	0	.204	-
1993 High Range	208	24	3	19	0	.242	

MATTINGLY, DON - Yankees 1B - BL - Age 31

Mattingly had his best year since 1989, but isn't anywhere near approaching his peak years of 1985-1987. What we saw in 1992 is about as good as it's going to get; Mattingly was healthy enough to play all year. In 1993 or any other year, the medical prognosis is that his back may flare up any time.

	AB	R	HR	RBI	SB	BA	$
1992 New York AL	640	89	14	86	3	.288	20
1993 Low Range	443	54	7	56	1	.263	
1993 Base Case	554	74	11	81	2	.291	21
1993 High Range	629	92	15	101	4	.315	

MAURER, ROB - Rangers 1B - BL - Age 26

A September callup each of the past two seasons, Maurer's hitting regressed at AAA in 1992. Even so, he is regarded as the Rangers' best hitting prospect in the near term. Maurer was slated to have minor knee surgery in the offseason, but should be fully recovered by spring 1993.

	AB	R	HR	RBI	SB	BA	$
1992 Texas AL	9	1	0	1	0	.222	-
1992 Okla. City AAA	493	76	10	82	1	.288	
1993 Base Case	224	31	4	27	1	.272	4
1993 High Range	319	49	7	44	2	.303	

MAY, DERRICK - Cubs OF - BL - Age 24

The son of Dave May has shown good power which should increase as he develops. He hit well enough to force his way into the lineup two different times last year. May hit .295 or better in each of his seven minor league seasons. From August 1 to the end of the year, he hit .303 with 4 HR, 26 RBI in 185 AB.

	AB	R	HR	RBI	SB	BA	$
1992 Chicago NL	351	33	8	45	5	.274	11
1993 Low Range	332	36	6	39	3	.256	
1993 Base Case	495	58	11	67	7	.283	19
1993 High Range	555	72	14	85	11	.315	

MAYNE, BRENT - Royals C - BL - Age 24

Mayne will get more playing time against righthanders and could work his way up to a platoon role with better hitting. Not likely to play full-time until he learns to hit lefties. A better defensive player than Mike Macfarlane and should eventually win the job outright. Mayne has little power or speed. He can help a team with BA if he returns to his 1991 level. Mayne would be a good $1 second catcher; a former number one pick (1989); may eventually blossom into a more valuable catcher.

	AB	R	HR	RBI	SB	BA	$
1992 Kansas City AL	213	16	0	18	0	.225	-
1993 Low Range	175	14	0	16	0	.212	
1993 Base Case	240	21	2	27	1	.241	1
1993 High Range	345	33	4	38	2	.253	

McCARTY, DAVID - Twins OF/1B - BL - Age 23

David McCarty has tremendous potential for power and average. McCarty was the third overall draft pick in '91. Promoted to AAA Portland, he hit like Lou Gehrig, peaking in the PCL playoffs with two 2-homer games. The Twins will make a place for him in their lineup sometime in '93.

	AB	R	HR	RBI	SB	BA	$
1992 Orlando AA	457	75	18	79	6	.271	
1992 Portland AAA	26	7	1	8	1	.500	
1993 Base Case	167	20	5	23	1	.252	2
1993 High Range	313	41	11	49	2	.282	

McCLENDON, LLOYD - Pirates OF/1B - BR - Age 34

He followed a horrid regular season with a torrid 1992 National League Championship Series, going 8 for 11 in the seven game loss to the Braves. Still just a utility player at best.

	AB	R	HR	RBI	SB	BA	$
1992 Pittsburgh NL	190	26	3	20	1	.253	2
1993 Base Case	222	30	4	23	1	.253	2
1993 High Range	305	46	6	37	2	.283	

McCONNELL, CHAD - Phillies OF - BR - Age 21

The Phillies made this power hitting outfielder from Creighton their top pick in 1992. As a member of the U.S. Olympic team, he did not play last year in the minors but will likely play at least at Double-A this season

	AB	R	HR	RBI	SB	BA	$
1992 Creighton U	220	68	14	73	29	.400	

McCRAY, RODNEY - Mets OF - BR - Age 29

McCray, if he's known at all, is known as the player who ran through that outfield wall in Portland in 1991. He does cover some ground, but his overall defense is erratic, as is his baserunning, and he hasn't a clue how to reach base. Rodney's one and only asset is his speed.

	AB	R	HR	RBI	SB	BA	$
1992 Tidewater AAA	10	1	0	0	3	.000	
1992 New York NL	1	3	0	1	2	1.000	-
1993 Base Case	25	9	0	2	6	.160	-
1993 High Range	221	39	1	25	22	.261	

McDANIEL, TERRY - Reds OF - BB - Age 26

Good speed, but has been a consistent .240 hitter over seven minor league seasons. Not likely to be a factor anywhere in 1993.

	AB	R	HR	RBI	SB	BA	$
1992 Chattanooga AA	19	1	0	3	0	.263	
1992 Nashville AAA	38	5	1	9	1	.289	

McDAVID, RAY - Padres OF - BL - Age 22

The 21-year-old McDavid was rated the best prospect in the California League by Baseball America. A ninth round pick in the 1989 draft, McDavid is a potential four-category hitter, blessed with a great combination of power and speed.

	AB	R	HR	RBI	SB	BA	$
1992 High Desert A	428	94	24	94	43	.276	

McGEE, WILLIE - Giants OF - BB - Age 34

Many people don't think of McGee as a two-time NL batting champ, but this 34 year-old still hits for high average. The RBI, extra base hits, and home runs have declined precipitously since 1987 when he had 59 extra base hits and 105 RBI.

	AB	R	HR	RBI	SB	BA	$
1992 San Francisco NL	474	56	1	36	13	.297	14
1993 Low Range	391	39	3	34	5	.260	
1993 Base Case	455	50	5	46	10	.287	16
1993 High Range	558	67	7	65	17	.318	

McGINNIS, RUSS - Rangers C/IF - BR - Age 29

McGinnis is a reasonably good AAA-level power hitter, but his age and defensive shortcomings make it very unlikely that he would be more than a fringe major leaguer.

McGRIFF, FRED - Padres 1B - BL - Age 29

The "Crime Dog" possesses one of the most consistent bats in the NL. His HR/RBI stats over the last three years: 35/88, 31/106 and 35/104, making him one of the most bankable sluggers in the game. Frankly, McGriff has been the dominant hitter in the National League for the last two years and may still come at a favorable price due to the relative anonymity of all Padres.

	AB	R	HR	RBI	SB	BA	$
1992 San Diego NL	531	79	35	104	8	.286	34
1993 Low Range	506	68	27	85	4	.248	
1993 Base Case	536	79	36	105	8	.275	31
1993 High Range	559	90	41	116	11	.306	

McGWIRE, MARK - Athletics 1B - BR - Age 29

Last season McGwire bounced back from a miserable 1991 season with 42 homers and 104 RBI, despite missing three weeks with a pulled muscle in his rib cage. Probably the best home run stroke in the majors. Somebody is likely to hit 50 home runs in 1993.

	AB	R	HR	RBI	SB	BA	$
1992 Oakland AL	467	87	42	104	0	.268	26
1993 Low Range	459	80	31	87	0	.205	
1993 Base Case	501	96	42	110	0	.246	24
1993 High Range	556	117	50	130	0	.276	

McINTOSH, TIM - Brewers C - BR - Age 28

Was a credible backup catcher / 1B /part-time DH / OF fill-in a couple of years ago, but now it may be too late. Excellent minor league hitting stats, with good power at all levels are probably nothing more now than evidence of what might have been.

	AB	R	HR	RBI	SB	BA	$
1992 Milwaukee AL	77	7	0	6	1	.182	-
1993 High Range	203	20	4	23	2	.274	
1993 Base Case	160	15	3	16	1	.244	0
1993 High Range	203	20	4	23	2	.274	

McKNIGHT, JEFF - Mets OF/IF - BB - Age 30

Tidewater's leading hitter (.307), McKnight is an aging journeyman who had surfaced briefly with Baltimore in 1990 and 1991. His stint with the 1992 Mets was due to their running out of healthy major leaguers, and probably won't happen again.

	AB	R	HR	RBI	SB	BA	$
1992 Tidewater AAA	352	43	4	43	3	.307	
1992 New York NL	85	10	2	13	0	.271	0
1993 Base Case	50	7	1	9	1	.240	
1993 High Range	203	21	2	25	1	.290	

McLEMORE, MARK - Orioles IF - BB - Age 28

Once the Angels' "2B of the Future," McLemore is another of the Orioles' reclamation projects. At age 28, he has a chance to become an everyday player. It's more likely that Oates will utilize a cast of characters at 2B and Mac will be a part. If you believe McLemore will get 450 at-bats, then ratchet his SB totals to 25.

	AB	R	HR	RBI	SB	BA	$
1992 Baltimore AL	228	40	0	27	11	.246	4
1993 Low Range	106	16	0	12	7	.217	
1993 Base Case	206	33	0	25	10	.240	1
1993 High Range	314	53	0	39	21	.261	

McNAMARA, JIM - Unsigned C - BL - Age 27

Both expansion teams were showing interest after McNamara became available, but he won't play much anywhere in the majors in 1993.

	AB	R	HR	RBI	SB	BA	$
1992 Phoenix AAA	67	5	0	3	0	.209	
1992 San Francisco NL	74	6	1	9	0	.216	-
1993 Low Range	108	8	1	11	0	.177	
1993 Base Case	229	19	3	28	0	.216	-
1993 High Range	304	27	5	42	0	.248	

McNEELY, JEFF - Red Sox OF - BR - Age 23

Had surgery on right shoulder after a disappointing season. Best Red Sox speed prospect in years. Stole 84 bases in 1990-1991. Will begin 1993 in the minors and will have to do well to get a callup before September.

	AB	R	HR	RBI	SB	BA	$
1992 New Britain AA	261	30	2	11	10	.218	

McRAE, BRIAN - Royals OF - BB - Age 25

As long as Dad manages the club, Brian will play. McRae produced fewer runs per out used-up than any other regular player in 1992. Looks confused at the plate and was overmatched by mediocre pitchers last year. Still, he's young enough to be improving, and the one quality that characterized his career from 1989-1991 is that he exceeded everyone's expectations. For people who need to take chances, McRae offers high potential at a low price based on his 1992 stats. For people who need a solid value however, McRae presents the dangers of someone who'll get 500 AB without many extras and won't get benched no matter how bad he gets. I think he'll come back, but there is that risk.

	AB	R	HR	RBI	SB	BA	$
1992 Kansas City AL	533	63	4	52	18	.223	6
1993 Low Range	509	56	3	43	12	.201	
1993 Base Case	529	64	4	52	20	.242	10
1993 High Range	602	80	6	67	31	.272	

McREYNOLDS, KEVIN - Royals OF - BR - Age 33

A fastball hitter who hasn't adjusted to the breaking ball league. Getting 13 HR is good for Royals Stadium; injuries limited his playing time. Batting fifth and playing full-time will get McReynolds back to the 70 RBI range, but he'll never again reach 25 HR. His good batting eye will keep his BA near .250. Long term trend is down, but after that bad 1992 season he can bounce back for one good year before fading further.

	AB	R	HR	RBI	SB	BA	$
1992 Kansas City AL	373	45	13	49	7	.247	10
1993 Low Range	293	30	7	34	3	.199	
1993 Base Case	413	49	15	66	7	.248	11
1993 High Range	539	68	20	82	13	.269	

MEDINA, LUIS - Royals 1B - BR - Age 30

Good power prospect during the late 1980's, but like so many Indians hitters he just didn't fit in anywhere other than Colorado Springs. If he surfaces somewhere, he'll pop a home run or two -- has 10 major league jacks in 150 at bats.

	AB	R	HR	RBI	SB	BA	$
1992 Omaha AAA	341	37	16	49	1	.276	

MELVIN, BOB - Royals C - BR - Age 31
The .314 BA was a fluke. He's a .235 career hitter. In 1993 he will be very hard pressed for playing time.

	AB	R	HR	RBI	SB	BA	$
1992 Kansas City AL	70	5	0	6	0	.314	0
1993 Base Case	50	4	0	5	0	.233	-
1993 High Range	177	16	2	19	0	.264	

MERCED, ORLANDO - Pirates 1B - BB - Age 26
A disappointment in 1992 after a solid rookie season in 1991. He hit five of his homers in a six-week span and showed no noticeable improvements in any aspect of his game. Biggest factor in his favor is that he got the major leagues young, and has time to make progress.

	AB	R	HR	RBI	SB	BA	$
1992 Pittsburgh NL	405	50	6	60	5	.247	8
1993 Low Range	385	43	4	49	3	.229	
1993 Base Case	408	50	6	60	6	.260	9
1993 High Range	508	69	9	84	11	.290	

MERCEDES, HENRY - Athletics C - BR - Age 23
Never hit above .258 in five minor league seasons, but jumped from A to AAA to the majors in 1992. Has a little power and a little speed but would hit for very low average if he played all of 1993 in the majors. Look for a start at AAA and no callup unless he is a revelation.

	AB	R	HR	RBI	SB	BA	$
1992 Oakland AL	5	1	0	1	0	.800	-
1992 Tacoma AAA	246	36	0	20	1	.232	
1993 Base Case	50	4	1	4	1	.224	0
1993 High Range	207	28	2	20	2	.247	

MERCEDES, LUIS - Orioles OF - BR - Age 25
In four minor league seasons, Mercedes has won two batting titles and finished second twice. His stolen base totals have also been high throughout his minor league career. On the negative side, Oriole management has been disappointed with his three brief appearances in the majors and he is considered somewhat of a hothead and often appears disoriented in game situations (e.g. "runs into too many outs" on the bases). Still, in many ways he may be just what the doctor ordered for the Orioles' offense -- a high-average, spray hitter with speed -- and Mercedes can be expected to get an opportunity to bat second and at least platoon in RF if his glovework is passable.

	AB	R	HR	RBI	SB	BA	$
1992 Rochester AAA	409	62	3	29	35	.313	
1992 Baltimore AL	50	7	0	4	0	.140	-
1993 Low Range	105	13	0	7	2	.250	
1993 Base Case	206	29	0	16	8	.277	5
1993 High Range	381	59	1	35	20	.308	

MERULLO, MATT - White Sox C/1B - BL - Age 27
Third catcher for the past couple of years. Unlikely to make any significant impact; good pick for a few HR.

	AB	R	HR	RBI	SB	BA	$
1992 Chicago AL	50	3	0	3	0	.180	-
1993 Base Case	127	7	3	14	0	.222	-
1993 High Range	309	20	8	39	0	.251	

MEULENS, HENSLEY - Yankees 3B - BR - Age 25

"Bam Bam" told me he would be happy if taken by an expansion team. "It's time to move on." And the Yankees left him exposed. But Charlie Hayes was the one taken, and now Meulens will compete for time at third base. He's a good power hitter. If he hadn't come up young and had those false starts in the major leagues, he would be on the top of everyone's rookie list this year.

	AB	R	HR	RBI	SB	BA	$
1992 Columbus AAA	534	96	26	100	15	.275	
1992 New York AL	5	1	1	1	0	.600	-
1993 Low Range	368	46	10	40	2	.215	
1993 Base Case	424	58	14	54	4	.256	11
1993 High Range	513	77	21	74	7	.286	

MILLER, KEITH - Royals 2B - BR - Age 29

The arrival of Jose Lind doesn't help Miller, who has never had a full healthy season. KC considered Miller as a left fielder in early 1992 and will have to look at that possibility again. Full time play in 1992 let Miller display the full range of his baseball skills. Does many things well; would have had much better numbers without five-week DL stint.

	AB	R	HR	RBI	SB	BA	$
1992 Kansas City AL	416	57	4	38	16	.284	14
1993 Low Range	368	41	3	28	8	.247	
1993 Base Case	407	50	4	36	15	.273	12
1993 High Range	505	68	5	50	25	.304	

MILLER, N. KEITH - Rangers OF - BB - Age 30

The former Phillie (not the current Royal) went to learn catching in the instructional league. He last played in the majors in 1989, but one positive development was the Rangers adding him to the 40-man winter roster after the season's end.

	AB	R	HR	RBI	SB	BA	$
1992 Okla. City AAA	459	82	7	56	8	.257	
1993 Base Case	60	8	0	3	1	.200	-
1993 High Range	120	17	1	7	2	.218	

MILLER, ORLANDO - Astros SS - BR - Age 24

Has had two good seasons at A-ball and now one decent year at Double-A. Miller is not a top prospect, but he could become a factor if Andujar Cedeno doesn't come around and Houston doesn't get a free agent.

	AB	R	HR	RBI	SB	BA	$
1992 Jackson AA	378	51	5	53	7	.265	
1992 Tucson AAA	37	4	2	8	0	.243	

MILLETTE, JOE - Phillies SS - BR - Age 26

Millette is caught in the logjam of shortstops with the Phillies. He's competent defensively, but has neither power nor speed nor much ability to get on base. With Bell, Duncan, and possibly a recycled Kim Batiste in his way, there isn't much hope of significant playing time above AAA for Millette.

	AB	R	HR	RBI	SB	BA	$
1992 Scranton AAA	256	24	1	23	3	.266	
1992 Philadelphia NL	78	5	0	2	1	.205	-
1993 Base Case	50	4	0	2	0	.180	-
1993 High Range	100	10	1	7	1	.230	

MILLIGAN, RANDY - Orioles 1B - BR - Age 31

In the spring the O's were thankful that they did not trade "Moose" as was often rumored. Still, it was a disappointing year for Milligan, one of the chief culprits in the mid-lineup crisis that plagued the Orioles. Despite his bulk, Milligan is most effective in the second spot in the lineup where his patience (106 walks) and ability to hit to the opposite field are assets.

	AB	R	HR	RBI	SB	BA	$
1992 Baltimore AL	462	71	11	53	0	.240	5
1993 Low Range	325	43	6	35	1	.204	
1993 Base Case	407	59	9	50	2	.245	5
1993 High Range	507	80	13	72	3	.275	

MITCHELL, KEITH - Braves OF - BR - Age 23

Kevin Mitchell's cousin couldn't continue his meteoric rise through the minors in 1992. Still a decent prospect, though, with a good batting eye and some speed. A big first half could earn him a callup.

	AB	R	HR	RBI	SB	BA	$
1992 Richmond AAA	403	45	4	50	14	.226	
1993 Base Case	80	11	1	9	5	.245	1
1993 High Range	225	26	3	17	11	.276	

MITCHELL, KEVIN - Reds OF - BR - Age 31

Mitchell will benefit from the return to the National League. He spent all of 1992 wondering if any AL pitcher would ever throw him a fastball. But there were other problems, too. After being traded during the off-season, Mitchell came to spring training overweight and with a wrist injury. For the third straight year, his HR and RBI decreased. However, he maintained his RBI rate of one per 5.4 AB and his batting average went back up to 1989-1990 level. Mitchell went on the DL twice -- once with a rib cage injury and a second time with a broken foot.

	AB	R	HR	RBI	SB	BA	$
1992 Seattle AL	360	48	9	67	0	.286	11
1993 Low Range	362	46	14	57	0	.247	
1993 Base Case	489	66	23	85	0	.274	20
1993 High Range	543	84	31	106	0	.305	

MOLITOR, PAUL - Brewers 1B/DH - BR - Age 36

The trade for Kevin Reimer raises the danger that Molitor will be pushed out of the DH slot and onto the field. There have been no signs of decline for two years. Like Dwight Evans he may build a Hall of Fame career after age 30. The key has been Milwaukee's refusal to play him anywhere in the field but 1B, and that only rarely, limiting Molitor's susceptibility to injuries that previously caused frequent trips to the DL. If he stays a DH, or is carefully used at 1B, expect more of the same; if he's moved out to play second or third regularly, however, assume a 120-game season at best.

	AB	R	HR	RBI	SB	BA	$
1992 Milwaukee AL	609	89	12	89	31	.320	37
1993 Low Range	407	52	7	51	12	.271	
1993 Base Case	507	71	11	74	24	.299	29
1993 High Range	605	93	16	97	36	.321	

MONDESI, RAUL - Dodgers OF - BR - Age 22

Mondesi is considered the jewel of the Dodger farm system despite his small stature (5'11", 150) and despite some less-than-sparkling numbers in the minors. Scouts love him. In 1991, he hit a combined .277-8-39-17 at three minor league stops. His 1992 season ended prematurely with an injury and was interrupted by a demotion inspired by Mondesi's open displeasure (he went AWOL) when the Dodgers' didn't recall him when Davis and Strawberry went down. He has all the classic tools except "big" power and is probably a year away from regular major league playing time.

	AB	R	HR	RBI	SB	BA	$
1992 San Antonio AA	68	8	2	14	3	.265	
1992 Albuquerque AAA	138	23	4	15	2	.312	
1993 Base Case	75	10	3	15	4	.283	2
1993 High Range	303	32	5	35	3	.275	

MOORE, BOBBY - Braves OF - BR - Age 27

Always had good speed. Surfaced briefly with KC in 1991. Now he's far down on the depth charts.

	AB	R	HR	RBI	SB	BA	$
1992 Richmond AAA	316	41	0	25	14	.250	

MOORE, KERWIN - Marlins OF - BR - Age 22

A speed demon with good defensive skills. Must hit for a better average and not strikeout as much (over 100 K in each of the last three minor league seasons). If he's willing to cut down his swing to make contact, he could become an Alex Cole type player.

	AB	R	HR	RBI	SB	BA	$
1992 Baseball City A	248	39	1	10	26	.238	
1992 Memphis AA	179	27	4	17	16	.235	
1993 High Range	70	12	0	3	8	.212	

MORANDINI, MICKEY - Phillies 2B - BL - Age 26

Jim Fregosi mentioned Nellie Fox and Morandini in the same breath, not exactly as a comparison, but to make the point that Morandini stands a reasonable chance of developing into a .280-range slap hitter with moderate speed and good on-base skills. His job is presently secure, there's nobody pushing him, and he's pretty good with the glove. Inability to hit left-handed pitching (.198 last year, .185 in 1991) has been a problem.

	AB	R	HR	RBI	SB	BA	$
1992 Philadelphia NL	422	47	3	30	8	.265	7
1993 Low Range	323	30	2	20	3	.233	
1993 Base Case	425	43	3	31	7	.268	7
1993 High Range	527	59	4	43	13	.295	

MORMAN, RUSS - Reds 1B/OF - BR - Age 30

Spent parts of five seasons with the White Sox and Royals (1986-1991) but isn't likely to make it back. If he does, he'll hit about .240 without much power or speed.

	AB	R	HR	RBI	SB	BA	$
1992 Nashville AAA	384	53	14	63	5	.310	

MORRIS, HAL - Reds 1B - BL - Age 27

Injuries hampered Morris in 1992. A ball fouled off his knee in spring training affected him all year (bone chips in the knee were removed in the off season). Hal also pulled a hamstring warming up in the on-deck circle. A decision on his role would help; at this point the Reds can't decide whether Morris should set the table or clean it. Expect a return to his 1991 form.

	AB	R	HR	RBI	SB	BA	$
1992 Cincinnati NL	395	41	6	53	6	.271	11
1993 Low Range	368	32	9	41	3	.260	
1993 Base Case	440	42	13	57	6	.288	18
1993 High Range	484	51	17	72	9	.320	

MORRIS, JOHN - Angels OF - BL - Age 32

No matter what team he's with in '93, Morris' role is utility outfielder and pinch hitter. He's a 7-year veteran with a career BA of .237, and career totals of 7 HR and 14 SB. He was "designated for assignment" by the Angels in August and chose to become a free agent.

	AB	R	HR	RBI	SB	BA	$
1992 California AL	57	4	1	3	1	.193	-
1993 Base Case	95	6	1	6	1	.189	-
1993 High Range	178	17	3	18	5	.251	

MOSEBY, LLOYD - Japan OF - BL - Age 33

Moseby passed up a shot at signing with the Oakland A's after the '91 season, and had given up baseball when the Yomiuri Giants contacted him. Lloyd put together a good season in Japan, and seems to have found a home there, so he's therefore not very likely to return to the U.S., but you never know.

	AB	R	HR	RBI	SB	BA	$
1992 Japan	293	54	22	56	---	.295	

MOSES, JOHN - Seattle OF - BB - Age 36

Only 43 major league at bats in the past two years. Hit .254 at Calgary. If he makes it back, he might be good as a fill-in for just one stolen base.

	AB	R	HR	RBI	SB	BA	$
1992 Seattle AL	22	3	0	1	0	.136	-
1993 High Range	91	14	1	9	2	.242	

MOTA, ANDY - Astros 2B - BR - Age 27

Surfaced briefly with the Astros in 1991, but no longer a prospect. In 1992 he hit .240 at Tucson, with three home runs and seven steals.

MOTA, GARY - Astros OF - BR - Age 22

Astros' 2nd round draft choice in 1990 had breakthrough season in 1992, taking MVP honors in Class A South Atlantic League. He's probably 2 or 3 years away but bears watching now. The fourth of Manny's six sons should be the third to appear in the majors. He is legally entitled to use the name "Manny Mota Junior" and would rise faster if he made that change.

	AB	R	HR	RBI	SB	BA	$
1992 Ashville A	484	82	24	90	22	.291	
1993 High Range	40	5	1	6	1	.200	

MOTA, JOSE - Royals IF/OF - BB - Age 28

Once had a shot with the Padres, and they really needed a second baseman. If Jose couldn't reach the bigs in that situation, he isn't going to fare any better in 1993. In this whole book, you get one pun: if the Tigers acquired all of Manny's offspring and namesakes, they would call Detroit "Mota City."

	AB	R	HR	RBI	SB	BA	$
1992 Omaha AAA	469	45	3	28	21	.230	

MOTTOLA, CHAD - Reds OF - BR - Age 21

Fifth pick in the first round of the 1992 draft, from Central Florida University. Great power prospect.

	AB	R	HR	RBI	SB	BA	$
1992 Billings R	213	53	12	37	12	.286	

MULLINIKS, RANCE - Blue Jays DH/3B - BL - Age 37

If he hasn't retired by the time you read this, he should do so without delay. Base Case is zero at bats.

	AB	R	HR	RBI	SB	BA	$
1992 Toronto AL	2	1	0	0	0	.500	-
1993 High Range	183	21	2	19	0	.257	

MUNOZ, PEDRO - Twins OF - BR - Age 24

1992 was Munoz' first full season in the show, and he produced. Unfortunately, he was often the man on the bench, missing 35 games as Manager Tom Kelly gave playing time to older players as is his practice. Munoz is one of my top picks to go up in value from 1992 to 1993.

	AB	R	HR	RBI	SB	BA	$
1992 Minnesota AL	418	44	12	71	4	.270	13
1993 Low Range	373	37	10	47	3	.258	
1993 Base Case	463	50	15	68	7	.285	20
1993 High Range	532	63	20	87	11	.316	

MURPHY, DALE - Phillies OF - BR - Age 37

Murphy's career, which began a rapid fade back around 1988, may have come to a more official close. His ability to come back from rather severe knee problems is extremely questionable, although he is just two homers short of 400, and, if semi-healthy, may be tempted to hang around to give it a shot.

	AB	R	HR	RBI	SB	BA	$
1992 Philadelphia NL	62	5	2	7	0	.161	-
1993 Base Case	228	18	5	26	0	.228	0
1993 High Range	409	36	16	53	0	.257	

MURRAY, CALVIN - Giants OF - BR - Age 21

Left fielder for Team USA, and the seventh pick overall in 1992. He was the 11th pick overall (Indians) in 1989 but wouldn't sign. Terrific speed.

	AB	R	HR	RBI	SB	BA	$
1992 Univ. of Texas	250	70	4	40	45	.356	

MURRAY, EDDIE - Mets 1B - BB - Age 37

Murray was the Mets' MVP by far in 1992. This year Eddie will have more RBI opportunities if the offense doesn't go on the disabled list again.

	AB	R	HR	RBI	SB	BA	$
1992 New York NL	551	64	16	93	4	.261	18
1993 Low Range	464	48	12	66	3	.230	
1993 Base Case	507	57	16	94	5	.261	18
1993 High Range	548	68	21	100	8	.291	

MYERS, GREG - Angels C - BL - Age 26

Getting virtually no playing time in Toronto behind Pat Borders, Myers was traded to California in mid-season, immediately becoming the Angels top catcher. Unfortunately, he broke his hamate bone and had to miss a large part of the season. Still young enough to reach new high levels in 1993. For example, he had untapped power potential (20 home runs in the California League in 1986).

	AB	R	HR	RBI	SB	BA	$
1992 Two Teams AL	78	4	1	13	0	.231	-
1993 Low Range	128	10	2	11	0	.218	
1993 Base Case	305	26	6	30	0	.239	1
1993 High Range	388	36	9	43	0	.269	

NAEHRING, TIM - Red Sox SS/2B - BR - Age 26

In Boston, his 1993 possibilities are feast or famine. Absent Jody Reed, Naehring would have been the starting second baseman if the Red Sox had to field a team the day after the expansion draft; but they were looking actively for a free agent to play 2B, in which case Naehring would be benched or traded. People were bidding Naehring up to 20 dollars a couple years ago, a lesson in caution about unproven youngsters, especially those with injuries.

	AB	R	HR	RBI	SB	BA	$
1992 Boston AL	186	12	3	14	0	.231	-
1993 Low Range	135	8	2	9	0	197	
1993 Base Case	233	15	4	18	0	.238	-
1993 High Range	309	22	6	27	0	.268	

NATAL, BOB - Marlins C - BR - Age 27

A light-hitting mediocre prospect, Natal had a big first half last season and was selected to play in the Class AAA All-Star Game. He then got a brief promotion to the majors. His arrival in Florida tells you more about the Marlins' inclination toward Expos, than it does about baseball talent.

	AB	R	HR	RBI	SB	BA	$
1992 Indianapolis AAA	344	50	12	50	3	.302	
1992 Montreal NL	6	0	0	0	0	.000	-
1993 Base Case	224	23	5	27	0	.239	1
1993 High Range	324	34	10	38	1	.268	

NAVARRO, TITO - Mets SS - BR - Age 22

Tito Navarro is the Mets' great shortstop hope for the future - their hope to bring an end to the string of Rafael Santanas, Kevin Elsters, and Dick Schofields. Tony Fernandez is a temporary idea. Navarro is a slick fielder who had reached AA in 1991, where he stole 42 bases, drew 72 walks, and batted .288.

	AB	R	HR	RBI	SB	BA	$
1992 Tidewater AAA			(Did not play - Injured)				
1993 Base Case	75	9	0	6	3	.227	-
1993 High Range	150	19	1	13	7	.260	

NEEL, TROY - Athletics OF/1B - BL - Age 27

Sweet swinger, led the Pacific Coast League in batting at .351 with 17 HR. Finally achieved prospect status at a late age. Never hit over .292 anywhere before last year, but that's what the PCL will do for you when you reach your peak in the right place.

	AB	R	HR	RBI	SB	BA	$
1992 Oakland AL	53	8	3	9	0	.264	0
1992 Tacoma AAA	396	61	17	74	2	.351	
1993 Base Case	90	10	2	11	0	.260	0
1993 High Range	173	25	5	24	1	.278	

NEVIN, PHIL - Astros 3B - BR - Age 21

What a resume! BBA College Player of the Year, U.S. Olympic cleanup hitter (.347 BA), Number One pick overall in the June draft, and Big West Conference triple crown, to name just a few accomplishments. Should reach the majors as fast as any 1992 collegiate player, say 1994.

	AB	R	HR	RBI	SB	BA	$
1992 Cal State Fullerton	200	66	20	75	5	.390	

NEWMAN, AL - Rangers 2B/3B/SS - BB - Age 32

Strictly a utility infielder at this point, although his versatility makes it likely that he will remain in the big leagues. His only Rotisserie value is his ability to steal a few bases, and his low batting average tends to offset that. Has over 2,000 AB since his last homer.

	AB	R	HR	RBI	SB	BA	$
1992 Texas AL	246	25	0	12	9	.220	0
1993 Low Range	140	14	0	7	3	.193	
1993 Base Case	208	21	0	10	8	.220	
1993 High Range	334	37	0	19	17	.248	

NEWSON, WARREN - White Sox OF - BL - Age 28

Newson is one of many possible right fielders for the White Sox this season. If he plays, it will be strictly in a platoon situation. Good talent, just in a crowded situation.

	AB	R	HR	RBI	SB	BA	$
1992 Chicago AL	136	19	1	11	3	.221	-
1993 Low Range	162	22	2	15	3	.246	
1993 Base Case	288	42	5	32	8	.273	9
1993 High Range	404	65	9	51	16	.304	

NIEVES, MELVIN - Braves OF - BB - Age 21

Has been compared to Ruben Sierra, because he has power from both sides of the plate, hits for average, plays well in right field and has some speed. Sierra was a major league star at age 21, so Nieves better hurry.

	AB	R	HR	RBI	SB	BA	$
1992 Durham A	106	18	8	32	4	.302	
1992 Greenville AA	350	61	18	76	6	.283	
1993 Base Case	170	19	3	19	1	.251	1
1993 High Range	306	37	7	39	3	.282	

NILSSON, DAVE - Brewers C - BL - Age 23

The real thing. Nilsson didn't embarrass himself in his rookie season, too much of which was spent watching in Milwaukee rather than playing everyday in Denver. Despite being one of the youngest players in his league every year, Nilsson has hit well at each level of the minors, and just needs time to develop as a major-league hitter. His defensive skills are very good, equal to or better than Surhoff's even now. Already has better power than Surhoff, and is certain to take the catching job within the next two years, with Surhoff going elsewhere or moving to 3B.

	AB	R	HR	RBI	SB	BA	$
1992 Denver AAA	240	38	3	39	10	.317	
1992 Milwaukee AL	164	15	4	25	2	.232	1
1993 Low Range	226	26	3	27	2	.248	
1993 Base Case	345	43	6	48	4	.275	10
1993 High Range	402	55	9	64	7	.306	

NIXON, OTIS - Braves OF - BB - Age 34

Returned to normal in 1992. His circumstances have changed little, so the prognosis for 1993 is similar; his age and growing competition point towards decline. Pay attention to his strikeout/walk ratio; about 1-to-1 before 1992, but fell to about 3-to-2 last year - a sign of decline. The Braves must choose Nixon or Deion Sanders, not both; Ron Gant and David Justice have the other two regular OF jobs.

	AB	R	HR	RBI	SB	BA	$
1992 Atlanta NL	456	79	2	22	41	.294	24
1993 Low Range	401	60	1	15	21	.255	
1993 Base Case	490	80	1	22	42	.283	24
1993 High Range	601	108	2	31	62	.314	

NOBOA, JUNIOR - Reds IF/OF - BR - Age 28

Career high point was a .340 batting average for AAA Indianapolis in 1989. Could still be a useful pinch hitter in the National League. He could even develop into a Rex Hudler type if given the opportunity.

	AB	R	HR	RBI	SB	BA	$
1992 Tidewater AAA	20	1	0	3	0	.200	
1992 New York NL	47	7	0	3	0	.149	-
1993 Base Case	35	4	0	3	2	.229	-
1993 High Range	100	16	1	9	5	.270	

NOKES, MATT - Yankees C - BL - Age 29

Good power hitter and adequate defense. The 1992 batting average was a downward blip, not a true indication of anything gone wrong.

	AB	R	HR	RBI	SB	BA	$
1992 New York AL	384	42	22	59	0	.224	8
1993 Low Range	263	29	10	37	0	.220	
1993 Base Case	323	39	16	53	1	.244	8
1993 High Range	446	59	26	82	1	.272	

OBERKFELL, KEN - Angels IF - BL - Age 36

Oberkfell is a journeyman utility infielder one step away from retirement or Japan.

	AB	R	HR	RBI	SB	BA	$
1992 Edmonton AAA	202	33	1	34	2	.282	
1992 California AL	91	6	0	10	0	.264	-
1993 Base Case	50	4	0	6	0	.280	-
1993 High Range	155	11	1	17	0	.269	

O'BRIEN, CHARLIE - Mets C - BR - Age 31

He can't hit now and never could, but O'Brien does throw well and the pitchers love throwing to him. It's not much to put on a resume, but it keeps him in the league. 1992 was one of his better years.

	AB	R	HR	RBI	SB	BA	$
1992 New York NL	156	15	2	13	0	.212	-
1993 Low Range	75	3	0	4	0	.146	
1993 Base Case	187	18	2	16	0	.202	-
1993 High Range	305	32	5	29	0	.245	

O'BRIEN, PETE - Mariners 1B - BL - Age 35

Six or seven years ago, O'Brien was a clear (though distant) second best 1B in the American League. Now he's just barely in the American League.

	AB	R	HR	RBI	SB	BA	$
1992 Seattle AL	396	40	14	52	2	.222	5
1993 Low Range	253	21	5	27	1	.197	
1993 Base Case	335	31	9	42	3	.237	4
1993 High Range	442	44	14	63	5	.266	

OCHOA, ALEX - Orioles OF - BL - Age 21

Baseball America tabbed Ochoa as the fifth best prospect in the Midwest (A) League. He was the O's third-round pick in 1991. Ochoa is one of the many good defense/speed OF prospects in the organization.

	AB	R	HR	RBI	SB	BA	$
1992 Kane County A	491	65	1	59	31	.295	

OFFERMAN, JOSE - Dodgers SS - BB - Age 24

While everyone focuses on the 42 errors, many forget that Offerman put together a respectable rookie season with an on-base percentage of .331 and a batting average over .300 in the second half. Offerman will continue to improve in all phases of his game and will get opportunities in the leadoff spot, especially if his platoon differential diminishes.

	AB	R	HR	RBI	SB	BA	$
1992 Los Angeles NL	534	67	1	30	23	.260	12
1993 Low Range	473	62	2	26	17	.233	
1993 Base Case	507	73	2	32	30	.264	16
1993 High Range	552	87	3	40	42	.295	

OLANDER, JIM - Reds OF - BR - Age 30

Surfaced for nine at bats with the Brewers in 1991; that was his reward for a dozen years of minor league toil. Not a factor for 1993.

	AB	R	HR	RBI	SB	BA	$
1992 Denver AAA	78	23	5	15	2	.372	

O'LEARY, TROY - Brewers OF - BL - Age 23

Texas League MVP and batting champ. Not considered a good defensive outfielder. Base Case is a September callup with a home run or two.

	AB	R	HR	RBI	SB	BA	$
1992 El Paso AA	506	92	5	79	28	.334	
1993 High Range	289	30	3	26	4	.275	

OLERUD, JOHN - Blue Jays 1B - BL - Age 24

Olerud can hit lefty pitchers fine now. 1993 should be his break-out year. If you don't get him cheap this year, you will never have another chance.

	AB	R	HR	RBI	SB	BA	$
1992 Toronto AL	458	68	16	66	1	.284	15
1993 Low Range	426	62	14	54	0	.260	
1993 Base Case	496	79	20	73	1	.287	22
1993 High Range	537	94	26	88	1	.319	

OLIVA, JOSE - Rangers 3B - BR - Age 22

One of the Rangers' top prospects, Oliva had a solid season at AA Tulsa in 1992 at the age of 21. Barring an injury to someone at the big league level, in which case Oliva could appear any time now, he is probably a year or two away. Needs to become more selective at the plate (36 walks and 123 strikeouts in 405 AB).

	AB	R	HR	RBI	SB	BA	$
1992 Tulsa AA	445	57	16	75	3	.270	
1993 Base Case	50	6	1	5	0	.220	-
1993 High Range	231	18	5	22	3	.268	

OLIVER, JOE - Reds C - BR - Age 27

Challenged for his job after a dismal 1991 season, Oliver lost weight and responded with the best season of his career. It wasn't the first time as Oliver repeated the scenario in 1989-90. A key to his season was not trying to pull everything and he should continue as a regular in 1993 (if he can remain motivated).

	AB	R	HR	RBI	SB	BA	$
1992 Cincinnati NL	485	42	10	57	2	.270	12
1993 Low Range	138	11	2	14	0	.208	
1993 Base Case	252	21	5	30	1	.249	3
1993 High Range	488	45	12	66	4	.279	

OLSON, GREG - Braves C - BR - Age 32
Gradually dropping down to a level you would expect of a career minor leaguer. Olson's days of good Rotisserie numbers are gone.

	AB	R	HR	RBI	SB	BA	$
1992 Atlanta NL	302	27	3	27	2	.238	1
1993 Base Case	220	18	1	20	2	.231	0
1993 High Range	301	27	2	32	4	.261	

O'NEILL, PAUL - Yankees OF - BL - Age 30
Good swing for the short right field line at Yankee Stadium. The trade should help for other reasons too. O'Neill regressed from his career best 1991 performance. A sore wrist contributed to a horrible second half and Paul and Lou Piniella were not best of friends.

	AB	R	HR	RBI	SB	BA	$
1992 Cincinnati NL	496	59	14	66	6	.246	13
1993 Low Range	411	44	16	44	3	.215	
1993 Base Case	490	57	25	61	5	.256	17
1993 High Range	554	71	33	77	8	.286	

OQUENDO, JOSE - Cardinals 2B/SS - BL - Age 29
Cardinals color man and former third baseman-outfielder Mike Shannon calls Oquendo "The Secret Weapon". However, Oquendo was just a secret last season. A recurring heel injury limited him to just 14 major league games. Oquendo is a slick fielder, a true shortstop stuck at second base for years.

	AB	R	HR	RBI	SB	BA	$
1992 Louisville AAA	64	8	0	6	0	.266	
1992 St. Louis NL	35	3	0	3	0	.257	-
1993 Low Range	190	15	0	14	0	228	
1993 Base Case	286	25	0	25	0	.259	1
1993 High Range	417	39	0	41	0	.289	

ORSULAK, JOE - Orioles OF - BL - Age 30
After a very slow start, Orsulak came out of it to hit .289 overall to lead the Orioles. He spent some time on the DL late in the season with a sprained thumb. The past five years have shown that Orsulak is a consistent .270-.290 hitter. Baltimore management has always wanted Orsulak to become the classic "fourth outfielder" because he is capable of playing all three OF positions well and has the mental makeup for pinch-hitting.

	AB	R	HR	RBI	SB	BA	$
1992 Baltimore AL	391	45	4	39	5	.289	10
1993 Low Range	307	33	3	26	3	261	
1993 Base Case	355	42	4	34	5	.278	9
1993 High Range	471	61	6	52	9	.299	

ORTIZ, JUNIOR - Indians C - BR - Age 33
Ortiz' role is backup catcher. He will hit .250 with a possible short .300 hot streak in a good year, but won't give you much else.

	AB	R	HR	RBI	SB	BA	$
1992 Cleveland AL	244	20	0	24	1	.250	0
1993 Low Range	87	7	0	8	0	.224	
1993 Base Case	197	19	0	22	1	.244	-
1993 High Range	339	31	0	38	2	.280	

ORTIZ, RAY - Twins OF - BL - Age 25

Good for a couple of home runs, but Ortiz really can't match the offensive value of the numerous other Twins outfield prospects. Base Case is zero at bats.

	AB	R	HR	RBI	SB	BA	$
1992 Orlando AA	266	40	10	47	0	.263	
1992 Portland AAA	134	17	3	22	0	.328	
1993 High Range	167	13	3	17	1	.259	

ORTON, JOHN - Angels C - BR - Age 27

Once thought to be the Angels catcher of the future, Orton has struggled at the plate in every year he's been in the majors. The Angels finally ran out of patience and traded for Greg Myers with Orton slated to be the backup catcher.

	AB	R	HR	RBI	SB	BA	$
1992 Edmonton AAA	149	28	3	25	3	.255	
1992 California AL	114	11	2	12	1	.219	-
1993 Base Case	124	12	2	13	1	.219	
1993 High Range	239	25	5	29	3	.248	

OWEN, SPIKE - Expos SS - BB - Age 31

He heard the footsteps of hot Expos prospect Wil Cordero each of the past two seasons but held on to the starting shortstop job anyway. Owen isn't the prettiest player but he always gets the job done with great leadership qualities. Likely to find a new team for 1993.

	AB	R	HR	RBI	SB	BA	$
1992 Montreal NL	386	52	7	40	9	.269	11
1993 Low Range	154	20	2	13	2	.199	
1993 Base Case	283	39	4	29	6	.240	3
1993 High Range	405	62	7	47	13	.270	

> *"The Ancient Mariner: an aging shortstop who now stoppeth only one in three."*
>
> *-- Red Smith*

PAGLIARULO, MIKE - Twins 3B - BL - Age 33

Pags was slated to be the lefty half of the platoon at third base but spent a long time on the DL with a broken hamate bone. Eligible for free agency, he was looking for another team in late 1992.

	AB	R	HR	RBI	SB	BA	$
1992 Minnesota AL	105	10	0	9	1	.200	-
1993 Base Case	189	18	4	22	1	.229	-
1993 High Range	388	41	9	51	2	.258	

PAGNOZZI, TOM - Cardinals C - BR - Age 30

Pagnozzi continued to be a solid offensive catcher in 1992, his second full season as a starter. However, he works a lot of games and may start wearing down. He loves catching, says his goal is to catch all 162 games some season. His goal. Not yours.

	AB	R	HR	RBI	SB	BA	$
1992 St. Louis NL	485	33	7	44	2	.249	6
1993 Low Range	342	18	5	25	1	.204	
1993 Base Case	427	24	8	37	1	.245	4
1993 High Range	509	32	11	50	2	.275	

PALMEIRO, RAFAEL - Rangers 1B - BL - Age 28

Palmeiro's 1992 average was his lowest since his rookie season, yet his power statistics were second only to his outstanding 1991 season. His 1992 strikeout total was a career high, suggesting that he is becoming more of a power-oriented hitter as he matures.

	AB	R	HR	RBI	SB	BA	$
1992 Texas AL	608	84	22	85	2	.268	18
1993 Low Range	464	58	15	62	1	.268	
1993 Base Case	582	79	24	91	2	.296	29
1993 High Range	635	95	31	106	4	.328	

PALMER, DEAN - Rangers 3B/OF - BR - Age 24

Ever since I first saw him put on a week-long power display during spring training 1989, I have believed he was a hitter of destiny. A streaky, free-swinging young power hitter, he reminds some of a young Mike Schmidt. He made progress in 1992, raising his batting average 42 points and cutting his strikeout ratio. He should continue to make progress, and could break through in a big way.

	AB	R	HR	RBI	SB	BA	$
1992 Texas AL	541	74	26	72	10	.229	14
1993 Low Range	506	60	19	56	6	.193	
1993 Base Case	506	66	24	65	9	.233	12
1993 High Range	552	78	31	86	14	.280	

PAPPAS, ERIK - Royals C/IF - BR - Age 26

Career .258 BA in nine minor league season. Maybe good for a home run or two, but not likely to be called up in 1993. Appeared briefly with the White Sox in 1991.

	AB	R	HR	RBI	SB	BA	$
1992 Omaha AAA	138	18	1	11	4	.217	
1992 Vancouver AAA	98	17	4	17	4	.276	

PAQUETTE, CRAIG - Athletics 3B/DH - BR - Age 24
Good speed/power combination. Not much for defense, so he will have to hit to get a callup in 1993.

	AB	R	HR	RBI	SB	BA	$
1992 Huntsville AA	450	59	17	71	13	.258	
1992 Tacoma AAA	66	10	2	11	3	.273	

PAREDES, JOHNNY - Unsigned 2B - BR - Age 30
Back in 1987 he was a good prospect with the Expos: high average, high speed. Now over the hill.

	AB	R	HR	RBI	SB	BA	$
1992 Toledo AAA	83	6	2	5	3	.193	

PARENT, MARK - Orioles C - BR - Age 31
Back-up catcher with a little home run power. He had several trials with the Padres but hit only .197 in 488 at-bats.

	AB	R	HR	RBI	SB	BA	$
1992 Rochester AAA	356	52	17	69	4	.287	
1992 Baltimore AL	34	4	2	4	0	.235	-
1993 Base Case	225	18	5	24	0	.213	-
1993 High Range	302	26	9	37	1	.245	

PARKER, RICK - Astros 3B/OF - BR - Age 30
Appeared briefly with the Giants in 1990-1991. Good hitter. If you're looking for one stolen base in July, and Parker comes up, he might be worth having for a week or two. Base Case is clearly zero at bats.

	AB	R	HR	RBI	SB	BA	$
1992 Tucson AAA	319	51	4	38	20	.323	

PARKS, DEREK - Twins C - BR - Age 24
Once considered as one of the Twins' top prospects, Parks has struggled around the Mendoza line in the minors.

	AB	R	HR	RBI	SB	BA	$
1992 Portland AAA	249	33	12	49	0	.245	
1992 Minnesota AL	6	1	0	0	0	.333	-
1993 Base Case	59	6	1	5	0	.223	-
1993 High Range	207	24	3	22	0	.263	

PARRISH, LANCE - Mariners C - BR - Age 36
Near the end of his major league career. Parrish isn't very effective behind the plate and doesn't hit well enough to play any other position. He has hit under .240 in four of the last five seasons.

	AB	R	HR	RBI	SB	BA	$
1992 Two Teams AL	275	26	12	32	1	.233	4
1993 Base Case	246	23	9	28	1	.220	1
1993 High Range	377	39	16	49	2	.249	

PASQUA, DAN - White Sox OF - BL - Age 31
Out part of the season with an injury. Strictly platoon. When healthy, he is helped by New Comiskey.

	AB	R	HR	RBI	SB	BA	$
1992 Chicago AL	265	26	6	33	0	.211	-
1993 Low Range	254	22	5	28	0	.201	
1993 Base Case	340	33	8	43	0	.242	3
1993 High Range	420	44	12	61	0	.272	

PATTERSON, JOHN - Giants 2B - BB - Age 26

Spring training phenom last season, Patterson may finally be on the verge of earning a major league position. Good speed, good range at second base, decent bat.

	AB	R	HR	RBI	SB	BA	$
1992 San Francisco	103	10	0	4	5	.184	-
1992 Phoenix AAA	362	52	2	37	22	.301	
1993 Low Range	123	12	0	7	3	.193	
1993 Base Case	153	17	0	10	6	.233	0
1993 High Range	308	37	1	23	16	.262	

PAULINO, ELVIN - Cubs 1B - BL - Age 25

Paulino was a Cubs top 1B prospect until he struggled at AAA and was demoted to AA. He led the Southern League with 24 HR and 91 RBI in 1991. His home runs increased each year from 2 to 8 to 14 to 24 before falling to 5 last year.

	AB	R	HR	RBI	SB	BA	$
1992 Iowa AAA	157	15	1	16	0	.217	
1992 Charlotte AA	142	18	4	21	1	.225	

PEARSON, EDDIE - White Sox 1B/DH - BR - Age 20

Batted a thin .235 for Sarasota GCL Rookie league. Has good raw power but needs to learn a lot. Came from a junior college (Bishop State) that didn't face the toughest collegiate pitching.

PECOTA, BILL - Mets IF - BR - Age 33

Pecota is a veteran glove man who spurred interest last off-season as he was coming off his most productive year in 1991. Bill does provide a manager with versatility and good defense at all infield positions, but he can't hit, and in view of that, and his age, and the Mets' rebuilding philosophy, it doesn't seem likely that he'll be here any longer than it takes for Tito Navarro or any halfway decent young infielder to get off the plane at LaGuardia.

	AB	R	HR	RBI	SB	BA	$
1992 New York NL	269	28	2	26	9	.227	3
1993 Low Range	189	18	2	16	4	.197	
1993 Base Case	259	27	3	25	8	.237	2
1993 High Range	296	34	4	32	13	.266	

PEDRE, JORGE - Cubs C - BR - Age 26

Injuries have hampered Pedre's career, and he has become a journeyman player. He hit 13 HR in 233 AB in 1987, but hasn't shown that kind of power in the five seasons since. The Cubs gave him a brief look during the last week of the year when Girardi was injured.

	AB	R	HR	RBI	SB	BA	$
1992 Iowa AAA	296	31	6	34	2	.253	
1993 Base Case	50	3	0	4	0	.236	-
1993 High Range	182	14	2	15	1	.265	

PEGUERO, JULIO - Phillies OF - BB - Age 24

Peguero is basically a less-experienced version of Ruben Amaro, and Amaro's going to have to fight for the playing time he gets. But if the Phillies entire outfield gets hurt again, Peguero can play.

	AB	R	HR	RBI	SB	BA	$
1992 Scranton AAA	289	41	1	21	14	.256	
1992 Philadelphia NL	9	3	0	0	0	.222	-
1993 Base Case	25	4	0	2	2	.240	-
1993 High Range	204	29	2	16	10	.269	

PEGUES, STEVE - Padres OF - BR - Age 24
A little bit of speed and a little bit of power, but not a good hitter. Not likely to reach the majors in 1993.

	AB	R	HR	RBI	SB	BA	$
1992 Las Vegas AAA	376	51	9	56	12	.263	

PELTIER, DAN - Rangers OF - BL - Age 24
Peltier has been one of the Rangers' better prospects for several years. He made the jump from rookie ball to AA in 1990 at the age of 21, and spent the last two years in Oklahoma City. He has the potential to hit for high average (.402 in 1989), with fair HR and RBI totals. His lack of big speed or big power may make it difficult for him to play regularly in the major leagues.

	AB	R	HR	RBI	SB	BA	$
1992 Texas AL	24	1	0	2	0	.167	-
1992 Okla. City AAA	450	65	7	53	1	.296	
1993 Base Case	121	13	2	11	2	.232	1
1993 High Range	298	36	5	32	5	.261	

PEMBERTON, RUDY - Tigers OF - BR - Age 23
Just spent his fifth year in Rookie/A-ball. Good speed but really hasn't progressed.

	AB	R	HR	RBI	SB	BA	$
1992 Lakeland A	343	41	3	43	25	.265	

PENA, GERONIMO - Cardinals 2B - BB - Age 26
One of the best candidates to have a career year in 1993. Quietly, he has become a solid offensive player, showing power and speed in a part-time role. He is somewhat lazy in the field, though, and that keeps him from being a regular. If he improves his attitude, he has a chance to be a star.

	AB	R	HR	RBI	SB	BA	$
1992 Louisville AAA	101	16	3	12	4	.248	
1992 St. Louis NL	203	31	7	31	13	.305	13
1993 Low Range	289	39	6	27	10	.238	
1993 Base Case	351	53	9	39	19	.270	15
1993 High Range	506	83	16	63	35	.301	

PENA, TONY - Red Sox C - BR - Age 35
Since he went to Boston, Pena, a pretty productive player in the National League, has experienced a pronounced offensive downturn. The Red Sox say they are committed to him, and showed that commitment by leaving Eric Wedge exposed. Still, he'll be 36 in June.

	AB	R	HR	RBI	SB	BA	$
1992 Boston AL	410	39	1	38	3	.241	2
1993 Low Range	232	19	0	20	1	.202	
1993 Base Case	332	31	1	33	2	.243	0
1993 High Range	402	41	1	46	3	.273	

PENDLETON, TERRY - Braves 3B - BB - Age 32
Another great year from Pendleton, but not quite MVP caliber (look at Barry Bonds' numbers to see why). All his stats were down slightly from 1991 and his GDP are climbing, but that's quibbling. Pendleton's aging, ailing knees are the only real question at this point. He's a gamer.

	AB	R	HR	RBI	SB	BA	$
1992 Atlanta NL	640	98	21	105	5	.311	33
1993 Low Range	464	67	11	68	2	.256	
1993 Base Case	595	95	18	102	4	.283	25
1993 High Range	635	111	23	115	7	.314	

PENNYFEATHER, WILLIAM - Pirates OF - BR - Age 24

Pennyfeather made it to the majors last season, mainly on his speed and overall athleticism. He still did not show major-league hitting ability and struggled against off-speed and breaking pitches. He was a wide receiver at Syracuse before signing with the Pirates out of a tryout camp in 1988.

	AB	R	HR	RBI	SB	BA	$
1992 Carolina AA	199	28	6	25	7	.337	
1992 Buffalo AAA	160	19	1	12	3	.238	
1992 Pittsburgh NL	9	2	0	0	0	.222	-
1993 Base Case	75	10	1	7	2	.230	-
1993 High Range	214	30	3	21	5	.272	

PEREZ, EDUARDO - Angels 3B - BR - Age 23

Son of Tony Perez, Eduardo was the Angels' first round draft pick in '91. He needs to find his power stroke, and get more experience, but he could progress rapidly.

	AB	R	HR	RBI	SB	BA	$
1992 Palm Springs A	204	37	3	35	14	.314	
1992 Midland AA	235	27	3	23	19	.230	

PEREZ, ROBERT - Blue Jays OF - BR - Age 23

Had a big year in the FSL in 1991 and showed steady progress again in 1992. Not likely to be a factor this year, but for 1994 he is a good possibility. Make a note to check his status in July.

	AB	R	HR	RBI	SB	BA	$
1992 Knoxville AA	526	59	9	59	11	.260	

PEREZCHICA, TONY - Indians IF - BR - Age 26

Utility infielder without any power punch. Looked like a super prospect in 1987 but never made much progress after that.

	AB	R	HR	RBI	SB	BA	$
1992 Col. Sp. AAA	70	8	2	9	1	.171	
1992 Cleveland AL	20	2	0	1	0	.100	-
1993 High Range	142	10	1	11	1	.232	

PERRY, GERALD - Cardinals 1B - BL - Age 32

Wasn't it just yesterday the Braves were touting him as a future star? It never quite worked out for Perry and he was ineffecitive in limited playing time last year. He won't even come close to matching the career of his uncle, Dan Driessen.

	AB	R	HR	RBI	SB	BA	$
1992 St. Louis NL	143	13	1	18	3	.238	0
1993 Low Range	127	11	1	14	2	.206	
1993 Base Case	163	15	1	21	3	.247	1
1993 High Range	286	29	2	41	8	.277	

PETRALLI, GENO - Rangers C - BL - Age 33

After several years of providing a decent left-handed bat off the bench, Petralli's performance declined markedly in 1992. Defense and calling a game have never been his claim to fame, so another year like 1992 could spell the end of his career. At one point last season, Petralli was so frustrated that he tried switch-hitting, a practice he had abandoned in 1988, but it didn't help. He is unlikely to post numbers which would help to a Rotisserie team.

	AB	R	HR	RBI	SB	BA	$
1992 Texas AL	192	11	1	18	0	.198	-
1993 Low Range	193	10	1	16	0	.190	
1993 Base Case	228	13	1	21	0	.230	-
1993 High Range	303	19	2	32	0	.259	

PETTIS, GARY - Tigers OF - BB - Age 34

The old guy can still run, so if you need some cheap steals he'll fill the bill. Watch that BA though.

	AB	R	HR	RBI	SB	BA	$
1992 Two Teams AL	159	27	1	12	14	.201	3
1993 Base Case	195	30	1	15	16	.211	2
1993 High Range	290	48	2	26	32	.244	

PHILLIPS, J.R. - Angels 1B - BL - Age 22

Phillips hurt his progress by hitting only .237 for Class AA Midland where nearly everyone hits over .300. Hit 20 home runs and stole 15 base in 1991.

	AB	R	HR	RBI	SB	BA	$
1992 Midland AA	497	58	14	77	5	.237	

PHILLIPS, TONY - Tigers IF/OF - BB - Age 33

His ability to play so many positions, and perform so well offensively are valuable assets. His runs scored correlate closely with Cecil Fielder's RBI in 1992. Tony's aging.

	AB	R	HR	RBI	SB	BA	$
1992 Detroit AL	606	114	10	64	12	.276	18
1993 Low Range	474	78	7	42	5	.238	
1993 Base Case	530	96	10	54	10	.270	15
1993 High Range	610	122	13	71	15	.301	

PIAZZA, MIKE - Dodgers C - BR - Age 24

After being a courtesy pick in the 60th round of the draft because he is the godson of Tom Lasorda, Piazza has blossomed into one of the more interesting stories around. He is on the fast track to major league success as evidenced by his promotions from AA to AAA to the majors all in 1992 season. Piazza even had three hits in his major league debut. His dad was one of the investors in the Tampa offer for the Giants. Outstanding stats speak for themselves and Piazza is becoming a good catcher with a fine arm.

	AB	R	HR	RBI	SB	BA	$
1992 San Antonio AA	114	18	7	20	0	.377	
1992 Albuquerque AAA	358	54	16	69	1	.341	
1992 Los Angeles NL	69	5	1	7	0	.232	-
1993 Low Range	161	13	3	16	0	.230	
1993 Base Case	299	27	7	34	1	.262	6
1993 High Range	422	43	12	54	2	.292	

PIRKL, GREG - Mariners 1B - BR - Age 22

Has received midseason promotions in two consecutive years. The best factor a player can have going for him, other than pure talent, is someone in the front office watching his career with interest.

	AB	R	HR	RBI	SB	BA	$
1992 Jacksonville AA	227	25	10	29	0	.291	
1992 Calgary AAA	286	30	6	32	4	.266	
1993 High Range	201	13	4	17	1	.272	

PLANTIER, PHIL - Red Sox OF - BL - Age 24

Plantier had a nerve injury that wasn't disclosed until after he fell into a horrendous slump. At the end of 1991, when he hit 11 home runs in 148 at bats for Boston, Plantier looked and talked like one of the great sluggers of the 1990's. He told me, "I have a goal of hitting one home run a week, and put some streaks on top of that." Now, he doesn't look any better than Kevin Maas, for example, and has the injury question to clear up. High potential if you want to take a risk, but not a solid investment.

	AB	R	HR	RBI	SB	BA	$
1992 Boston AL	349	46	7	30	2	.246	4
1993 Low Range	303	37	7	27	1	.210	
1993 Base Case	420	57	12	43	2	.251	7
1993 High Range	518	77	17	60	3	.281	

POLONIA, LUIS - Angels OF - BL - Age 28

Speedster Luis Polonia had another excellent year, and the outlook for '93 is for more of the same, especially with Junior Felix out of the picture.

	AB	R	HR	RBI	SB	BA	$
1992 California AL	577	83	0	35	51	.286	29
1993 Low Range	404	52	0	20	21	.257	
1993 Base Case	502	71	0	29	43	.284	25
1993 High Range	573	89	0	38	59	.316	

POSE, SCOTT - Reds OF - BL - Age 26

A slap hitting, fast outfielder. The Reds signed about a hundred outfielders during November, or so it seemed. Good talent; crowded situation. Check in during spring training.

	AB	R	HR	RBI	SB	BA	$
1992 Chattanooga AA	526	87	2	45	20	.342	

POUGH, CLYDE - Indians OF - BR - Age 23

A third round pick in 1988, Pough had a big year in the SAL in 1991 but hasn't progressed since then.

	AB	R	HR	RBI	SB	BA	$
1992 Kinston A	411	59	11	58	12	.226	

POWELL, ALONZO - Mariners OF/1B - BR - Age 28

Reached the majors with Montreal in 1987 and Seattle in 1991, and hit way over .300 for four consecutive years in Triple-A, but it wasn't enough.

	AB	R	HR	RBI	SB	BA	$
1992 Calgary AAA	35	7	1	7	0	.343	

PRATT, TODD - Phillies C/1B - BR - Age 26

Pratt's late-season play (albeit only 46 at-bats) has earned him a chance to win the number two catcher position behind Darren Daulton. Todd was salvaged from the Red Sox organization in the December 1991 draft. He won't be a .280 hitter over the course of 200 AB, but he'll get some PT when Daulton gets hurt and/or slumps.

	AB	R	HR	RBI	SB	BA	$
1992 Reading AA	132	20	6	26	2	.333	
1992 Scranton AAA	125	20	7	28	1	.320	
1992 Philadelphia NL	46	6	2	10	0	.283	0
1993 Low Range	75	7	2	13	0	.227	
1993 Base Case	150	14	6	24	0	.253	-
1993 High Range	185	19	3	23	0	.264	

PRESLEY, JIM - Unsigned 3B - BR - Age 31

Sharing the Oklahoma City infield corners with Steve Balboni in 1992, Presley showed why he's no longer a major leaguer. Career total 135 major league home runs and holding.

	AB	R	HR	RBI	SB	BA	$
1992 Okla City AAA	173	16	4	28	3	.237	

PRINCE, TOM - Pirates C - BR - Age 28

Has been considered a prospect since 1987 but has yet to spend a full season in the majors. Prince has shown little ability to hit major-league pitching in any of his past six seasons in the majors. Why is he still called a prospect? Just a six-year habit.

	AB	R	HR	RBI	SB	BA	$
1992 Buffalo AAA	244	34	9	35	3	.262	
1992 Pittsburgh NL	44	1	0	5	1	.091	-
1993 High Range	162	8	1	14	2	.197	

PRITCHETT, CHRIS - Angels 1B - BL - Age 23

A former UCLA star, Pritchett was the Midwest League's all-star 1B. He led his club in HR and RBI and was voted loop's best defensive 1B. He will not be a factor in 1993.

	AB	R	HR	RBI	SB	BA	$
1992 Quad City A	448	79	13	72	9	.290	

PUCKETT, KIRBY - Twins OF - BR - Age 32

Puckett had another outstanding year in '92, showing no signs of slowing down.

	AB	R	HR	RBI	SB	BA	$
1992 Minnesota AL	639	104	19	110	17	.329	39
1993 Low Range	504	72	10	73	9	.283	
1993 Base Case	584	91	15	98	17	.311	36
1993 High Range	655	112	20	117	25	.338	

PULLIAM, HARVEY - Royals OF - BR - Age 25

Just barely hanging on to the prospect label. Steady minor league progress; had decent AAA numbers in 1992. Unless the whole Royals outfield goes on the DL (it can happen -- look at Boston in 1992) Pulliam won't get much major league playing time. The departure of Conine helps a little.

	AB	R	HR	RBI	SB	BA	$
1992 Omaha AAA	359	55	16	60	4	.270	
1992 Kansas City AL	5	2	0	0	0	.200	-
1993 Base Case	175	19	3	19	0	.236	
1993 High Range	323	38	6	40	1	.266	

QUINLAN, TOM - Blue Jays 3B - BR - Age 25

Career has been characterized by terrific fielding and lots of strikeouts, with a few home runs. Quinlan has put in two years at Syracuse, so it's now time to use him or lose him. Won't be a big stat player anyway.

	AB	R	HR	RBI	SB	BA	$
1992 Syracuse AAA	349	43	6	36	1	.215	
1992 Toronto AL	15	2	0	2	0	.067	-
1993 High Range	203	22	2	21	2	.242	

QUINONES, LUIS - Twins IF - BB - Age 30
Five year veteran Luis Quinones is a utility infielder with a career BA of .226, little power, and no speed.

	AB	R	HR	RBI	SB	BA	$
1992 Portland AAA	276	45	12	49	1	.243	
1992 Minnesota AL	5	0	0	1	0	.200	-
1993 Base Case	58	5	1	6	0	.229	-
1993 High Range	192	19	2	23	2	.259	

QUINTANA, CARLOS - Red Sox 1B - BR - Age 27
His major injuries prior to the 1992 season kept him out the whole year. How much is left? Watch the boxes for winter ball and his spring training role. Minor league rehab is likely until May or June. One good sign was that the Red Sox protected him in November.

	AB	R	HR	RBI	SB	BA	$
1992 Boston AL	(Did not play - Injured)						
1993 Base Case	249	25	3	27	0	.270	4
1993 High Range	406	45	7	51	1	.301	

QUIRK, Jamie - Athletics C - BL - Age 38
Quirk has been a backup for almost his entire 18 year career, during which he has compiled a .240 average and all of 43 home runs.

	AB	R	HR	RBI	SB	BA	$
1992 Oakland AL	177	13	2	11	0	.220	-
1993 Low Range	157	10	1	8	0	.181	
1993 Base Case	203	15	2	13	0	.220	-
1993 High Range	309	25	4	22	0	.249	

RAINES, TIM - White Sox OF - BB - Age 33
Despite age, still a fast runner. Will continue to be White Sox leadoff hitter. Doesn't bat as well against lefties and might sit down against the occasional Mark Langston type of lefty. Raines is still young enough and clever enough that, if he ever gets the hang of American League breaking balls, he could become a power hitter.

	AB	R	HR	RBI	SB	BA	$
1992 Chicago AL	551	102	7	54	45	.294	32
1993 Low Range	419	69	5	39	21	.258	
1993 Base Case	510	93	8	55	41	.285	29
1993 High Range	589	118	11	72	59	.316	

RAMIREZ, MANNY - Indians OF - BR - Age 20
Cleveland's No. 1 draft pick in '91. Moving up from Rookie ball, he had trouble with Carolina League breaking pitches at first, then started hitting until he went down because of a bruised hand.

	AB	R	HR	RBI	SB	BA	$
1992 Kinston A	291	52	13	63	1	.278	

RAMIREZ, RAFAEL - Astros SS - BR - Age 34
Sometimes in 1991-1992, it was only the thought of Rafael Ramirez that caused Andujar Cedeno's name to be written into the lineup at shortstop.

	AB	R	HR	RBI	SB	BA	$
1992 Houston NL	176	17	1	13	0	.250	-
1993 Base Case	137	13	1	10	0	.242	-
1993 High Range	278	29	2	23	0	.272	

RAMOS, JOHN - Yankees C - BR - Age 27
Good hitting catcher (.308 and .314 at AA/AAA in 1991-1992), but the Yankees decided to go with defense and pitcher handling for their righty-hitting platoon catcher, and acquired Mike Stanley. That was just about the end for Ramos' career.

RAMOS, KEN - Indians OF - BL - Age 25
Won the batting title, hitting .339 in the pitching-rich Eastern League. He's a line drive hitter with speed. Base Case is zero at bats for 1993; may hit for decent average and get an SB or two as a September callup. There are just too many Tribe outfielders.

	AB	R	HR	RBI	SB	BA	$
1992 Canton AA	442	94	5	42	13	.339	
1993 High Range	202	23	2	16	4	.280	

RAMSEY, FERNANDO - Cubs OF - BR - Age 27
Good speed, with 119 SB in three years. And he's risen from A to AA to AAA with hardly a ripple in his stats. There are just too many Cubbie outfielders; sometimes it looks like major league teams have an implicit agreement to keep these guys around, just so developing pitchers have somebody to practice on. Base Case is zero at bats.

	AB	R	HR	RBI	SB	BA	$
1992 Iowa AAA	480	62	1	38	39	.269	
1992 Chicago NL	25	0	0	2	0	.120	-
1993 High Range	234	20	0	15	10	.262	

RANDOLPH, WILLIE - Mets 2B - BR - Age 38
Randolph could probably hang around for a couple more years as a utility player, but his days as a big offensive contributor are over. Future coach or manager.

	AB	R	HR	RBI	SB	BA	$
1992 New York NL	286	29	2	15	1	.252	1
1993 Low Range	150	18	0	7	0	.233	
1993 Base Case	256	25	2	13	1	.254	0
1993 High Range	309	33	2	18	1	.284	

RATLIFF, DARYL - Pirates OF - BR - Age 23
Good speed, and he knows how to draw a walk. But Ratliff is about two years away. Hit .240 with 25 SB for AA Carolina last year.

READY, RANDY - Athletics IF - BR - Age 33
Prototypical journeyman, from afar Ready looks like a major leaguer.

	AB	R	HR	RBI	SB	BA	$
1992 Oakland AL	125	17	3	17	1	.200	-
1993 Base Case	117	16	2	16	1	.220	-
1993 High Range	238	36	6	37	3	.249	

REBOULET, JEFF - Twins SS/3B - BR - Age 28
Utility infielder. He spent seven years in the minors, and at age 28, doesn't have much upside potential except as a role player. Consistently hit in the .240 range during his minor league career, before 1992.

	AB	R	HR	RBI	SB	BA	$
1992 Portland AAA	161	21	2	21	3	.286	
1992 Minnesota AL	137	15	1	16	3	.190	
1993 Base Case	121	13	1	13	1	.207	-
1993 High Range	303	41	3	38	5	.238	

REDFIELD, JOE - Pirates IF/OF - BR - Age 32

The Pirates' third base woes got Redfield into the major leagues back in 1991, but he had already become a career minor leaguer before that. Best year was 1987 at Midland: .321 with 30 HR and 17 SB.

REDINGTON, TOM - Padres 3B - BR - Age 24

At his young age, Redington has already been a prospect and then an ex-prospect with two organizations, and is working on his third. The Braves made him a third round pick in 1987 but waived him in 1990. Padres picked him up and got a good year from him at AA Wichita in 1991 but then obtained Gary Sheffield for their 3B needs. Redington hit .231 with little power or speed at AA Birmingham in 1992.

REDUS, GARY - Pirates 1B/OF - BR - Age 36

Looked like he was over the hill through most of the 1992 season. However, he came on late in the regular season and starred in the National League Championship Series, keeping alive hopes for 1993.

	AB	R	HR	RBI	SB	BA	$
1992 Pittsburgh NL	176	26	3	12	11	.256	5
1993 Low Range	105	14	1	7	4	.210	
1993 Base Case	185	25	3	14	12	.251	5
1993 High Range	305	49	6	24	26	.281	

REED, DARREN - Mets OF - BR - Age 27

Once a top prospect, Reed was acquired by Minnesota from Montreal late in the season in a trade for Bill Kreuger, and then passed along to New York for Pat Howell during the winter. When he first came up with the Mets in 1990, I asked Reed what single factor had contributed most to his promotion. "The fly balls go farther now," he said. Seriously, he started swinging harder when he could see that he wasn't going to become a major leaguer with warning track power. Reed missed all of '91 due to a broken right forearm; and '92 was almost a total loss as he struggled to regain his skills.

	AB	R	HR	RBI	SB	BA	$
1992 W. Palm B. A	40	6	2	12	0	.250	
1992 Montreal NL	81	10	5	10	0	.173	-
1992 Minnesota AL	33	2	0	4	0	.182	
1993 Low Range	136	13	6	18	4	.213	-
1993 Base Case	242	24	8	32	3	.215	0
1993 High Range	357	39	13	54	5	.247	

REED, JEFF - Reds C - BL - Age 30

Reed's collapse coincided with Joe Oliver's comeback. Don't expect much for 1993.

	AB	R	HR	RBI	SB	BA	$
1992 Cincinnati NL	25	2	0	2	0	.160	-
1993 Base Case	98	7	1	8	0	.218	-
1993 High Range	203	16	2	19	0	.250	

REED, JODY - Dodgers 2B - BR - Age 30

Reed was down in just about every offensive category in 1992, but there were a few hopeful signs. He got a career high for SB; and his strikeout/walk ratio improved over 1990-1991. Reed was in the doghouse in Boston for being too independent and outspoken. The Dodgers obviously believe he can come back. Just don't expect any more .288 hitting.

	AB	R	HR	RBI	SB	BA	$
1992 Boston AL	550	64	3	40	7	.247	5
1993 Low Range	238	24	1	15	2	.209	
1993 Base Case	374	41	2	27	5	.250	3
1993 High Range	512	62	3	42	9	.280	

REESE, CALVIN - Reds SS - BR - Age 20

Cincinnati's No. 1 draft pick in '91, out of high school. Voted the Sally League's best defensive SS. He's the type of player who has to bring his skills up to the level of his talent (makes spectacular plays, blows routine grounders).

	AB	R	HR	RBI	SB	BA	$
1992 Charleston A	380	50	6	53	19	.268	

REIMER, KEVIN - Brewers OF/DH - BL - Age 28

Given a choice between Paul Molitor in the field and Kevin Reimer in the field, the Brewers are likely to choose Molitor. Reimer's future is at DH - he is probably the worst defensive outfielder in the AL, and has been playing the outfield largely because former teammate Brian Downing doesn't own a glove. Reimer's 1992 season was not up to 1991 standards, and most of the decline was in the second half, when he had only 16 RBI. One theory is that he is less effective as a regular than as a part-time player; 1992 was the first season that he had more than 400 AB.

	AB	R	HR	RBI	SB	BA	$
1992 Texas AL	494	56	16	58	2	.267	13
1993 Low Range	334	33	9	31	1	.215	
1993 Base Case	412	44	13	44	2	.256	9
1993 High Range	495	58	19	60	3	.287	

REYNOLDS, HAROLD - Mariners 2B - BB - Age 32

Reynolds has been a solid defensive player throughout his career, but his offense is slipping. He was never an effective basestealer and no longer steals 25-30 bases per year. In 1987 he stole 60 bases to break Rickey Henderson's streak of league SB titles. Hit a career high .300 in 1989 but has hovered near .250 ever since. After the expansion draft, the interested teams included Boston and Baltimore.

	AB	R	HR	RBI	SB	BA	$
1992 Seattle AL	458	55	3	33	15	.247	8
1993 Low Range	408	44	2	24	10	.210	
1993 Base Case	440	53	2	30	18	.251	8
1993 High Range	620	81	4	49	33	.281	

REYNOLDS, R.J. - Japan OF - BB - Age 32

Reynolds' average declined from .316 to .252 in his second season in the Central League and his power is nothing much, yet R.J. still possesses adequate speed and could be a credible fourth- or fifth-string outfielder in the majors.

	AB	R	HR	RBI	SB	BA	$
1992 Japan	397	54	18	61	---	.252	

RHODES, KARL - Astros OF - BL - Age 24

Began the 1991 season as the Astros starting right fielder but couldn't hold the job. Spent most of 1991 and 1992 at Tucson with limited success except for a strong finish in the last month. Does not appear to have enough power or speed to hold a regular job in the majors.

	AB	R	HR	RBI	SB	BA	$
1992 Tucson AAA	332	62	2	54	8	.289	
1992 Houston NL	4	0	0	0	0	.000	-
1993 Base Case	50	7	0	6	2	.220	-
1993 High Range	247	21	3	19	6	.255	

RICHARDSON, JEFF - Pirates IF - BR - Age 27
Marginal utility type. No value.

RIESGO, NIKCO - Unsigned 1B/3B/OF - BR - Age 26
Appeared with Montreal in 1991, and played at AA Memphis in 1992. Stole 104 bases in 1988-1990, but now appears to be finished.

RILES, ERNEST - Astros IF - BL - Age 32
Veteran utilityman played all 4 infield positions in limited stint with Astros in 1992. Released at the end of the season, his best chance is to hook up somewhere as a lefthanded pinch-hitter and utility infielder. Has shown some power, especially in 1990 with the Giants, when he hit 8 homers in only 155 at-bats. Base Case for 1993 is zero at bats.

	AB	R	HR	RBI	SB	BA	$
1992 Tucson AAA	202	37	1	35	2	.307	
1992 Houston NL	61	5	1	4	1	.262	-
1993 High Range	150	20	4	25	1	.250	

RIPKEN, BILLY - Orioles 2B - BR - Age 28
Ripken lost some playing time to Mark McLemore, but finished the 1992 season still as the Orioles' number one second baseman. One free agent signing could change that fast. And there are younger players making footsteps behind him, too. I wouldn't want B Ripken in 1993.

	AB	R	HR	RBI	SB	BA	$
1992 Baltimore AL	330	35	4	36	2	.230	1
1993 Base Case	194	19	2	21	1	.229	-
1993 High Range	344	37	4	42	3	.258	

RIPKEN, CAL - Orioles SS - BR - Age 32
Ripken followed his '91 career-best season with his worst in '92. Among the "low lights" was a 73-game streak without a homer. Ripken conceded that contract talks were a major distraction affecting his play. Another observer, former Brooklyn Dodger and broadcast host Rex Barney, believed that Ripken was playing with an injured back that he suffered while trying to get out of the way of a pitched ball in early July. Other observers believe that he needs to be receptive to batting coaches other than his father, something that we didn't hear during his career year in 1991. The outlook for '93 is for a comeback to another good, but not so spectacular, year.

	AB	R	HR	RBI	SB	BA	$
1992 Baltimore AL	637	73	14	72	4	.251	12
1993 Low Range	502	66	15	70	2	.247	
1993 Base Case	602	87	23	98	3	.274	24
1993 High Range	653	103	39	112	5	.300	

RIVERA, LUIS - Red Sox SS - BR - Age 29
John Valentin should get the lion's share of time at short. Rivera is a good late inning defensive replacement who will add nothing to your team. Away from Fenway, he will hit even worse.

	AB	R	HR	RBI	SB	BA	$
1992 Boston AL	288	17	0	29	4	.215	-
1993 Base Case	178	10	0	18	2	.226	-
1993 High Range	305	19	0	35	5	.255	

ROBBINS, DOUG - Orioles C - BR - Age 26

Has now hit .300 at each level -- A, AA, and AAA -- in just four years of effort. With luck he could reach the majors in mid 1993, but the Base Case is still zero at bats.

	AB	R	HR	RBI	SB	BA	$
1992 Rochester AAA	288	45	6	46	8	.309	
1993 High Range	158	14	1	13	2	.278	

ROBERSON, KEVIN - Cubs OF - BB - Age 25

Has shown both power and speed in the minors; best year was 1991 when he hit 19 home runs and stole 17 bases for AA Charlotte. Suffering from the major league outfielder overpopulation problem. Base Case is zero at bats.

	AB	R	HR	RBI	SB	BA	$
1992 Iowa AAA	197	25	6	34	0	.305	
1993 High Range	221	18	4	18	3	.245	

ROBERTS, BIP - Reds OF/2B - BB - Age 29

The trade for Kevin Mitchell means that Roberts becomes the everyday 2B. He was the team's 1992 MVP and the best Reds leadoff hitter since Pete Rose. Led the team in average, hits, runs, doubles, triples, and steals. A strong September (including 10 straight hits) put Bip into the NL batting race.

	AB	R	HR	RBI	SB	BA	$
1992 Cincinnati NL	532	92	4	45	44	.323	34
1993 Low Range	453	75	6	36	20	.275	
1993 Base Case	525	95	8	48	38	.303	33
1993 High Range	551	109	11	58	51	.330	

RODRIGUEZ, CARLOS - Yankees SS - BB - Age 25

Looked like a good prospect three years ago, and appeared with the Yankees in 1991, but hasn't really made any progress. Played at AA Albany in 1992 (a demotion) and hit .260.

RODRIGUEZ, HENRY - Dodgers OF - BL - Age 25

Rodriguez has decent tools. The Dodger outfield will not be set until the spring, and Rodriguez has the best chance of any young OF in the organization to be given significant playing time.

	AB	R	HR	RBI	SB	BA	$
1992 Albuquerque AAA	365	59	14	72	1	.304	
1992 Los Angeles NL	146	11	3	14	0	.219	-
1993 Low Range	121	12	2	13	0	.208	
1993 Base Case	311	35	7	38	1	.249	4
1993 High Range	442	54	12	62	3	.279	

RODRIGUEZ, IVAN - Rangers C - BR - Age 21

One of the youngest regulars in the major leagues, Rodriguez' 1992 numbers should be indicative of his performance in the near future. Two areas of concern surfaced in 1992: Rodriguez experienced back problems, and his work habits were not exemplary. His offensive output declined in the second half of the season for the second straight year. Having said all this, however, he has the talent to have a long major league career, and his hitting improves every year.

	AB	R	HR	RBI	SB	BA	$
1992 Texas AL	420	39	8	37	0	.260	
1993 Low Range	403	31	4	30	0	.215	
1993 Base Case	478	40	7	41	1	.256	6
1993 High Range	505	47	8	50	1	.287	

ROHDE, DAVE - Indians IF - BB - Age 28

If he makes the parent club, Rohde's role is utility infielder. He's hit for high averages in AAA, and can steal a few bases.

	AB	R	HR	RBI	SB	BA	$
1992 Col. Sp. AAA	448	85	4	55	13	.295	
1992 Cleveland AL	7	0	0	0	0	.000	-
1993 Low Range	95	11	0	13	2	.221	
1993 Base Case	109	14	1	15	4	.239	
1993 High Range	143	19	1	19	5	.252	

ROMERO, MANDY - Pirates C - BB - Age 25

Spent his second year at AA Carolina in 1992, hitting just .216. Hasn't looked like a good prospect since 1990.

ROSARIO, VICTOR - Tigers SS - BR - Age 26

Appeared with the Braves in 1990, but was traded for Dan Petry in 1991, and has since slipped in the Tigers depth charts. Hit just .202 for AAA Toledo last year.

ROSE, BOBBY - Japan IF/OF - BR - Age 26

Rose was the starting second baseman until he was injured in the bus accident between New York and Philadelphia. Luis Sojo then took over and kept the job. In October, Rose's contract was sold to a Japanese team.

	AB	R	HR	RBI	SB	BA	$
1992 Edmonton AAA	74	11	2	11	1	.270	
1992 California AL	84	10	2	10	1	.214	-

ROSSY, RICO - Royals SS - BR - Age 29

A career minor leaguer. Weak hitter, weaker glove. Rossy is a safety valve in case of injury to David Howard. You're better off with a marginal minor league prospect than with Rossy.

	AB	R	HR	RBI	SB	BA	$
1992 Omaha AAA	174	29	4	17	3	.316	
1992 Kansas City AL	149	21	1	12	0	.215	-
1993 Low Range	109	13	1	8	1	.185	
1993 Base Case	190	24	1	16	1	.225	-
1993 High Range	302	42	2	28	3	.254	

ROWLAND, RICH - Tigers C - BR - Age 26

During spring training 1992, in the Tigers' dugout, I saw the linep card spelled his name "Roland," a sign that he didn't figure prominently. Rowland can hit, though. Knowing what Sparky Anderson likes, Rowland began swinging harder at Toledo in 1992. He produced 25 home runs (previous career high was 13); 112 strikeouts (another career high); and dropped his BA to .235 (a career low). Maybe he's ready for Tiger Stadium now.

	AB	R	HR	RBI	SB	BA	$
1992 Toledo AAA	473	75	25	82	9	.235	
1992 Detroit AL	14	2	0	0	0	.214	
1993 Base Case	185	20	3	20	1	.242	0
1993 High Range	290	35	6	35	2	.272	

ROYER, STAN - Cardinals 3B - BR - Age 25

Has shown decent power in Class AAA over the past two seasons. Though many consider him a top prospect, he doesn't hit for a high average and appears more like a platooner or role player. He does add versatility with his ability to play either corner. But the Cards had a chance to put Royer at 3B when they sent Todd Zeile down last year, and they opted for Tracy Woodson.

	AB	R	HR	RBI	SB	BA	$
1992 Louisville AAA	444	55	11	77	0	.282	
1992 St. Louis NL	31	6	2	9	0	.323	0
1993 Base Case	150	15	3	20	0	.257	0
1993 High Range	252	30	5	39	1	.287	

RUPP, BRIAN - Cardinals SS - BR - Age 21

Drafted in the 43rd round of last June's draft from the University of Missouri as a roster filler. He proved to be much more than that, leading the Arizona Rookie League in six offensive categories. He was ranked the league's second-best prospect in a poll of league managers by Baseball America. At 6-4, 190, he may be too big to play shortstop, though.

	AB	R	HR	RBI	SB	BA	$
1992 Chandler R	208	34	0	40	9	.385	

RUSSELL, JOHN - Rangers OF - BR - Age 32

Russell has hung on, largely because he hasn't minded being stashed on the disabled list whenever the Rangers have needed a roster spot. He hasn't been anything but a spare part since 1986, and is at, or near, the end of his career. He may become a coach in 1993.

	AB	R	HR	RBI	SB	BA	$
1992 Texas AL	10	1	0	2	0	.100	-
1992 Tulsa AA	163	26	10	27	0	.258	
1993 Base Case	24	1	0	2	0	.167	
1993 High Range	125	11	2	13	0	.240	

RUSSO, PAUL - Twins 3B - BR - Age 23

Power hitter Paul Russo could be in the Metrodome soon if he finds some plate discipline (he struck out 122 times in 420 class AA at-bats) -- if the Twins other Twins third basemen sign with others, falter, move to other positions, or get hurt. Most likely, Russo will spend most of the year at AAA Portland with a cup of coffee in September.

	AB	R	HR	RBI	SB	BA	$
1992 Orlando AA	420	63	22	74	0	.255	
1993 Base Case	83	9	2	13	0	.217	-
1993 High Range	177	18	6	24	1	.270	

SABO, CHRIS - Reds 3B - BR - Age 31

Sabo ruined his season by sliding feet first into first base the first week of the season, severely spraining his ankle (which required off season surgery to repair). Sabo tried to play through the injury but did more harm than good. At age 31, he has reached the point of probable decline. Willie Greene is ready, too.

	AB	R	HR	RBI	SB	BA	$
1992 Cincinnati NL	344	42	12	43	4	.244	9
1993 Low Range	308	34	9	33	2	.226	
1993 Base Case	420	50	15	52	4	.257	11
1993 High Range	538	71	23	76	7	.287	

SALAZAR, LUIS - Cubs 3B - BR - Age 36

Salazar is on the downside of a solid, if unspectacular, career. His HR and RBI totals in 1992 were his lowest since 1987 when he played only 84 games for the Padres. Just a reserve, if he doesn't retire.

	AB	R	HR	RBI	SB	BA	$
1992 Chicago NL	255	20	5	25	1	.208	-
1993 Base Case	209	18	4	21	1	.230	0
1993 High Range	287	27	8	33	1	.266	

SALMON, TIM - Angels OF - BR - Age 24

Lots of honors: The Sporting News' top position-playing prospect. Baseball America's top Pacific Coast League prospect and Triple-A player of the year. PCL MVP led the league in HR and RBI despite an August call-up. Above-average arm and decent speed. Cautions: Before last season, he was a .253 career hitter in the minors, and he struck out 126 times in '92. Could have big trouble with AL slow stuff.

	AB	R	HR	RBI	SB	BA	$
1992 Edmonton AAA	409	101	29	105	9	.347	
1992 California AL	79	8	2	6	1	.177	-
1993 Low Range	287	36	7	35	2	.199	
1993 Base Case	497	68	16	70	6	.240	10
1993 High Range	537	81	21	84	10	.270	

SAMUEL, JUAN - Royals 2B - BR - Age 32

Samuel can't catch the ball well enough to play the field and doesn't hit well enough to be a regular DH. It's hard to see Samuel as more than a backup or pinch-hitter. KC was just another stop on his road to retirement; they released him.

	AB	R	HR	RBI	SB	BA	$
1992 Los Angeles NL	122	7	0	15	2	.262	-
1992 Kansas City AL	102	15	0	8	6	.284	2
1993 Base Case	248	28	4	25	9	.251	5
1993 High Range	491	60	9	57	25	.281	

SANCHEZ, REY - Cubs SS - BR - Age 25

Sanchez is one of the Cubs SS clones -- very good field, very little hit. Sanchez made it to the majors faster than expected due to injuries to players ahead of him on the depth chart. He has never hit more than 2 HR or driven in more than 50 runs in a season. He made 35 errors at AA and 29 at AAA, but led his league in assists and total chances both years.

	AB	R	HR	RBI	SB	BA	$
1992 Iowa AAA	76	12	0	3	6	.342	
1992 Chicago NL	255	24	1	19	2	.251	1
1993 Low Range	65	6	0	4	0	.211	
1993 Base Case	345	34	2	26	2	.253	2
1993 High Range	451	49	3	39	3	.283	

SANDBERG, RYNE - Cubs 2B - BR - Age 33
If you need to read this to know who Sandberg is, you haven't been on the planet long. While his MVP season was nine years ago, Sandberg has remained one of the top five players in the league in 1990-1992. He has lost maybe half a step in the field and running bases, but he's still a superstar.

	AB	R	HR	RBI	SB	BA	$
1992 Chicago NL	612	100	26	87	17	.304	37
1993 Low Range	500	77	18	61	9	.262	
1993 Base Case	592	100	27	83	18	.290	34
1993 High Range	604	112	33	94	25	.306	

SANDERS, DEION - Braves OF - BL - Age 25
When not moonlighting as a football player, he gave NL pitchers fits, bashing triples and stealing bases. Every time you looked up, Deion was standing on third. Nevertheless, two things stand between Sanders and greatness, only one of which he can control (no, it's not football). His strikeout-to-walk ratio is terrible and he can't reach his expected level until he reverses this 3-to-1 whiff ratio. A crowded Braves OF means that, barring injury to one of the other three starters, Sanders can only play part-time.

	AB	R	HR	RBI	SB	BA	$
1992 Atlanta NL	303	54	8	28	26	.304	20
1993 Low Range	266	41	5	23	13	.252	
1993 Base Case	404	68	10	41	32	.279	23
1993 High Range	523	97	15	60	51	.310	

SANDERS, REGGIE - Reds OF - BR - Age 25
A strong spring put Sanders in the Reds starting lineup and Reggie had the good sense to get off to a good start, which protected his job when major league pitchers began to pay more attention to him. Sanders did have trouble with RHP (.233 BA) and will need to improve to develop into the 20/20 hitter that the organization expects.

	AB	R	HR	RBI	SB	BA	$
1992 Cincinnati NL	385	62	12	36	16	.270	16
1993 Low Range	380	54	9	36	8	.249	
1993 Base Case	457	71	13	50	15	.276	19
1993 High Range	550	94	19	69	26	.307	

SANDERS, TRACY - Indians OF - BL - Age 23
Sanders is a power hitter who belted 21 homers in the pitching-rich Eastern League. With the glut of good outfielders in Cleveland, Sanders' best chance may be in another organization.

	AB	R	HR	RBI	SB	BA	$
1992 Canton AA	381	66	21	87	3	.241	

SANTIAGO, BENITO - Padres C - BR - Age 28
Santiago missed 40 games with a broken pinky finger and disappointed many owners by failing to post expected "salary drive" numbers. The Padres are so set on ridding themselves of Santiago's attitude problems that they stated they would not even exercise their arbitration rights, thus forfeiting two draft picks when Santiago leaves town. A full season in a positive environment could result in 1991-like stats (.267-17-87-8); like Sheffield in Milwaukee, Santiago hates his "current" management so much that he has allowed it to affect his play. The talent is there, will the head follow?

	AB	R	HR	RBI	SB	BA	$
1992 San Diego NL	386	37	10	42	2	.251	8
1993 Low Range	340	30	8	30	1	.229	
1993 Base Case	393	39	11	41	1	.260	8
1993 High Range	534	58	18	63	3	.290	

SANTOVENIA, NELSON - White Sox C/1B - BR - Age 31
Now on the downside of his career. Unlikely to play anywhere other than AAA unless an injury occurs.

	AB	R	HR	RBI	SB	BA	$
1992 Vancouver AAA	281	24	6	42	0	.263	
1992 Chicago AL	3	1	1	2	0	.333	-
1993 Base Case	20	2	1	4	0	.250	-
1993 High Range	204	18	5	26	0	.262	

SASSER, MACKEY - Mets C - BL - Age 30
Mackey serves the Mets fairly well in his capacity as a left-handed pinch hitter, but there's not much room on a roster for a catcher who can't catch. His at bats have dropped from 270 to 228 to 141 over the past three seasons.

	AB	R	HR	RBI	SB	BA	$
1992 New York NL	141	7	2	18	0	.241	0
1993 Low Range	134	8	2	15	0	.238	
1993 Base Case	211	14	3	27	0	.270	3
1993 High Range	303	22	7	44	0	.301	

SAX, STEVE - White Sox 2B - BR - Age 33
Considered by many to be poor defensively, he was not aided by the fact he played with five different shortstops in 1992. Always good for stolen bases and usually can be counted on for a helpful BA. Good comeback candidate for 1993.

	AB	R	HR	RBI	SB	BA	$
1992 Chicago AL	567	74	4	47	30	.236	13
1993 Low Range	492	60	3	37	16	.238	
1993 Base Case	572	77	4	50	30	.270	21
1993 High Range	608	90	5	61	41	.305	

SCARSONE, STEVE - Orioles 2B - BR - Age 26
The IL All Star 2B, Scarsone is a speedy infielder obtained from the Phillies in a trade for Juan Bell. At the end of 1992, he faced a battle with Billy Ripken and Mark McClemore for playing time.

	AB	R	HR	RBI	SB	BA	$
1992 Two Teams AAA	407	56	12	60	13	.270	
1992 Baltimore AL	17	2	0	0	0	.176	-
1993 Base Case	128	14	2	14	2	.231	-
1993 High Range	242	30	5	29	6	.260	

SCHAEFER, JEFF - Mariners IF - BR - Age 32
Refused minor league assignment at the of 1992 and became a free agent. Not much future.

	AB	R	HR	RBI	SB	BA	$
1992 Seattle AL	70	5	1	3	0	.114	-
1993 High Range	202	16	3	10	0	.214	

SCHOFIELD, DICK - Mets SS - BR - Age 30
Looked like a comeback player in April, but started swinging too freely again. Won't be back in New York.

	AB	R	HR	RBI	SB	BA	$
1992 Two Teams	423	52	4	36	11	.206	1
1993 Low Range	135	15	1	12	2	.179	
1993 Base Case	308	37	3	31	8	.208	-
1993 High Range	475	63	6	54	17	.241	

SCHU, RICK - Phillies IF - BR - Age 31
Still hanging around at AAA Scranton in 1992. Even if he gets back to the majors, he won't help you.

SCHULZ, JEFF - Cubs OF/1B - BL - Age 31
Former KC prospect, appeared with Royals and Pirates and passed through Reds organization.

SCIOSCIA, MIKE - Dodgers C - BL - Age 34
Maybe all those plate-blocking collisions finally caught up to Scioscia in 1992 as his stats took a tumble. Scioscia had nine errors and only 12 extra-base hits all season. At age 34 it appears his days as a regular are over. Dodger management wants Mike Piazza to assume the full-time role and Scioscia will either be Piazza's backup or be wearing a new uniform.

	AB	R	HR	RBI	SB	BA	$
1992 Los Angeles NL	348	19	3	24	3	.221	-
1993 Low Range	133	5	1	7	0	.193	
1993 Base Case	249	11	2	16	1	.233	-
1993 High Range	355	17	3	25	3	.262	

SCOTT, GARY - Marlins 3B - BR - Age 24
An Opening Day starter in 1991 and 1992, he played his way back to Triple-A both years. Was the Cubs' minor league player of the year in 1990. He has looked badly outmatched against major league pitchers. At age 24, it's still too early to give up on Scott. Expected to share time with Chris Donnels in 1993.

	AB	R	HR	RBI	SB	BA	$
1992 Chicago NL	96	8	2	11	0	.156	-
1993 Low Range	256	21	3	25	0	.182	
1993 Base Case	322	32	6	35	1	.222	-
1993 High Range	405	44	9	51	2	.251	

SCRUGGS, TONY - Rangers OF - BR - Age 27
A career minor leaguer. Played for Tulsa and Oklahoma City in 1992. Appeared with the Rangers in 1991.

SEGUI, DAVID - Orioles 1B/OF - BB - Age 26
During the winter, it was the O's intention to trade Randy Milligan (if anyone would take him) and install Segui at first base. Segui is an outstanding defensive first baseman, and a good line drive hitter who just needs to play regularly. Segui can also play the outfield where he's made a number of "highlight" catches.

	AB	R	HR	RBI	SB	BA	$
1992 Baltimore AL	189	21	1	17	1	.233	-
1993 Low Range	230	23	1	18	1	.212	
1993 Base Case	307	43	3	36	3	.258	4
1993 High Range	487	68	5	60	6	.283	

SEITZER, KEVIN - Brewers 3B - BR - Age 31
A nice comeback season for a typical Brewer: little power, advanced age, and unlikely to show any significant improvement, with a substantial chance of decline. The fact that Milwaukee has no prospect behind Seitzer in the high minors means that the opportunity for playing time will exist in the Brewer lineup. Caution is advised for two reasons: (1) a major second-half dropoff; and (2) a lousy (54%) SB success ratio, which can lead to a decline in attempts.

	AB	R	HR	RBI	SB	BA	$
1992 Milwaukee AL	540	74	5	71	13	.270	15
1993 Low Range	335	44	3	38	4	.234	
1993 Base Case	439	63	5	58	10	.266	11
1993 High Range	531	84	7	78	16	.297	

SERVAIS, SCOTT - Astros C - BR - Age 25

1988 Olympian was third round draft choice by Astros. Spent entire 1992 season in platoon role. Struggled to keep average above .200 for most of the year; then had a September surge when he hit .457! Strong finish could lead to more playing time in 1993. Hard worker with sound defensive skills.

	AB	R	HR	RBI	SB	BA	$
1992 Houston NL	205	12	0	15	0	.239	-
1993 Low Range	180	10	1	11	0	.191	
1993 Base Case	238	14	1	17	0	.231	-
1993 High Range	308	20	1	26	0	.260	

SHABAZZ, BASIL - Cardinals OF - BR - Age 21

One of the most gifted athletes in professional baseball. As a high school senior in 1991, he had major-college scholarship offers in baseball, football, basketball, and track. He has great speed but must learn to make better contact. Expect just minor league play for 1993.

	AB	R	HR	RBI	SB	BA	$
1992 Johnson City A	223	33	3	20	41	.229	

SHARPERSON, MIKE - Dodgers IF - BR - Age 31

The fact that Sharperson was Los Angeles' lone All-Star representative was indicative of what a disastrous season it was for the Dodgers. After the Break, Sharperson played just 17 games at 3B. Lenny Harris is the more useful player (he can play 2B and SS, too). The arrival of Jody Reed creates another crowd at third base, not good for Sharperson.

	AB	R	HR	RBI	SB	BA	$
1992 Los Angeles NL	317	48	3	36	2	.300	9
1993 Low Range	277	36	2	25	2	.255	
1993 Base Case	333	48	3	34	3	.282	8
1993 High Range	427	67	5	50	6	.313	

SHAVE, JON - Rangers 2B - BR - Age 25

Shave had a very solid year at AA Tulsa, but at 24 was a bit old to be considered a prospect. He should play at AAA in 1993.

	AB	R	HR	RBI	SB	BA	$
1992 Tulsa AA	453	57	2	36	6	.287	
1993 Base Case	50	6	0	2	1	.220	-

SHEFFIELD, GARY - Padres 3B - BR - Age 24

Sheffield and Brady Anderson were the two players who increased in value most from 1991 to 1992. Dwight Gooden's nephew flirted with the NL Triple Crown for much of the season and ultimately led the league in BA. Over a full year, these numbers are not produced by accident. Realistically, Sheffield cannot be expected to repeat his career year, but he is just 24 years old and may have the quickest bat in baseball. He has always been highly touted; now we know why. The fact that he may be a free agent after the 1993 season could cut both ways for Sheffield -- adding pressure or incentive. Remember, Sheffield got to start 1992 in anonymity; he has a fragile ego and may react poorly to lofty expectations.

	AB	R	HR	RBI	SB	BA	$
1992 Padres NL	557	87	33	100	5	.330	40
1993 Low Range	477	62	14	66	6	.262	
1993 Base Case	539	77	19	86	11	.290	28
1993 High Range	579	91	25	102	17	.325	

SHELBY, JOHN - Unsigned OF - BB - Age 35

Spent 1992 at Pawtucket. Best year was 1987 when he hit .277 with 21 HR and 16 SB. Not likely to see the major leagues again.

SHELTON, BEN - Pirates 1B/OF - BR - Age 23

Pittsburgh's number two pick, out of high school in '87. Made Baseball America's list of the Pirates' top 10 prospects after the '91 season, but didn't advance much in 1992. Can play good defense. Struck out more than 100 times each of the last five seasons. Watch for a September callup in 1993, if he has a good 1993 season; otherwise the ETA is 1994.

	AB	R	HR	RBI	SB	BA	$
1992 Carolina AA	368	57	10	51	4	.234	

SHERMAN, DARRELL - Padres OF - BL - Age 25

Sherman was selected by Baltimore in the Rule V draft before the 1992 season but was returned to the Padres when Brady Anderson established himself as the LF and leadoff man. Sherman combined for a .307 average in stops at Wichita and Las Vegas, piling up 52 SBs and 108 runs scored in the process. Because of his speed and glove, Sherman is a serious candidate for extensive time in LF, and a major reason why the Padres let Jerald Clark go to the Rockies. New manager Riggleman is a Sherman fan, which never hurt any player.

	AB	R	HR	RBI	SB	BA	$
1992 Wichita AA	220	60	6	25	26	.332	
1992 Las Vegas AAA	269	48	3	22	26	.286	
1993 Low Range	54	6	0	3	3	.225	
1993 Base Case	306	42	4	25	21	.256	10
1993 High Range	483	63	8	41	42	.285	

SHIELDS, TOMMY - Orioles OF/3B - BR - Age 28

Former top prospect. The key word is former.

	AB	R	HR	RBI	SB	BA	$
1992 Rochester AAA	431	58	10	59	13	.302	
1993 Base Case	86	9	1	7	4	.233	-
1993 High Range	108	12	1	9	5	.241	

SHIPLEY, CRAIG - Padres 2B/SS - BR - Age 30

Aussie-born Shipley can be a candidate for the SS job now that Fernandez is dealt. The Padres would see a big dropoff if they elect that route. Like most Australian prospects, he is older than his peers.

	AB	R	HR	RBI	SB	BA	$
1992 San Diego NL	105	7	0	7	1	.248	-
1993 Low Range	128	9	1	8	1	.228	
1993 Base Case	256	19	1	18	3	.250	-
1993 High Range	450	30	4	30	6	.277	

SHIRLEY, AL - Mets OF - BR - Age 19

New York's number one pick in 1991, out of high school. In his second season in Rookie ball, he was named the top prospect in the Appalachian League in the Baseball America managers' poll, even though his season ended abruptly after he suffered a broken wrist. He has both speed and power. For 1993, a good year in A-ball would be solid progress.

	AB	R	HR	RBI	SB	BA	$
1992 Kingsport R	99	26	7	22	9	.313	

SHUMPERT, TERRY - Royals 2B - BR - Age 26

Benched due to unsteady fielding and weak hitting, then shipped back to AAA. At age 26, Shumpert could return but it seems unlikely at this point. He's a remote candidate for part-time play at best. Let him prove himself before taking a chance here.

	AB	R	HR	RBI	SB	BA	$
1992 Omaha AAA	210	23	1	14	3	.200	
1992 Kansas City AL	94	6	1	11	2	.149	-
1993 Base Case	102	7	1	12	2	.219	-
1993 High Range	220	15	3	29	7	.248	

SIERRA, RUBEN - Athletics OF - BB - Age 27

Former Texas superstar, Sierra was key part of package traded for Jose Canseco. A quiet superstar who has failed to live up to expectations. Never more than 30 HR in a season.

	AB	R	HR	RBI	SB	BA	$
1992 Two Teams AL	601	83	17	87	14	.278	23
1993 Low Range	511	74	20	79	7	.260	
1993 Base Case	601	96	29	108	13	.288	35
1993 High Range	656	115	38	125	20	.320	

SILVESTRI, DAVE - Yankees SS - BR - Age 25

Played SS for the gold medal-winning U.S. Olympic team in '88, the year he was drafted in the second round by Houston. May not have enough glove to make it in the majors at SS; in fact, the Yanks were shopping for an SS during the offseason. Has enough power to play 3B; however, he struck out 100-plus times each of the last two seasons.

	AB	R	HR	RBI	SB	BA	$
1992 ColumbusAAA	420	83	13	73	19	.279	
1992 New York AL	13	3	0	1	0	.308	-
1993 Base Case	99	15	2	13	2	.255	0
1993 High Range	354	59	9	52	8	.285	

SIMMS, MIKE - Astros OF - BR - Age 26

Strong minor league player has failed to impress in 3 major league trials. Once considered the logical replacement for Glenn Davis at first base for the Astros, he hit 39 homers for Asheville in 1987. Strikes out too much and fields too poorly to play regularly in the majors.

	AB	R	HR	RBI	SB	BA	$
1992 Tucson AAA	404	73	11	75	7	.282	
1992 Houston NL	24	1	1	3	0	.250	-
1993 Base Case	56	7	2	7	0	.230	-
1993 High Range	263	34	9	37	2	.259	

SINATRO, MATT - Mariners C - BR - Age 33

Released at the end of 1992. In ten ML seasons, he never had more than 81 at bats, and when he played that much (1982) hit just .136.

SKINNER, JOEL - Indians C - BR - Age 32

Joel Skinner missed all of the '92 season due to a bad rotator cuff. His rehab didn't take and more surgery was necessary. He may miss all of '93. If and when he returns, he will back up Sandy Alomar.

SLAUGHT, DON - Pirates C - BR - Age 34

He defied baseball logic in 1992. He had his best season despite playing a demanding position at an age when most players are past their prime. He has hit at least .295 in each of his three seasons as a platoon catcher with the Pirates. An exceedingly bright guy, with an economics degree from UCLA.

	AB	R	HR	RBI	SB	BA	$
1992 Pittsburgh NL	255	26	4	37	2	.345	12
1993 Low Range	178	17	3	17	1	.252	
1993 Base Case	207	22	4	24	1	.279	5
1993 High Range	302	35	7	39	2	.310	

SMITH, BUBBA - Mariners 1B - BR - Age 23

The Carolina League MVP led the minors in home runs last year. A one-dimensional player, he struck out 138 times. With a good year at Double-A, he could get a late season callup; but more likely we won't see him until 1994 or 1995.

	AB	R	HR	RBI	SB	BA	$
1992 Peninsula A	482	70	32	93	4	.261	

SMITH, DWIGHT - Cubs OF - BL - Age 29

A three-time all star selection in the minor leagues, Smith was runner up for Rookie of the Year in 1989. He hasn't put up good numbers since, and was demoted briefly last year. However, he is a good enough hitter that he gets in the lineup even though he is a poor fielder. An everyday job could revitalize his career. Has good speed that doesn't show when he's sitting on the bench.

	AB	R	HR	RBI	SB	BA	$
1992 Chicago NL	217	28	3	24	9	.276	7
1993 Low Range	282	35	4	29	6	.247	
1993 Base Case	330	48	5	41	12	.274	12
1993 High Range	526	78	11	71	26	.305	

SMITH, GREG - Tigers 2B - BB - Age 25

Got a peek into the major leagues in 1989, 1990, and 1991. Now faded. Played at Toledo last year, and hit just .234, though he did steal 24 bases.

SMITH, LONNIE - Braves OF - BR - Age 37

Smith appears done after a long and fruitful career. Was a good PH late in 1992 after a terrible start; produced one RBI per five at bats. No longer a good hitter, though, and will probably lose his roster spot to one of the Braves rising young stars.

	AB	R	HR	RBI	SB	BA	$
1992 Atlanta NL	158	23	6	33	4	.247	5
1993 Base Case	70	9	2	12	3	.238	0
1993 High Range	294	42	7	37	7	.277	

SMITH, MARK - Orioles OF - BR - Age 22

Smith was the O's first round draft pick in 1991, a power hitter out of Southern Cal. Although he hit .288 for Hagerstown in the Eastern League, he has yet to find his home run stroke. He's a year or two away. Will be at AAA Rochester in '93 with perhaps a September callup if he does well. Led the Eastern League with 32 doubles.

	AB	R	HR	RBI	SB	BA	$
1992 Hagerstown AA	472	51	4	62	15	.288	

SMITH, OZZIE - Cardinals SS - BB - Age 38

Still carrying a Gold Glove. Though he had sometimes bitter contract negotiations, Smith came through with another outstanding season in 1992. He wants to play at least two more years. He is in great shape and should continue to be a productive player for as long as he wants. The man has had a movie made about him. How many active players can make that claim?

	AB	R	HR	RBI	SB	BA	$
1992 St. Louis NL	518	73	0	31	43	.295	26
1993 Low Range	355	48	0	23	14	.250	
1993 Base Case	508	75	0	38	34	.277	20
1993 High Range	588	96	0	50	50	.308	

SNOW, J.T. - Angels 1B - BB - Age 25

The International League batting champion, MVP and Rookie of the Year. Smooth-swinging and smooth-fielding. Hits better against righthanders than against lefties. New York's fifth-round pick in '89 out of the U. of Arizona. Son of Rams wide receiver-turned-broadcaster Jack Snow. Only problem was, he was stuck behind another guy who had the same type of Columbus stats, at a younger age -- Don Mattingly.

	AB	R	HR	RBI	SB	BA	$
1992 Columbus AAA	492	81	15	78	3	.313	
1992 New York AL	14	1	0	2	0	.143	-
1993 Low Range	63	7	1	7	0	.228	
1993 Base Case	232	28	4	30	0	.262	3
1993 High Range	329	41	9	43	2	.293	

SNYDER, CORY - Dodgers OF/IF - BR - Age 30

Former All Star with the Indians, Snyder was resurrected from the scrap heap by the Giants last season. Cory is once again a productive major leaguer, but don't count on another season like 1992; his slumps are among the longest and deepest in history, his back isn't 100%, and it's time for the Giants to rebuild.

	AB	R	HR	RBI	SB	BA	$
1992 San Francisco NL	390	48	14	57	4	.269	14
1993 Low Range	219	25	6	25	1	.203	
1993 Base Case	256	32	8	34	2	.244	4
1993 High Range	376	51	15	57	5	.274	

SOJO, LUIS - Angels 2B - BR - Age 27

Sojo was in the minors in early '92 as the Angels wanted him to learn to be an all-purpose utility player. He got called up after the bus accident injury to Bobby Rose, who has now gone to Japan.

	AB	R	HR	RBI	SB	BA	$
1992 Edmonton AAA	145	22	1	24	4	.297	
1992 California AL	368	37	7	43	7	.272	9
1993 Low Range	386	35	5	34	4	.228	
1993 Base Case	510	51	8	52	10	.259	11
1993 High Range	535	59	10	62	14	.289	

SORRENTO, PAUL - Indians 1B - BL - Age 27

Sorrento got out from under Kent Hrbek, and made the most of it in Cleveland. He hit only .156 against lefties but .281 against the righties.

	AB	R	HR	RBI	SB	BA	$
1992 Cleveland AL	458	52	18	60	0	.269	13
1993 Low Range	398	42	11	47	1	.240	
1993 Base Case	461	54	16	64	1	.272	15
1993 High Range	518	67	22	80	2	.303	

SOSA, SAMMY - Cubs OF - BR - Age 24

Sosa is a poor contact hitter (3:1 K:BB ratio) with good speed and moderate power. The Cubs traded George Bell for him because they think Sosa will develop power and better selectivity. Injuries reduced his playing time last year, but he could become a star soon.

	AB	R	HR	RBI	SB	BA	$
1992 Chicago NL	262	41	8	25	15	.260	11
1993 Low Range	358	49	9	38	11	.209	
1993 Base Case	460	69	14	57	23	.250	17
1993 High Range	519	85	19	73	33	.280	

SPEARMAN, VERN - Dodgers OF - BL - Age 23

A fine leadoff prospect. Now has 107 steals in two years as a pro.

	AB	R	HR	RBI	SB	BA	$
1992 Vero Beach A	276	50	0	16	33	.304	
1992 San Antonio AA	184	24	0	11	18	.281	

SPEHR, TIM - Royals C - BR - Age 26

Small chance of any major league impact, but could hit for power if he ever gets playing time.

	AB	R	HR	RBI	SB	BA	$
1992 Omaha AAA	336	48	15	42	4	.253	
1993 Base Case	60	4	1	5	0	.220	-
1993 High Range	202	15	5	15	2	.249	

SPIERS, BILL - Brewers SS - BL - Age 26

Although they won't say so for the record, Brewers insiders are pessimistic about Spiers's ability to make a full comeback from his back problems. The injury was severe, and the most strenuous infield position is an unforgiving location from which to forge a recovery. Before the injury, Spiers showed the promise of becoming one of the AL's best at a rather weak position; now, all bets are off. If he does make it back, expect Listach to keep SS, with Spiers moving to 2B.

	AB	R	HR	RBI	SB	BA	$
1992 Milwaukee AL	16	2	0	2	1	.313	-
1993 Low Range	198	23	2	18	3	.231	
1993 Base Case	334	42	3	35	9	.262	7
1993 High Range	468	64	6	55	18	.292	

SPRAGUE, ED - Blue Jays C - BR - Age 25

Good young catcher who can hit, he just needs playing time.

	AB	R	HR	RBI	SB	BA	$
1992 Syracuse AAA	369	49	16	50	0	.276	
1992 Toronto AL	47	6	1	7	0	.234	-
1993 Base Case	56	6	1	7	0	.238	-
1993 High Range	260	31	5	36	2	.268	

SPRINGER, STEVE - Mets 2B/3B - BR - Age 32

Surfaced very briefly with the Indians in 1990 and the Mets in 1992. Had his best pro season, hitting .290 for AAA Tidewater, but he's not a prospect.

STAIRS, MATT - Expos OF - BR - Age 24

After winning the Mexican Winter League batting title following the 1990 season then doing the same in the Class AA Eastern League in 1991, Stairs struggled in his first look at major-league pitching in 1992. Hitting, not defense, is what will get him to the majors. The Expos still had Ivan Calderon after the expansion draft, and they like Moises Alou as much as Calderon, so Stairs will need a new team or a great streak of good luck to be on the field in a major league uniform on Opening Day. Still young, with big offensive potential.

	AB	R	HR	RBI	SB	BA	$
1992 Indianapolis AAA	401	57	11	56	11	.267	
1992 Montreal NL	30	2	0	5	0	.167	-
1993 Low Range	177	21	3	20	4	.213	
1993 Base Case	262	35	6	35	9	.254	7
1993 High Range	497	73	13	74	25	.284	

STANKIEWICZ, ANDY - Yankees 2B/SS - BR - Age 28
Just had his career year. Don't expect another. Stankiewicz' presence in the lineup was unplanned and the result of multiple injuries. He never hit for average in the minors.

	AB	R	HR	RBI	SB	BA	$
1992 New York AL	400	52	2	25	9	.268	7
1993 Low Range	201	21	1	10	3	.208	
1993 Base Case	292	34	1	17	6	.249	2
1993 High Range	403	52	2	27	19	.279	

STANLEY, MIKE - Yankees C - BR - Age 29
A steady, established platoon catcher, nothing more.

	AB	R	HR	RBI	SB	BA	$
1992 New York AL	173	24	8	27	0	.249	3
1993 Low Range	183	20	4	21	0	.204	
1993 Base Case	220	27	5	29	0	.244	2
1993 High Range	266	35	8	40	0	.274	

STATON, DAVID - Padres 1B/3B/OF - BR - Age 24
A robust power hitter, Staton appears to be best suited for a DH role because of his weak glove at each of the three positions he has tried (3B, 1B and LF). With 19 HRs in just 335 at-bats, he was the only player in double figures in Vegas' high-average, low-power park; however, Staton also struck out 95 times and did not steal a base. The Padres' stated need for more speed and Riggleman's hit-and-run approach dim Staton's chances for 1993. He has been compared to Dave Kingman, with good reason. DH may be his best position. With Jerald Clark gone, he could get a look in left field for San Diego.

	AB	R	HR	RBI	SB	BA	$
1992 Las Vegas AAA	335	47	19	76	0	.281	
1993 Base Case	192	22	7	28	0	.233	1
1993 High Range	324	40	15	59	2	.260	

STEINBACH, TERRY - Athletics C - BR - Age 31
Steinbach is among the best at his profession, but isn't going to get any better.

	AB	R	HR	RBI	SB	BA	$
1992 Oakland AL	438	48	12	53	2	.279	12
1993 Low Range	334	31	6	36	1	.238	
1993 Base Case	412	42	10	52	2	.270	11
1993 High Range	458	51	13	66	3	.301	

STEPHENS, RAY - Rangers C - BR - Age 30
Peaked in 1990 with 15 at bats for the Cardinals. Not a factor for 1993.

STEPHENSON, PHIL - Padres 1B/OF - BL - Age 32

Has surfaced every year for four years, but never did enough to stick. Now he's strictly an injury backup who will be stored at Triple-A.

	AB	R	HR	RBI	SB	BA	$
1992 San Diego NL	71	5	0	8	0	.155	-
1993 Base Case	162	17	2	17	1	.204	-
1993 High Range	304	35	5	36	3	.242	

STEVENS, LEE - Angels 1B - BL - Age 25

Stevens struggled in '92, and he has yet to show that he can hit major league pitching. The issue is whether he can hit lefties, which he finally did well at Edmonton in 1991. The Angels were running out of patience at the end of 1992.

	AB	R	HR	RBI	SB	BA	$
1992 California AL	312	25	7	37	1	.221	1
1993 Low Range	209	21	6	27	1	.209	
1993 Base Case	403	46	10	53	2	.249	7
1993 High Range	508	63	20	88	3	.280	

STILLWELL, KURT - Padres 2B/SS - BB - Age 27

Stillwell's 1992 numbers proved that the Royals were not wrong in letting him go after the 1991 season. He is hardly guaranteed of another 379 at-bats in 1993 if he doesn't hit, so at least the negative impact of a low batting average will be limited. Stillwell also had a slugging percentage under .300. His future is behind him.

	AB	R	HR	RBI	SB	BA	$
1992 San Diego NL	379	35	2	24	4	.227	0
1993 Low Range	288	24	2	23	2	.208	
1993 Base Case	357	33	3	34	3	.249	3
1993 High Range	483	48	4	52	6	.279	

STOCKER, KEVIN - Phillies SS - BB - Age 23

A second-round pick in the '91 draft from the Univ. of Washington, he could reach Triple-A this season with the hope that he makes the Phillies in 1994. Hit a composite .266 with 32 SB in his first pro season, split between A Clearwater and AA Reading.

STRANGE, DOUG - Cubs IF - BB - Age 28

A former Tiger farmhand who has not been productive since his 13 HR and 70 RBI in 1987. Had brief stints with the Cubs in 1991 and 1992.

	AB	R	HR	RBI	SB	BA	$
1992 Iowa AAA	212	32	4	26	3	.307	
1992 Chicago NL	94	7	1	5	1	.160	-
1993 Base Case	20	1	0	1	0	.171	-
1993 High Range	207	17	3	13	3	.238	

STRAWBERRY, DARRYL - Dodgers OF - BL - Age 31

Strawberry now must be associated with the two ugliest words in Rotisserie baseball -- "back surgery." Early in his career, Strawberry was very durable, but he has not played a full season since 1990, his last year with the Mets. Dodger Stadium has had its normal negative impact on his power figures, reducing Strawberry's HR frequency from 1 HR every 14.7 at-bats (1990) to 1 every 20.0 at-bats (1991 and 1992 combined). Still, he will be the cleanup hitter if healthy and should have talented offensive players hitting in front of him, creating RBI chances.

	AB	R	HR	RBI	SB	BA	$
1992 Los Angeles NL	156	20	5	25	3	.237	3
1993 Low Range	277	39	10	38	3	.228	
1993 Base Case	410	63	19	66	8	.259	16
1993 High Range	547	92	30	96	15	.289	

STUBBS, FRANKLIN - Brewers 1B/DH - BL - Age 32

Another disappointing season for Stubbs in 1992, although his power numbers show decent productivity on a per at bat basis. Garner benched him for a long late-summer stretch, and Stubbs took the demotion well; his big contract must have eased the pain. That contract is the primary reason why the Brewers didn't just release Stubbs after his pitiful 1991. Now, with only one year remaining on that contract, Stubbs's skills have eroded to the point where the contract may no longer be enough to save his job.

	AB	R	HR	RBI	SB	BA	$
1992 Milwaukee AL	288	37	9	42	11	.229	6
1993 Low Range	171	20	4	20	4	.190	
1993 Base Case	225	29	6	31	8	.230	3
1993 High Range	312	43	10	49	15	.259	

SUERO, WILLIAM - Brewers 2B - BR - Age 26

Rapidly becoming a former top prospect, Suero attracted wide attention three years ago when he hit .263 with 16 home runs and 40 stolen bases for AA Knoxville. But then he fell off to .198 the next year, and the Jays were happy to give up Suero in a trade to get Candy Maldonado.

	AB	R	HR	RBI	SB	BA	$
1992 Denver AAA	276	42	1	25	16	.257	
1992 Milwaukee AL	16	4	0	0	1	.188	-
1993 Base Case	86	14	1	8	5	.207	-
1993 High Range	224	39	4	25	17	.245	

SURHOFF, B.J. - Brewers C/1B - BL - Age 28

The first pick overall in the 1985 draft, Surhoff has spent his major league career trying to prove that he deserved to be selected that high, and developing a major league crisis of self-confidence when he invariably fails to do so. His trademarks are a lack of power, a BA that has settled in between .250 and .280, second-half productivity surges, and great speed for a catcher -- although the longer he catches, the more his speed will diminish. He's unlikely now to show any dramatic improvement as a hitter (although his defense has improved in the last year), which means that Surhoff likely will continue to frustrate himself. You will share in the frustration only if you pay for the potential he once had, or if you drop him at midseason and watch some other owner get all the good numbers.

	AB	R	HR	RBI	SB	BA	$
1992 Milwaukee AL	480	63	4	62	14	.252	11
1993 Low Range	372	49	4	40	8	.238	
1993 Base Case	426	62	5	53	14	.270	14
1993 High Range	508	81	7	72	24	.301	

SUTKO, GLENN - Reds C - BR - Age 24

Sutko surfaced with the Reds in 1990 and 1991. Although still young, he has been classified as a good defense, no offense type of catcher, a label that became even more indelible when he hit .187 for AA Chattanooga last year, lowering his career minor league BA to .207. Get the idea?

SUTTON, LARRY - Royals 1B - BL - Age 23

Classic lefty power-hitting first baseman with a good batting eye. Expect a promotion to AA Memphis in

1993. At least two years away.

	AB	R	HR	RBI	SB	BA	$
1992 Appleton A	2	1	0	0	0	.000	
1992 Eugene A	238	45	15	58	3	.311	

SVEUM, DALE - White Sox IF - BB - Age 29

Sveum was acquired from the Phillies in 1992, to use while Ozzie Guillen was injured. Sveum can play all four infield positions when needed. He was considered a potential star until he broke his leg in 1988.

	AB	R	HR	RBI	SB	BA	$
1992 Chicago AL	114	15	2	12	1	.219	-
1992 Philadelphia NL	135	13	2	16	0	.178	-
1993 Base Case	175	20	3	20	1	.220	
1993 High Range	224	32	5	27	3	.251	

SZEKELY, JOE - Unsigned C - BR - Age 31

A college All American and second round pick way back in 1982, Szekely never made it to the major leagues, largely because of injuries. Played for AAA Richmond in 1992.

TABLER, PAT - Blue Jays DH/1B - BR - Age 35

Once a good hitter, Tabler now is noteworthy only for his high career batting average with the bases loaded. For your roster, he is nothing more than a last resort fill-in for 1993.

	AB	R	HR	RBI	SB	BA	$
1992 Toronto AL	135	11	0	16	0	.252	-
1993 Base Case	90	7	0	8	0	.244	-
1993 High Range	196	18	1	26	0	.273	

TACKETT, JEFF - Orioles C - BR - Age 27

Tackett is an eight-year minor league veteran who got his big break when he made the Orioles out of spring training as the backup to Chris Hoiles. He became the starter when Hoiles was injured. He's a low-average hitter who pops an occasional home run. During the off season Tackett was injured in a bicycle accident but was expected to be OK for spring training.

	AB	R	HR	RBI	SB	BA	$
1992 Baltimore AL	179	21	5	24	0	.240	1
1993 Low Range	107	9	1	7	0	.159	
1993 Base Case	230	27	3	19	1	.223	-
1993 High Range	340	43	7	32	2	.252	

TARASCO, TONY - Braves OF - BL - Age 22

A good combination of power and speed. He's a distant prospect at this point, but developing well. Spent four years at Rookie and A-ball.

	AB	R	HR	RBI	SB	BA	$
1992 Greenville AA	489	73	15	54	33	.286	

TARTABULL, DANNY - Yankees OF/DH - BR - Age 30

Great when he plays. Tartabull still has one of the highest RBI per at bat rates in the game today. Unfortunately, he usually finds a way to get hurt. Hasn't had 490 at bats in a season since 1988.

	AB	R	HR	RBI	SB	BA	$
1992 New York AL	421	72	25	85	2	.266	18
1993 Low Range	342	54	16	60	1	.240	
1993 Base Case	446	77	27	92	2	.272	22
1993 High Range	547	104	39	119	4	.303	

TATUM, JIM - Rockies 3B/1B - BR - Age 25

Strong stats as a hitter in Denver. Tatum was the American Association MVP and batting leader. After being released by San Diego and Cleveland, he came into his own in '91, batting .320 at El Paso. Also has played SS, and is especially adept at fielding balls to his left. The only rumblings are about his attitude, including a report that he almost didn't start last year's Triple-A All-Star Game because he showed up late. The fans in Denver like him just fine, and his signing is largely PR.

	AB	R	HR	RBI	SB	BA	$
1992 Denver AAA	492	74	19	101	8	.329	
1992 Milwaukee AL	8	0	0	0	0	.125	-
1993 Base Case	192	21	4	26	2	.259	3
1993 High Range	311	37	10	49	3	.290	

TAUBENSEE, EDDIE - Astros C - BL - Age 24

In his first season with the Astros, Taubensee rates as a mild disappointment. He spent the year in a platoon situation, but he hit slightly better against left-handers than he did against right-handers (.234 vs.220). A mid-season slump resulted in a brief trip to AAA Tucson. Defensively, he has a strong arm but is not the take-charge type that is desirable in catchers, and the Astros thought he took a long time to learn their complex signal system during spring training 1992. Toward the end of the season, his hitting improved and he could still become the standout the Astros were hoping for when they gave up Kenny Lofton to get him.

	AB	R	HR	RBI	SB	BA	$
1992 Tucson AAA	74	13	1	10	0	.338	
1992 Houston NL	297	23	5	28	2	.222	-
1993 Low Range	291	28	5	27	2	.206	
1993 Base Case	335	36	7	36	3	.246	4
1993 High Range	406	48	10	50	6	.276	

TAVAREZ, JESUS - Marlins OF - BR - Age 22

Stole 109 bases in his first two pro seasons, but now there are questions about a leg injury. If he's 100%, he could displace the weak-hitting Chuck Carr in CF quickly, but everyone including the Marlins will just have to wait and see.

	AB	R	HR	RBI	SB	BA	$
1992 Jacksonville AA	392	38	3	25	29	.258	
1993 Base Case	113	10	0	6	9	.234	-
1993 High Range	311	25	2	24	22	.266	

TAYLOR, DWIGHT - Reds OF - BL - Age 33

Stole 165 bases in three seasons at Triple-A, and surfaced with the Royals in 1986. Too old now.

TAYLOR, WILL - Padres OF - BR - Age 24

Appeared headed for the major leagues after 1991, when he got 62 stolen bases for AAA Las Vegas. But then he got off to a slow start in 1992 and went all the way back to A-ball to get re-oriented.

TETTLETON, MICKEY - Tigers C - BB - Age 32

At this point, he's the prime Rotisserie catcher in the game. I just have this nagging suspicion that he will slump back to his old level, pre-1989, when he hit just eight or ten home runs per year and often produced a very low batting average. At a position that attracts high bids, Tettleton is a big risk in 1993.

	AB	R	HR	RBI	SB	BA	$
1992 Detroit AL	525	82	32	83	0	.238	15
1993 Low Range	358	50	15	46	1	.219	
1993 Base Case	452	69	24	67	2	.234	10
1993 High Range	529	89	33	87	3	.263	

TEUFEL, TIM - Padres 3B/2B - BR - Age 34

Teufel is a decent utility player with modest power. His modest Rotisserie value should diminish in 1993. Expect the penny-pinching Padres to go with kids at 2B and SS. Gutierrez, Gardner, Shipley and Faries are simply cheaper alternatives than Teufel.

	AB	R	HR	RBI	SB	BA	$
1992 San Diego NL	246	23	6	25	2	.224	2
1993 Base Case	175	17	4	20	2	.230	-
1993 High Range	369	38	11	43	4	.253	

THOMAS, FRANK - White Sox 1B - BR - Age 24

Thomas is a former first round pick who worked out just fine. One of the top hitters in the American League. Still room for improvement. Numbers could be huge.

	AB	R	HR	RBI	SB	BA	$
1992 Chicago AL	573	108	24	115	6	.323	34
1993 Low Range	520	80	20	80	2	.295	
1993 Base Case	564	108	29	115	5	.329	43
1993 High Range	586	123	36	126	8	.349	

THOME, JIM - Indians 3B - BL - Age 22

Rookie Jim Thome was tabbed as the Indians starting third baseman in '92. The expectations were high with some experts picking him as their preseason favorite for rookie of the year, and comparing him to hitting talents like Wade Boggs and George Brett. Unfortunately, an elbow injury placed Thome on the DL for much of the season. He pressed too hard when he finally was healed resulting in a trip to AAA. The talent is still there, and the outlook is to be the Indians' starting third baseman in '93.

	AB	R	HR	RBI	SB	BA	$
1992 Canton AA	107	16	1	14	0	.336	
1992 Col. Sp. AAA	48	11	2	14	0	.313	
1992 Cleveland AL	117	8	2	12	2	.205	-
1993 Low Range	188	18	2	18	1	.220	
1993 Base Case	304	32	4	34	3	.254	4
1993 High Range	411	48	6	53	6	.290	

THOMPSON, MILT - Phillies OF - BL - Age 34

He is an example of the disappearing middle class in baseball. Though he has been a dependable fourth outfielder for many years, St. Louis refused to pay his $1.95 million salary for 1993 and bought him out for $300,000 at the end of last season. He can still help a lot of clubs but at a lower price tag.

	AB	R	HR	RBI	SB	BA	$
1992 St. Louis NL	208	31	4	17	18	.293	11
1993 Low Range	206	23	3	14	8	.250	
1993 Base Case	273	38	4	20	17	.277	9
1993 High Range	383	58	7	36	32	.308	

THOMPSON, ROBBY - Giants 2B - BR - Age 30

Decent mix of power and speed, but has a chronic sore back; cannot get through an entire season healthy. Often an indicator of decline, Thompson stole only 5 bases in 14 attempts last season.

	AB	R	HR	RBI	SB	BA	$
1992 San Francisco NL	443	54	14	49	5	.260	13
1993 Low Range	318	35	8	29	3	.228	
1993 Base Case	427	51	11	46	7	.259	10
1993 High Range	504	66	18	62	13	.289	

THOMPSON, RYAN - Mets OF - BR - Age 25

Toronto's 13th-round pick in '87, out of high school. Last year's bull market on Thompson's stock really skyrocketed when the Mets obtained him in a trade for David Cone. On the positive side, he is fast enough to play CF (which the Mets need) and has a strong enough arm to play RF, and he plays so hard that he literally knocked himself out diving for a line drive last season. On the down side, before last year he never batted better than .273, and that was in a short-season. Struck out 138 times last season. He also has been injury-prone. On the plus side, Thompson made progress by cutting his swing to be more compact, generating even more power than he had with his big looping swing. Another plus: the Mets are very likely to let him play frequently, to show value from the Cone deal.

	AB	R	HR	RBI	SB	BA	$
1992 Syracuse AAA	429	74	14	46	10	.282	
1992 New York NL	108	15	3	10	2	.222	0
1993 Low Range	241	29	5	22	4	.195	
1993 Base Case	330	40	8	36	8	.235	6
1993 High Range	483	61	12	52	14	.264	

THON, DICKIE - Rangers SS - BR - Age 34

Played in only 93 games, his lowest total since 1987, due mainly to injuries and his declining abilities as a fielder. His days as a front-line shortstop are over, and he was released by Texas at the end of the season.

	AB	R	HR	RBI	SB	BA	$
1992 Texas AL	275	30	4	37	12	.247	7
1993 Low Range	146	14	2	16	3	.204	
1993 Base Case	194	20	3	25	7	.245	3
1993 High Range	338	39	5	49	16	.275	

THURMAN, GARY - Royals OF - BR - Age 28

A fifth outfielder at best; got 200 AB only because others were hurt. Speed is his only asset. Not much future with KC.

	AB	R	HR	RBI	SB	BA	$
1992 Kansas City AL	200	25	0	20	9	.245	3
1993 Low Range	100	12	0	10	4	.229	
1993 Base Case	178	28	0	20	9	.260	4
1993 High Range	404	55	0	46	25	.290	

TINGLEY, RON - Angels C - BR - Age 33

Tingley is a substitute catcher who's been around forever. He will be 34 in May. Doesn't give you much even if he plays. He's a good pitcher handler, but that won't help you.

	AB	R	HR	RBI	SB	BA	$
1992 California AL	127	15	3	8	0	.197	-
1993 Low Range	76	9	1	11	0	.211	
1993 Base Case	95	10	1	12	0	.221	-
1993 High Range	143	15	2	17	1	.231	

TINSLEY, LEE - Mariners OF - BB - Age 24

Tinsley is a very fast base stealer who has struggled at the plate. The Indians released him at season's end, and he was signed by Seattle, his third organization.

	AB	R	HR	RBI	SB	BA	$
1992 Canton AA	349	65	5	38	18	.287	
1992 Col. Sp. AAA	81	19	0	4	3	.235	
1993 Base Case	95	11	0	8	5	.239	-
1993 High Range	201	25	3	20	9	.268	

TOLENTINO, JOSE - Pirates OF/1B - BL - Age 31

Looked like a possible late bloomer at first base in Houston, before the emergence of Jeff Bagwell. If he got a few pinch hit appearances in the majors during 1993, that would be a big year for him.

TOVAR, EDGAR - Expos SS - BR - Age 19

Tovar is a decent hitter, but scouts feel it's the outstanding defense that will get him to the major leagues, probably as a second baseman.

	AB	R	HR	RBI	SB	BA	$
1992 Jamestown A	281	38	4	31	13	.267	

TRAMMELL, ALAN - Tigers SS - BR - Age 35

During his last visit to Yankee Stadium in 1992, Trammell told me his ankle was fully healed, and that he could do everything physically, was just sitting out as a precaution because the season was almost over. Can be valuable as a DH or third baseman.

	AB	R	HR	RBI	SB	BA	$
1992 Detroit AL	102	11	1	11	2	.275	1
1993 Low Range	234	22	3	24	4	.236	
1993 Base Case	334	36	7	40	7	.268	9
1993 High Range	481	57	12	66	13	.299	

TREADWAY, JEFF - Braves 2B - BL - Age 30

Lost most of the year to injury, then hit very little after his return. Can still contribute as a lefty PH. He'll do better in 1993, but will never again be a regular for the Braves.

	AB	R	HR	RBI	SB	BA	$
1992 Atlanta NL	126	5	0	5	1	.222	-
1993 Low Range	108	10	1	8	0	.234	
1993 Base Case	189	19	3	16	1	.266	2
1993 High Range	319	36	6	30	2	.297	

TUCKER, MICHAEL - Royals SS - BB - Age 20

1992 first round draft pick. Played with the US Olympic team. Good power and speed.

TUCKER, SCOOTER - Astros C - BR - Age 26

Aggressive receiver hit well at Tucson but did not hit well at all in brief trial with the Astros. Sound defense gives him a chance to stick as a backup, but strong finishes by Taubensee and Servais will make it tough for him to make it in 1993.

	AB	R	HR	RBI	SB	BA	$
1992 Tucson AAA	288	36	1	29	5	.302	
1992 Houston NL	50	5	0	3	1	.120	-
1993 Base Case	78	8	0	7	1	.224	
1993 High Range	236	27	2	25	3	.253	

TURNER, SHANE - Mariners OF/IF - BL - Age 30

Finally produced two good seasons at Triple-A in 1991-1992, hitting .280 with a handful of stolen bases each year for Rochester and Calgary. If he plays in the majors in 1993, it will be a small role with no attractive numbers, maybe .240 with half a dozen SB if he gets 200 at bats.

TWARDOSKI, MIKE - Red Sox 1B - BL - Age 28
Former Indians farmhand, about what you would expect from a minor league first baseman: can hit .280 with 10+ home runs in a good, full season. Base Case is zero at bats. Here's the upside:

	AB	R	HR	RBI	SB	BA	$
1993 High Range	176	19	2	15	3	.269	

URIBE, JOSE - Giants SS - BB - Age 33
Former glove wizard, Uribe has been relegated to part time status the last two seasons during which he amassed 12 and 13 RBI's respectively.

	AB	R	HR	RBI	SB	BA	$
1992 San Francisco NL	162	24	2	13	2	.241	0
1993 Low Range	100	8	0	7	1	.191	
1993 Base Case	189	17	1	15	2	.231	-
1993 High Range	308	31	1	27	5	.260	

VALENTIN, JOHN - Red Sox SS - BR - Age 26
He is highly touted, and did pretty well in 58 games for Boston last year, but he is a late arrival who never hit above .270 at any level before 1992. Caveat City.

	AB	R	HR	RBI	SB	BA	$
1992 Boston AL	185	21	5	25	1	.276	4
1993 Low Range	159	13	2	15	0	.200	
1993 Base Case	315	27	5	35	1	.240	2
1993 High Range	507	48	10	65	3	.275	

VALENTIN, JOSE - Brewers SS - BB - Age 23
Got three at bats with the Brewers, after hitting .240 with 3 HR and 9 SB for AAA Denver. With maturity he could hit .270 with 5-10 home runs and 5-10 steals in the majors, but he isn't there yet. Expect a September callup.

VALLE, DAVE - Mariners C - BR - Age 32
For the fifth straight year his RBI total decreased, even though his playing time increased. On the other hand, he had his highest batting average since 1987. In six words: the expansion teams didn't want him.

	AB	R	HR	RBI	SB	BA	$
1992 Seattle AL	367	39	9	30	0	.240	3
1993 Low Range	194	18	3	14	0	.201	
1993 Base Case	304	30	7	25	0	.229	0
1993 High Range	383	42	10	35	0	.258	

VANDERWAL, JOHN - Expos OF - BL - Age 26
After showing promise in 1991, VanderWal played little in his first full major-league season last year. He is a line-drive hitter with occasional power and looks like he will be a journeyman.

	AB	R	HR	RBI	SB	BA	$
1992 Montreal NL	213	21	4	20	3	.239	2
1993 Low Range	183	19	2	15	1	.204	
1993 Base Case	253	28	4	25	3	.245	2
1993 High Range	357	44	7	40	6	.275	

VAN BURKLEO, TY - Angels 1B - BL - Age 29
Van Burkleo spent 1987-91 playing in Japan where he learned to hit breaking pitches. It's very rare to see power and speed in a first baseman, so Van Burkleo can be a valuable player. Furthermore, since Tim Salmon received most of the publicity at Edmonton, Van Burkleo is a virtual unknown. If Lee Stevens

continues to have difficulty with major league pitching, Van Burkleo may get the call to Anaheim.

	AB	R	HR	RBI	SB	BA	$
1992 Edmonton AAA	458	83	19	88	20	.273	
1993 Low Range	77	11	3	12	6	.221	
1993 Base Case	77	11	2	12	5	.221	-
1993 High Range	263	43	10	39	12	.243	

VAN SLYKE, ANDY - Pirates OF - BL - Age 32

It took three herniated discs in his lower back to get Van Slyke to truly understand hitting. Because of the problem, he cut down on his swing in 1992. While just concentrating on making contact, he had his best season since 1988. A five-time Gold Glove winner.

	AB	R	HR	RBI	SB	BA	$
1992 Pittsburgh NL	614	103	14	89	12	.324	33
1993 Low Range	408	63	9	49	5	.257	
1993 Base Case	519	88	14	73	11	.284	22
1993 High Range	605	107	19	94	16	.315	

VARSHO, GARY - Reds OF - BL - Age 31

He was a pleasant surprise for the Pirates in 1991 after being acquired from the Cubs in a spring training trade. However, he slipped considerably in 1992, though he still wound up being the Pirates' most-frequently used pinch hitter. He aspires to be a manager and his poor 1992 probably hastened a move in that direction. Was released.

	AB	R	HR	RBI	SB	BA	$
1992 Pittsburgh NL	162	22	4	22	5	.222	2
1993 Base Case	118	13	2	12	4	.233	0
1993 High Range	307	40	5	33	13	.265	

VATCHER, JIM - Padres OF - BR - Age 26

In the minor leagues, in different seasons, he has stolen 26 bases, poked 17 home runs, and hit over .300; but he doesn't seem to have a major league cut on his jib.

	AB	R	HR	RBI	SB	BA	$
1992 Las Vegas AAA	280	41	8	35	2	.275	
1992 San Diego NL	16	1	0	2	0	.250	-
1993 Base Case	76	7	1	9	1	.249	-
1993 High Range	292	30	5	40	3	.279	

VAUGHN, GREG - Brewers OF - BR - Age 27

We've seen the best of Greg Vaughn: solid power, but much too streaky. When he's on a tear, he can hit .350 for a month, but then he always follows up by hitting .150 for a month. If you like the "last 4 weeks" stats in USAT BB Weekly, Vaughn will often grab your attention. Just beware. He is most valuable in leagues that allow movement on and off the active roster. And he's a good pickup late in the season if you get desperate and have nothing to lose.

	AB	R	HR	RBI	SB	BA	$
1992 Milwaukee AL	501	77	23	78	15	.228	16
1993 Low Range	402	57	15	55	6	.198	
1993 Base Case	499	78	24	79	12	.239	16
1993 High Range	540	93	31	95	18	.269	

VAUGHN, MO - Red Sox 1B/DH - BL - Age 25

Vaughn tells me he is a good second half player: "Sure, it's not how you begin that counts. It's how you finish." Vaughn was hitting .194 at the All Star break with 5 homers and 20 RBI. His second half performance was better: .257 BA with 8 HR and 37 RBI. If you factor his second half into a 570 AB season, Vaughn's numbers would look like this: .257 BA, 20 HR, 93 RBI. Realistic? Sure. You could argue that he was just a platooner in 1992, and wouldn't have done as well if he had to face lefty pitching every day, but the key point is that he's young and improving.

	AB	R	HR	RBI	SB	BA	$
1992 Pawtucket AAA	149	15	6	28	1	.282	
1992 Boston AL	355	42	13	57	3	.234	7
1993 Low Range	374	38	9	51	2	.236	
1993 Base Case	484	54	15	76	4	.268	16
1993 High Range	537	65	20	93	6	.299	

VELARDE, RANDY - Yankees 3B/SS - BR - Age 30

Just had his career year. Even if he's handed the shortstop job, which isn't likely, he won't do any better than he did in 1992.

	AB	R	HR	RBI	SB	BA	$
1992 New York AL	412	57	7	46	7	.272	11
1993 Low Range	229	25	3	23	2	.219	
1993 Base Case	336	40	6	40	6	.250	6
1993 High Range	445	59	10	60	10	.278	

VELASQUEZ, GUILLERMO - Padres 1B - BL - Age 24

Velasquez was the PCL's All-Star 1B, but he is blocked by Fred McGriff. To get any playing time, Velasquez will have to develop OF skills. He looked good in a brief September call-up. Velasquez' home run total dropped from 21 at AA Wichita to 7 at Vegas (a high-average, low-HR park); he also added 44 doubles.

	AB	R	HR	RBI	SB	BA	$
1992 Las Vegas AAA	512	68	7	99	3	.309	
1992 San Diego NL	23	1	1	5	0	.304	-
1993 Base Case	120	8	2	10	0	.260	-
1993 High Range	234	25	5	33	2	.291	

VENABLE, MAX - Unsigned OF - BL - Age 35

Venable could be useful to a team as a left-handed pinch-hitter or late-inning defensive specialist. Like most American players in Japan, Max doesn't have nearly the power or run-producing ability that his stats say he does.

	AB	R	HR	RBI	SB	BA	$
1992 Japan	410	55	13	50	---	.273	

VENTURA, ROBIN - White Sox 3B - BL - Age 25

First round pick of White Sox and former Olympian. Everyday third baseman. One of the premier cornermen defensively. Approaching his prime years.

	AB	R	HR	RBI	SB	BA	$
1992 Chicago AL	592	102	16	93	2	.282	19
1993 Low Range	503	73	13	72	1	.250	
1993 Base Case	565	90	18	94	3	.276	21
1993 High Range	608	107	23	109	4	.307	

VERAS, QUILVIO - Mets 2B - BB - Age 22

Led the minor leagues in SB, and the Sally League in BA. Named the league's best baserunner and best defensive 2B in the Baseball America poll.

	AB	R	HR	RBI	SB	BA	$
1992 Columbia A	414	97	2	40	66	.319	

VIDRO, JOSE -Expos - 2B - Age 18

He showed a quick bat with power and good defense in Rookie ball after being selected from a Puerto Rican high school in 1992 draft.

	AB	R	HR	RBI	SB	BA	$
1992 Gulf Coast Expos R	200	29	4	31	10	.330	

VILLANUEVA, HECTOR - Cardinals C/1B - BR - Age 28

Career has been held back by the fact that Paul White doesn't own the Cubs. Hits both righties and lefties well; a dead fastball hitter. He has tremendous power (22 HR in 418 ML AB), but poor defense will keep him from being an everyday player. He was an all-star three times in the minors. Released at year end.

	AB	R	HR	RBI	SB	BA	$
1992 Iowa AAA	159	21	9	35	0	.239	
1992 Chicago NL	112	9	2	13	0	.152	-
1993 Low Range	60	7	2	9	0	.210	
1993 Base Case	120	15	7	19	0	.245	0
1993 High Range	227	20	7	30	0	.260	

VITIELLO, JOE - Royals 1B - BR - Age 22

First round pick in 1991. Overmatched at Memphis (AA) in 1991. Hit for average last year and should eventually develop moderate power. Strikes out too much and has a long way to go.

	AB	R	HR	RBI	SB	BA	$
1992 Baseball City A	400	52	8	65	0	.283	

VIZCAINO, JOSE - Cubs 3B/SS - BB - Age 25

Like Rey Sanchez and Alex Arias, he is a good field, no hit player. Though still young, he is a utility infielder who didn't produce good Rotisserie stats even when he played everyday.

	AB	R	HR	RBI	SB	BA	$
1992 Chicago NL	285	25	1	17	3	.225	-
1993 Low Range	121	9	0	7	1	.200	
1993 Base Case	303	25	1	21	4	.240	1
1993 High Range	403	36	2	31	8	.270	

VIZQUEL, OMAR - Mariners SS - BB - Age 25

He went from a career .230 hitter to having a .300 average until the final month of the season. Hitting at the top of the order helped a lot; he also tried to run more often but had a terrible success rate. His glove should keep him an everyday player for years to come.

	AB	R	HR	RBI	SB	BA	$
1992 Seattle AL	483	49	0	21	15	.294	12
1993 Low Range	423	40	1	16	6	.229	
1993 Base Case	502	52	1	22	12	.260	7
1993 High Range	521	59	1	26	18	.290	

VOIGT, JACK - Orioles OF - BR - Age 26

Voigt will be 27 in May. Seems to have a future as a career minor leaguer.

	AB	R	HR	RBI	SB	BA	$
1992 Rochester AAA	443	74	16	64	9	.284	

WAKAMATSU, DON - Dodgers C - BR - Age 30
Was in the major leagues only because he had experience handling the knuckleball (Charlie Hough in Chicago) and the Dodgers didn't know what to expect with Tom Candiotti on the mound. No value for 1993.

WALKER, CHICO - Mets OF/3B - BB - Age 35
Winner of the 1992 Dave Gallagher award, given annually to the best-performing Met player who shouldn't really be playing every day major league lineup. Walker, who began his professional career during the Ford administration, gives a club speed, pretty good defense, and options. About the only position he can't play is behind the plate.

	AB	R	HR	RBI	SB	BA	$
1992 Two Teams NL	253	26	4	38	15	.289	12
1993 Low Range	114	11	1	8	3	.220	
1993 Base Case	200	21	3	25	8	.252	4
1993 High Range	290	33	6	43	16	.287	

WALKER, HUGH - Royals OF - BL - Age 23
1988 first round draft pick. Has developed slowly. Good speed, hasn't hit sufficiently for average while striking out too much. At least a year away. 1992 was a down year.

	AB	R	HR	RBI	SB	BA	$
1992 Baseball City A	74	9	1	5	0	.203	
1992 Memphis AA	278	38	5	31	11	.259	

WALKER, LARRY - Expos OF/1B - BL - Age 26
Walker continues to be one of the game's most underrated players. He hits for power and average, steals bases and has the strongest outfield arm in the National League. His career highs are 23 in homers and 21 in steals. It's not out of the question to see him joining the 30-30 club soon.

	AB	R	HR	RBI	SB	BA	$
1992 Montreal NL	528	85	23	93	18	.301	34
1993 Low Range	499	76	15	74	11	.269	
1993 Base Case	543	91	21	93	20	.300	35
1993 High Range	582	107	27	107	29	.322	

WALLACH, TIM - Expos 3B/1B - BR - Age 35
If he was going to stage a comeback, 1992 would have been the year. He's been in a slump since late 1990.

	AB	R	HR	RBI	SB	BA	$
1992 Montreal NL	537	53	9	59	2	.223	4
1993 Low Range	394	34	6	39	1	.199	
1993 Base Case	484	46	9	55	1	.234	3
1993 High Range	579	60	13	75	3	.263	

WALLING, DENNY - Astros IF/OF - BL - Age 38
Not worth a look, even if he surfaces somewhere during spring training.

WALTERS, DAN - Padres C - BR - Age 26
After an impressive stint when recalled during Santiago's DL time, Walters was expected to become the regular in 1993. Defensively, he can handle the role. Unfortunately, former manager Greg Riddoch failed to give much September seasoning time to Walters even after the Padres had been essentially eliminated from the NL West. That may have stunted Walters' development some. Minor league stats suggest a steady, but unspectacular talent.

	AB	R	HR	RBI	SB	BA	$
1992 San Diego NL	179	14	4	22	1	.251	2
1992 Las Vegas AAA	124	16	2	25	0	.394	
1993 Low Range	104	8	1	9	0	.199	
1993 Base Case	302	21	4	26	0	.240	2
1993 High Range	410	35	8	42	1	.270	

WALTON, JEROME - Cubs OF - BR - Age 27

The NL Rookie of the Year in 1987. Injuries and ineffective play have marked his career since then. He has never walked or stolen enough to be a lead-off man. He does not have much power but is a good defensive replacement. Despite being penciled in as an opening day starter in each of his four years, he has only averaged 298 AB per year.

	AB	R	HR	RBI	SB	BA	$
1992 Chicago NL	55	7	0	1	1	.127	-
1993 Low Range	202	28	1	15	4	.209	
1993 Base Case	251	39	2	21	9	.250	3
1993 High Range	428	72	3	42	21	.280	

WARD, KEVIN - Unsigned OF/1B - BR - Age 31

Ward created brief excitement with three quick home runs when he was called up. Realistically, Ward was just a 30-year-old rookie. He was released after the 1992 season.

	AB	R	HR	RBI	SB	BA	$
1992 San Diego NL	147	12	3	12	2	.197	-
1993 High Range	239	21	6	22	5	.249	

WARD, TURNER - Blue Jays OF - BB - Age 27

A career minor leaguer, Ward was stuck underneath the Indians' overloaded outfield in 1990-1991. Now his potential is all behind him. Could be a safe PH/utility type, but nothing more.

	AB	R	HR	RBI	SB	BA	$
1992 Syracuse AAA	280	41	10	29	7	.239	
1992 Toronto AL	29	7	1	3	0	.345	0
1993 Base Case	93	15	1	9	1	.280	1
1993 High Range	311	55	6	36	4	.311	

WEBSTER, LENNY - Twins C - BR - Age 28

Webster's role is strictly backup to Brian Harper. Webster hits better than the typical backup catcher, and can slam an occasional home run.

	AB	R	HR	RBI	SB	BA	$
1992 Minnesota AL	118	10	1	13	0	.280	1
1993 Base Case	205	21	2	22	0	.260	1
1993 High Range	309	35	4	37	0	.290	

WEBSTER, MITCH - Dodgers OF - BB - Age 33

Webster played in 135 games only because of injuries to Davis and Strawberry. It is highly unlikely that Webster can match 262 at bats in 1993. He is still an adequate reserve outfielder and pinch hitter with SB potential and modest power, and the same people who got hurt last year can always get hurt again.

	AB	R	HR	RBI	SB	BA	$
1992 Los Angeles NL	262	33	6	35	11	.267	10
1993 Low Range	109	12	2	12	3	.207	
1993 Base Case	227	27	5	29	9	.248	5
1993 High Range	253	35	7	40	14	.278	

WEDGE, ERIC - Rockies C - BR - Age 25

Pena was signed "for the rest of his career" and Wedge became expendable in Boston. He is a bright prospect who should hit with good power in Denver. Defensive limitations and a sore elbow will put a cap on playing time.

	AB	R	HR	RBI	SB	BA	$
1992 Pawtucket AAA	211	28	11	40	0	.299	
1992 Boston AL	68	11	5	11	0	.250	1
1993 Low Range	159	16	3	16	0	.208	
1993 Base Case	272	31	7	32	0	.249	3
1993 High Range	334	40	10	45	0	.279	

WEHNER, JOHN - Pirates 3B - BR - Age 25

After hitting .340 in 37 games as a rookie, Wehner's batting average dropped 161 points last season. The Pirates went from considering the Pittsburgh native as a potential starting third baseman to trying to convert him into a utility player.

	AB	R	HR	RBI	SB	BA	$
1992 Buffalo AAA	223	37	7	27	10	.269	
1992 Pittsburgh NL	123	11	0	4	3	.179	-
1993 High Range	214	24	1	19	7	.270	

WEISS, WALT - Marlins SS - BB - Age 29

All during the expansion draft, observers kept wondering: who plays shortstop for the Marlins? Florida clearly thinks he's valuable, but he's still just Walt Weiss. Started last season on the disabled list, with a pulled rib cage muscle, and never got going with the bat or the glove. Extra base hits were way down. Has missed a ton of games the past four seasons, and his defense has slipped noticeably too.

	AB	R	HR	RBI	SB	BA	$
1992 Oakland AL	316	36	0	21	6	.212	-
1993 Low Range	300	35	0	20	5	.217	
1993 Base Case	455	51	2	36	8	.229	0
1993 High Range	508	61	3	41	12	.261	

WHITAKER, LOU - Tigers 2B - BL - Age 35

Whitaker has had stunning success in the last three years as a power hitter. Leaving Detroit could cut his homers sharply.

	AB	R	HR	RBI	SB	BA	$
1992 Detroit AL	470	94	23	78	4	.279	18
1993 Low Range	305	45	9	45	2	.239	
1993 Base Case	426	68	15	70	3	.269	15
1993 High Range	519	92	24	79	8	.288	

WHITE, DEVON - Blue Jays OF - BB - Age 30

If he would just cut down his swing and make contact better, White could hit .300 and get on base enough to steal 50 bases. He isn't likely to change at this age, however. At least you get 15 to 20 home runs with the big swing.

	AB	R	HR	RBI	SB	BA	$
1992 Toronto AL	641	98	17	60	37	.248	25
1993 Low Range	506	72	10	38	19	.210	
1993 Base Case	581	91	15	51	36	.251	22
1993 High Range	626	198	19	62	50	.281	

WHITE, RONDELL - Expos OF - BR - Age 21

Reminds many of a young Andre Dawson with outstanding all-around offensive talent and 30-30 potential. He led the Class A Florida State League in triples (12), was second in stolen bases, third in runs, fourth in on-base percentage (.384), and fifth in total bases (188), all before promotion to Class AA. He was selected third-best prospect in Florida State League in poll of league managers by Baseball America. Expect a September callup in 1993, but nothing more this year unless he surprises everyone including his avid supporters who drafted him number one in 1990.

	AB	R	HR	RBI	SB	BA	$
1992 West Palm Bch A	450	80	4	41	42	.316	
1992 Harrisburg AA	89	22	2	7	6	.303	

WHITEN, MARK - Indians OF - BB - Age 26

Only 26 years old, Whiten's career is on the upswing. He was talented enough to play for the World Champion Jays but wasn't, er, diplomatic enough. Cleveland's outfield, on the other hand, is not a breeding ground for future ambassadors.

	AB	R	HR	RBI	SB	BA	$
1992 Cleveland AL	508	73	9	43	16	.254	13
1993 Low Range	416	52	7	39	10	.238	
1993 Base Case	502	67	11	56	15	.270	18
1993 High Range	557	81	17	75	21	.301	

WHITMORE, DARRELL - Marlins OF - BL - Age 24

Has power and speed, but most of the good players his age are farther along by now. Florida planned to use him as a backup right fielder if they couldn't find anyone with higher level experience, but more likely he will be their AAA starter.

	AB	R	HR	RBI	SB	BA	$
1992 Kinston A	443	71	10	52	17	.280	

WHITT, ERNIE - Unsigned C - BL - Age 40

If by some miracle he surfaces again during spring training, don't look.

WILKERSON, CURTIS - Royals IF - BB - Age 31

A marginal hitter who rebounded from off years in the NL to post respectable part-time numbers for KC. The obvious question about Wilkerson is whether he can do it again. The odds are good that he'll come close. He fits in well on any team as a backup infielder; his mediocre glove doesn't hurt you much in that role while he contributes some with the bat. Wilkerson showed surprising speed in 1992 - don't count on it for 1993, though; he hadn't reached double digit steals since 1985.

	AB	R	HR	RBI	SB	BA	$
1992 Kansas City AL	296	27	2	29	18	.250	9
1993 Base Case	206	18	1	20	8	.229	0
1993 High Range	309	32	3	34	17	.254	

WILKINS, RICK - Cubs C - BL - Age 25

A rarity: a young, lefthanded-hitting catcher with power. He led his league in caught stealing percentage twice. Despite the power, his RBI totals are low.

	AB	R	HR	RBI	SB	BA	$
1992 Iowa AAA	155	20	5	28	0	.277	
1992 Chicago NL	244	20	8	22	0	.270	5
1993 Low Range	265	21	7	26	0	.211	
1993 Base Case	390	35	12	45	1	.252	8
1993 High Range	479	52	18	61	1	.282	

WILLARD, JERRY - Expos C - BL - Age 33
In the Senior League, he'd be a star. Not likely to play major league ball in 1993 unless someone gets hurt, like Greg Olson did in 1992

WILLIAMS, BERNIE - Yankees OF - BB - Age 24
The trade of Roberto Kelly solidified Williams as the logical everyday CF. The International League All-Star has speed, on-base ability and some power, and he can hit for average. The Baseball America poll named him both the IL's best hitting prospect and best defensive OF.

	AB	R	HR	RBI	SB	BA	$
1992 Columbus AAA	363	68	8	50	20	.306	
1992 New York AL	261	39	5	26	7	.280	8
1993 Low Range	382	55	9	35	10	.248	
1993 Base Case	509	80	14	55	23	.275	23
1993 High Range	593	103	20	73	34	.306	

WILLIAMS, CARY - Phillies OF - BR - Age 25
A little power, a little speed, has never hit for average (career .254 in four minor league seasons).

WILLIAMS, GERALD - Yankees OF - BR - Age 26
An exception to the rule that players who reach age 26 before reaching the major leagues are no longer prospects. Williams somehow remained in the Yankee organization long enough to get some playing time. For years New York had no idea where he could fit in, but didn't trade him. Nickname "Ice" for his cool disposition. Good second half player: "I come on strong at the end, always have." Expect a platoon with Paul O'Neill.

	AB	R	HR	RBI	SB	BA	$
1992 Columbus AAA	547	92	16	86	36	.285	
1992 New York AL	27	7	3	6	2	.296	1
1993 Low Range	209	28	5	24	5	.214	
1993 Base Case	298	43	9	39	12	.255	9
1993 High Range	458	73	16	69	26	.285	

WILLIAMS, KENNY - Unsigned OF - BR - Age 28
Last up with Expos in 1991. Still able to play, he was at AAA Denver in 1992. Best season was 1987 with the White Sox, when he hit .281 with 11 home runs and 28 steals.

WILLIAMS, MATT - Giants 3B - BR - Age 27
Former 30+ home run hitter and league RBI champ, Williams suffered through a woeful 1992 season, unable to produce in the clean-up spot. Good signs: still just age 27, and is likely to return to the number five slot in the batting order, which he likes. Could be the Mark McGwire of 1993.

	AB	R	HR	RBI	SB	BA	$
1992 San Francisco NL	529	58	20	66	7	.227	13
1993 Low Range	465	51	21	74	3	.218	
1993 Base Case	511	61	29	94	6	.251	19
1993 High Range	601	80	40	117	10	.278	

WILLIAMS, REGGIE - Angels OF - BB - Age 26
Williams is a good defensive outfielder with base-stealing speed. He won't hit enough to win a starting position, but he could earn a roster spot as a utility outfielder and pinch runner.

	AB	R	HR	RBI	SB	BA	$
1992 Edmonton AAA	519	96	3	64	44	.272	
1992 California AL	26	5	0	2	0	.231	-
1993 Base Case	110	16	0	8	10	.209	-
1993 High Range	162	27	1	13	15	.241	

WILSON, BRANDON - White Sox SS - BR - Age 24

Chicago's 18th-round pick in '90, out of the U. of Kentucky. His maturity shows in his leadership and take-charge attitude. Protected from expansion draft. Expect a September callup.

	AB	R	HR	RBI	SB	BA	$
1992 Sarasota A	399	68	4	54	30	.296	
1992 Birmingham AA	107	10	0	4	5	.271	

WILSON, CRAIG - Cardinals IF/OF - BR - Age 28

A good line-drive hitter who shows the ability to hit off the bench. He can play many positions. Never received a true chance in the major leagues. In the right situation, he could be a productive role player.

	AB	R	HR	RBI	SB	BA	$
1992 Louisville AAA	81	13	0	5	3	.296	
1992 St. Louis NL	106	6	0	13	1	.311	1
1993 Base Case	64	5	0	6	0	.263	-
1993 High Range	226	21	1	24	2	.294	

WILSON, DAN - Reds C - BR - Age 24

Cincinnati's No. 1 draft pick in '90. A top defensive catcher, whose arm is more accurate than strong. Hasn't yet hit for power or average, but he could improve suddenly.

	AB	R	HR	RBI	SB	BA	$
1992 Nashville AAA	366	27	4	34	1	.251	
1992 Cincinnati NL	25	2	0	3	0	.360	-
1993 Base Case	223	14	1	15	1	.240	-
1993 High Range	357	25	5	30	2	.270	

WILSON, NIGEL - Marlins OF - BL - Age 23

Expecting him to produce from Opening Day would be unreasonable. Fortunately the Marlins have a long-term approach and won't rush him. Expect a simple September callup, or a June-July appearance if he gets off to a really hot start.

	AB	R	HR	RBI	SB	BA	$
1992 Knoxville AA	521	85	26	69	13	.274	
1993 Base Case	124	17	4	14	3	.255	1
1993 High Range	297	50	15	41	7	.275	

WILSON, WILLIE - Athletics OF - BB - Age 37

At age 37, Wilson can still steal some bases and hit, especially on Astroturf. He was helped by the many injuries to the Oakland outfield in 1992, a factor that can't be so extreme in 1993. His best days are way behind him, but Willie is still a decent fourth outfielder.

	AB	R	HR	RBI	SB	BA	$
1992 Oakland AL	396	38	0	37	28	.270	15
1993 Low Range	195	17	0	15	7	.229	
1993 Base Case	288	28	1	25	17	.260	8

WINFIELD, DAVE - Blue Jays OF - BR - Age 41
Obviously an exception to the age rules that affect mortals. Winfield's departure from the game should be at least as graceful as Dave Parker's. Comparisons are appropriate, because Winfield succeeded in exactly the same role where Parker failed: Blue Jays veteran DH and team leader. Winfield is only four months younger than Parker. Toronto did not offer Winfield arbitration.

	AB	R	HR	RBI	SB	BA	$
1992 Toronto AL	583	92	26	108	2	.290	26
1993 Low Range	384	49	10	50	1	.229	
1993 Base Case	492	69	16	74	1	.260	13
1993 High Range	577	89	22	95	2	.290	

WINNINGHAM, HERM - Red Sox OF - BL - Age 31
Strictly a platoon player who does nothing especially well.

	AB	R	HR	RBI	SB	BA	$
1992 Boston AL	234	27	1	14	6	.235	1
1993 Low Range	167	18	1	9	3	.195	
1993 Base Case	201	20	1	10	5	.233	-
1993 High Range	308	39	3	18	9	.259	

WITMEYER, RON - Athletics 1B - BL - Age 25
Has failed to hit for average in two PCL seasons, a condemnation to a first baseman. Doesn't have enough power to compensate, either. Rapidly becoming a former prospect.

WOOD, TED - Giants OF - BL - Age 26
Good line drive hitter. Wood was leading his Triple-A team in hitting when he was called up to majors.

	AB	R	HR	RBI	SB	BA	$
1992 Phoenix AAA	418	70	7	63	9	.304	
1992 San Francisco NL	58	5	1	3	0	.207	-
1993 Low Range	116	13	2	11	2	.214	
1993 Base Case	230	29	4	25	5	.247	3
1993 High Range	405	55	9	50	13	.277	

WOODSON, TRACY - Cardinals 3B - BR - Age 30
After not playing in the majors since 1989, he was called up from St. Louis in August when slumping Todd Zeile was sent down. Surprisingly, Woodson played exceptionally well, driving in 22 runs in 31 games. While he may not win a job in the majors, he must again be considered a good extra. He has power; his 46 home runs are the North Carolina State career record.

	AB	R	HR	RBI	SB	BA	$
1992 Louisville AAA	412	62	12	59	4	.296	
1992 St. Louis NL	114	9	1	22	0	.307	2
1993 Base Case	94	8	1	12	1	.243	0
1993 High Range	255	24	3	38	1	.280	

WORTHINGTON, CRAIG - Indians 3B - BR - Age 27
Worthington may be without a job after being "designated for assignment" in September. If he does hook on with a major league team and plays regularly as he did with Baltimore in 1989, he can still hit.

	AB	R	HR	RBI	SB	BA	$
1992 Col. Sp. AAA	319	47	6	57	0	.295	
1992 Cleveland AL	24	0	0	2	0	.167	-
1993 Base Case	101	10	2	12	0	.241	-
1993 High Range	242	25	5	35	1	.271	

WRONA, RICK - Reds C - BR - Age 29
A perennial third string catcher. If he plays he will hit about .230 with no power. Not what you want.

YELDING, ERIC - Reds IF/OF - BR - Age 28
Fast outfielder and a former shortstop. Likely to play at Nashville in 1993.

	AB	R	HR	RBI	SB	BA	$
1992 Tuscon AAA	338	47	0	29	32	.263	

YOUNG, DMITRI - Cardinals 3B - BB - Age 19
A first-round pick in 1991, the switch-hitting Young hits for power and average from both sides of the plate. His fielding is below average and he is a little chunky. He realizes his defensive problems, though, saying "I know I have to improve but I still have some mistakes in my brain." Voted the top prospect in the Class A Midwest League in 1992 in a poll of league managers by Baseball America.

	AB	R	HR	RBI	SB	BA	$
1992 Springfield A	493	74	14	72	14	.310	

YOUNG, ERIC - Rockies 2B - BR - Age 25
One of the most underrated players at the end of 1992. Young will get plenty of playing time with Colorado. After a fantastic year at Albuquerque, Young was brought up and appeared overmatched, batting just .209 in his first 86 at-bats. He rallied in September, however, batting .348 in his last 46 at bats. Young was in the running for his fourth straight minor league SB crown before being called up. He was a three-year starter at wide receiver for the Scarlet Knights. Contact hitter; struck out just 27 times last season.

	AB	R	HR	RBI	SB	BA	$
1992 Albuquerque AAA	350	61	3	49	28	.337	
1992 Los Angeles NL	132	9	1	11	6	.258	2
1993 Low Range	298	31	1	22	12	.233	
1993 Base Case	453	55	2	40	29	.264	11
1993 High Range	535	66	3	50	40	.296	

YOUNG, GERALD - Rockies OF - BB - Age 28
Posted fourth straight disappointing season since breaking in with .321 average in 1987 and team record of 65 stolen bases in 1988. Released by Astros at the end of the 1992 season, he could catch on somewhere as a spare outfielder. A one category player, he could have some Rotisserie value just for stolen bases.

	AB	R	HR	RBI	SB	BA	$
1992 Tucson AAA	74	15	0	2	13	.311	
1992 Houston NL	76	14	0	4	6	.184	-
1993 Base Case	149	16	0	8	9	.220	0
1993 High Range	303	37	0	23	25	.252	

YOUNG, KEVIN - Pirates 3B - BR - Age 23
In his first taste of the major leagues in 1992, Young looked like a rising star. He showed a quick, line-drive stroke and above-average speed. He played in Class A, AA, and AAA in 1991, his first full professional season. Ranked as the top prospect in the American Association in 1992 in a poll of league managers by Baseball America. In the second half he raised his average some 60 points and cut down his errors.

	AB	R	HR	RBI	SB	BA	$
1992 Buffalo AAA	490	91	8	65	18	.314	
1992 Pittsburgh NL	7	2	0	4	1	.571	-
1993 Low Range	173	25	3	21	5	.246	
1993 Base Case	302	45	6	41	13	.273	11
1993 High Range	416	71	10	68	26	.304	

YOUNT, ROBIN - Brewers OF - BR - Age 37

Past glory and career achievements mean nothing in Rotisserie, except maybe high prices. Yount's power is gone, his batting eye is slipping fast, but he still has above-average speed on the basepaths. At this point, Yount is hurting the team in CF, but there are logjams already at first base, left field, and DH.

	AB	R	HR	RBI	SB	BA	$
1992 Milwaukee AL	557	71	8	77	15	.264	16
1993 Low Range	409	45	6	51	6	.238	
1993 Base Case	488	60	9	71	12	.259	13
1993 High Range	569	76	14	91	19	.289	

ZEILE, TODD - Cardinals 3B - BR - Age 27

After showing much promise in his two full major-league seasons, he hit bottom and spent most of last August back in Class AAA. Zeile looked much better when he returned but he is a question mark until he proves he can bounce all the way back in 1993.

	AB	R	HR	RBI	SB	BA	$
1992 Louisville AAA	74	11	5	13	0	.311	
1992 St. Louis NL	439	51	7	48	7	.257	10
1993 Low Range	389	40	6	41	4	.236	
1993 Base Case	433	49	9	54	7	.260	11
1993 High Range	548	68	13	77	12	.284	

ZINTER, ALAN - Mets 1B - BB - Age 25

A former top catching prospect with good power, he's been converted to first base, but he has a way to go before becoming a major-league quality player. Zinter has patience at the plate, but his swing is way too big, he has zero speed, and isn't much of a first baseman either. Expect a year at Triple-A.

	AB	R	HR	RBI	SB	BA	$
1992 Binghamton AA	431	63	16	50	0	.223	

ZOSKY, EDDIE - Blue Jays SS - BR - Age 25

Toronto's first pick in 1989, out of Fresno State. In two years at Triple-A, he has played well only during the second half of '91. He has shown nothing in his brief major league trials (34 AB) and was a major disappointment in spring training 1992 when it became clear that he wasn't making progress.

	AB	R	HR	RBI	SB	BA	$
1992 Syracuse AAA	342	31	4	38	3	.231	
1992 Toronto AL	7	1	0	1	0	.286	-
1993 Base Case	111	10	1	12	1	.236	-
1993 High Range	309	30	3	38	5	.265	

ZUPCIC, BOB - Red Sox OF - BR - Age 26

Took a second-half nosedive after teasing owners with a .328 BA at the All Star break. If Burks and or Greenwell return, Zupcic will sit or even return to the minors.

	AB	R	HR	RBI	SB	BA	$
1992 Boston AL	392	46	3	43	2	.276	7
1993 Base Case	291	32	2	29	2	.247	1
1993 High Range	440	52	5	49	4	.277	

ABBOTT, JIM - Yankees - TL - Age 25
Abbott pitched well enough to win 15-20 games in 1992 but suffered from a remarkable lack of run support and won only seven. Equally remarkable is the fact that the Angels then put Abbott on the trading block.

	W	SV	ERA	IP	H	BB	SO	BPI	$
1992 California AL	7	0	2.77	211	208	68	130	1.31	11
1993 Base Case	17	0	2.97	212	202	67	132	1.27	18

ABBOTT, KYLE - Phillies - TL - Age 25
Went 0-12 in 1992 in his first regular stint in the majors. But the Phillies think this acquisition from California can still be a useful pitcher though he may end up working in relief. A first round pick and a major talent.

	W	SV	ERA	IP	H	BB	SO	BPI	$
1992 Philadelphia NL	1	0	5.13	133	147	45	88	1.43	-
1993 Base Case	6	0	4.57	147	154	43	97	1.34	-

ABBOTT, PAUL - Twins - TR - Age 25
Abbott has struggled in several trials with the Twins. He showed good stuff in the minors by striking out more than one batter per inning, but he also walks many. He was plagued with shoulder problems in '92.

	W	SV	ERA	IP	H	BB	SO	BPI	$
1992 Portland AAA	4	0	2.33	46	30	31	46	1.31	
1992 Minnesota AL	0	0	3.27	11	12	5	13	1.54	-
1993 Base Case	1	0	4.28	28	25	18	28	1.56	-

ACKER, JIM - Mariners - TR - Age 34
Finished the year on the DL. Near the end of the trail.

	W	SV	ERA	IP	H	BB	SO	BPI	$
1992 Seattle AL	0	0	5.28	30	45	12	11	1.86	-
1993 Base Case	1	0	5.23	60	67	24	26	1.52	-

AGOSTO, JUAN - Mariners - TL - Age 35
Once an ultra-safe Rotisserie reliever, now he's risky and may not even have a role in 1993.

	W	SV	ERA	IP	H	BB	SO	BPI	$
1992 Two Teams	2	0	6.12	50	66	12	25	1.56	-
1993 Base Case	4	1	4.84	74	87	25	34	1.51	-

AGUILERA, RICK - Twins - TR - Age 31
Aguilera is one of the top relievers in baseball, and he should continue his outstanding pitching in '93. He may have a few poor outings at the start of the season, no cause for panic.

	W	SV	ERA	IP	H	BB	SO	BPI	$
1992 Minnesota AL	2	41	2.84	67	60	17	52	1.16	34
1993 Base Case	3	36	2.65	65	52	21	53	1.13	34

AKERFELDS, DARREL - Orioles - TR - Age 30
Pitched well for the Rangers in 1989 and the Phillies in 1990, but now he's about done.

	W	SV	ERA	IP	H	BB	SO	BPI	$
1992 Oklahoma City AAA	3	1	6.95	33	48	19	18	1.99	
1992 Buffalo AAA	0	1	4.18	32	34	17	14	1.58	

ALDRED, SCOTT - Rockies - TL - Age 24

Aldred was a top prospect just a couple years ago, but hasn't had a really good season higher than A-ball. Was hit hard after his call up by the Tigers. High potential, but at this point he does not have our seal of approval. Will get a real chance to pitch regularly for the Rockies, anyway, which makes him a dangerous pick.

	W	SV	ERA	IP	H	BB	SO	BPI	$
1992 Detroit AL	3	0	6.78	65	80	33	34	1.74	-
1993 Base Case	9	0	4.65	157	162	65	88	1.45	-

ALEXANDER, GERALD - Rangers - TR - Age 25

Dominant in the low minors, but still struggling in the big leagues. Similar to Tom Gordon: if he gets his curveball over for a strike one, he's very tough; if he misses and falls behind, he's in deep fondue.

	W	SV	ERA	IP	H	BB	SO	BPI	$
1992 Texas AL	1	0	27.00	1	5	1	1	3.59	-
1993 Base Case	3	0	4.86	37	41	18	21	1.60	-

ALLISON, DANA - Athletics - TL - Age 26

Pitched for Oakland in 1991 but went back down in 1992. Has previously done well at AA; didn't show any real progress in 1992.

	W	SV	ERA	IP	H	BB	SO	BPI	$
1992 Huntsville AA	4	1	2.93	61	51	5	40	0.91	
1992 Tacoma AAA	2	0	4.84	44	63	17	17	1.79	

ALVAREZ, TAVO - Expos - TR - Age 21

He is polished at a young age with a variety of pitches and outstanding poise. His fastball and changeup are already considered major league quality. His 17 wins ties for third in all the minor leagues and his 1.84 ERA tied for second.

	W	SV	ERA	IP	H	BB	SO	BPI	$
1992 W Palm Beach A	13	0	1.49	139	124	24	83	1.07	
1992 Harrisburg AA	4	0	2.85	47	42	8	18	1.06	

ALVAREZ, WILSON - White Sox - TL - Age 23

Will finally get a chance to be in the rotation in 1993. Major talent, just a bit emotional. For a low price I would want him on my team. Very high upward potential.

	W	SV	ERA	IP	H	BB	SO	BPI	$
1992 Chicago AL	5	1	5.20	100	103	65	66	1.67	-
1993 Base Case	10	0	3.71	132	121	61	107	1.38	4

ANDERSEN, LARRY - Padres - TR - Age 39

At age 39, Andersen's contract was not expected to be picked up by the Padres. He pitched only 35 innings in 1992 and had arm and neck problems. With a ratio of 0.97, Andersen will still attract someone's interest in the free agent market if he doesn't retire.

	W	SV	ERA	IP	H	BB	SO	BPI	$
1992 San Diego NL	1	2	3.34	35	26	8	35	0.97	2
1993 Base Case	2	6	3.27	47	38	14	44	1.11	6

ANDERSON, ALLAN - Yankees - TL - Age 29

American League ERA champ in 1988, and won 17 games in 1989, but he's lost it.

APPIER, KEVIN - Royals - TR - Age 25

September shoulder stiffness was the only sour note in his stellar season. Appier rose to the occasion, replacing Bret Saberhagen as the Royals' staff ace. He won't duplicate his 1992 numbers, but he'll be a strong starter among the league's best. Don't pay for his 1992 performance, it's more than he can achieve.

	W	SV	ERA	IP	H	BB	SO	BPI	$
1992 Kansas City AL	15	0	2.46	208	167	68	150	1.13	21
1993 Base Case	13	0	2.91	196	172	62	145	1.20	18

AQUINO, LUIS - Royals - TR - Age 27

He's rarely around long enough to acquire the necessary runs (or innings) to get a W. He's a good long reliever and would revert to that role if he loses his starting role as seems likely. Injuries have diminished two of Aquino's last three years. His value to the Royals is much greater than it is to his Rotisserie owners.

	W	SV	ERA	IP	H	BB	SO	BPI	$
1992 Omaha AAA	0	0	2.61	10.1	13	4	3	1.65	
1992 Kansas City AL	3	0	4.52	67.2	81	20	11	1.49	-
1993 Base Case	6	1	3.83	115	123	34	40	1.36	2

ARD, JOHNNY - Giants - TR - Age 25

The guy traded for Steve Bedrosian. Hasn't exactly blossomed, although he did have a good year at Shreveport in 1991. Giants pitchers have a way of appearing from nowhere and doing well.

	W	SV	ERA	IP	H	BB	SO	BPI	$
1992 Phoenix AAA	5	0	4.46	113	130	69	56	1.76	

ARMSTRONG, JACK - Marlins - TR - Age 28

In his whole career, he's pitched well for exactly one half of one season. It was the first half of 1990, and he got to start the All-Star game that year. People keep paying for a performance level that long since disappeared. Armstrong is talented but very erratic. After getting hammered numerous times, he lost his spot in the rotation and was sent to the bullpen where he was effective in a middle and long relief role.

	W	SV	ERA	IP	H	BB	SO	BPI	$
1992 Cleveland AL	6	0	4.64	167	176	67	114	1.46	-
1993 Base Case	7	0	4.56	152	162	64	100	1.49	-

ARNSBERG, BRAD - Indians - TR - Age 29

Arnsberg had a good year in '90 as a set-up man with Texas. Since then he's had arm problems and disappointing years.

	W	SV	ERA	IP	H	BB	SO	BPI	$
1992 Colo. Spr. AAA	1	0	7.56	25	34	13	11	1.88	
1992 Cleveland AL	0	0	11.81	11	13	11	5	2.25	-

AROCHA, RENE - Cardinals - TR - Age 27

When Arocha pitched for the Cuban team, he didn't get much respect. Most scouts in the U.S. rated him around the high Double-A level. Arocha proved that he was better than that, with a superb year at Triple-A in 1992. Do you think the Cardinals would have risked exposing him to the draft with a callup in September? No way. Arocha has a huge repertoire. Any pitch you can name, he can throw. Had 100 wins and 1,000 strikeouts in his career with the Cuban National Team.

	W	SV	ERA	IP	H	BB	SO	BPI	$
1992 Louisville AAA	12	0	2.70	167	145	65	128	1.26	
1993 Base Case	9	0	3.54	155	149	67	90	1.39	4

ASHBY, ANDY - Rockies - TR - Age 25

Philadelphia targeted him as one of the few solid prospects from their awful farm system, but a broken thumb wiped out much of his 1992 season and when he returned, Ashby was a disappointment. At least in Colorado, he won't have to fight for a job.

	W	SV	ERA	IP	H	BB	SO	BPI	$
1992 Philadelphia NL	1	0	7.54	37	42	21	24	1.70	-
1993 Base Case	6	0	4.66	46	48	24	30	1.56	-

ASSENMACHER, PAUL - Cubs - TL - Age 32

Over the past five years, Assenmacher has been a solid middle reliever. His strikeout to walk ratio fell from nearly 4:1 to 2.5:1 last year. If given a defined role, he has the pitches and experience to be very effective. Had a knee injury in 1992.

	W	SV	ERA	IP	H	BB	SO	BPI	$
1992 Chicago NL	4	8	4.10	68	72	26	67	1.44	4
1993 Base Case	5	10	3.69	80	79	28	84	1.32	8

ASTACIO, PEDRO - Dodgers - TR - Age 23

Only David Cone and Tom Glavine had more NL shutouts than Astacio, who had 4 in just 11 starts. Although he was extremely impressive, do not overlook the fact that Astacio was hit hard at Albuquerque before his recall. His low strikeout numbers suggest that the NL hitters will catch up.

	W	SV	ERA	IP	H	BB	SO	BPI	$
1992 Albuquerque AAA	6	0	5.47	99	115	44	66	1.61	
1992 Los Angeles NL	5	0	1.98	82	80	20	43	1.22	5
1993 Base Case	5	0	3.21	104	116	29	54	1.39	2

AUGUST, DON - Tigers - TR - Age 29

Had one good year with the Brewers in 1988, but has been struggling ever since. Needs to get the sharp curveball over the plate, and hasn't been doing it.

	W	SV	ERA	IP	H	BB	SO	BPI	$
1992 London AA	3	0	2.72	53	47	10	39	1.07	
1992 Toledo AAA	0	0	8.59	14	25	7	6	2.18	

AUSANIO, JOE - Expos - TR - Age 27

Pitched extremely well at A and AA in 1988-1990, and finally achieved success at AAA in 1992. It's not too late for him to be a major league success. Pirates released him.

	W	SV	ERA	IP	H	BB	SO	BPI	$
1992 Buffalo AAA	6	15	2.90	83	64	40	66	1.24	
1993 Base Case	2	3	3.80	52	48	20	33	1.31	2

AUSTIN, JAMES - Brewers - TR - Age 29

A potential successor to Doug Henry as closer, with much greater upside potential. Austin was often untouchable in 1992 (only 5.6 hits per nine innings), and Garner's practice of using him exclusively as a setup man to ease him through his rookie season kept him obscure. Definitely worth acquiring, because he will be cheap, and he is good.

	W	SV	ERA	IP	H	BB	SO	BPI	$
1992 Milwaukee AL	5	0	1.85	58	38	32	30	1.20	5
1993 Base Case	6	5	2.27	49	36	29	33	1.33	9

AVERY, STEVE - Braves - TL - Age 22

The Braves won most of his 1992 starts, but many of the W's went to relievers. He'll continue to be an effective pitcher for a number of years. Use his "down" year (only 11 Wins) to grab him cheaply.

	W	SV	ERA	IP	H	BB	SO	BPI	$
1992 Atlanta NL	11	0	3.20	233	216	71	129	1.23	9
1993 Base Case	14	0	3.40	220	204	64	128	1.22	12

AYALA, BOBBY - Reds - TR - Age 23

Signed as a minor league free agent in 1988, Ayala was moved to a starter role with AA Chattanooga in 1992 and earned a look from the Reds in September. His mechanics are similar to Rob Dibble's, with a high leg kick and 3/4 delivery. Projected to compete for the 5th starter role in 1993.

	W	SV	ERA	IP	H	BB	SO	BPI	$
1992 Chattanooga AA	12	0	3.54	162	152	58	154	1.29	
1992 Cincinnati NL	2	0	4.34	29	33	13	23	1.59	-
1993 Base Case	11	0	4.20	152	157	57	111	1.41	1

AYRAULT, BOB - Phillies - TR - Age 26

Looked good in a trial with the Phillies, but since 1990 he has generally struggled above the AA level.

	W	SV	ERA	IP	H	BB	SO	BPI	$
1992 Scranton AAA	5	6	4.97	25	19	15	30	1.34	
1992 Philadelphia NL	2	0	3.12	43	32	17	27	1.13	0
1993 Base Case	5	0	4.05	74	62	32	58	1.28	0

BACKLUND, BRETT - Pirates - TR - Age 23

A fifth round pick in 1992, Backlund attracted attention by earning quick promotions. He has a full assortment of pitches and good poise. Selected from the University of Iowa in the fifth round of last year's draft then did not sign until July, but still rose farther than any other 1992 draftee.

	W	SV	ERA	IP	H	BB	SO	BPI	$
1992 Augusta A	3	0	0.36	25	10	4	31	0.56	
1992 Carolina AA	1	0	1.89	19	11	3	17	0.74	
1992 Buffalo AAA	3	0	2.16	25	15	11	9	1.04	
1993 Base Case	3	0	3.66	55	50	24	24	1.34	1

BAILES, SCOTT - Angels - TR - Age 30

Bailes is a lefty set-up reliever who usually provides some awful Rotisserie stats. Furthermore, he hasn't had a save since 1987. The Angels released Bailes in October.

	W	SV	ERA	IP	H	BB	SO	BPI	$
1992 California AL	3	0	7.45	39	59	28	25	2.25	-
1993 Base Case	3	0	5.23	52	58	28	36	1.67	-

BALLARD, JEFF - Cardinals - TL - Age 29

Big year with the Orioles in 1989 (18-8, 3.43 ERA). Since then, he's been a classic example of why you should avoid soft throwers. Had two elbow operations after 1990 season. Longshot for a comeback, but if anyone can salvage him, the Cards can.

	W	SV	ERA	IP	H	BB	SO	BPI	$
1992 Louisville AAA	12	0	2.52	160	164	34	76	1.23	
1993 Base Case	4	0	3.80	40	40	15	16	1.38	0

BALLER, JAY - Phillies - TR - Age 31

Baller's role in life is to illustrate why Rotisserians should ignore minor league saves. Baller keeps piling them up at Triple-A, but he can't get anyone out in the majors.

	W	SV	ERA	IP	H	BB	SO	BPI	$
1992 Scranton AAA	4	22	1.42	63	48	25	67	1.16	
1992 Philadelphia NL	0	0	8.18	11	10	10	9	1.82	-
1993 Base Case	0	0	5.11	21	22	14	17	1.68	-

BANKHEAD, SCOTT - Red Sox - TR - Age 29

The Reds gambled a rare free agent signing that Scott Bankhead would be healthy in 1992, after two years of arm miseries. Bankhead pitched extremely well in the first half setting up Norm Charlton and Rob Dibble, but faded in the second half. Held opponents to .218 BA, but his role is unlikely to expand in 1993.

	W	SV	ERA	IP	H	BB	SO	BPI	$
1992 Cincinnati NL	10	1	2.93	70	57	29	53	1.22	5
1993 Base Case	6	0	3.60	65	63	24	41	1.34	1

BANKS, WILLIE - Twins - TR - Age 24

Highly regarded prospect. He overpowered the PCL in the first half of '92, and it appeared that he had finally gotten it together. However, he was hammered when called up to the Twins, and he is a prime example that there is a big difference between AAA and the majors. Even the PCL does not have hitters like Cecil Fielder, Frank Thomas, etc. Ask Banks. He knows.

	W	SV	ERA	IP	H	BB	SO	BPI	$
1992 Portland AAA	6	0	1.92	75	62	34	41	1.28	
1992 Minnesota AL	4	0	5.70	71	80	37	37	1.65	-
1993 Base Case	6	0	5.14	99	108	54	44	1.64	-

BANNISTER, FLOYD - Rangers - TL - Age 37

Oh, to be born lefthanded! He can still get the lefties out (.174 BA), but otherwise he is atrocious. Very uncertain big league future.

	W	SV	ERA	IP	H	BB	SO	BPI	$
1992 Texas AL	1	0	6.32	37	39	21	30	1.62	-
1993 Base Case	1	0	5.73	40	41	21	30	1.57	-

BARBER, BRIAN - Cardinals - TR - Age 20

St. Louis' second pick in the first round of the '91 draft, out of Orlando's Dr. Phillips High School. A power pitcher, he has averaged better than a strikeout per inning in 1 1/2 pro seasons. Eccentric habits make him a crowd pleaser.

	W	SV	ERA	IP	H	BB	SO	BPI	$
1992 Springfield A	3	0	3.73	51	39	24	56	1.24	
1992 St. Petersburg A	5	0	3.26	113	99	46	102	1.28	

BARFIELD, JOHN - Rangers - TL - Age 28

Basically a finesse/control pitcher, Barfield had some good outings with the Rangers in 1989-1991, but now his career is going the wrong way.

	W	SV	ERA	IP	H	BB	SO	BPI	$
1992 Oklahoma City AAA	7	2	4.14	71	75	26	26	1.42	
1992 Charlotte A	0	1	7.71	7	10	1	4	1.57	

BARNES, BRIAN - Expos - TL - Age 26
The Mets hitters are fairly unanimous in telling me that Barnes is tougher than Chris Nabholz, for comparison to another Expos lefty. Tabbed as a hot prospect, Barnes had a disappointing 1991 then found himself in the minors at the start of 1992. He returned to the Expos in the middle of last season and pitched well. He has good stuff but needs to throw strikes.

	W	SV	ERA	IP	H	BB	SO	BPI	$
1992 Indianapolis AAA	4	0	3.69	83	69	30	77	1.19	
1992 Montreal NL	6	0	2.97	100	77	46	65	1.23	3
1993 Base Case	9	0	3.61	160	128	78	113	1.28	4

BARTON, SHAWN - Mariners - TL - Age 29
Long-time Phillies/Mets farmhand. Reaching the majors in 1992 was his career highlight.

	W	SV	ERA	IP	H	BB	SO	BPI	$
1992 Calgary AAA	3	4	4.25	53	57	24	31	1.53	
1992 Seattle AL	0	0	2.92	12	10	7	4	1.38	-
1993 Base Case	1	0	3.56	22	24	9	11	1.47	-

BATISTA, MIGUEL - Expos - TR - Age 22
Pittsburgh manager Jim Leyland was frosted to find Batista on his roster as a Rule Five pick. It didn't last. Batista is an exciting, hard thrower with poor control.

	W	SV	ERA	IP	H	BB	SO	BPI	$
1992 West Palm Beach A	7	0	3.79	135	130	54	92	1.36	
1992 Pittsburgh NL	0	0	9.00	2	4	3	1	3.50	-
1993 Base Case	2	0	4.96	51	58	27	31	1.54	-

BAUTISTA, JOSE - Royals - TR - Age 28
Pitched for Baltimore, 1988-1991 (career 4.79 ERA). Now just hanging on.

	W	SV	ERA	IP	H	BB	SO	BPI	$
1992 Omaha AAA	2	2	4.90	108	125	28	60	2.82	
1992 Memphis AA	1	0	4.50	6	6	2	7	1.33	

BEASLEY, CHRIS - Angels - TR - Age 30
The Angels are Beasley's third organization. He's a career minor leaguer.

	W	SV	ERA	IP	H	BB	SO	BPI	$
1992 Edmonton AAA	2	3	4.05	33	44	11	28	1.65	

BEATTY, BLAINE - Expos - TL - Age 28
Surfaced with the Mets and did OK in 1989 and 1991, but he's just a lefty journeyman.

	W	SV	ERA	IP	H	BB	SO	BPI	$
1992 Indianapolis AAA	7	0	4.31	94	109	24	54	1.41	

BECK, ROD - Giants - TR - Age 24
Beck is a good example of why you should look at strikeout/walk ratios when fishing for ace relievers. He was superb in the K/BB department in 1991. Roger Craig noticed. Beck has a good fastball, works inside, doesn't waste pitches or try to fool anyone.

	W	SV	ERA	IP	H	BB	SO	BPI	$
1992 San Francisco NL	3	17	1.76	92	62	15	87	0.84	26
1993 Base Case	3	17	2.40	72	54	18	61	1.00	22

BECKETT, ROBBIE - Padres - TL - Age 20
Beckett was the Padres' No. 1 pick in the 1990 draft and is starting to make progress after a disastrous 2-14, 8.23 season at Charleston (A) in 1991. While he led Padre minor leaguers with 147 Ks, he also had 140 walks in 121 IP. Obviously, he can throw hard; when he starts to figure out where it's going, Beckett could be dangerous.

	W	SV	ERA	IP	H	BB	SO	BPI	$
1992 Waterloo A	4	0	4.77	121	77	140	147	1.79	

BELCHER, TIM - Reds - TR - Age 31
Tim Belcher's 1992 record is a lesson in the difference between pitching in Chavez Ravine and Riverfront Stadium. Belcher is a solid #2 starter, and has now made 33 or more starts in 4 of the last 5 years.

	W	SV	ERA	IP	H	BB	SO	BPI	$
1992 Cincinnati NL	15	0	3.91	227	201	80	149	1.23	6
1993 Base Case	15	0	3.53	215	193	74	148	1.24	10

BELINDA, STAN - Pirates - TR - Age 26
Though he had a career-high 18 saves in 1992, he has not developed into the first-rate closer many expected. His inconsistent season came to a brutal close in Game 7 of the National League Championship Series when he blew a 2-0 lead in the ninth inning. That blown save could prove damaging, based on the history of similar cases.

	W	SV	ERA	IP	H	BB	SO	BPI	$
1992 Pittsburgh NL	6	18	3.15	71	58	29	57	1.22	18
1993 Base Case	6	15	3.43	73	56	32	61	1.20	14

BELL, ERIC - Indians - TL - Age 29
Bell's 3.73 ERA for Colorado Springs was good, for the hitting-rich PCL. The Indians' rotation was a mess at the end of 1992, so Bell will be a candidate for a big workload in 1993. You don't want him anyway.

	W	SV	ERA	IP	H	BB	SO	BPI	$
1992 Colo. Sp. AAA	10	1	3.73	139	161	30	56	1.38	
1992 Cleveland AL	0	0	7.36	15	22	9	10	2.02	-
1993 Base Case	2	0	4.99	19	20	9	11	1.48	-

BENES, ANDY - Padres - TR - Age 25
Despite posting solid stats, 1992 was not the expected breakthrough year for Benes. The losing record and the 230 hits were disappointments. As the rotation weakens due to the Padres' financial constraints, Benes will be asked to be the stopper. He has the stuff to respond favorably. Note Benes' history of big second half streaks.

	W	SV	ERA	IP	H	BB	SO	BPI	$
1992 San Diego NL	13	0	3.35	231	230	61	169	1.26	8
1993 Base Case	16	0	3.13	222	206	59	164	1.19	16

BENNETT, ERIK - Angels - TR - Age 24
Bennett has been a success in the lower minors, but still has a lot to prove before pitching in Anaheim.

	W	SV	ERA	IP	H	BB	SO	BPI	$
1992 Quad City A	3	0	2.68	57	46	22	59	1.19	
1992 Palm Sp. A	4	1	3.64	42	27	15	33	1.00	
1992 Midland AA	1	0	3.91	46	47	16	36	1.37	

BERENGUER, JUAN - Royals - TR - Age 38

It's a stretch to imagine Berenguer remaining valuable in 1993. He's been down and up and down repeatedly since 1987.

	W	SV	ERA	IP	H	BB	SO	BPI	$
1992 Two Teams	4	1	5.42	78	77	36	45	1.45	-
1993 Base Case	3	0	4.08	88	79	37	57	1.38	-

BEVIL, BRIAN - Royals - TR - Age 21

Bevil's a hard thrower with a shot at the bigs in 1994-1995.

	W	SV	ERA	IP	H	BB	SO	BPI	$
1992 Appleton A	9	0	3.40	156	129	63	168	1.23	

BIELECKI, MIKE - Braves - TR - Age 33

An injury cut short his successful 1992 season. Bielecki pitched very well but couldn't do what he'd always managed to do before - win. He'll fight for a fifth spot in 1993.

	W	SV	ERA	IP	H	BB	SO	BPI	$
1992 Atlanta NL	2	0	2.57	80	77	27	62	1.29	1
1993 Base Case	6	0	3.55	104	100	34	53	1.29	2

BIRKBECK, MIKE - Mets - TR - Age 32

Symbolic of the Mets' futility in 1992. Birkbeck pitched for the Brewers in the late 1980's, producing a career ERA above 5.00. Steer clear.

	W	SV	ERA	IP	H	BB	SO	BPI	$
1992 New York NL	0	0	9.00	7	12	1	2	1.86	-
1993 Base Case	0	0	5.21	15	21	4	7	1.68	-

BLACK, BUD - Giants - TL - Age 35

Generally a disappointment since coming to SF, Black is still a lefty who can change speeds effectively and move the ball around. Such pitchers usually succeed in the NL.

	W	SV	ERA	IP	H	BB	SO	BPI	$
1992 San Francisco NL	10	0	3.97	177	178	59	82	1.34	0
1993 Base Case	11	0	3.93	193	191	66	91	1.33	1

BLAIR, WILLIE - Rockies - TR - Age 27

Split the season between majors and minors for third straight year. Started eight games for Astros, but only two were good outings. Throws in the low 90's. High risk, borderline major leaguer.

	W	SV	ERA	IP	H	BB	SO	BPI	$
1992 Tucson AAA	4	2	2.39	53	50	12	35	1.17	
1992 Houston NL	5	0	4.00	78	74	25	48	1.26	-
1993 Base Case	9	0	4.35	134	140	42	74	1.35	-

BLYLEVEN, BERT - Angels - TR - Age 41

Blyleven gave the Angels 24 starts after not appearing in 1991. That's the good news. The bad news? His performance. Still, Blyleven will be given an opportunity to go for his 300th victory as an Angel; you don't want to be a part of the history.

	W	SV	ERA	IP	H	BB	SO	BPI	$
1992 California AL	8	0	4.74	133	150	29	70	1.35	-
1993 Base Case	6	0	4.66	96	106	23	48	1.34	-

BODDICKER, MIKE - Royals - TR - Age 35
Boddicker had won at least 10 games in every professional season since 1978, a string broken in 1992. He barely managed one win and was talking retirement. He's not fooling batters anymore with his "fosh" pitch.

	W	SV	ERA	IP	H	BB	SO	BPI	$
1992 Kansas City AL	1	3	4.98	86	92	37	47	1.49	-
1993 Base Case	6	1	4.28	114	120	41	54	1.42	-

BOEVER, JOE - Astros - TR - Age 32
Rubber armed reliever led the league in appearances by pitching in half of Houston's games. Came to spring training 1992 with a minor league contract. Success in 1992 was largely the result of a better mix of fastballs with his forkball/palmball. Former closer had 21 saves for 1989 Braves and could return to that role in the right situation.

	W	SV	ERA	IP	H	BB	SO	BP	$
1992 Houston NL	3	2	2.51	111	103	45	67	1.33	4
1993 Base Case	3	1	3.16	102	95	48	76	1.40	2

BOHANON, BRIAN - Rangers - TL - Age 24
As a #1 pick, he'll get more chances to prove himself, but 1992 was not encouraging. Bohanon failed as a starter and as a reliever. One positive sign was his work at Oklahoma City, but he has not been able to translate AAA success into major league effectiveness. He had surgery in October 1992 in an attempt to locate the cause of pain in his left bicep.

	W	SV	ERA	IP	H	BB	SO	BPI	$
1992 Texas AL	1	0	6.31	45	57	25	29	1.79	-
1992 Okla. City AAA	4	0	2.73	56	53	15	24	1.24	
1993 Base Case	2	0	5.72	61	63	24	37	1.42	-

BOLTON, TOM - Tigers - TL - Age 30
Acquired for Billy Hatcher in mid-summer, Bolton was a major disappointment for the Reds. A lefty curveball pitcher, Bolton was effective when he threw it for strikes, which rarely occured in 1992. Bolton will need a strong spring in 1993 to remain in the majors.

	W	SV	ERA	IP	H	BB	SO	BPI	$
1992 Two Teams	4	0	4.54	75	86	37	50	1.63	-
1993 Base Case	6	0	4.85	104	123	50	58	1.67	-

BONES, RICKY - Brewers - TR - Age 23
Couldn't hold a job in an otherwise solid Brewer rotation, largely because of a lack of concentration that led to blown leads and mid-game explosions. In retrospect, Bones could have used another year in Triple-A, but the Brewers were under pressure to show some return for trading MVP candidate Gary Sheffield. It's unlikely that Bones will ever dominate hitters, because his stuff is not overpowering, but the on-the-job training he received in 1992 probably will make him a credible fourth or fifth starter sometime in the future, if not in 1993.

	W	SV	ERA	IP	H	BB	SO	BPI	$
1992 Milwaukee AL	9	0	4.57	163	169	48	65	1.33	2
1993 Base Case	9	0	4.50	115	121	34	50	1.35	0

BORBON, PEDRO - Braves - TL - Age 26
Pedro, Jr., son of the former Reds pitcher, is a marginal prospect at best. He still walks too many.

	W	SV	ERA	IP	H	BB	SO	BPI	$
1992 Greenville AA	8	3	3.06	94	73	42	79	1.22	
1992 Atlanta NL	0	0	6.75	1	2	1	1	2.25	-
1993 Base Case	0	0	3.41	13	12	5	8	1.33	-

BORLAND, TOBY - Phillies - TR - Age 23
Outstanding performer at A and AA in 1990-1991. Still developing.

	W	SV	ERA	IP	H	BB	SO	BPI	$
1992 Scranton AAA	0	1	7.24	27	25	26	25	1.89	
1992 Reading AA	2	5	3.43	42	39	32	45	1.69	

BOSIO, CHRIS - Mariners - TR - Age 29
Year-in, year-out, one of the 10 best starters in the AL. Unlikely to return to Milwaukee, so watch his new team and park context closely. Bosio's hot temper makes his relationship with his manager crucial. Also, watch his weight. Bosio's mechanics place great stress on his bad knee. One spring training photograph means more than anything you'll see in the box scores.

	W	SV	ERA	IP	H	BB	SO	BPI	$
1992 Milwaukee AL	16	0	3.62	231	223	44	120	1.15	16
1993 Base Case	14	0	3.61	220	205	47	119	1.20	13

BOSKIE, SHAWN - Cubs - TR - Age 26
Even when Boskie pitched well in the minor leagues, his ERA was high. In 1992 he produced only five quality starts in 18 tries, the lowest percentage of any NL starter with at least 10 starts. Still young.

	W	SV	ERA	IP	H	BB	SO	BPI	$
1992 Chicago NL	5	0	5.01	91	96	36	39	1.44	-
1993 Base Case	4	0	5.42	98	112	40	43	1.56	-

BOTTENFIELD, KENT - Expos - TR - Age 24
He made a good first impression in the major leagues last year and should stick as a starting pitcher. He is a workhorse. Writes contemporary Christian music on the side.

	W	SV	ERA	IP	H	BB	SO	BPI	$
1992 Indianapolis AAA	12	0	3.43	152	139	58	111	1.30	
1992 Montreal NL	1	1	2.23	32	26	11	14	1.14	1
1993 Base Case	7	0	3.58	132	127	44	60	1.29	4

BOUCHER, DENIS - Rockies - TL - Age 25
Some observers have likened prospect Denis Boucher to Jimmy Key. Boucher needs pinpoint control to be effective, and thus far, it has eluded him. But he had a very good '92 record with Colorado Springs in the hitting-rich PCL, and he will likely be in the Rockies rotation in '93.

	W	SV	ERA	IP	H	BB	SO	BPI	$
1992 Col. Sp. AAA	11	0	3.48	124	119	30	40	1.20	
1992 Cleveland AL	2	0	6.37	41	48	20	17	1.66	-
1993 Base Case	8	0	4.44	158	161	55	56	1.37	-

BOWEN, RYAN - Marlins - TR - Age 25

Astros' 1986 first round draft choice experienced a nightmare season in 1992. Won six games after a July 1991 callup and was expected to be a part of the rotation in 1992. Struggled in spring training and did even worse when the season started. Poor outings in his first 4 starts earned him a trip to Tucson in May where he stayed until September. Started 5 more games with the Astros in September with similar bad results. Didn't have command of any of his pitches. Still has a fine arm if he can get straightened out.

	W	SV	ERA	IP	H	BB	SO	BPI	$
1992 Tucson AAA	7	0	4.12	122	128	64	94	1.57	
1992 Houston NL	0	0	10.96	33	48	30	22	2.32	-
1993 Base Case	3	0	4.75	76	78	38	51	1.53	-

BRANTLEY, CLIFF - Phillies - TR - Age 24

A former second-round draft choice who has only recently shown promise and who could end up sticking in a middle-relief role. Hard thrower, but needs better location.

	W	SV	ERA	IP	H	BB	SO	BPI	$
1992 Scranton AAA	3	0	1.76	30	19	14	26	1.08	
1992 Philadelphia NL	2	0	4.60	76	71	58	32	1.69	-
1993 Base Case	2	0	4.18	55	48	39	28	1.58	-

BRANTLEY, JEFF - Giants - TR - Age 29

One of the best pitchers in the NL in September. Only question is whether he is a starter or reliever in 1993. And that question depends on who's managing. He will be valuable no matter what the role. Large repertoire would be most useful as a starter.

	W	SV	ERA	IP	H	BB	SO	BPI	$
1992 San Francisco NL	7	7	2.95	91	67	45	86	1.22	10
1993 Base Case	12	4	3.04	133	104	67	124	1.29	11

BRINK, BRAD - Phillies - TR - Age 28

Steady progress up the Phillies minor league ladder, though it took six years. Will have a shot at the fifth starter job, or long relief.

	W	SV	ERA	IP	H	BB	SO	BPI	$
1992 Reading AA	1	0	3.29	13	14	3	12	1.24	
1992 Scranton AAA	8	0	3.48	111	100	34	92	1.20	
1992 Philadelphia NL	0	0	4.14	41	53	13	16	1.60	-
1993 Base Case	1	0	4.09	47	56	13	22	1.41	-

BRISCOE, JOHN - Athletics - TR - Age 25

Oh, those bases on balls! Can't possibly pitch in the majors until he throws strikes.

	W	SV	ERA	IP	H	BB	SO	BPI	$
1992 Tacoma AAA	2	0	5.88	78	78	68	66	1.87	
1992 Oakland AL	0	0	6.43	7	12	9	4	3.00	-

BROCAIL, DOUG - Padres - TR - Age 25

Brocail, at 6'5", 220, was a first-round pick in 1986 and spent three years at Wichita before his 1992 promotions to Las Vegas and San Diego. He is now a modest prospect who could get a starting opportunity at the big league level but would likely produce below-average results.

	W	SV	ERA	IP	H	BB	SO	BPI	$
1992 Las Vegas AAA	10	0	3.97	172	187	63	103	1.45	
1992 San Diego NL	0	0	6.43	14	17	5	15	1.57	-
1993 Base Case	0	0	5.79	17	20	6	16	1.50	-

BRONKEY, JEFF - Rangers - TR - Age 27

Bronkey has had a checkered career in the minors, including an injury-plagued 1991 season. By the end of the 1991 season, he was throwing well again, but at the age of 27 he is a long shot to become an effective pitcher in the majors. His primary asset is a "take-charge" attitude on the mound that characterizes effective relievers. He was added to the 40-man roster following the 1992 season.

	W	SV	ERA	IP	H	BB	SO	BPI	$
1992 Okla. City AAA	0	3	7.47	16.2	26	7	10	1.98	
1992 Tulsa AA	2	13	2.55	71.2	51	25	58	1.07	

BROSS, TERRY- Padres - TR - Age 27

The former Met pitched well in middle relief at Las Vegas and still has a chance to break into the big leagues as the Padres rid themselves of expensive contracts.

	W	SV	ERA	IP	H	BB	SO	BPI	$
1992 Las Vegas AAA	7	0	3.26	86	83	30	42	1.31	

BROWN, KEITH - Reds - TR - Age 29

One year ago, Mo Sanford was the Reds top minor league starter, but when it came time to reach into the farm for help in 1992, Brown was the one selected.

	W	SV	ERA	IP	H	BB	SO	BPI	$
1992 Nashville AAA	12	0	3.61	150	157	43	102	1.33	
1992 Cincinnati NL	0	0	4.50	8	10	5	5	1.87	-
1993 Base Case	1	0	3.86	25	29	12	12	1.60	-

BROWN, J. KEVIN - Rangers - TR - Age 28

He's the "Real McCoy"; 1992 was no fluke. Excellent sinking fastball. At 28, injury and bad luck are the only impediments to duplicating last year's performance. Since Brown is a ground-ball pitcher, any improvement in the infield defense behind him should improve his overall numbers significantly. Look what Pendleton and Bream did for Tom Glavine.

	W	SV	ERA	IP	H	BB	SO	BPI	$
1992 Texas AL	21	0	3.32	265	262	76	173	1.26	17
1993 Base Case	15	0	3.59	238	235	75	138	1.30	11

BROWN, KEVIN D. - Mariners - TL - Age 27

Needs terrific control to be successful; didn't have it in 1992. Caution advised for 1993.

	W	SV	ERA	IP	H	BB	SO	BPI	$
1992 Calgary AAA	6	0	4.84	151	163	64	49	1.50	
1992 Seattle AL	0	0	9.00	3	4	3	2	2.33	-
1993 Base Case	1	0	5.81	28	30	16	14	1.64	-

BROWNING, TOM - Reds - TL - Age 32

Browning's season was ended when he ruptured a knee ligament trying to score a run against Houston. Browning relies on a screwball and perfect location to be effective. Given his performance in 1991 and 1992, and his age, one has to question Browning's ability to come back in 1993.

	W	SV	ERA	IP	H	BB	SO	BPI	$
1992 Cincinnati NL	6	0	5.07	87	108	28	33	1.56	-
1993 Base Case	8	0	4.42	127	140	34	59	1.36	-

BULLINGER, JIM - Cubs - TR - Age 27

A converted SS who finally made it to the majors as a closer. Bullinger recorded five saves in a two week stretch shortly after his promotion. Even after the hot streak, I found him quiet and unassuming, too much so to be an ace reliever. He finished the year with only seven saves and in the starting rotation. His career minor league stats before 1992 were weak. It's hard to get seven saves and have a zero value, but Bullinger did it in 1992.

	W	SV	ERA	IP	H	BB	SO	BPI	$
1992 Iowa AAA	1	14	2.45	22	17	12	15	1.32	
1992 Chicago NL	2	7	4.66	85	72	54	36	1.48	0
1993 Base Case	2	3	4.78	78	69	46	37	1.46	-

BURBA, DAVE - Giants - TR - Age 26

A throw-in in the Kevin Mitchell trade, as if Seattle wasn't giving enough. Burba pitched well for Calgary and Seattle in 1991 but hasn't yet clicked in the NL.

	W	SV	ERA	IP	H	BB	SO	BPI	$
1992 San Francisco NL	2	0	4.97	70	80	31	47	1.57	-
1993 Base Case	2	0	4.42	51	54	21	31	1.49	-

BURKE, JOHN - Rockies - TR - Age 23

Former Denver high school star was Colorado's first-ever draft pick, out of the U. of Florida. Also was Houston's first pick in the '91 draft, but didn't sign.

	W	SV	ERA	IP	H	BB	SO	BPI	$
1992 Bend A	2	0	2.41	41	38	18	32	1.37	

BURKE, TIM - Reds - TR - Age 34

Tim Burke's sinker didn't sink enough in 1992, and he had elbow tendinitis. He has fallen a long way since June 1991 when Tom Runnells handed the Montreal closer job to Barry Jones.

	W	SV	ERA	IP	H	BB	SO	BPI	$
1992 Two Teams	3	0	4.15	43	52	18	15	1.62	-
1993 Base Case	5	2	3.60	75	78	22	36	1.33	4

BURKETT, JOHN - Giants - TR - Age 28

Your basic fastball/curveball pitcher. Burkett is talented enough that he should have one good season in the majors. Soon.

	W	SV	ERA	IP	H	BB	SO	BPI	$
1992 San Francisco NL	13	0	3.84	189	194	45	107	1.26	4
1993 Base Case	13	0	3.94	194	203	50	114	1.30	3

BURLINGAME, DENNIS - Braves - TR - Age 23

Another fine young Braves arm. Burlingame has made consistent minor league progress. Will start the 1993 season at AAA Richmond.

	W	SV	ERA	IP	H	BB	SO	BPI	$
1992 Greenville AA	9	0	3.09	151	137	62	84	1.31	

BURNS, TODD - Rangers - TR - Age 29

Burns revived his flagging career in 1992. He remained injury-free while switching from the rotation to the bullpen. Burns doesn't look impressive; the Texas writers generally laughed at his comeback attempt as a non-roster invitee during spring training 1992. But he gets people out.

	W	SV	ERA	IP	H	BB	SO	BPI	$
1992 Texas AL	3	1	3.84	103	97	32	55	1.28	5
1993 Base Case	2	1	3.60	65	62	22	32	1.30	2

BUTCHER, MIKE - Angels - TR - Age 22

Butcher is a hard-throwing reliever who fared well in a brief appearance in the majors. He should be an integral part of the Angels bullpen in 1993, with Bryan Harvey gone.

	W	S	ERA	IP	H	BB	SO	BPI	$
1992 Edmonton AAA	5	4	3.07	29	24	18	32	1.45	
1992 California AL	2	0	3.25	28	29	13	24	1.52	-
1993 Base Case	3	1	3.42	64	59	30	40	1.39	1

BYRD, PAUL - Indians - TR - Age 22

Byrd had a good year in AA ball last year. He's a good prospect and may be in Cleveland by midseason if the other Tribe starters have problems.

	W	SV	ERA	IP	H	BB	SO	BPI	$
1992 Canton AA	14	0	3.01	152	124	74	118	1.30	

CADARET, GREG - Reds - TL - Age 31

In relief work his ERA has been under 3.00 with the Yankees, but they insist on ruining his full year stats by giving him work as a starter every year. With Norm Charlton gone, the Reds will use Cadaret wisely, and he should have a good comeback year in 1993.

	W	SV	ERA	IP	H	BB	SO	BPI	$
1992 New York AL	4	0	4.25	103	104	74	73	1.71	-
1993 Base Case	5	4	3.76	102	95	45	84	1.37	3

CAMPBELL, KEVIN - Athletics - TR - Age 28

Matured late, after developing a good slider. Was 9-2 with a 1.80 ERA for Tacoma in 1991.

	W	SV	ERA	IP	H	BB	SO	BPI	$
1992 Oakland AL	2	1	5.12	65	66	45	38	1.71	-
1993 Base Case	1	1	4.63	49	46	35	31	1.66	-

CAMPBELL, MIKE - Rangers - TR - Age 29

Failed in three trials with the Mariners, 1987-1989. Really too late now.

	W	SV	ERA	IP	H	BB	SO	BPI	$
1992 Oklahoma City AAA	2	0	5.71	41	43	12	25	1.34	
1992 Texas AL	0	0	9.82	3	3	2	2	1.32	-
1993 Base Case	0	0	5.54	10	10	5	6	1.46	-

CANDELARIA, JOHN - Dodgers - TL - Age 39

Another Dodger free agent, the ageless Candy Man may be retained because the Dodgers have very little lefthanded pen talent. He is still murder on lefties and strikes out almost a batter an inning. Those skills alone should keep Candelaria in baseball in 1993.

	W	SV	ERA	IP	H	BB	SO	BPI	$
1992 Los Angeles AL	2	5	2.84	25	20	13	23	1.30	3
1993 Base Case	2	3	3.20	34	28	15	34	1.28	2

CANDIOTTI, TOM - Dodgers - TR - Age 35

Candiotti battled through some injuries to be the Dodgers' most consistent starter. He benefited from being a knuckleballer in a league which had not seen one for five years. He is reliable for 200-plus innings, double figures in victories and 150-plus Ks.

	W	SV	ERA	IP	H	BB	SO	BPI	$
1992 Los Angeles NL	11	0	3.00	203	177	63	152	1.18	11
1993 Base Case	13	0	3.01	209	181	66	152	1.18	16

CAPEL, MIKE - Astros - TR - Age 31

Veteran reliever spent all season at Tucson and had some success in first opportunity as a closer since 1986. Expansion should provide another chance in the majors. Could be a sleeper in 1993 if he finds work with access to saves.

	W	SV	ERA	IP	H	BB	SO	BPI	$
1992 Tucson AAA	6	18	2.19	82	68	36	70	1.27	

CARLSON, DAN - Giants - TR - Age 23

Texas League All-Star has won 31 games the last two seasons.

	W	S	ERA	IP	H	W	SO	BPI	$
1992 Shreveport AA	15	0	3.19	186	166	60	157	1.22	

CARMAN, DON - Rangers - TL - Age 33

Hasn't been a good pitcher since 1986, but lefties keep getting try-outs. During the mid 1980's I had a young man working for me, who had been a lefty pitcher with the University of Connecticut. Nothing special, he had trouble reaching 70 MPH on the radar gun at a country fair. Nonetheless, every six months or so, someone would call and ask if we would come for a try-out. It went on for years. Probably still going on.

	W	SV	ERA	IP	H	BB	SO	BPI	$
1992 Texas AL	0	0	7.71	2	4	0	2	1.71	-
1993 Base Case	0	0	5.53	16	19	8	8	1.65	-

CARPENTER, CRIS - Marlins - TR - Age 27

Though he had his best season in 1992, he has never come close to reaching the expectations placed on him when St. Louis selected him in the first round of the 1987 draft. He has finally gained some consistency in the majors but he's a long way from stardom. One big plus for 1993 is the depth of the Florida middle relief corps. Carpenter should be used wisely and not overworked.

	W	SV	ERA	IP	H	BB	SO	BPI	$
1992 St. Louis NL	5	1	2.97	88	69	27	46	1.09	5
1993 Base Case	7	0	3.57	77	64	24	45	1.15	4

CARTER, LARRY - Giants -TR - Age 27

Carter's presence in SF was just an experiment, not a reward or legitimate promotion. The trial isn't likely to lead to a major league job in 1993.

	W	SV	ERA	IP	H	BB	SO	BPI	$
1992 Phoenix AAA	11	0	4.37	185	188	62	126	1.35	
1992 San Francisco NL	1	0	4.64	33	34	18	21	1.58	-
1993 Base Case	1	0	4.73	31	30	16	18	1.50	-

CARY, CHUCK - Japan - TL - Age 33

Cary had some success with the Yankees in 1989 after developing a screwball during the preceding winter. But he developed bone chips in 1990 and faded. He is still the type of crafty lefty who can resurface at any time and be effective if used in the right situations.

CASIAN, LARRY - Twins - TL - Age 27

If he makes the Twins roster, Casian will be a lefty setup man. But Gary Wayne and Mark Guthrie were doing very well as the lefty setup men, so Casian may see more AAA action in '93.

	W	SV	ERA	IP	H	BB	SO	BPI	$
1992 Portland AAA	4	11	2.32	62	54	13	43	1.08	
1992 Minnesota AL	1	0	2.70	7	7	1	2	1.20	0
1993 Base Case	1	0	5.40	13	17	4	4	1.61	-

CASTILLO, FRANK - Cubs - TR - Age 24

The fomer Cubs top pitching prospect was 10-1 with a 2.29 ERA in 1987 and 6-1 with a 0.71 ERA in 1988 (at ages 18 and 19, respectively). His earned run average had increased each year as he was promoted, but he stopped the trend and dropped his major league ERA from 1991 to 1992. Two-thirds of his games were quality starts last year and he should improve with age.

	W	SV	ERA	IP	H	BB	SO	BPI	$
1992 Chicago NL	10	0	3.46	205	179	63	135	1.18	8
1993 Base Case	11	0	3.67	166	150	50	108	1.20	7

CASTILLO, TONY - Tigers - TL - Age 30

Bounced around the majors with the Blue Jays, Braves, and Mets in 1988-1991. Now just another lefty stored on the farm.

	W	SV	ERA	IP	H	BB	SO	BPI	$
1992 Toledo AAA	2	2	3.63	44	48	14	24	1.39	

CERUTTI, JOHN - Unsigned - TL - Age 32

Good pitcher back in 1989. Last up with Tigers in 1991. Soft thrower.

	W	SV	ERA	IP	H	BB	SO	BPI	$
1992 Pawtucket AAA	7	0	4.63	105	128	23	43	1.44	
1992 Buffalo AAA	4	0	5.36	45	53	7	13	1.32	

CHAPIN, DARRIN - Phillies - TR - Age 27

Had a big year as a co-closer for AAA Columbus in 1991, but got just four saves with a 5.11 ERA for Scranton last year.

	W	SV	ERA	IP	H	BB	SO	BPI	$
1992 Philadelphia NL	0	0	9.00	2	2	0	1	1.00	-
1993 Base Case	1	0	4.09	18	17	7	12	1.39	-

CHARLTON, NORM - Mariners - TL - Age 30

A fastball/forkball pitcher, Charlton benefited from Rob Dibble's spring training tendinitis to grab a share of the closer role. Charlton was shut down in September (shoulder tendinitis). If Charlton is healthy and effective, he could be a thirty-save gem. Even if he struggles, and shares the closer role with a righty, Seattle will still try to make Charlton look valuable -- which is exactly what you want in a pen man.

	W	SV	ERA	IP	H	BB	SO	BPI	$
1992 Cincinnati NL	4	26	2.99	81	79	26	90	1.29	23
1993 Base Case	3	19	3.25	87	81	28	78	1.25	20

CHIAMPARINO, SCOTT - Marlins - TR - Age 26

The Rangers now have nothing remaining from the Harold Baines trading debacle of 1990. Major elbow surgery in '91, but recovery looks promising. Got back to majors last year, but was not at full strength.

	W	SV	ERA	IP	H	BB	SO	BPI	$
1992 Texas AL	0	0	3.55	25	25	5	13	1.18	1
1993 Base Case	8	0	3.70	146	152	44	68	1.34	1

CHITREN, STEVE - Athletics - TR - Age 25
Formerly "the next Dennis Eckersley." Now hoping to be the next Todd Burns.

	W	SV	ERA	IP	H	BB	SO	BPI	$
1992 Tacoma AAA	4	0	6.82	62	64	46	37	1.77	

CHOUINARD, BOB - Orioles - TR - Age 20
Chouinard led the Midwest League in ERA and had 10 complete games. He will not be a candidate for major league time for at least a year or two.

	W	SV	ERA	IP	H	BB	SO	BPI	$
1992 Kane County A	10	0	2.08	182	152	38	112	1.04	

CHRISTOPHER, MIKE - Indians - TR - Age 29
With Cleveland's solid bullpen and prospects Mike Soper and Bill Wertz knocking on the door, Christopher has an uphill battle earning a roster spot. If he does make it, his roles will be middle reliever and setup man.

	W	SV	ERA	IP	H	BB	SO	BPI	$
1992 Colo. Sp. AAA	4	26	2.91	59	59	13	39	1.23	
1992 Cleveland AL	0	0	3.00	18	17	10	13	1.50	-
1993 Base Case	2	0	3.66	64	66	21	43	1.36	-

CLARK, DERA - Royals - TR - Age 27
Pitched at three levels during 1992. Has a 4.00 career minor league ERA.

CLARK, MARK - Cardinals - TR - Age 24
Many scouts feel he has the stuff to be a staff ace someday. Threw extremely well at times as a rookie in 1992 but was awful in other starts. One bad inning hurts him in many games. If he's on your roster, don't watch the games; it could harm your nerves.

	W	SV	ERA	IP	H	BB	SO	BPI	$
1992 Louisville AAA	4	0	2.80	61	56	15	38	1.16	
1992 St. Louis NL	3	0	4.45	113	117	36	44	1.35	-
1993 Base Case	6	0	4.34	158	160	56	66	1.36	1

CLEMENS, ROGER - Red Sox - TR - Age 30
There was talk of trading Clemens to Texas. Not likely to happen, but for grins, consider that Fenway is considered to be the worst park in which to pitch so, if he is anywhere else it should only help him, as if he needs help. He could retire right now and he'd be in the Hall of Fame in five years.

	W	SV	ERA	IP	H	BB	SO	BPI	$
1992 Boston AL	18	0	2.41	246	203	62	208	1.07	30
1993 Base Case	19	0	2.53	249	207	61	215	1.08	30

CLEMENTS, PAT - Orioles - TL - Age 31
Clements came to Baltimore on waivers from the Padres and was a garden variety lefty reliever. If Poole returns to health and Pennington gets a chance with the major league club, Clements will be out of a job, at least in Baltimore.

	W	SV	ERA	IP	H	BB	SO	BPI	$
1992 San Diego NL	2	0	2.66	24	25	12	11	1.56	-
1992 Baltimore AL	2	0	3.28	24	23	11	9	1.38	-
1993 Base Case	4	0	3.67	44	44	22	19	1.49	-

COLE, VICTOR - Pirates - TR - Age 25

Cole was ineffective in the major leagues last season. He made four starts and tired in all of them once he got to the fifth inning. First big leaguer from Russia in 60 years.

	W	SV	ERA	IP	H	BB	SO	BPI	$
1992 Buffalo AAA	11	0	3.11	116	102	61	69	1.41	
1992 Pittsburgh NL	0	0	5.48	23	23	14	12	1.61	-
1993 Base Case	0	0	5.01	28	28	20	18	1.70	-

COMBS, PAT - Phillies - TL - Age 26

Elbow problems and lack of overall development as a pitcher have set back this former first-round draft pick who was once among the NL's top pitching prospects.

	W	SV	ERA	IP	H	BB	SO	BPI	$
1992 Philadelphia NL	1	0	7.71	18	20	12	11	1.71	-
1993 Base Case	2	0	4.87	41	42	21	25	1.54	-

COMPRES, FIDEL - Cardinals - TR - Age 27

Career minor leaguer, he's been waiting for nine years.

	W	SV	ERA	IP	H	BB	SO	BPI	$
1992 Arkansas AA	4	28	3.28	57	55	23	39	1.35	

CONE, DAVID - Royals - TR - Age 30

When Cone is on a streak, he's as tough as any pitcher ever. He has a career ERA of 4.01 for the month of April, which often creates opportunities in leagues where people get nervous about lousy pitching stats early in the season, so be alert.

	W	SV	ERA	IP	H	BB	SO	BPI	$
1992 New York NL	13	0	2.88	196	162	82	214	1.24	10
1992 Toronto AL	4	0	2.55	53	39	29	47	1.28	3
1993 Base Case	16	0	3.21	236	199	96	244	125	17

CONVERSE, JIM - Mariners - TR - Age 21

A rarity: a 5'9" league strikeout leader. Has a good fastball and slider. Seattle's 16th-round pick in '90.

	W	SV	ERA	IP	H	BB	SO	BPI	$
1992 Jacksonville AA	12	0	2.66	159	134	82	157	1.36	

COOK, DENNIS - Indians - TL - Age 30

Two factors helped Cook in 1992. He developed a new pitch, a third type of sinker to go with his slider and forkball. And the Indians gave Cook great run support in '92, about six runs per game. At his best, Cook draws comparisons to Chuck Finley. At his worst, Charles O. Finley.

	W	SV	ERA	IP	H	BB	SO	BPI	$
1992 Cleveland AL	5	0	3.82	158	156	50	96	1.30	4
1993 Base Case	10	0	3.73	160	154	53	88	1.29	6

COOKE, STEVE - Pirates - TL - Age 23

He made a quick leap to the major leagues, going from a short-season Class A league to the Pirates in two years. Most of Cooke's experience has come as a starting pitcher but he was effective in the bullpen after his promotion to Pittsburgh last season.

	W	SV	ERA	IP	H	BB	SO	BPI	$
1992 Carolina AA	2	0	3.00	36	31	12	38	1.19	
1992 Buffalo AAA	6	0	3.75	74	71	36	52	1.45	
1992 Pittsburgh NL	2	1	3.52	23	22	4	10	1.13	0
1993 Base Case	2	1	3.69	28	28	8	14	1.27	0

CORBIN, ARCHIE - Expos - TR - Age 25
Maybe just a slow developer. Spent three years in Rookie ball, two years in A-ball, and now two in Double-A. Should reach the majors in 1995 at that rate. Actually, he surfaced with the Royals for two innings in 1991, and could reappear in the majors any time.

	W	SV	ERA	IP	H	BB	SO	BPI	$
1992 Memphis AA	7	0	4.73	112	115	72	100	1.66	
1992 Harrisburg AA	0	0	0.00	3	2	1	3	1.00	

CORMIER, RHEAL - Cardinals - TL - Age 25
The little left-hander finally showed his promise in the second half of last season when he reeled off a six-game winning streak. He started the season 0-5 and came very close to going back to the minors. The New Brunswick native pitched for Canada in the 1988 Olympics and used to work as a lumberjack in the offseason. Great pick to be undervalued in 1993.

	W	SV	ERA	IP	H	BB	SO	BPI	$
1992 Louisville AAA	0	0	6.75	4	8	0	1	2.00	
1992 St. Louis NL	10	0	3.68	186	194	33	117	1.20	5
1993 Base Case	12	0	3.54	141	146	22	86	1.18	8

CORSI, JIM - Marlins - TR - Age 31
Can still throw in the high 80's. I like the depth in the Florida middle relief corps, because it means everyone will be used in just the right situations.

	W	SV	ERA	IP	H	BB	SO	BPI	$
1992 Oakland AL	4	0	1.43	44	44	18	19	1.41	2
1993 Base Case	3	3	2.85	66	66	24	36	1.35	3

COSTELLO, JOHN - Unsigned - TR - Age 32
Good pitcher with the Cardinals in 1988-1989, and had a fair year with the Padres in 1991. Now done.

	W	SV	ERA	IP	H	BB	SO	BPI	$
1992 Calgary A	0	0	13.50	5	11	2	0	2.44	

COURTRIGHT, JOHN - Reds - TL - Age 22
A 1991 8th round draft pick, Courtright allowed only 7.6 Hits per 9 IP and struck out 147 in 173.0 IP at AA Charleston.

	W	SV	ERA	IP	H	BB	SO	BPI	$
1992 Charleston A	10	0	2.50	173	147	55	147	1.17	

COX, DANNY - Blue Jays - TR - Age 33
His comeback stalled then took on new life last season. Cox, who did not pitch in the majors in 1989-90 after undergoing reconstructive elbow surgery, struggled in the Phillies' rotation and was released when he refused a minor-league assignment. He resurfaced in Pittsburgh in late August and gave the shaky Pirates' bullpen a boost down the stretch, notching his first three career saves.

	W	SV	ERA	IP	H	BB	SO	BPI	$
1992 Buffalo AAA	1	0	1.70	42	28	18	30	1.10	
1992 Two Teams	5	3	4.60	62	66	27	48	1.48	-
1993 Base Case	5	2	4.16	76	74	30	45	1.36	0

CREWS, TIM - Dodgers - TR - Age 31
Just about the only Dodger pitcher you don't want.

	W	SV	ERA	IP	H	BB	SO	BPI	$
1992 Los Angeles NL	0	0	5.19	78	95	20	43	1.47	-
1993 Base Case	1	2	4.53	75	84	18	46	1.37	-

CRIM, CHUCK - Angels - TR - Age 31
Crim led the Angels' staff in games but was unable to regain the form he displayed in Milwaukee through 1990. His career shows signs of a permanent downward trend.

	W	SV	ERA	IP	H	BB	SO	BPI	$
1992 California AL	7	1	5.17	87	100	29	30	1.48	-
1993 Base Case	8	2	4.60	86	99	26	31	1.45	0

CROSS, JESSE - Blue Jays - TR - Age 25
Solid progress through minors. Drafted by Twins last year, but returned to Toronto.

	W	SV	ERA	IP	H	BB	SO	BPI	$
1992 Syracuse AAA	0	0	9.45	6	11	3	3	2.10	
1992 Knoxville AA	8	0	3.45	147	136	44	126	1.22	

CUMMINGS, STEVE - Tigers - TR - Age 28
A second round pick in 1986, Cummings went downhill after the Blue Jays traded him away in 1990.

	W	SV	ERA	IP	H	BB	SO	BPI	$
1992 Toledo AAA	0	0	8.10	20	26	8	6	1.70	

DALTON, MIKE - Pirates - TL - Age 30
Good minor league career but never found a role in the majors. In a Leyland pen, everyone gets used perfectly, so he's OK if he surfaces in Pittsburgh in 1993.

	W	SV	ERA	IP	H	BB	SO	BPI	$
1992 Buffalo AAA	3	10	3.66	71	56	18	25	1.04	

DARLING, RON - Athletics - TR - Age 32
Classic case of Oakland revival: healthy pitcher with history of major league success finds himself again with help from Dave Duncan and Tony LaRussa. Good, cheap pick for 1993.

	W	SV	ERA	IP	H	BB	SO	BPI	$
1992 Oakland AL	15	0	3.66	206	198	72	99	1.31	10
1993 Base Case	12	0	3.74	200	191	70	110	1.31	7

DARWIN, DANNY - Red Sox - TR - Age 37
He's getting a bit creaky to expect much. In the Astrodome, he was a valuable Rotisserie pitcher. In Fenway, he's dangerous.

	W	SV	ERA	IP	H	BB	SO	BPI	$
1992 Boston AL	9	3	3.96	161	159	53	124	1.31	7
1993 Base Case	6	1	4.06	135	132	42	99	1.29	3

DAVIS, MARK - Braves - TL - Age 32
The Cy Young guy, who stopped throwing strikes inexplicably. Still has good stuff, incredibly. For the Braves he was striking out a hitter per inning.

	W	SV	ERA	IP	H	BB	SO	BPI	$
1992 Kansas City AL	1	0	7.18	36	42	28	19	1.93	-
1993 Atlanta NL	1	0	7.02	16	22	13	15	2.10	-
1993 Base Case	4	2	4.43	65	64	30	47	1.44	-

DAVIS, RAY - Cardinals - TR - Age 20

Only a 61st-round draft pick in 1991, Davis came on strong at the end of the Arizona Rookie League season in 1992. He threw four shutouts in his last six starts and missed a fifth because of an error. Ranked fifth-best prospect in a league in poll of league managers by Baseball America.

	W	SV	ERA	IP	H	BB	SO	BPI	$
1992 Chandler R	5	0	2.49	76	57	22	74	1.03	

DAVIS, STORM - Athletics - TR - Age 31

Davis became an effective pitcher in middle relief. He found enough comfort in the role that he resisted opportunities to go into the starting rotation. Nagging leg injuries affected his September performance (5.23, ratio of 1.45), but his fastball looked good all year. Expect a similar role in 1992.

	W	SV	ERA	IP	H	BB	SO	BPI	$
1992 Baltimore AL	7	4	3.43	89	79	36	53	1.28	2
1993 Base Case	6	3	4.24	95	102	39	54	1.48	0

DAYLEY, KEN - Blue Jays - TL - Age 34

Former top setup man for St. Louis, still recovering from 1992 surgery

	W	SV	ERA	IP	H	BB	SO	BPI	$
1992 Syracuse AAA	0	0	17.18	3	3	6	4	2.45	

DEJESUS, JOSE - Phillies - TR - Age 28

Had a 100 MPH fastball that attracted a small crowd in the bullpen when he first arrived at Phillies camp in 1990. Now trying to come back from a sore arm.

DELEON, JOSE - Phillies - TR - Age 32

An enigma in three previous organizations, the Phillies picked DeLeon off the scrap heap in hopes that he can finally become a winner. Has excellent stuff and a career W/L record 30 games under .500.

	W	SV	ERA	IP	H	BB	SO	BPI	$
1992 Philadelphia NL	2	0	4.37	117	111	48	79	1.36	-
1993 Base Case	3	0	3.57	127	116	52	89	1.32	1

DELUCIA, RICH - Mariners - TR - Age 28

In 1990, he had an ERA of 2.11 at AA. His ERA of 5.09 in 1991 and 7.09 in the first half of last year mean he is not ready to be a major league starter. In the second half of last year, he was moved to the bullpen and posted a respectable 3.55 ERA. If he stays out of the rotation, his minor league numbers suggest success.

	W	SV	ERA	IP	H	BB	SO	BPI	$
1992 Seattle AL	3	1	5.49	83	100	35	66	1.61	1
1993 Base Case	8	1	4.66	118	121	51	76	1.46	-

DESHAIES, JIM - Twins - TL - Age 32

Despite a 4-7 record, DeShaies re-established his career when he pitched effectively in 15 late-season starts after two poor seasons in Houston. However, don't forget that he is only one year removed from a season in which he won only 5 games with an ERA of nearly 5.00.

	W	SV	ERA	IP	H	BB	SO	BPI	$
1992 Las Vegas AAA	6	1	4.03	58	60	17	46	1.33	
1992 San Diego NL	4	0	3.28	96	92	33	46	1.30	0
1993 Base Case	5	0	3.89	139	135	49	73	1.32	0

DESILVA, JOHN - Tigers - TR - Age 25
Good Double-A performance in 1991 (2.81 ERA) but no big progress since then.

	W	SV	ERA	IP	H	BB	SO	BPI	$
1992 Toledo AAA	0	0	8.53	19	26	8	21	1.79	
1992 London AA	2	0	4.13	52	51	13	53	1.22	

DEWEY, MARK - Mets - TR - Age 28
Decent reliever with the Giants in 1990, and a good performer at AAA Tidewater in 1991, but Dewey's performance dipped last year despite making it back to the majors. Doesn't look good for 1993.

	W	SV	ERA	IP	H	BB	SO	BPI	$
1992 New York NL	1	0	4.32	33	37	10	24	1.41	-
1993 Base Case	1	0	4.32	37	43	12	27	1.45	-

DIBBLE, ROB - Reds - TR - Age 29
Pre-season tendinitis, a slow start, a couple of blown saves, and the "fight" with Lou Piniella left the impression that Rob Dibble had an off-year. An opponent BA of .193 and 14.1 K's per 9 innings (extending his own all-time record of last year) suggest otherwise. The tussle with Piniella and its aftermath were completely overblown by the press. New GM Jim Bowden says that Dibble will be the sole closer in 1993.

	W	SV	ERA	IP	H	BB	SO	BPI	$
1992 Cincinnati NL	3	25	3.07	70	48	31	110	1.12	24
1993 Base Case	4	32	2.84	75	53	26	119	1.07	30

DICKSON, LANCE - Cubs - TL - Age 23
In 1990, he combined for a 7-3 record and a 0.94 ERA in his first year out of the University of Arizona. He was 4-4 with a 3.11 ERA at Triple A in 1991. He missed almost all of last year due to a foot injury. He is still considered one of the top pitching prospects in the NL but may not be ready until the latter half of 1993.

	W	SV	ERA	IP	H	BB	SO	BPI	$
1992 Iowa AAA	0	0	19.29	2	6	2	2	3.43	

DIPINO, FRANK - Cardinals - TL - Age 36
Like many other Cardinals' pitchers recently, DiPino has battled back from arm problems. Missed a season-and-a-half with an elbow injury, before making nine major-league relief appearances in September. He threw well, though. He is the answer to a trivia as he was the winning pitcher in the first night game at Wrigley Field.

	W	SV	ERA	IP	H	BB	SO	BPI	$
1992 Louisville AAA	0	0	3.97	23	28	8	10	1.57	
1992 St. Louis NL	0	0	1.64	11	9	3	8	1.09	-
1993 Base Case	0	0	3.00	12	11	4	8	1.20	-

DIPOTO, GERRY - Indians- TR - Age 24
Although the PCL tends to inflate pitchers' stats, Dipoto's are in the stratosphere.

	W	SV	ERA	IP	H	BB	SO	BPI	$
1992 Colo. Sp. AAA	9	2	4.94	122	148	66	62	1.75	

DOHERTY, JOHN -Tigers - TR - Age 25
One of the problems of pitching for a team with a weak starting rotation: good relievers often get pressed into starter duty. Doherty had a few good outings, and should be worth something in 1993.

	W	SV	ERA	IP	H	BB	SO	BPI	$
1992 Detroit AL	7	3	3.88	116	131	25	37	1,34	5
1993 Base Case	5	2	3.80	76	87	15	24	1.35	2

DOPSON, JOHN - Red Sox - TR - Age 29

Classic example proving the rule: avoid Red Sox starters. You can find a few cheap wins on other AL teams with a much lower downside risk than Dopson and friends.

	W	SV	ERA	IP	H	BB	SO	BPI	$
1992 Boston AL	7	0	4.08	141	159	38	55	1.39	1
1993 Base Case	7	0	4.03	152	161	49	60	1.38	1

DOWNS, KELLY - Athletics - TR - Age 32

Still coming back from rotator cuff surgery two years ago. Knows how to pitch; and if he pitches badly he won't be used much. Safer than many young pitchers who have higher potential.

	W	SV	ERA	IP	H	BB	SO	BPI	$
1992 Oakland AL	5	0	3.29	82	72	46	38	1.44	0
1992 San Francisco NL	1	0	3.47	62	65	24	33	1.43	-
1993 Base Case	8	0	3.69	132	120	59	67	1.36	3

DRABEK, DOUG - Astros - TR - Age 30

Without fanfare, he is one of the game's best starting pitchers. In the same workmanlike way he attacks hitters, throwing four pitches for strikes, he consistently puts up good numbers. He has a string of five straight winning seasons, posting at least 14 in each of them. Reminds me of Catfish Hunter.

	W	SV	ERA	IP	H	BB	SO	BPI	$
1992 Pittsburgh NL	15	0	2.77	256	218	54	177	1.06	22
1993 Base Case	16	0	2.89	243	226	57	158	1.16	22

DRAHMAN, BRIAN - White Sox - TR - Age 26

A closer-in-waiting in the ChiSox farm system for seven years, Drahman finally became a true ace for Vancouver in 1992. Has good major league possibilities, but he is blocked by Roberto Hernandez and Scott Radinsky in Chicago, and his control still poses a question.

	W	SV	ERA	IP	H	BB	SO	BPI	$
1992 Vancouver AAA	2	30	2.01	58	44	31	34	1.29	
1992 Chicago AL	0	0	2.57	7	6	2	1	1.14	-
1993 Base Case	2	0	3.32	36	28	18	16	1.28	1

DRAPER, MIKE - Yankees - TR - Age 26

Won 11 or more games three years in a row as a starter, then was moved to the bullpen. Demolished the International League saves record, and set a Triple-A mark. Unfortunately for Draper, the Yankees have enough second-tier bullpen arms.

	W	SV	ERA	IP	H	BB	SO	BPI	$
1992 Columbus AAA	5	37	3.60	80	70	28	42	1.23	

DREES, TOM - Mariners - TL - Age 29

Long time White Sox prospect. Never made it. Not likely to reach a new high level in 1993.

	W	SV	ERA	IP	H	BB	SO	BPI	$
1992 Oklahoma City AAA	2	0	5.20	36	43	13	22	1.54	
1992 Calgary AAA	7	0	5.18	92	108	37	38	1.58	

DRESSENDORFER, KIRK - Athletics - TR - Age 23

First round pick in 1990. Made it to the A's in 1991, but ended his season with shoulder surgery. He was supposed to be ready for spring training 1992, but is, shall we say, behind schedule. If you want farm system picks, take some nice speedy outfielders, and leave the pitchers to your oopenents.

DUNNE, MIKE - White Sox - TR - Age 30

Yes, it's the same guy -- the rookie pitcher of the year from 1987. He didn't have a good year after that, and is just barely knocking on the door for 1993.

	W	SV	ERA	IP	H	BB	SO	BPI	$
1992 Vancouver AAA	10	0	2.78	133	128	46	78	1.31	
1992 Chicago AL	2	0	4.26	12	12	6	6	1.42	-
1993 Base Case	2	0	4.23	29	28	14	13	1.45	-

ECKERSLEY, DENNIS - Athletics - TR - Age 38

MVP, Cy Young. Good strikeout/walk ratio.

	W	SV	ERA	IP	H	BB	SO	BPI	$
1992 Oakland AL	7	51	1.91	80	62	11	93	0.91	49
1993 Base Case	7	40	2.38	77	60	10	89	0.91	44

EDDY, CHRIS - Royals - TL - Age 23

Lefty Eddy throws very hard and had some success as a relief ace in his first professional season. When he learns to get control of more than his fastball, he'll move up quickly. Look for a 1995 arrival.

	W	SV	ERA	IP	H	BB	SO	BPI	$
1992 Eugene A	4	5	1.59	45	25	23	63	1.06	

EDENS, TOM - Astros - TR - Age 31

Edens is a middle reliever who had his career-best year in 1992, after starting the season with a 4.50 career ERA. All he needed was a better changeup.

	W	SV	ERA	IP	H	BB	SO	BPI	$
1992 Minnesota AL	6	3	2.83	76	65	36	57	1.32	5
1993 Base Case	4	2	3.54	56	53	26	40	1.41	0

EDWARDS, WAYNE - White Sox - TL - Age 29

Long groomed to be a starter, Edwards finally found a major league role in 1990 as a lefty versus lefty relief specialist. But he slipped in 1991 and was still trying to get back a similar job last year. He is not a major talent.

	W	SV	ERA	IP	H	BB	SO	BPI	$
1992 Syracuse AAA	4	3	4.48	130	127	76	108	1.55	

EGLOFF, BRUCE - Indians - TR - Age 27

Was supposed to be the heir to Doug Jones' role, but he ran into a couple of rotator cuff operations and a broken hand along the way.

EICHHORN, MARK - Blue Jays - TR - Age 32

"I throw doo-doo," says Eichhorn. Right. But everyone has had trouble hitting it, up until late 1992 that is. Although Eichhorn had a good year overall in 1992, he was a disappointment to the Jays, who let him go after the season ended.

	W	SV	ERA	IP	H	BB	SO	BPI	$
1992 Two Teams AL	4	2	3.08	87	86	25	61	1.27	6
1993 Base Case	4	2	2.88	83	79	20	55	1.20	7

EILAND, DAVE - Padres - TR - Age 26
Eiland is one of those pitchers that can hurt a Rotisserie team: can get lots of innings, while pitching badly. Avoid him.

	W	SV	ERA	IP	H	BB	SO	BPI	$
1992 San Diego NL	0	0	5.67	27	33	5	10	1.41	-
1993 Base Case	1	0	5.47	51	61	13	15	1.47	-

ELDRED, CAL - Brewers - TR - Age 25
Prorate these stats and you get Dwight Gooden, 1984. (Before one late-September pounding, it was Bob Gibson, 1968.) Such comparisons are unrealistic, but Mike Mussina 1992 is not out of reach. Eldred has a good curve and good control. He did not lose effectiveness the second time around the league, and he kept his composure as a rookie starter in a pennant race. Trouble is, none of this is a secret, so everyone in your league will know who Eldred is, and he is therefore unlikely to be a bargain, if he's available at all.

	W	SV	ERA	IP	H	BB	SO	BPI	$
1992 Denver AAA	10	0	3.00	141	122	42	99	1.16	
1992 Milwaukee AL	11	0	1.79	100	76	23	62	0.99	14
1993 Base Case	14	0	3.01	165	143	44	102	1.14	17

ELLIOTT, DON - Braves - TR - Age 24
Such a good prospect, three organizations wanted him during 1992 (Mariners drafted and returned him).

	W	SV	ERA	IP	H	BB	SO	BPI	$
1992 Clearwater A	1	0	3.00	18	12	8	12	1.11	
1992 Reading AA	3	0	2.52	35	37	11	23	1.34	
1992 Greenville AA	7	0	2.08	103	76	35	100	1.07	

ELVIRA, NARCISO - Rangers - TL - Age 25
Mexican League veteran. Surfaced with the Brewers in 1990. Still a prospect.

	W	SV	ERA	IP	H	BB	SO	BPI	$
1992 Oklahoma City AAA	4	0	4.97	88	87	28	45	1.30	

EMBREE, ALAN - Indians - TL - Age 22
Beginning the '92 season at Class A Kinston, talented flame thrower Alan Embree's career made major jumps all the way to Cleveland where he made his major league debut starting against Toronto. He was shaky against the Blue Jays, but has a great future. Because he may not get as much publicity as Sam Militello, Bob Wickman, etc., Embree will be a good sleeper pick in many leagues.

	W	SV	ERA	IP	H	BB	SO	BPI	$
1992 Kinston A	10	0	3.30	101	89	32	115	1.20	
1992 Canton AA	7	0	2.28	79	61	28	56	1.13	
1992 Cleveland AL	0	0	7.00	18	19	8	12	1.50	-
1993 Base Case	10	0	4.05	122	111	55	92	1.36	2

ERB, MIKE - Mariners - TR - Age 27
Long-time Angels farmhand, never made it to California. No value.

	W	SV	ERA	IP	H	BB	SO	BPI	$
1992 Edmonton AAA	0	5	27.00	2	6	6	3	5.15	
1992 Jacksonville AA	0	0	10.38	4	12	1	2	3.00	

ERICKS, JOHN - Cardinals - TR - Age 25
Very hard thrower. Went from being a first pick in 1988 to being released in 1992.

	W	SV	ERA	IP	H	BB	SO	BPI	$
1992 Arkansas AA	2	0	4.08	75	69	29	71	1.31	

ERICKSON, SCOTT - Twins - TR - Age 25
Erickson successfully altered his pitching style in '92 resulting in an very good second half: 2.92 ERA and a 1.215 ratio in 110 innings. He should continue to be effective in '93. Still young, still learning.

	W	SV	ERA	IP	H	BB	SO	BPI	$
1992 Minnesota AL	13	0	3.40	212	197	83	101	1.32	10
1993 Base Case	15	0	3.38	200	192	78	106	1.35	9

ERWIN, SCOTT - Athletics - TR - Age 25
Fifth round pick, he's been held back by injuries.

	W	SV	ERA	IP	H	BB	SO	BPI	$
1992 Huntsville AA	3	1	3.28	35	25	27	39	1.46	

ESTES, SHAWN - Mariners - TL - Age 20
Seattle's No. 1 draft pick in '91, out of high school. In his second year at Bellingham, the hard thrower cut his walks considerably, from 14.6 to 5.2 per nine innings.

	W	S	ERA	IP	H	BB	SO	BPI	$
1992 Bellingham A	3	0	4.32	77	84	45	77	1.68	

> *"Natural grass is a wonderful thing --*
> *for little bugs and sinkerball pitchers."*
>
> *-- Dan Quisenberry*

FAJARDO, HECTOR - Rangers - TR - Age 22

After starting five games in the majors in 1991 (and becoming the youngest pitcher since Steve Avery to do so), Fajardo spent the entire 1992 season battling injuries in the minors. Texas called him up to the major league roster in September, but allowed him to return home when his house was burglarized. Although he ended the season with a clean bill of health, he had more pain in winter ball (November 1992) and was clocked with a fastball under 80 MPH. Big talent. Big problems.

	W	SV	ERA	IP	H	BB	SO	BPI	$
1992 Okla. City AAA	1	0	0.00	7	8	2	6	1.43	
1992 Tulsa AA	2	0	2.16	25	19	7	26	1.04	
1992 Charlotte A	2	0	2.78	23	22	8	12	1.30	
1992 Rangers R	0	0	5.68	6	5	2	9	1.17	
1993 Base Case	4	0	4.15	60	56	27	44	1.38	2

FARMER, HOWARD - Expos - TR - Age 27

Six-year Expos farmhand, he surfaced in Montreal in 1990, did poorly in four starts, and has been essentially the same pitcher ever since, although he works out of the pen more now.

	W	SV	ERA	IP	H	BB	SO	BPI	$
1992 Indianapolis AAA	3	0	3.75	84	89	24	64	1.35	

FARR, STEVE - Yankees - TR - Age 36

Farr went on the DL with a sore back in 1992, but came back stronger than ever late in the season. He pitches best when he pitches frequently; when the Yankees created enough save opportunities he became very sharp.

	W	SV	ERA	IP	H	BB	SO	BPI	$
1992 New York AL	2	30	1.56	52	34	19	37	1.02	27
1993 Base Case	4	28	2.27	49	43	22	45	1.09	26

FARRELL, JOHN - Angels - TR - Age 30

Farrell has not pitched in the majors since September 1990 when he required elbow surgery. After rehabilitation, he tore an elbow ligament again and required the "Tommy John" surgery. Farrell won 14 games for a bad Cleveland club in 1988 and hopes to pitch in 1993; still, it's hard to excited about Farrell's chances given his medical history.

FASSERO, JEFF - Expos - TL - Age 30

A journeyman who has blossomed late in his career to become one of the NL's better lefthanded setup relievers. He throws hard and his ball sinks, making him the perfect guy to get a double play. Also has a good forkball.

	W	SV	ERA	IP	H	BB	SO	BPI	$
1992 Montreal NL	8	1	2.84	85	81	34	63	1.34	3
1993 Base Case	6	2	2.89	70	62	25	53	1.29	6

FERNANDEZ, ALEX - White Sox - TR - Age 23

Very young and very talented. Full repertoire and good velocity. Was a first round pick twice, 1988 and 1990. Fernandez will be a great pitcher. But for those of you who suffered with Fernandez in 1991 and 1992, take a note: Koufax, Gibson and Ryan all struggled for a couple of years when they reached the majors. It's always better to let someone else carry the top young hurlers when they first arrive.

	W	SV	ERA	IP	H	BB	SO	BPI	$
1992 Chicago AL	8	0	4.27	187	199	50	95	1.33	3
1993 Base Case	11	0	4.17	189	196	162	113	1.29	6

FERNANDEZ, SID - Mets - TL - AGE 30
Consistently underrated and consistently excellent. Over the years he has been the best Rotisserie pitcher for the money, without a doubt.

	W	SV	ERA	IP	H	BB	SO	BPI	$
1992 New York NL	14	0	2.73	214	162	67	193	1.07	18
1993 Base Case	16	0	2.60	144	111	43	121	1.07	19

FETTERS, MIKE - Brewers - TR - Age 28
Like his fellow newcomers Cal Eldred and Jim Austin, Fetters put up numbers so impressive that they don't quite register. Fetters' weak minor league record, complete with classic "attitude problems," caution against investing too much in his '92 performance. It seems, however, that Garner knows exactly how to use him, which suggests that if Fetters continues as a middle reliever, he'll be a valuable acquisition with a low price tag.

	W	SV	ERA	IP	H	BB	SO	BPI	$
1992 Milwaukee AL	5	2	1.87	62	38	24	43	0.99	9
1993 Base Case	3	10	3.07	55	45	27	35	1.31	10

FILER, TOM - Mets - TR - Age 36
Before 1992, Filer's last major league season was 1990, when he gave the Brewers a 6.14 ERA. Filer gave the Mets 22 decent innings, but his presence was a comment on a decimated staff.

	W	SV	ERA	IP	H	BB	SO	BPI	$
1992 New York NL	0	0	2.05	22	18	6	9	1.09	
1993 Base Case	0	0	3.04	30	27	9	11	1.22	0

FINLEY, CHUCK - Angels - TL - Age 30
Since being the best lefthanded starter in baseball in 1990, Finley has fallen on hard times with his ERA and ratio rising and victory totals falling in 1991 and 1992. A nagging foot injury may be to blame; a sore toe sounds minor but can really affect a pitcher's motion. Finley appeared healthy late in the season and posted a 3-1, 2.60 mark over his last four weeks. After warning people off for two years (because of the high price), I now like Finley as a buy for 1993.

	W	SV	ERA	IP	H	BB	SO	BPI	$
1992 California AL	7	0	3.96	204	212	98	124	1.52	-
1993 Base Case	13	0	3.64	217	198	100	147	1.37	6

FIREOVID, STEVE - Rangers - TR - Age 34
Appeared with four major league teams 1981-1986 but had been in the minors ever since, before the Rangers gave him a callup. Look at the Triple-A BPI ratio and you can see why I don't think he is suddenly a major league pitcher again

	W	SV	ERA	IP	H	BB	SO	BPI	$
1992 Oklahoma City AAA	7	0	3.10	105	130	28	54	1.51	
1992 Texas AL	1	0	4.05	6	10	4	0	2.10	-
1993 Base Case	1	0	4.43	8	12	4	1	1.92	-

FISHER, BRIAN - Mariners - TR - Age 31
Yankee fans remember Fisher's 14 saves in 1985. Later he bombed with the Pirates and Astros and was fortunate to get back to the major leagues in 1992.

	W	SV	ERA	IP	H	BB	SO	BPI	$
1992 Seattle AL	4	1	4.53	91	80	47	26	1.39	0
1993 Base Case	3	1	4.51	97	88	47	140	1.40	-

FLANAGAN, MIKE - Orioles - TL - Age 41
After a great comeback year in 1991, Flanny was awful in 1992 and probably will retire.

	W	SV	ERA	IP	H	BB	SO	BPI	$
1992 Baltimore AL	0	0	8.05	35	50	23	17	2.09	-
1993 Base Case	0	0	4.95	35	37	18	16	1.59	-

FLEMING, DAVE - Mariners - TL - Age 23
In two minor league seasons, he had combined for a 19-9 record and a 2.56 ERA. Like most control pitchers, Fleming had some horrible outings on days when he wasn't sharp, which inflated his year end ERA. He should continue to star as he matures. Consistency is the key.

	W	SV	ERA	IP	H	BB	SO	BPI	$
1992 Seattle AL	17	0	3.39	228	225	60	112	1.25	14
1993 Base Case	11	0	3.61	143	142	33	72	1.23	9

FORTUGNO, TIMOTHY - Angels - TL - Age 30
Fortugno was a first round pick in 1984 but did not make his rookie debut until the summer of 1992 as a 30 year old. A shutout of Detroit highlighted his season if not his career. He has little chance of making the rotation but could contribute as a reliever.

	W	SV	ERA	IP	H	BB	SO	BPI	$
1992 Edmonton AAA	6	1	3.56	73	69	33	82	1.40	
1992 California AL	1	1	5.18	42	37	19	31	1.34	-
1993 Base Case	1	1	5.06	53	48	31	36	1.48	-

FOSSAS, TONY - Red Sox - TL - Age 35
A lefty, Fossas is the AL answer to John Candelaria.

	W	SV	ERA	IP	H	BB	SO	BPI	$
1992 Boston AL	1	2	2.43	29	31	14	19	1.52	1
1993 Base Case	2	2	3.67	47	44	22	27	1.44	0

FOSTER, STEVE - Reds - TR - Age 26
A 12th round draft pick in 1988, Foster has made steady progress up the Reds system. He features a good fastball and slider and has performed well in two brief trials with the Reds. Steve has been groomed as a relief pitcher and will compete for a middle relief role in 1993.

	W	SV	ERA	IP	H	BB	SO	BPI	$
1992 Nashville AAA	5	1	2.68	50	53	22	28	1.49	
1992 Cincinnati NL	1	2	2.88	50	52	13	34	1.30	1
1993 Base Case	0	2	2.84	53	58	17	32	1.40	1

FRANCO, JOHN - Mets - TL - Age 32
Franco says the elbow surgery he underwent following the premature end of his 1992 season was successful, and he was expected to be able to throw before spring training. Franco was used rather sparingly by Jeff Torborg even before his breakdown, averaging barely an inning per appearance and taking the mound only in save situations. The Mets did not often find themselves in the position of leading in the late innings in 1992.

	W	SV	ERA	IP	H	BB	SO	BPI	$
1992 New York NL	6	15	1.64	33	24	11	20	1.06	16
1993 Base Case	7	24	2.60	49	44	16	34	1.23	22

FRASER, WILLIE - Angels - TR - Age 28
After several other stops, veteran Willie Fraser is back in the Angels' organization where he began his career. Failing as a starter, he has been effective in a middle relief role.

	W	SV	ERA	IP	H	BB	SO	BPI	$
1992 Edmonton AAA	7	6	4.90	90	110	24	49	1.49	
1993 Base Case	4	1	3.93	71	76	22	26	1.38	0

FREEMAN, MARVIN - Braves - TR - Age 29
Freeman had surprising success in a long relief role in 1992. He still looks like the odd man out as the Braves young pitchers develop.

	W	SV	ERA	IP	H	BB	SO	BPI	$
1992 Atlanta NL	7	3	3.22	64	61	29	41	1.40	3
1993 Base Case	5	2	3.30	57	50	23	38	1.34	3

FREY, STEVE - Angels - TL - Age 29
Frey posted respectable numbers for the Angels but don't let the numbers make you think that Frey is anything but an average bullpen lefty. He is just one year removed from a 4.99 ERA and a 1.64 BPI ratio for Montreal in 1991, and he wasn't too fine in clutch situations for the Angels in 1992. The departure of Bryan Harvey definitely helps Frey's value, however, if the Anaheims don't pick up another lefty.

	W	SV	ERA	IP	H	BB	SO	BPI	$
1992 California AL	4	4	3.57	45	39	22	24	1.35	4
1993 Base Case	3	8	4.01	52	48	27	28	1.44	5

FRITZ, JOHN - Angels - TR - Age 24
Fritz became the first 20-game winner in baseball while at Quad City (A), capping an undefeated second half. This marked a startling turnaround; Fritz had won just 14 games in the four prior seasons! Although the strikeouts were plentiful, Fritz is not a power pitcher and is several years away from the majors.

	W	SV	ERA	IP	H	BB	SO	BPI	$
1992 Quad City A	20	0	3.03	172	129	69	143	1.15	

FROHWIRTH, TODD - Orioles - TR - Age 30
I liked Frohwirth when he was with the Phillies in 1989, but he never really clicked in the NL. In the slowball league, he has been a revelation. Frohwirth produced two excellent setup seasons for the Orioles in 1991-1992.

	W	SV	ERA	IP	H	BB	SO	BPI	$
1992 Baltimore AL	4	4	2.46	106	97	41	58	1.30	9
1993 Base Case	5	3	2.56	99	82	36	63	1.20	11

GAKELER, DAN - Tigers - TR - Age 28
About the last thing you want in 1993 is a mediocre Tiger starter. Gakeler had a 5.74 ERA for Detroit in 1991 and spent most of 1992 rehabbing.

	W	SV	ERA	IP	H	BB	SO	BPI	$
1992 London AA	0	0	0.00	2	3	1	1	2.00	
1992 Toledo AAA	0	0	7.11	12	14	4	11	1.42	

GARCES, RICH - Twins - TR - Age 21
Great things were expected from Garces following his sensational performance as a closer with the Twins at the end of '90. Then 1991 was pretty much lost due to personal problems, and '92 saw Garces restarting his career in AA-ball. He's still very young.

	W	SV	ERA	IP	H	BB	SO	BPI	$
1992 Orlando AA	3	3	4.54	73	76	39	72	1.59	

GARCIA, RAMON - White Sox - TR - Age 23
The White Sox like Garcia so much, they brought him up before Wilson Alvarez in 1991.

	W	SV	ERA	IP	H	BB	SO	BPI	$
1992 Vancouver AAA	9	0	3.71	170	165	56	79	1.30	

GARCIA, VICTOR - Indians - TR - Age 26
From 1988 to 1991 Garcia could do no wrong; he swept through all five levels of the Reds farm system in just four years. In 1992 he couldn't do anything right. Worth watching to see if he gets back on track, but won't reach the majors until he turns it around.

	W	SV	ERA	IP	H	BB	SO	BPI	$
1992 Canton AA	5	1	6.07	102	115	57	56	1.68	

GARDELLA, MIKE - Yankees - TL - Age 26
Led his league in saves in 1989 and 1990, but now he needs someone to take notice and promote him. Hasn't really been as tough on AA hitters as he was in the low minors.

	W	SV	ERA	IP	H	BB	SO	BPI	$
1992 Albany AA	3	5	2.00	18	18	10	18	1.56	
1992 Canton Akrn. AA	2	7	3.60	55	43	32	45	1.36	

GARDINER, MIKE - Expos - TR - Age 27
In 1990 Gardiner was the best pitcher in the pitching-rich Eastern League, but he hasn't developed much in the two years since. All Red Sox pitchers must be regarded as dangerous.

	W	SV	ERA	IP	H	BB	SO	BPI	$
1992 Boston AL	4	0	4.75	130	126	58	79	1.41	-
1993 Base Case	6	0	4.80	149	140	68	79	1.39	1

GARDNER, CHRIS - Astros - TR - Age 24
Splendid pitcher at Rookie, A, and AA in 1988-1991 and got a visit to the big leagues in 1991. Obviously needs a little more work at the Triple-A level.

	W	SV	ERA	IP	H	BB	SO	BPI	$
1992 Tucson AAA	6	0	5.69	110	141	63	49	1.84	

GARDNER, MARK - Royals - TR - Age 31
With one of the game's best curveballs, Gardner should be a big winner. However, lack of consistent control and a disturbing trend of wilting in pressure situations make him only average. After age 30, the chances of him getting much better are minimal.

	W	SV	ERA	IP	H	BB	SO	BPI	$
1992 Expos NL	12	0	4.36	179	179	60	132	1.33	0
1993 Base Case	11	0	4.25	167	155	59	115	1.28	1

GARRELTS, SCOTT - Giants - TR - Age 31
Been on the comeback trail a long time. His last good season was 1989.

	W	SV	ERA	IP	H	BB	SO	BPI	$
1992 San Jose A	0	0	2.25	4	3	3	1	1.50	
1992 Shreveport AA	0	0	1.86	9	4	3	15	0.72	
1992 Phoenix AAA	0	0	8.49	11	14	5	7	1.63	

GEORGE, CHRIS - Brewers - TR - Age 26
After he produced a 1.78 ERA and 13 saves at AA El Paso in 1990, the Brewers thought highly enough of George to make him one of the two players they sent to the first official major league "orientation" seminar for rookies in the spring of 1991. He's still waiting to use what he learned about the big league lifestyle.

	W	SV	ERA	IP	H	BB	SO	BPI	$
1992 Denver AAA	2	0	4.64	42	54	10	20	1.50	

GIBSON, PAUL - Mets - TL - Age 33
Developed a tired arm in May 1991 -- while on the streak of his career -- and hasn't been the same since.

	W	SV	ERA	IP	H	BB	SO	BPI	$
1992 New York NL	0	0	5.23	62	70	25	49	1.53	-
1993 Base Case	2	3	4.74	72	80	33	46	1.57	-

GLAVINE, TOM - Braves - TL - Age 27
Another 20 win season from the man who can do no wrong. Glavine didn't suffer the Cy Slump after winning in 1991. The main thing Glavine did differently in 1992 was eliminate the gopher ball, allowing 6 in 1992 after surrendering 55 over the previous three seasons. He'll be good in 1993, but expensive.

	W	SV	ERA	IP	H	BB	SO	BPI	$
1992 Atlanta NL	20	0	2.76	225	197	70	129	1.19	17
1993 Base Case	19	0	2.91	223	192	69	149	1.17	20

GLEATON, JERRY DON - Pirates -TL - Age 35
Just a journeyman, and near the end of his journey.

	W	SV	ERA	IP	H	BB	SO	BPI	$
1992 Pittsburgh NL	1	0	4.26	31	34	19	18	1.67	-
1993 Base Case	2	1	3.89	55	56	27	33	1.50	-

GOHR, GREG - Tigers - TR - Age 25
Tigers' first pick in 1989. Has 90 MPH fastball.

	W	SV	ERA	IP	H	BB	SO	BPI	$
1992 Toledo AAA	8	0	3.99	130	124	46	94	1.30	

GOMEZ, PAT - Rangers - TL - Age 25
Ever since 1991, he's been untouchable at AA Greenville and unmentionable at AAA Richmond.

	W	SV	ERA	IP	H	BB	SO	BPI	$
1992 Richmond AAA	3	0	5.45	71	79	42	48	1.70	
1992 Greenville AA	7	0	1.13	47	25	19	38	0.92	

GOODEN, DWIGHT - Mets - TR - Age 28
Because of his early start at age 18, and the incomparable success he enjoyed all those years ago, Gooden is thought of as a pitcher who is going downhill fast, but: He's only 28. His most relevant stats (BPI, ERA, K/BB) are substantially the same as those of pitchers like Benes, Harnisch, and Schilling, who are all considered to be up-and-comers. And he was pitching very well in September with a AAA team behind him.

	W	SV	ERA	IP	H	BB	SO	BPI	$
1992 New York NL	10	0	3.67	206	197	70	145	1.30	3
1993 Base Case	12	0	3.61	194	188	60	142	1.28	6

GORDON, TOM - Royals - TR - Age 25

Gordon seems like he's forever disappointing fans who expect him to suddenly blossom into a great starting pitcher. He's had a few battles recently with manager Hal McRae; his future in KC may be dim. Gordon has been dismal as a starter the last few years, he's much better in relief but doesn't like that job. He'll have to find better control -- specifically throwing the curve for strike one -- or it's the bullpen for Flash.

	W	SV	ERA	IP	H	BB	SO	BPI	$
1992 Kansas City AL	6	0	4.59	117	116	55	98	1.45	-
1993 Base Case	8	0	4.02	128	112	68	124	1.41	0

GOSSAGE, GOOSE - Athletics - TR - Age 41

Still throws strikes, and still pitches inside. Gossage comes with one built-in safety factor: If he pitches badly, he will stop pitching. Might retire anyway.

	W	SV	ERA	IP	H	BB	SO	BPI	$
1992 Oakland AL	0	0	2.84	38	32	19	26	1.34	0
1993 Base Case	1	0	3.29	47	39	22	32	1.30	0

GOTT, JIM - Dodgers - TR - Age 33

Gott was a member in good standing of the LA arson squad although his numbers were the best of the bunch. He will never regain his old Pittsburgh closer form, but he could be a reliable set-up man and provide saves for a dollar apiece. If the Dodgers don't acquire somone new, Gott could actually begin the season as the closer.

	W	SV	ERA	IP	H	BB	SO	BPI	$
1992 Los Angeles NL	3	6	2.45	88	72	41	75	1.28	7
1993 Base Case	4	8	2.91	80	67	37	70	1.30	8

GOZZO, MAURO - Twins -TR - Age 27

Gozzo has been in a number of organizations. He's had some good years in the minors but usually struggles in the majors.

	W	SV	ERA	IP	H	BB	SO	BPI	$
1992 Portland AAA	10	1	3.33	157	155	50	108	1.31	
1992 Minnesota AL	0	0	27.00	2	7	0	1	4.20	-
1993 Base Case	1	0	4.77	14	16	7	8	1.58	-

GRAHE, JOE - Angels - TR - Age 25

The Angels gave Grahe the stopper role when Bryan Harvey went down with elbow problems and he exceeded expectations with 21 saves. With Harvey gone, Grahe is the logical choice to remain in the closer role. California paved the way by trading Eichhorn to Toronto. Be wary of Grahe's 7.56 ERA and 2.04 ratio during September.

	W	SV	ERA	IP	H	BB	SO	BPI	$
1992 California AL	5	21	3.52	95	85	39	39	1.31	18
1993 Base Case	4	23	3.73	82	80	35	35	1.40	20

GRANT, MARK - Mariners - TR - Age 27

The journeyman middle reliever was signed by the Mariners to help their shorthanded staff. He was 8-2 with a 3.33 ERA in 1989 for the Padres. He struggled in 1990 and did not appear in the majors in 1991. He looks like he has returned to old form, which is simpy adequate.

	W	SV	ERA	IP	H	BB	SO	BPI	$
1992 Seattle AL	2	0	3.89	81	100	22	42	1.51	-
1993 Base Case	2	0	3.88	56	70	14	29	1.51	-

GRATER, MARK - Cardinals - TR - Age 29

Top minor league closer -- 32 saves in 1989 led the FSL.Cardinals are clearly not inclined to give him a shot at the majors, although he did get three innings with St. Louis in 1991.

	W	SV	ERA	IP	H	BB	SO	BPI	$
1992 Louisville AAA	7	24	2.13	76	74	15	46	1.17	

GRAY, JEFF - Red Sox - TR - Age 29

Suffered a stroke in the middle of a fine season in 1991. Very unlikely to make it back, although he keeps trying.

GREEN, OTIS - Brewers - TL - Age 29

Minor league outfielder 1983-1990. Tried pitching in 1991 and did well at A and AA. Still working on AAA.

	W	SV	ERA	IP	H	BB	SO	BPI	$
1992 Denver AAA	11	0	4.61	152	148	70	114	1.43	

GREEN, TYLER - Phillies - TR - Age 23

Drafted No. 1 out of Wichita State in '91. Doesn't throw above 90 mph, but uses a knuckle-curve as his out pitch. Went on the disabled list with tendinitis, and had shoulder surgery, but is expected to be ready for spring training 1993. Good gamble, but not a safe pick.

	W	SV	ERA	IP	H	BB	SO	BPI	$
1992 Reading AA	6	0	1.88	62	46	20	67	1.06	
1992 Scranton AAA	0	0	6.10	10	7	12	15	1.90	

GREENE, TOMMY - Phillies - TR - Age 25

Seemingly on the verge of stardom, Greene spent most of 1992 rehabilitating a sore arm and made only 12 starts. He pitched a no-hitter in '91 when he was overpowering.

	W	SV	ERA	IP	H	BB	SO	BPI	$
1992 Philadelphia NL	3	0	5.32	64	75	34	39	1.69	-
1993 Base Case	7	0	3.90	122	117	45	84	1.33	0

GRIFFITHS, BRIAN - Astros - TR - Age 24

Had a dominant season in A-ball in 1991, but found the going tougher in Double-A. Still a prospect.

	W	SV	ERA	IP	H	BB	SO	BPI	$
1992 Jackson AA	3	0	3.80	97	95	42	91	1.41	

GRIMSLEY, JASON - Astros - TR - Age 25

Hard thrower obtained from Phillies for Curt Schilling spent entire season at AAA Tucson. Improved his control but was hit hard. Needs a strong AAA year in 1993 to have a chance for another shot in the majors.

	W	SV	ERA	IP	H	BB	SO	BPI	$
1992 Tucson AAA	8	0	5.05	125	152	55	90	1.66	

GROOM, BUDDY - Tigers - TL - Age 27

A lefty, Groom posted a 0-3 W/L record in the first half, and followed with 0-2 (total 0-5) in the second with an ERA in the mid 5.00 range over the whole year.

	W	SV	ERA	IP	H	BB	SO	BPI	$
1992 Toledo AAA	7	0	2.80	109	102	23	71	1.14	
1992 Detroit AL	0	1	5.82	38	48	22	15	1.81	-
1993 Base Case	1	1	5.08	61	68	28	28	1.57	-

GROSS, KEVIN - Dodgers - TR - Age 31

After a disappointing year in 1991, Gross quietly put together a steady season in 1992, highlighted by the only no-hitter in baseball. He reduced his ERA by half a run and his ratio by 0.23. With the lack of support afforded by the L.A. offense and defense, Gross won only eight games; with a better team, he could easily have been in the mid-teens.

	W	SV	ERA	IP	H	BB	SO	BPI	$
1992 Los Angeles NL	8	0	3.17	205	182	77	158	1.27	6
1993 Base Case	10	0	3.45	167	154	66	127	1.32	5

GROSS, KIP - Dodgers - TR - Age 28

A curveball pitcher, Gross needs fine control to be effective. He didn't have it in 1992 in LA, but is clearly capable of doing better.

	W	SV	ERA	IP	H	BB	SO	BPI	$
1992 Albuquerque AAA	6	8	3.51	108	96	36	58	1.22	
1992 Los Angeles NL	1	0	4.18	23	32	10	14	1.77	-
1993 Base Case	3	0	3.72	53	60	21	27	1.52	-

GUBICZA, MARK - Royals - TR - Age 30

After nine major league seasons, Gubicza is still only 30. He came back from 1990 shoulder surgery to perform near his previous level in late 1992, with full command of his pitches. Stamina is the only question at this point. Gubicza is an excellent late pick; he'll be overlooked by many people focused only on full season stats.

	W	SV	ERA	IP	H	BB	SO	BPI	$
1992 Kansas City AL	7	0	3.72	111	110	36	81	1.31	3
1993 Base Case	7	0	3.90	98	106	31	68	1.40	1

GUETTERMAN, LEE - Mets - TL - Age 34

Too many sinkers stayed up in the strike zone in 1992. Guetterman looked as bad as his numbers. A soft thrower with little stamina. Needs pinpoint control to get anyone out.

	W	SV	ERA	IP	H	BB	SO	BPI	$
1992 Two Teams AL/NL	4	2	7.09	66	92	27	20	1.80	-
1993 Base Case	4	4	4.70	88	93	28	30	1.38	-

GULLICKSON, BILL - Tigers - TR - Age 34

The righthander came back to earth with a 14-13 record, and an ERA over 4.00 after his stunning 20-9 season in 1991. If you get hung with a Tiger pitcher, this should be your guy.

	W	SV	ERA	IP	H	BB	SO	BPI	$
1992 Detroit AL	14	0	4.34	221	228	50	64	1.25	7
1993 Base Case	15	0	4.39	217	238	47	72	1.31	3

GUNDERSON, ERIC - Giants - TL - Age 27

Gunderson has been terrific at Double-A for years, including two great seasons for Shreveport and one for Jacksonville. His fastball just isn't good enough for the better, more disciplined hitters.

	W	SV	ERA	IP	H	BB	SO	BPI	$
1992 Jacksonville AA	2	2	2.31	23	18	7	23	1.07	
1992 Calgary AAA	0	5	6.02	52	57	31	50	1.68	
1992 Seattle AL	2	0	8.68	9	12	5	2	1.82	-
1993 Base Case	2	0	5.50	29	32	10	18	1.44	-

GUTHRIE, MARK - Twins - TL - Age 27

Guthrie is a good middle reliever and set-up man giving you a few wins and saves and reasonable ERA and ratio numbers in 75-100 innings every year. He needs fine control to be effective, and failed as a starter for that reason -- they had to send him out there when scheduled, even if he wasn't sharp. Working out of the pen, he can be used only when he's in good form. If he becomes a starter, dump him fast.

	W	SV	ERA	IP	H	BB	SO	BPI	$
1992 Minnesota AL	2	5	2.88	75	59	23	76	1.09	8
1993 Base Case	4	4	3.45	80	78	28	71	1.32	5

GUZMAN, JOHNNY - Athletics - TL - Age 22

Good prospect, he got a brief callup to Oakland in 1991. Still needs to prove himself above AA.

	W	SV	ERA	IP	H	BB	SO	BPI	$
1992 Huntsville AA	8	0	3.71	89	87	26	55	1.26	
1992 Oakland AL	0	0	12.00	3	8	0	0	2.67	-
1993 Base Case	3	0	4.55	36	41	10	16	1.42	-

GUZMAN, JOSE - Cubs - TR - Age 29

Less than 2 years ago, some Ranger insiders believed he would never pitch again at Major League level; but he surprised everyone winning 29 games in '91 & '92. He set career highs in '92 for wins, innings pitched, and strikeouts, and did not miss a start all year. Solid #2 starter in prime of career. He got a huge multi-year contract.

	W	SV	ERA	IP	H	BB	SO	BPI	$
1992 Texas AL	16	0	3.66	224	229	73	179	1.35	9
1993 Base Case	15	0	3.39	199	193	78	158	1.36	9

GUZMAN, JUAN - Blue Jays - TR - Age 26

Classic flame-thrower. He achieved major league success by finding the strike zone in 1991. The sore arm in 1992 unfortunately puts him in the speculation category; but if you have to speculate, it's always better to get someone whose success is as recent as Guzman's.

	W	SV	ERA	IP	H	BB	SO	BPI	$
1992 Toronto AL	16	0	2.64	180	135	72	165	1.15	18
1993 Base Case	13	0	2.95	149	113	66	132	1.21	14

HAAS, DAVE - Tigers - TR - Age 27

Haas is a righthanded workhorse, and should get a lot more work in 1993. Regardless, he won't help you. Something to do with the stadium.

	W	SV	ERA	IP	H	BB	SO	BPI	$
1992 Toledo AAA	9	0	4.18	148	149	53	112	1.76	
1992 Detroit AL	5	0	3.94	61	68	16	29	1.36	1
1993 Base Case	6	0	4.16	108	116	36	52	1.40	-

HABYAN, JOHN - Yankees - TR - Age 29

A sinker/slider pitcher, Habyan threw too many fastballs that stayed up in 1992. He filled in as a closer while Steve Farr was out with a sore back in mid summer, but isn't assured of any saves in 1993. The return of Steve Howe won't help Habyan's chances to get stopper duty.

	W	SV	ERA	IP	H	BB	SO	BPI	$
1992 New York AL	5	7	3.84	72	84	21	44	1.44	5
1993 Base Case	4	4	3.51	74	78	20	52	1.31	4

HAMILTON, JOEY - Padres - TR - Age 23

San Diego's No. 1 pick in '91 out of Georgia Southern U. Throws a mid-90-mph fastball rated best in the California League by Baseball America. Playing time limited last year because of a pulled groin muscle.

	W	SV	ERA	IP	H	BB	SO	BPI	$
1992 Charleston A	2	0	3.38	35	37	4	35	1.17	
1992 High Desert A	4	0	2.74	49	46	18	43	1.31	
1992 Wichita AA	3	0	2.86	35	33	11	26	1.26	

HAMMOND, CHRIS - Reds - TL - Age 27

A curveball/changeup pitcher, Chris Hammond did not develop as expected in 1992. Hammond would pitch well for 5 or 6 innings, then collapse. Hammond was dropped from the rotation in September while the Reds looked at Tim Pugh and Bobby Ayala. Like many young pitchers, Chris will be good if he harnesses his control. Lefties with good changeups should be successful in the NL.

	W	SV	ERA	IP	H	BB	SO	BPI	$
1992 Cincinnati NL	7	0	4.21	147	149	55	79	1.38	-
1993 Base Case	6	0	4.31	122	124	48	65	1.41	-

HANCOCK, CHRISTOPHER - Giants - TL - Age 23

Dominated two A-ball leagues in 1990-1991 but didn't advance far in 1992. Second round pick in 1988.

	W	SV	ERA	IP	H	BB	SO	BPI	$
1992 San Jose A	7	0	4.04	111	104	55	80	1.43	
1992 Shreveport AA	2	0	3.10	49	37	18	30	1.11	

HANEY, CHRIS - Royals - TL - Age 24

The son of major league catcher Larry Haney, Chris got to the majors very quickly, spending slightly more than a year on various farm teams before making his 1991 debut for Montreal. After the Royals got him and Bill Sampen for Sean Berry, Haney became an instant success for Kansas City. He's highly regarded although he's been erratic, and has a very good chance to open the season in the Royals' rotation.

	W	SV	ERA	IP	H	BB	SO	BPI	$
1992 Indianapolis AAA	5	0	5.14	84	88	42	61	1.55	
1992 Montreal NL	2	0	5.45	38	40	10	27	1.32	-
1992 Kansas City AL	2	0	3.86	42	35	16	27	1.21	1
1993 Base Case	5	0	4.41	98	98	38	64	1.39	1

HANSON, ERIK - Mariners - TR - Age 27

For the first time since he was 2-3 as a rookie, Hanson turned in a losing record last year. His ERA increased a full run from 1991, marking the third straight year it has risen. Only half of his starts were quality starts, as he never got going. Still has good control, and is certainly capable of a rebound.

	W	SV	ERA	IP	H	BB	SO	BPI	$
1992 Seattle AL	8	0	4.82	186	209	57	112	1.42	-
1993 Base Case	7	0	4.11	167	180	52	115	1.39	-

HARKEY, MIKE - Cubs - TR - Age 26

Harkey was 12-6 with a 3.26 ERA as a rookie in 1990. When he's healthy, he can be dominating, as he was in his seven starts last year. When he's hurt, he's not very good (but who is?). A freak injury turning a cartwheel ending his (and the Cubs) season last year. He should be recovered and is good enough to pitch in anyone's rotation.

	W	SV	ERA	IP	H	BB	SO	BPI	$
1992 Chicago NL	4	0	1.89	38	34	15	21	1.29	1
1993 Base Case	12	0	2.99	152	144	56	92	1.32	7

HARNISCH, PETE - Astros - TR - Age 26
Staff workhorse started 34 games -- 6 more than any other Astro pitcher. Fell short of outstanding 1991 season (12-9, 2.70 ERA, 1.16 BPI). Fierce competitor failed to go at least 5 innings only 3 times. Pitches well enough to give team a chance to win. Could be a big winner with improved command of off-speed and breaking pitches. Safest bet among Astro starters.

	W	SV	ERA	IP	H	BB	SO	BPI	$
1992 Houston NL	9	0	3.70	206	182	64	164	1.19	6
1993 Base Case	11	0	3.27	205	173	68	164	1.18	13

HARRIS, GENE - Padres - TR - Age 28
Six-year minor leaguer with Expos and Mariners organizations. Best year was 1991 as a reliever at Calgary. Not a safe pitcher unless used very carefully in the right situations.

	W	SV	ERA	IP	H	BB	SO	BPI	$
1992 Seattle AL	0	0	7.00	9	8	6	6	1.89	-
1992 San Diego NL	0	0	2.95	21	15	9	19	1.13	-

HARRIS, GREG - Red Sox - TR - Age 37
Ace reliever for Texas in 1986, has worked in all roles for Boston. I like his big curveball, which may be embarrassing in isolated cases of poor control but is a great weapon over a full season. If Harris stays with Boston in 1993, he is a good candidate to get saves while younger guys like Ken Ryan have time to develop.

	W	SV	ERA	IP	H	BB	SO	BPI	$
1992 Boston AL	4	4	2.51	107	82	60	73	1.32	8
1993 Base Case	6	5	3.39	132	116	63	92	1.36	8

HARRIS, GREG W. - Padres - TR - Age 29
Concern about Harris' career is well-founded after two straight injury-plagued seasons in which he could only pitch a total of 251 major league innings. One has to question the wisdom of Padre management in changing Harris from middle relief to stopper to starter at such a tender age. If truly healthy, Harris is capable of outstanding ERA and ratio. His curveball is as good as anyone's.

	W	SV	ERA	IP	H	BB	SO	BPI	$
1992 San Diego NL	4	0	4.12	118	113	35	66	1.25	0
1993 Base Case	12	0	3.30	121	111	30	75	1.16	9

HARRIS, REGGIE - Athletics - TR - Age 24
A Rule Five pick in December 1989, the A's were able to keep Harris by disabling him for the first half of 1990, while he pitched rehab in the minors. The walks were a minor nuisance with Oakland in 1991, but have a become a major block in his career now. Harris is a good hard thrower but hasn't made any progress in two years.

	W	SV	ERA	IP	H	BB	SO	BPI	$
1992 Tacoma AAA	6	0	5.71	149	141	117	111	1.72	

HARTLEY, MIKE - Twins - TR - Age 31
A journeyman middle reliever and spot starter who was originally a member of the Dodgers' organization and racks up decent strikeout numbers because of an effective split-finger fastball.

	W	SV	ERA	IP	H	BB	SO	BPI	$
1992 Philadelphia NL	7	0	3.44	55	54	23	53	1.40	-
1993 Base Case	6	1	3.98	67	63	33	58	1.44	-

HARTSOCK, JEFF - Cubs - TR - Age 26

A former Dodgers farm hand acquired for Steve Wilson. In his first two years of pro ball, he was 19-7 with a 2.64 ERA. In 1991, he was 12-6 with a 3.80 ERA at Albuquerque. That doesn't sound impressive until you realize that last year Pedro Astacio had an ERA of 5.47 there (and 1.98 in the majors) while Dodger phenom Pedro Martinez was 7-6 with a 3.81 ERA at Albuquerque. He had a brief trial with the Cubs in September and was ineffective.

	W	SV	ERA	IP	H	BB	SO	BPI	$
1992 Iowa AAA	5	0	4.36	173	177	61	87	1.37	
1992 Chicago NL	0	0	6.75	9	15	4	6	2.04	-
1993 Base Case	0	0	4.68	13	15	6	10	1.59	-

HARVEY, BRYAN - Marlins - TR - Age 29

Harvey was the AL's Fireman of the Year in 1991 (46 saves, 0.864 ratio) and regarded by many as the best pitcher anywhere. But he pitched in only 25 games in 1992 before suffering a serious, season-ending elbow injury. Because Harvey's bread-and-butter pitch is the forkball, which puts a tremendous strain on the elbow, the situation bears a close watch in the spring. The Marlins' interest is not a guaranteed bill of health, so be careful. Harvey had friends in the Florida organization, who were happy to take his word that he was going to be just fine. If you think about how many ace relievers have come back after missing a half season with surgery, it's a rare event in baseball.

	W	SV	ERA	IP	H	W	WO	BPI	$
1992 California AL	0	13	2.83	29	22	11	34	1.14	10
1993 Base Case	1	24	2.65	54	41	17	68	1.07	23

HATHAWAY, HILLY - Angels - TL - Age 23

Hathaway is a good young lefty prospect who did well last year in the hitting-rich Texas League. His good control keeps his ratio down. Although he may need more minor league experience, he's a good sleeper pick. Was protected in the expansion draft.

	W	SV	ERA	IP	H	BB	SO	BPI	$
1992 Palm Sp. A	2	0	1.50	24	25	3	17	1.17	
1992 Midland AA	7	0	3.22	95	90	10	69	1.05	
1992 California AL	0	0	7.94	6	8	3	1	1.94	-
1993 Base Case	0	0	4.17	41	46	7	21	1.30	-

HEATON, NEAL - Brewers - TL - Age 33

Developed shoulder trouble after a strong first half in 1990 leading to the All-Star game. Hasn't been the same since.

	W	SV	ERA	IP	H	BB	SO	BPI	$
1992 Two Teams AL	3	0	4.07	42	43	23	31	1.57	-
1993 Base Case	4	0	3.98	61	62	25	38	1.42	-

HENDERSON, KENNY - U. of Miami - TR - Age 20

Milwaukee's No. 1 pick in '91. He rejected the Brewers offer and instead took a scholarship to play for the Hurricanes. Eligible for the draft again in '94.

HENKE, TOM - Blue Jays - TR - Age 35

It doesn't matter where he plays in 1993; he will be the ace reliever no matter who else is in the pen. Henke has a long history of slow starts. It is a standard sucker ploy to trade for Henke on May 15 when he has a 5.00 ERA and just three saves, and enjoy four months of top value.

	W	SV	ERA	IP	H	BB	SO	BPI	$
1992 Toronto AL	4	34	2.26	55	40	22	46	1.11	29
1993 Base Case	1	34	2.41	54	39	17	49	1.04	32

HENNEMAN, MIKE - Tigers - TR - Age 31
Clearly Henneman is the best choice among all Tigers pitchers, but he is no longer a premier closer -- as his 3.96 ERA indicates. He should still rack up 20 saves or so.

	W	SV	ERA	IP	H	BB	SO	BPI	$
1992 Detroit AL	2	24	3.96	77	75	20	58	1.23	19
1993 Base Case	6	21	3.56	77	76	24	56	1.31	19

HENRY, BUTCH - Rockies - TL - Age 24
A long shot to make the squad in spring training, Henry started 28 games as the only left-hander in the rotation. Filled an obvious void, and team responded by winning half of his starts. Sat out the last 4 weeks with a sore shoulder. A control pitcher without overpowering stuff, he became more aggressive as he gained experience. He was in the major leagues in 1992 mainly because he dominated spring training. In the regular season the league batted .285 against him.

	W	SV	ERA	IP	H	BB	SO	BPI	$
1992 Houston NL	6	0	4.02	165	185	41	96	1.36	-
1993 Base Case	9	0	3.85	198	218	45	114	1.33	1

HENRY, DOUG - Brewers - TR - Age 29
His full-season stats won't reflect it, but by mid-September Henry had lost the full-time closer's job. Righthanders devoured him, and he gave up many extra-base hits. (Except for Jeff Reardon, Henry had the worst slugging percentage surrendered among AL closers.) Nothing about his stuff makes him stand apart from others in the Milwaukee pen who were far more effective, so extreme caution is advised; let Henry go to somebody who looks only at 1992's final save totals and ignores the context.

	W	SV	ERA	IP	H	BB	SO	BPI	$
1992 Milwaukee AL	1	29	4.02	65	64	24	52	1.35	21
1993 Base Case	1	12	3.52	51	45	19	41	1.25	10

HENRY. DWAYNE - Reds - TR - Age 31
Dwayne turned in a good year as a setup man for Rob Dibble and Norm Charlton, holding opponents to a .199 BA and striking out 7.7 batters per 9 IP. Control is still a problem with 44 walks in 83.2 IP and a team leading 12 wild pitches. Henry appears to have reached his career level.

	W	SV	ERA	IP	H	BB	SO	BPI	$
1992 Cincinnati NL	3	0	3.33	83	59	44	72	1.23	1
1993 Base Case	3	1	3.32	75	55	42	66	1.30	2

HENTGEN, PAT - Blue Jays - TR - Age 24
Hentgen's sore elbow was traced to a sprained ligament. The bad news is that the pain is linked to throwing the slider, his out pitch. Before the injury, he was a top prospect.

	W	SV	ERA	IP	H	BB	SO	BPI	$
1992 Toronto AL	5	0	5.36	50	49	32	39	1.61	-
1993 Base Case	2	0	5.50	28	26	18	21	1.58	-

HEREDIA, GIL - Expos - TR - Age 27
Tricky herky-jerky motion. He showed potential on the minor-league level in the Giants' organization, leading the Pacific Coast League in ERA in 1991, but has done little in the majors. Traded to Montreal last August, he is at an age where he must make his move now.

	W	SV	ERA	IP	H	BB	SO	BPI	$
1992 Phoenix AAA	5	1	2.01	81	83	13	37	1.19	
1992 Indianapolis AAA	2	0	1.02	18	18	3	10	1.17	
1992 Two Teams NL	2	0	4.23	44	44	20	22	1.43	-
1993 Base Case	2	0	4.12	49	46	19	23	1.32	-

HERNANDEZ, JEREMY - Padres - TR - Age 26

Hernandez started the season poorly in San Diego and was demoted to Las Vegas where he saved 11 games. With a 90-mph fastball he is a strong candidate for the committee of closers that will probably replace Myers.

	W	SV	ERA	IP	H	BB	SO	BPI	$
1992 San Diego NL	1	1	4.17	37	39	11	25	1.36	-
1992 Las Vegas AAA	2	11	2.91	56	53	20	38	1.30	
1993 Base Case	1	8	3.49	35	34	11	24	1.29	6

HERNANDEZ, ROBERTO - White Sox - TR - Age 28

Hernandez told me he never even thought about being a closer. He just found himself out there, at the end of one game, getting the final out and recording the save. Hard thrower who finally harnessed his control just enough.

	W	SV	ERA	IP	H	BB	SO	BPI	$
1992 Vancouver AAA	3	2	2.61	20	13	11	23	1.16	
1992 White Sox AL	7	12	1.65	71	45	20	68	0.92	19
1993 Base Case	5	16	2.20	54	38	14	49	0.96	21

HERNANDEZ, XAVIER - Astros - TR - Age 27

Former Texas High School Player of the Year quietly put together an outstanding season as the primary setup man for Doug Jones. Gained confidence and command of pitches, effectively mixing fastballs, sinkers and sliders. Primarily a starter until 1990, he appears to be better suited for relief. Should get additional save opportunities based on his success in 1992.

	W	SV	ERA	IP	H	BB	SO	BPI	$
1992 Houston NL	9	7	2.11	111	81	42	96	1.11	16
1993 Base Case	6	14	3.00	90	73	38	80	1.24	16

HERSHISER, OREL - Dodgers - TR - Age 34

Not surprisingly, Hershiser has not been the same since his drastic arm surgery. Don't underestimate his ability to put together one more good year, however. He did pitch more than 200 innings, an achievement in itself, and his ratio was respectable. He was also victimized by 15 unearned runs from the worst defense in baseball.

	W	SV	ERA	IP	H	BB	SO	BPI	$
1992 Los Angeles NL	10	0	3.67	211	209	69	130	1.32	2
1993 Base Case	9	0	3.61	167	168	52	105	1.32	3

HESKETH, JOE - Red Sox - TL - Age 34

Hesketh was touted as the "poor mans' John Tudor" after his fine performance in 1991. Hesketh had wanted to be a starter again, ever since losing that role in Montreal in 1986. The thrill carried him in 1991 but has apparently worn off.

	W	SV	ERA	IP	H	BB	SO	BPI	$
1992 Boston AL	8	1	4.36	148	162	58	104	1.48	0
1993 Base Case	10	1	4.04	142	148	54	98	1.43	1

HIBBARD, GREG - Cubs - TL - Age 28

Drafted just long enough to be traded across town. Hibbard should do at least as well in the NL as he did with the White Sox.

	W	SV	ERA	IP	H	BB	SO	BPI	$
1992 White Sox AL	10	1	4.40	176	187	57	69	1.39	1
1993 Base Case	10	0	3.67	174	172	56	67	1.31	3

HICKERSON, BRYAN - Giants - TL - Age 29

Hickerson did well in 1992 mainly because he was used carefully in situations that suited him, and because he got regular work. If used less frequently with longer outings in 1993, his quality numbers will suffer.

	W	SV	ERA	IP	H	BB	SO	BPI	$
1992 San Francisco NL	5	0	3.09	87	74	21	68	1.09	4
1993 Base Case	4	0	3.39	71	65	19	56	1.19	3

HIGUERA, TEDDY - Brewers - TL - Age 34

Will likely never pitch in the majors again. All those Mexican League innings as a teenager took their toll.

	W	SV	ERA	IP	H	BB	SO	BPI	$
1992 Beloit A	1	0	3.27	11	13	1	11	1.27	
1992 El Paso AA	0	0	3.60	5	4	2	3	1.20	
1992 Denver AAA	1	0	4.15	9	7	8	4	1.67	

HILL, KEN - Expos - TR - Age 27

Hill may have been the steal of the year as Montreal acquired him from St. Louis in a trade for first baseman Andres Galarraga after the 1991 season. He looks like he will be a consistent winner for a long time. A forkball developed at Louisville in 1990 (producing a 1.79 ERA) accelerated his rise to excellence.

	W	SV	ERA	IP	H	BB	SO	BPI	$
1992 Montreal NL	16	0	2.68	218	187	75	150	1.20	15
1993 Base Case	15	0	3.03	200	170	70	139	1.20	15

HILL, MILT - Reds - TR - Age 27

A fastball/slider pitcher, Hill has impressed in two brief stints with the Reds. Groomed as a relief pitcher, Hill led Nashville with 18 saves and struck out 70 in 74.1 IP. Will compete with Steve Foster for a middle relief/setup role in 1993.

	W	SV	ERA	IP	H	BB	SO	BPI	$
1992 Nashville AAA	0	18	2.66	74	56	17	70	0.98	
1992 Cincinnati NL	1	1	3.15	20	15	5	10	1.00	0
1993 Base Case	0	1	3.44	29	26	7	16	1.15	0

HILL, TYRONE - Brewers - TL - Age 21

Milwaukee's first round pick in 1991 and a Midwest League all-star in 1992, holding opponents to a .188 batting average. Shut down his 1992 season with a sore elbow in August. Needs to recover physically and demonstrate further progress before reaching major leagues. When healthy, throws 88 MPH and has three usable pitches. Ted Higuera, on a rehab assignment, was Hill's teammate at Beloit. Suppose Hill picked up any tricky pitches?

	W	SV	ERA	IP	H	BB	SO	BPI	$
1992 Beloit A	9	0	3.25	114	76	74	133	1.32	

HILLEGAS, SHAWN - Athletics - TR - Age 28

Was the Indians' closer for a month when Cleveland didn't win any games (June 1991). Good forkball worked for a while, but the hitters stopped swinging at it. Fairly risky as far as relievers go.

	W	SV	ERA	IP	H	BB	SO	BPI	$
1992 Two Teams AL	1	0	5.23	86	104	37	49	1.64	-
1993 Base Case	2	3	4.30	86	89	37	56	1.47	-

HILLMAN, ERIC - Mets - TL - Age 26

Not all tall pitchers throw like Randy Johnson. Eric Hillman is a large (6'10") person who evolved into a finesse pitcher, a la Ed Lynch, while Johnson often needs radar to locate home plate. Hillman once overpowered hitters in the lower minors, but took to nibbling, found his control, and misplaced his strikeout pitch. Created a stir in New York with two good outings when he first came up, but after that, not many hitters found the going to be very tough against Eric in '92.

	W	SV	ERA	IP	H	BB	SO	BPI	$
1992 Tidewater AAA	9	0	3.65	91	93	27	49	1.32	
1992 New York NL	2	0	5.33	52	67	10	16	1.48	-
1993 Base Case	5	0	4.48	77	88	18	28	1.38	-

HITCHCOCK, STERLING - Yankees - TL - Age 21

Throws a fastball and a curve. Victim of poor support in '92, when Albany averaged just 2.5 runs in his starts. In the majors, even the 5.5 runs he got weren't enough.

	W	SV	ERA	IP	H	BB	SO	BPI	$
1992 Albany AA	6	0	2.58	147	116	42	156	1.07	
1992 New York AL	0	0	8.31	13	23	6	6	2.23	-
1993 Base Case	2	0	4.16	57	65	22	53	1.51	-

HOFFMAN, TREVOR - Marlins - TR - Age 25

Hoffman converted to pitcher in 1991. Hoffman was considered one of the top pitching prospects in the Reds organization, reaching AAA Nashville after only one year as a pitcher and recording 75 K's in 47 IP in A and AA. Great natural talent with 95 MPH fastball. After big success as a starter at AA, he was tried as a closer by AAA Nashville, with mixed results. Will be one of many setup men for Bryan Harvey in 1993.

	W	SV	ERA	IP	H	BB	SO	BPI	$
1992 Chattanooga AA	3	0	1.52	30	22	11	31	1.10	
1992 Nashville AAA	4	6	4.27	65	57	32	63	1.37	
1993 Base Case	2	2	3.80	44	40	20	39	1.36	1

HOLLINS, JESSIE - Cubs - TR - Age 23

Still young enough that he can't be pigeonholed as a minor league closer. The Cubs showed their willingness to bring up minor leaguers in midseason, and give them saves, as they did for Jim Bullinger in 1992. If the Cubs pen remains unsettled through April-May, watch for Hollins to emerge.

	W	SV	ERA	IP	H	BB	SO	BPI	$
1992 Charlotte AA	3	25	3.20	70	60	32	73	1.31	
1992 Chicago NL	0	0	13.50	4	8	5	0	2.78	-
1993 Base Case	0	0	3.86	3	3	1	2	1.43	-

HOLMAN, BRIAN - Mariners - TR - Age 28

Holman missed the entire 1992 season after undergoing rotator cuff surgery, and will miss all or part of 1993 (depending on who you listen to). He was in double figures in wins in both 1990 and 1991 and could return to that level if he has recovered. Despite pitching in the Kingdome, his career ERA is 3.71.

HOLMES, DARREN - Rockies - TR - Age 26

The Colorado closer, on paper anyway, at the end of the expansion draft. May have saved his career with a solid '92 season in middle relief and in substituting for Doug Henry as closer when Henry blew leads or did time in Garner's doghouse. Holmes had excellent numbers at hitters' haven Albuquerque in Triple-A, so 1992 may be a fair sample of what he can do given a shot.

	W	SV	ERA	IP	H	BB	SO	BPI	$
1992 Milwaukee AL	4	6	2.55	42	35	11	31	1.09	8
1993 Base Case	4	19	3.58	64	64	20	48	1.30	16

HOLZEMER, MARK - Angels - TR - Age 23

Holzemer made good progress in the minors until he reached AAA-ball. If he can show more improvement, he may reach Anaheim sometime in '93.

	W	SV	ERA	IP	H	BB	SO	BPI	$
1992 Palm Sp. A	3	0	3.00	30	23	13	32	1.20	
1992 Midland AA	2	0	3.83	45	45	13	36	1.30	
1992 Edmonton AAA	5	0	6.67	89	114	55	49	1.90	

HONEYCUTT, RICK - Athletics - TL - Age 38

Old? Not compared to Rich Gossage, the righty setup guy in 1992. Honeycutt is useful and valuable because he is used carefully.

	W	SV	ERA	IP	H	BB	SO	BPI	$
1992 Oakland AL	1	3	3.69	39	41	10	32	1.31	2
1993 Base Case	2	2	3.66	46	48	16	36	1.37	1

HORSMAN, VINCE - Athletics - TL - Age 26

Useful lefty-versus-lefty setup man. Held LH hitters to .203 batting average; righties hit .296 off him. Just make sure he stays in the same role as 1992, and he's a good safe pick.

	W	SV	ERA	IP	H	BB	SO	BPI	$
1992 Oakland AL	2	1	2.49	43	39	21	18	1.38	1
1993 Base Case	2	1	2.77	55	51	23	26	1.35	2

HOUGH, CHARLIE - White Sox - TR - Age 45

Even while he pitched well through 1992, Hough was undrafted in many Rotisserie leagues. He's done too much damage over the years, statistically and emotionally. Watching him walk the bases around and around is worse than watching a grand slam yielded by your pitcher, because it takes so long.

	W	SV	ERA	IP	H	BB	SO	BPI	$
1992 Chicago AL	7	0	3.93	176	160	66	76	1.28	5
1993 Base Case	9	0	4.10	183	166	74	89	1.31	3

HOWARD, CHRIS - White Sox - TL - Age 27

Tantalizing strikeout pitcher with nerve-wracking control. Has been released by the Yankees and Indians already.

	W	SV	ERA	IP	H	BB	SO	BPI	$
1992 Vancouver AAA	3	0	2.92	24	18	22	23	1.62	

HOWE, STEVE - Yankees - TL - Age 35

Consistently leads the major leagues in number of hit batsmen divided by number of unintentional walks. Do you think he has excellent control and likes to pitch inside? You bet he does. Great slider.

	W	SV	ERA	IP	H	BB	SO	BPI	$
1992 New York AL	3	6	2.45	22	9	3	12	0.55	7
1993 Base Case	4	9	2.44	37	27	6	23	0.89	12

HOWELL, JAY - Dodgers - TR - Age 37

Howell suffered through his third injury-plagued season in a row and at his age that has to be viewed as a risk for the remainder of his career. He pitches effectively when healthy but his days as a top closer are over, although many teams would be willing to give him a chance at that job in 1993. If Tommy Lasorda liked Howell more, he could have had 15-20 saves in 1992.

	W	SV	ERA	IP	H	BB	SO	BPI	$
1992 Los Angeles NL	1	4	1.54	47	41	18	36	1.26	4
1993 Base Case	3	14	2.41	56	48	19	45	1.20	15

HOY, PETE - Red Sox - TR - Age 26
One more candidate for the Sox unsettled closer role. Hoy was a little behind Ken Ryan at the end of 1992, but can emerge during the summer, if Boston doesn't sign a top reliever.

	W	SV	ERA	IP	H	BB	SO	BPI	$
1992 Pawtucket AAA	3	5	4.81	73	83	25	38	1.48	
1992 Boston AL	0	0	7.36	3	8	2	2	2.72	-
1993 Base Case	0	0	5.02	6	10	3	2	2.16	-

HUISMAN, RICK - Giants - TR - Age 24
A '92 midseason promotion makes him one to keep your eye on for '93, especially with the Giants' history of arm troubles. Texas League All-Star. Not to be confused with Mark Huismann.

	W	SV	ERA	IP	H	BB	SO	BPI	$
1992 Shreveport AA	7	0	2.35	103	79	31	100	1.07	
1992 Phoenix AAA	3	0	2.41	56	45	24	44	1.23	

HUISMANN, MARK - Royals - TR - Age 34
Peaked with 33 saves for Omaha in 1985. Career minor league closer; that's all.

	W	SV	ERA	IP	H	BB	SO	BPI	$
1992 Omaha AAA	4	0	5.17	123	139	34	58	1.40	

HUNTER, JIM - Brewers - TR - Age 28
Just a reserve arm stored on the Triple-A roster in 1992.

	W	SV	ERA	IP	H	BB	SO	BPI	$
1992 El Paso AA	1	0	3.00	18	18	3	9	1.17	
1992 Denver AAA	6	2	3.68	134	144	46	56	1.41	

HURST, BRUCE - Padres - TL - Age 35
Hurst was on the trading block by the cash-poor Padres, and had rotator cuff surgery after the season. Hurst went 0-2, 7.56 in September and he is 35 years old. Still, there are about 15 major league clubs in need of 200 innings from a quality left-handed starter.

	W	SV	ERA	IP	H	BB	SO	BPI	$
1992 San Diego NL	14	0	3.85	217	223	51	131	1.26	5
1993 Base Case	12	0	3.89	208	208	50	122	1.24	5

HURST, JONATHAN - Expos - TR - Age 26
After playing for independent Miami in the Class A Florida State League in 1991, Hurst nearly made the Expos' rotation out of spring training last year. He lost out to Chris Haney then had a nondescript season.

	W	SV	ERA	IP	H	BB	SO	BPI	$
1992 Indianapolis AAA	4	0	3.77	119	135	29	70	1.38	
1992 Montreal NL	1	0	5.51	16	18	7	4	1.53	-
1993 Base Case	1	0	4.39	37	41	12	14	1.44	-

IGNASIAK, MIKE - Brewers - TR - Age 27
Got a callup in 1991 but went on the DL after just four games. Still trying to come back.

	W	SV	ERA	IP	H	BB	SO	BPI	$
1992 Denver AAA	7	10	2.93	92	83	33	64	1.26	

INNIS, JEFF - Mets - TR - Age 30

Steve Olin has proven that a submariner can in fact be a closer, but Jeff Innis has yet to find a manager who will give him a try in that role. Innis took a step forward last season in that Jeff Torborg would at least bring him into tied games, which accounts for the fact that he got 15 decisions in '92 vs. two the prior year, and Jeff did pick up 16 holds, third in the NL.

	W	SV	ERA	IP	H	BB	SO	BPI	$
1992 New York NL	6	1	2.86	88	85	36	39	1.38	2
1993 Base Case	3	3	2.79	83	72	30	39	1.24	5

IRVINE, DARYL - Red Sox - TR - Age 28

Just another Red Sox SP: dangerous.

	W	SV	ERA	IP	H	BB	SO	BPI	$
1992 Boston AL	3	0	6.11	28	31	14	10	1.61	-
1993 Base Case	2	0	5.78	30	35	15	11	1.68	-

> *"Man, what a pitcher's graveyard!"*
>
> *-- Satchel Paige when he first saw Fenway Park*

JACKSON, DANNY - Phillies - TL - Age 31
A flop for the Cubs, winning just five games and plagued by injuries over a season and half. Jackson occasionally flashed his old form after being traded to the Pirates. My advice is simple: stay away. Jackson holds some all-time records for bad Rotisserie damage.

	W	SV	ERA	IP	H	BB	SO	BPI	$
1992 Two Teams NL	8	0	3.84	201	211	77	97	1.43	-
1993 Base Case	8	0	4.30	144	158	62	70	1.52	-

JACKSON, MIKE - Giants - TR - Age 28
Good hard-throwing setup reliever. Just a little too wild (in my opinion) to be a closer.

	W	SV	ERA	IP	H	BB	SO	BPI	$
1992 San Francisco NL	6	2	3.73	82	76	33	80	1.33	1
1993 Base Case	6	4	3.81	81	70	34	74	1.29	4

JANICKI, PETE - Angels - TR - Age 21
Janicki was California's first round pick in the June 1992 draft and was signed in October after protracted negotiations. The transaction was made more complicated by the fact that Janicki suffered a stress fracture in his arm during the Olympic Trials. He will probably start the 1993 season at Class A Palm Springs. Fastball/forkball pitcher was at UCLA.

JEFFCOAT, MIKE - Rangers - TL - Age 33
Never a particularly effective pitcher, Jeffcoat suffered through a nightmarish 1992. An elbow injury limited him to 6 games in the majors. He had planned to change to a submarine-style delivery in an attempt to salvage his career. Became a free agent after the 1992 season.

	W	SV	ERA	IP	H	BB	SO	BPI	$
1992 Texas AL	0	0	7.32	19	28	5	6	1.68	-
1992 Oklahoma City AAA	2	0	4.22	32	33	6	20	1.22	
1993 Base Case	2	0	4.73	48	60	12	22	1.51	-

JOHNSON, JEFF - Yankees - TL - Age 26
Johnson was a sensation when he produced a 4-1 record with a 1.88 ERA after his callup in 1991, a classic lesson why a 4-1 record doesn't mean a darn thing in Rotisserie. When you get excited about this pitcher or that pitcher who is 4-1 in May 1993, stop and think about Jeff Johnson.

	W	SV	ERA	IP	H	BB	SO	BPI	$
1992 New York AL	2	0	6.66	52	71	23	14	1.78	-
1993 Base Case	3	0	6.23	73	88	23	31	1.51	-

JOHNSON, RANDY - Mariners - TL - Age 29
Much like Bobby Witt, Johnson is a hard thrower who can be incredibly wild. He walked more than six men per nine innings in each of the last two years. Despite a great spring training, Johnson showed only marginal improvement from 1991 to 1992. And despite a couple of solid outings in September, there's no reason to believe Johnson will suddenly harness his wildness.

	W	SV	ERA	IP	H	BB	SO	BPI	$
1992 Seattle AL	12	0	3.77	210	154	144	241	1.42	3
1993 Base Case	13	0	3.80	211	155	148	250	1.43	3

JOHNSTON, JOEL - Royals - TR - Age 26
Johnston couldn't live up to unrealistic projections after a great 1991 major league debut (0.40 ERA in 22.1 IP). This third round, 1988 draft pick throws hard but suffers control problems. His selection by Baseball America in 1991 as the Royals top prospect now appears premature.

	W	SV	ERA	IP	H	BB	SO	BPI	$
1992 Kansas City AL	0	0	13.50	2	3	2	0	1.88	-
1992 Omaha AAA	5	2	6.39	74	80	45	48	1.67	
1993 Base Case	1	1	4.45	37	35	19	29	1.46	-

JOHNSTONE, JOHN - Marlins - TR - Age 24
Good lively arm, one of the Mets' better prospects. Dominated the NY-Penn league in 1989 and the FSL in 1990. Still working on his stuff at Double-A in 1992.

JONES, BARRY - Phillies - TR - Age 30
Barry would have been deservedly unemployed after the Phillies dumped him in mid-season were it not for Jeff Torborg's memory of 1990, when he was on hand for Jones' one semi-effective year. Will have trouble finding major league role in 1993.

	W	SV	ERA	IP	H	BB	SO	BPI	$
1992 New York NL	7	1	5.68	69	85	35	30	1.72	-

JONES, BOBBY - Mets - TR - Age 25
Great prospect; will be especially valuable if he isn't rushed into major league service.

	W	SV	ERA	IP	H	BB	SO	BPI	$
1993 Binghamton AA	12	0	1.88	158	118	43	144	1.02	

JONES, CALVIN - Mariners - TR - Age 29
As successful as he was in 1991 with the Mariners (2.53 ERA in 46 IP), he was equally unsuccessful last year. Jones has a history of walking too many men, even when he pitched well. Major league hitters learned to take his forkballs (which often hit the dirt) and they hit his good stuff.

	W	SV	ERA	IP	H	BB	SO	BPI	$
1992 Seattle AL	3	0	5.69	61	50	47	49	1.57	-
1993 Base Case	2	1	4.42	55	41	38	44	1.46	-

JONES, DOUG - Astros - TR - Age 35
One of the great success stories of 1992, Jones was arguably the best relief pitcher in the National League. Clearly the Astros' most valuable player, he came to spring training with a minor league contract after being released by Cleveland. Jones told me in 1991 that he was still able to pitch effectively and just needed regular work to stay sharp. That was the year the Indians were generating about two save opportunities per month. The key is just having enough velocity on the fastball to make the changeup deceptive.

	W	SV	ERA	IP	H	BB	SO	BPI	$
1992 Houston NL	11	36	1.85	111	96	17	93	1.01	45
1993 Base Case	8	24	2.78	91	90	16	73	1.16	26

JONES, JIMMY - Astros - TR - Age 28
Off-season elbow surgery delayed the start of his season, but he finished with 10 wins, second on the Astros' staff. Essentially a stopgap starter until the Astros' young pitchers develop, Jones was the third player taken in the 1982 draft (ahead of Dwight Gooden) after an outstanding high school career in Dallas. Numerous arm injuries have taken their toll, but he gets by on location and changing speeds.

	W	SV	ERA	IP	H	BB	SO	BPI	$
1992 Jackson AA	1	0	2.50	18	20	6	20	1.44	
1992 Houston NL	10	0	4.07	139	135	39	69	1.25	2
1993 Base Case	9	0	4.13	138	138	44	76	1.32	0

JONES, STACY - Orioles - TR - Age 25
Pitched well in relief in 1991, rising from AA to AAA to Baltimore. Spent 1992 trying to regroup.

JONES, TODD - Astros - TR - Age 24
1989 compensation pick for Nolan Ryan. Made successful conversion from starter to closer in 1992. Hard thrower still needs better control before challenging for a big league job.

	W	SV	ERA	IP	H	BB	SO	BPI	$
1992 Jackson AA	3	25	3.14	66	53	44	60	1.47	
1992 Tucson AAA	0	0	4.50	4	1	10	4	2.75	

JUDEN, JEFF - Astros - TR - Age 22
Jumbo size hard thrower. Still working on control. Was 9-10 with 4.04 ERA and 149 hits in 147 IP at AAA.

KAMIENIECKI, SCOTT - Yankees - TR - Age 28
Despite the horrible full-season numbers, Kamieniecki actually pitched well after mid August 1992. In 1991 he had back trouble, but that wasn't a factor last year.

	W	SV	ERA	IP	H	BB	SO	BPI	$
1992 New York AL	6	0	4.36	188	193	74	88	1.42	-
1993 Base Case	6	0	4.21	138	140	53	70	1.40	-

KARCHNER, MATT - Royals - TR - Age 25
Terrific season at A-ball in 1991; struggled some at AA Memphis in 1992.

KEY, JIMMY - Blue Jays - TL - Age 31
Just when it looked like Key was fading from age, he put together one of his best streaks ever, and carried his team to the World Series. Key has a history of coming back marvelously rejuvenated from rehab stints in Dunedin, his home town.

	W	SV	ERA	IP	H	BB	SO	BPI	$
1992 Toronto AL	13	0	3.53	216	205	59	117	1.22	12
1993 Base Case	14	0	3.50	209	202	54	122	1.23	14

KIEFER, MARK - Brewers - TR - Age 24
Passed through AA El Paso in just half a season, but has been only so-so at Denver for two years.

KIELY, JOHN - Tigers - TR - Age 28
A bit old to be getting his feet wet in the majors, still he did little that would have been harmful to your team last year. A setup man.

	W	SV	ERA	IP	H	BB	SO	BPI	$
1992 Detroit AL	4	0	2.13	55	44	28	18	1.31	3
1993 Base Case	2	0	2.95	40	35	24	13	1.46	0

KILE, DARRYL - Astros - TR - Age 24
Highly touted young pitcher was a disappointment again in 1992. Started the year as the No. 3 man in the Astro rotation, but was sent back to Tucson for two months. Pitched better after returning, finishing with an eleven strikeout complete game win in his last start. Expect improvement in 1993 with occasional lapses.

	W	SV	ERA	IP	H	BB	SO	BPI	$
1992 Tucson AAA	4	0	3.99	56	50	32	43	1.46	
1992 Houston NL	5	0	3.95	125	124	63	90	1.49	-
1993 Base Case	9	0	3.80	163	157	81	112	1.47	-

KILGUS, PAUL - Unsigned - TL - Age 31
A regular starter with the Rangers and Cubs in 1988-1989, Kilgus is now just a minor league reserve.

KING, ERIC - Tigers - TR - Age 28
King is near finished. Too many aches and pains, including a bad back. Has been ineffective over most of the last two years, and not likely to regain his form soon, if ever.

	W	SV	ERA	IP	H	BB	SO	BPI	$
1992 Detroit AL	4	1	5.22	79	90	28	45	1.49	-
1993 Base Case	5	1	4.23	108	114	36	52	1.38	-

KIPPER, BOB - Twins - TL - Age 28
Kipper is a lefty setup man and middle reliever behind Mark Guthrie and Gary Wayne. He was worth more in the National League. These guys are supposed to be safe, but Kipper isn't.

	W	SV	ERA	IP	H	BB	SO	BPI	$
1992 Minnesota AL	3	0	4.42	39	40	14	22	1.40	-
1993 Base Case	3	2	4.26	55	58	20	33	1.43	-

KISER, GARLAND - Indians - TL - Age 24
Terrific in the low minors 1989-1991. Still stuck at AA in 1992 but young enough to make it.

KLINK, JOE - Athletics - TL - Age 31
Good lefty setup man in 1990. Over the hill now.

KNACKERT, BRENT - Mariners - TR - Age 23
A Rule Five pick in 1989, has been stuck at AA since spending a year in Seattle with a 6.51 ERA.

KNUDSEN, KURT - Tigers - TR - Age 26
Another setup man. He's the kind of pitcher who gets just enough opportunities to hurt you a little.

	W	SV	ERA	IP	H	BB	SO	BPI	$
1992 Detroit AL	2	5	4.58	70	70	41	51	1.57	-
1993 Base Case	1	3	4.90	50	50	29	39	1.57	-

KNUDSON, MARK - Unsigned - TR - Age 32
Worked at AAA Las Vegas in 1992 and had a couple teams interested. Best year was 1990 for Brewers.

KRAMER, TOM - Indians - TR - Age 25
Like many Indians pitchers he got a shock moving from AA Canton to AAA Colorado Springs. Produced eight wins and a 4.88 ERA in 1992.

KRIVDA, RICK - Orioles - TL - Age 23
Krivda led all O's minor leaguers with 17 wins and 188 Ks (in 179 innings) while splitting time between Baltimore's two Class A franchises.

	W	SV	ERA	IP	H	BB	SO	BPI	$
1992 Kane County	12	0	3.03	122	108	41	124	1.22	
1992 Frederick A	5	0	2.98	57	51	15	64	1.16	

KRUEGER, BILL - Tigers - TL - Age 34
The Expos acquired Krueger from Minnesota on Aug. 31 to help them in the NL East race. He was more of a hindrance, though, pitching woefully. Trading away Krueger after his hot start was one of the classic

sucker plays of 1992. I must have warned 50 people not to take him; but the Expos never called me.

	W	SV	ERA	IP	H	BB	SO	BPI	$
1992 Minnesota AL	10	0	4.30	161	166	46	86	1.31	4
1992 Montreal NL	0	0	6.75	17	23	7	13	1.73	-
1993 Base Case	9	0	4.42	165	186	55	90	1.46	-

LACOSS, MIKE - Expos - TR - Age 36
Last seen at AAA Indianapolis (7.30 ERA).

LAMP, DENNIS - Unsigned - TR - Age 40
Long past being valuable. Last good year was 1989.

	W	SV	ERA	IP	H	BB	SO	BPI	$
1992 Pittsburgh NL	1	0	5.14	28	33	9	15	1.50	-

LANCASTER, LES - Tigers - TR - Age 30
Sparky thought he had a rubber arm. He doesn't, just a very tired arm.

	W	SV	ERA	IP	H	BB	SO	BPI	$
1992 Detroit AL	3	0	6.33	86	101	51	35	1.75	-
1993 Base Case	5	1	4.54	109	115	46	60	1.48	-

LANDRUM, BILL - Expos - TR - Age 34
He led the majors in grievances filed in 1992. He filed one against the Pirates when they released him in spring training after he led them in saves each of the past three seasons. He filed another in early August, claiming he was injured when the Expos outrighted him to the minors. Chronic shoulder and knee injuries have all but ended his career.

	W	SV	ERA	IP	H	BB	SO	BPI	$
1992 Indianapolis AAA	1	0	3.95	27	27	4	23	1.15	
1992 Montreal NL	1	0	7.20	20	27	9	7	1.80	-
1993 Base Case	0	0	4.64	23	26	7	12	1.44	-

LANGSTON, MARK - Angels - TL - Age 32
Langston went from 19 wins and an ERA under 3.00 to a sub-par 1992. He still struck out 174 in 229 innings, indicating he has lost little off his fastball. One of the best picks to be a great pitcher for a fair price in 1993. Had a 2.70 ERA after July 31 last year.

	W	SV	ERA	IP	H	BB	SO	BPI	$
1992 California AL	13	0	3.66	229	206	74	174	1.22	12
1993 Base Case	17	0	3.31	235	196	82	181	1.18	20

LAYANA, TIM - Orioles - TR - Age 29
Last up with the Reds in 1991 (with a 6.97 ERA). Weak performance at Rochester last year.

LEACH, TERRY - White Sox - TR - Age 39
Wise usage by Gene Lamont made him a valuable pitcher again in 1992.

	W	SV	ERA	IP	H	BB	SO	BPI	$
1992 Chicago AL	6	0	1.95	73	57	20	22	1.05	8
1993 Base Case	5	0	2.93	71	66	17	26	1.17	5

LEARY, TIM - Mariners P - TR - Age 34
For one half of one season (1988) Leary was a top pitcher in the National League. The Mariners acquired him partly because they felt he could give innings, and partly because the Yankees paid them to take him. Even if someone pays you, don't make the same mistake.

	W	SV	ERA	IP	H	BB	SO	BPI	$
1992 Two Teams AL	8	0	5.36	141	131	87	46	1.55	-
1993 Base Case	5	0	5.59	124	134	72	57	1.66	-

LEE, MARK - Brewers - TL - Age 28

Didn't pitch in the majors at all in 1992, and if he's on the roster to open 1993, it only means that Angel Miranda isn't yet ready and no other lefties could be scavenged. Stay away.

LEFFERTS, CRAIG - Orioles - TL - Age 35

After Baltimore traded two good prospects to San Diego for one month of Lefferts, he posted a 4.09 ERA and won only one of his five September starts. This marred an otherwise effective year for Lefferts who won 13 games as a Padre starter after years of bullpen work.

	W	SV	ERA	IP	H	BB	SO	BPI	$
1992 San Diego NL	13	0	3.69	163	180	35	81	1.32	3
1992 Baltimore AL	1	0	4.09	33	34	6	23	1.21	0
1993 Base Case	12	0	3.86	141	152	30	78	1.29	6

LEIBRANDT, CHARLIE - Rangers - TL - Age 36

Still a big winner, Leibrandt has double-digit wins in 7 of his last 9 years. Leibrandt will retain the fourth starter role and will be among the league's best fourth starters, often matching up against much weaker opposing pitchers, thus helping his won/loss record. Don't risk more than a few bucks on him.

	W	SV	ERA	IP	H	BB	SO	BPI	$
1992 Atlanta NL	15	0	3.36	193	191	42	104	1.21	9
1993 Base Case	12	0	3.86	209	179	46	118	1.29	6

LEITER, AL - Blue Jays - TL - Age 27

Looked like a future star in 1988; but the future has arrived, and Leiter hasn't.

	W	SV	ERA	IP	H	BB	SO	BPI	$
1992 Toronto AL	0	0	9.00	1	1	2	0	3.00	-
1993 Base Case	0	0	4.80	15	14	7	10	1.40	-

LEITER, MARK - Tigers - TR - Age 29

Despite the 8 wins, Leiter is unproven and has the same tendency toward high ERA and ratio that plagues most Tiger pitchers.

	W	SV	ER	IP	H	BB	SO	BPI	$
1992 Detroit AL	8	0	4.18	112	116	43	75	1.42	1
1993 Base Case	8	0	4.09	111	107	40	77	1.32	2

LEON, DANNY - Rangers - TR - Age 25

Leon is a very hard thrower. Rangers found him in the Mexican League. Originally signed by the Expos at the age of 19, but injuries and a volatile temper impeded his progress. Like most power pitchers, he yields too many walks. He finished the season on the DL with elbow problems, but is expected to be ready in 1993.

	W	SV	ERA	IP	H	BB	SO	BPI	$
1992 Texas AL	1	0	5.89	18	18	10	15	1.53	-
1992 Tulsa AA	5	1	0.60	30	15	8	34	0.77	
1993 Base Case	1	0	5.32	18	17	9	14	1.42	-

LEWIS, JIM - Astros - TR - Age 23
Second round draft choice in 1991 is moving rapidly through the Astros' system. Hard thrower.

	W	SV	ERA	IP	H	BB	SO	BPI	$
1992 Osceola A	5	0	1.12	80	54	32	65	1.08	
1992 Jackson AA	3	0	4.11	70	64	30	43	1.34	
1992 Tucson AAA	0	0	0.00	1	0	2	0	2.00	

LEWIS, JIM - Orioles - TR - Age 28
Did much better at Las Vegas in 1991 than he did at Rochester in 1992, which means he slumped badly.

LEWIS, RICHIE - Marlins - TR - Age 27
Good curveball. Lewis had tremendous strikeout numbers for a little guy. He is a definite candidate for the fourth or fifth starter role.

	W	SV	ERA	IP	H	BB	SO	BPI	$
1992 Rochester AAA	10	0	3.28	159	136	61	154	1.24	
1992 Baltimore AL	1	0	10.80	7	13	7	4	3.00	-
1993 Base Case	8	0	3.94	160	160	60	90	1.38	1

LEWIS, SCOTT - Angels - TR - Age 27
Lewis was thrown into a starter's role in 1991 and failed miserably; in 1992, he appeared to turn his career around with successful stops at Edmonton (10 wins in 22 starts) and Anaheim. He has an outside shot at a starting job, but is more likely to be used in middle relief.

	W	SV	ERA	IP	H	BB	SO	BPI	$
1992 Edmonton AAA	10	0	4.17	147	159	40	88	1.35	
1992 California AL	4	0	3.99	38	36	14	18	1.30	0
1993 Base Case	4	0	4.99	55	55	20	29	1.36	-

LILLIQUIST, DEREK - Indians - TL - Age 27
As a lefty setup man, Lilliquist had an outstanding year. His '93 role will be the same with a few wins and saves; maybe a lot of saves if he's used to the full extent of his ability.

	W	SV	ERA	IP	H	BB	SO	BPI	$
1992 Cleveland AL	5	6	1.75	62	39	18	47	0.92	12
1993 Base Case	3	9	2.72	42	36	11	32	1.12	10

LINTON, DOUG - Blue Jays - TR - Age 28
Long-time Jays farmhand, he wasn't any better at Syracuse in 1992 than he had been in 1990.

	W	SV	ERA	IP	H	BB	SO	BPI	$
1992 Toronto AL	1	0	8.63	24	31	17	16	2.00	-
1992 Syracuse AAA	12	0	3.69	171	176	70	126	1.44	
1993 Base Case	1	0	4.71	26	26	17	17	1.66	-

LIVERNOIS, DEREK - Red Sox - TR - Age 25
Eight-year minor leaguer; still young enough to become a competent major league, but not a great one.

MacDONALD, BOB - Blue Jays - TL - Age 27
Has been plagued by control problems even in his good years. MacDonald will never be more than just a lefty-versus-lefty setup reliever, although he can be good in that role.

	W	SV	ERA	IP	H	BB	SO	BPI	$
1992 Syracuse AAA	2	2	4.63	23	25	12	14	1.59	
1992 Toronto AL	1	0	4.37	47	50	16	26	1.39	-
1993 Base Case	2	0	3.82	59	60	23	30	1.40	-

MACHADO, JULIO - Brewers - TR - Age 27
Big talent with big legal problems. Has been trying to get out of Venezuela for a year.

MADDUX, GREG - Braves - TR - Age 26
Over the past five years, he has started more games than any pitcher. Only Roger Clemens has more wins and more innings pitched. Not only is Maddux perhaps the best pitcher in baseball, he has never been on the disabled list.

	W	SV	ERA	IP	H	BB	SO	BPI	$
1992 Chicago NL	20	0	2.18	268	201	70	199	1.01	32
1993 Base Case	18	0	2.76	261	222	69	196	1.11	27

MADDUX, MIKE - Padres - TR - Age 31
Although he cannot compare to his brother Greg, this Maddux has put together two good, 5-save seasons in a row in middle relief. Maddux's role could grow slightly; and there is a chance Maddux will be asked to help in the rotation.

	W	SV	ERA	IP	H	BB	SO	BPI	$
1992 San Diego NL	2	5	2.37	80	71	24	60	1.19	7
1993 Base Case	4	4	2.78	87	76	25	60	1.15	9

MAGNANTE, MIKE - Royals - TL - Age 27
The Royals' attempt to make a starter of Magnante was a bona fide bust. He was 0-5 with an ERA of 5.47 as a starter; he was much better in relief. If he stays in the bullpen he'll get a few cheap wins and saves and won't hurt you with his ERA. But, if he becomes a starter, stay far away.

	W	SV	ERA	IP	H	BB	SO	BPI	$
1992 Kansas City AL	4	0	4.94	89	115	35	31	1.68	-
1993 Base Case	2	0	4.00	68	78	27	33	1.54	-

MAGRANE, JOE - Cardinals - TL - Age 28
After missing nearly two full seasons because of elbow surgery, Magrane pitched decently for the Cardinals in September. He showed signs of regaining his old form. Still just a speculation, but a good one.

	W	SV	ERA	IP	H	BB	SO	BPI	$
1992 Arkansas AA	0	0	1.50	18	14	5	15	1.06	
1992 Louisville AAA	3	0	5.40	53	60	29	35	1.68	
1992 St. Louis NL	1	0	4.02	31	34	15	20	1.56	-
1993 Base Case	1	0	3.97	33	35	14	20	1.50	-

MAHOMES, PAT - Twins - TR - Age 22
A very talented young pitcher with an outstanding 92 MPH fastball, a hard slider, and a good curve. He has all the tools to be an outstanding pitcher; it's just a question of time.

	W	SV	ERA	IP	H	BB	SO	BPI	$
1992 Portland AAA	9	0	3.41	111	97	43	87	1.26	
1992 Minnesota AL	3	0	5.04	70	73	37	44	1.58	-
1993 Base Case	7	0	4.13	84	81	37	55	1.41	1

MALDONADO, CARLOS - Royals - TR - Age 26
Maldonado has steadily progressed through the Royals system to become the AAA Omaha Royals' top relief ace in 1992. He's ready for the majors, but won't get a shot at saves unless Montgomery is injured.

	W	SV	ERA	IP	H	BB	SO	BPI	$
1992 Omaha AAA	7	16	3.60	75	61	35	60	1.28	
1993 Base Case	2	1	3.77	58	54	27	39	1.40	1

MALLICOAT, ROB - Astros - TL - Age 28
Originally drafted by Astros in 1984, he has been called up three times without much success. Missed entire 1988 and 1989 seasons due to shoulder surgery. Once the brightest pitching prospect in the organization, he put up good numbers at Tucson in 1992 and should be able to hang on as a lefthanded reliever.

	W	SV	ERA	IP	H	BB	SO	BPI	$
1992 Tucson AAA	1	3	2.32	50	36	21	53	1.14	
1992 Houston NL	0	0	7.23	23	26	19	20	1.90	-
1993 Base Case	0	0	5.41	28	30	15	23	1.58	-

MANUEL, BARRY - Rangers - TR - Age 27
A former minor league relief ace, Manuel had a brief stint with the Rangers in 1992. Rangers were desperate for relief help, and yet Manuel did not stick. He relies on location and changing speeds; didn't have good control in 1992.

	W	SV	ERA	IP	H	BB	SO	BPI	$
1992 Texas AL	1	0	4.76	5	6	1	9	1.24	-
1992 Okla. City AAA	1	5	5.27	27	32	26	11	2.14	
1993 Base Case	1	1	4.22	31	33	15	15	1.54	-

MANZANILLO, JOSIAS - Royals - TR - Age 25
Former Red Sox prospect. Was 7-10 with a 4.36 ERA at Omaha in 1992.

MARTEL, ED - Yankees - TR - Age 24
Six-year Yankee farmhand. Flopped at AAA Columbus last year, especially compared to his teammates.

MARTINEZ, DENNIS - Expos - TR - Age 37
The unquestioned ace of the Expos' staff. However, failure to win big games down the stretch raises questions if he can hold up over a full season at his age.

	W	SV	ERA	IP	H	BB	SO	BPI	$
1992 Montreal NL	16	0	2.47	226	172	60	147	1.03	23
1993 Base Case	16	0	2.42	220	175	57	136	1.05	29

MARTINEZ, JOSE - Marlins - TR - Age 22
Career 423 strikeouts and 67 walks tell the whole story. Has less than half a year above A-ball but could still be a major league contributor in 1993.

	W	SV	ERA	IP	H	BB	SO	BPI	$
1992 St. Lucie A	6	0	2.05	123	107	11	114	0.92	
1992 Binghamton AA	5	0	1.71	58	47	13	39	1.03	
1993 Base Case	6	0	3.66	60	55	21	33	1.27	2

MARTINEZ, PEDRO - Dodgers - TR - Age 21
The younger brother of Ramon, Pedro is considered an outstanding prospect and many observers were surprised to see Astacio get the extended call-up rather than Martinez. There are questions about his ability to deal with adversity and injuries, which have haunted him.

	W	SV	ERA	IP	H	BB	SO	BPI	$
1992 Albuquerque AAA	7	0	3.81	125	104	57	124	1.29	
1992 Los Angeles NL	0	0	2.25	8	6	1	8	0.88	0
1993 Base Case	4	0	3.27	88	68	38	64	1.20	3

MARTINEZ, RAMON - Dodgers - TR - Age 25
Martinez did not pitch in September and is a shadow of the 20-game winner of 1990. Lasorda wrecked another brilliant career by demanding complete games from young arms (Valenzuela, Hershiser, etc.).

	W	SV	ERA	IP	H	BB	SO	BPI	$
1992 Los Angeles NL	8	0	4.00	151	141	69	101	1.39	-
1993 Base Case	11	0	3.74	167	147	62	113	1.26	5

MASON, ROGER - Mets - TR - Age 34
At age 34, he finally spent a full season in the majors in 1992. He had a chance to help in the closer's role with the Pirates last year but was unreliable. He was particularly hurt by the home-run ball.

	W	SV	ERA	IP	H	BB	SO	BPI	$
1992 Pittsburgh NL	5	8	4.09	88	80	33	56	1.28	6
1993 Base Case	4	5	4.16	61	53	20	41	1.20	4

MASTERS, DAVE - Mariners - TR - Age 28
Long-time Giants farmhand, never made it to SF and won't likely make it anywhere.

MATHEWS, GREG - Phillies - TL - Age 30
Very tough lefty with St. Louis in 1986-1987, later succumbed to injury and missed all of 1991. Like many Cardinal expatriates from the same era (Danny Cox, Jim Lindeman, etc.) Mathews got a chance with the Phillies. Until he puts up some numbers, it's still just a human interest story.

	W	SV	ERA	IP	H	BB	SO	BPI	$
1992 Philadelphia NL	2	0	5.16	52	54	24	27	1.49	-

MATHEWS, TERRY - Rangers - TR - Age 28
Mathews followed a solid debut in 1991 with a disastrous performance in 1992. Every phase of his game deteriorated, and his future at the major league level is in doubt.

	W	SV	ERA	IP	H	BB	SO	BPI	$
1992 Texas AL	2	0	5.95	42	48	31	26	1.87	-
1992 Oklahoma City AAA	1	1	4.32	17	17	7	13	1.41	
1993 Base Case	2	0	4.66	62	64	31	29	1.54	-

MAUSER, TIM - Phillies - TR - Age 26
Surfaced with the Phillies in 1991. Worked 100 decent innings in relief at Scranton in 1992.

MAY, SCOTT - Cubs - TR - Age 31
Has appeared with Rangers and Cubs. His 1992 numbers at Iowa were nowhere near as good as 1991's.

MAYSEY, MATT - Expos - TR - Age 26
Once a hot prospect in the Padres' organization, Maysey is still trying to get to the major leagues. He finally made his debut in 1992, making two relief appearances for the Expos. The knuckle-curve is his out pitch.

	W	SV	ERA	IP	H	BB	SO	BPI	$
1992 Indianapolis AAA	5	5	4.30	67	63	28	38	1.36	
1992 Montreal NL	0	0	3.86	2	4	0	1	1.71	-
1993 Base Case	0	0	4.40	29	30	12	13	1.45	-

McANDREW, JAMIE - Dodgers - TR - Age 25
Dodgers top pick in 1989, consistently runs into trouble at AAA Albuquerque, but he's been good everywhere else. If you see good numbers at AAA in 1993, take a big interest.

McCASKILL, KIRK - White Sox - TR - Age 31

A former diamond-in-the-rough who never got polished, now he's a rolling stone with occasional flashes of brilliance.

	W	SV	ERA	IP	H	BB	SO	BPI	$
1992 Chicago AL	12	0	4.18	209	193	95	109	1.38	4
1993 Base Case	12	0	4.17	192	191	82	93	1.42	0

McCLELLAN, PAUL - Brewers - TR - Age 27

Got two shots with the Giants, 1990 and 1991. Just needs to mix other pitches in with his fastball to be successful, but he's been headstrong about learning that skill.

McCLURE, BOB - Cardinals - TL - Age 39

Has been around seemingly forever, long enough that he played Little League with Keith Hernandez. He hangs around because of his ability to get left-handed hitters out. He is still fairly effective in limited duty.

	W	SV	ERA	IP	H	BB	SO	BPI	$
1992 St. Louis NL	2	0	3.17	54	52	25	24	1.43	-
1993 Base Case	2	0	3.83	45	45	20	22	1.44	-

MCCULLERS, LANCE - Dodgers - TR - Age - 29

Once a top reliever with San Diego, McCullers has suffered through years of injuries (including blood clot surgery) and minor league obscurity to put himself in a position to get back to the majors after a decent year at Albuquerque. There may be a spot in the L.A. bullpen.

	W	SV	ERA	IP	H	BB	SO	BPI	$
1992 Texas AL	1	0	5.40	5	1	8	3	1.80	-
1992 Albuquerque AAA	4	12	1.84	44	34	10	35	1.00	
1993 Base Case	1	0	3.78	20	16	14	14	1.48	-

McDONALD, BEN - Orioles - TR - Age 25

On the negative side, McDonald's fastball is not as dominant as before he got a sore shoulder in 1991, and he led the league in HR allowed while assembling an ERA over 4.00. The longball tendency is especially problematic with the short RF wall at Camden Yards. He could be on the verge of a breakthrough year. Major talent.

	W	SV	ERA	IP	H	BB	SO	BPI	$
1992 Baltimore AL	13	0	4.24	227	213	74	158	1.26	7
1993 Base Case	10	0	4.21	184	175	62	127	1.29	3

McDOWELL, JACK - White Sox - TR - Age 27

A fine pitcher, but not quite as good as what we saw in 1992. Likely to be overvalued in most leagues.

	W	SV	ERA	IP	H	BB	SO	BPI	$
1992 Chicago AL	20	0	3.18	260	247	75	178	1.24	19
1993 Base Case	17	0	3.32	255	232	80	184	1.22	18

MCDOWELL, ROGER - Dodgers - TR - Age 32

McDowell's 14 saves were the result of his role, not his talent. McDowell is not likely to be re-signed by the Dodgers who are looking to pare their payroll; McDowell is a good place to start.

	W	SV	ERA	IP	H	BB	SO	BPI	$
1992 Los Angeles NL	6	14	4.09	84	103	42	50	1.73	5
1993 Base Case	7	5	3.86	91	99	40	47	1.54	2

McELROY, CHUCK - Cubs - TL - Age 25

The league caught up to McElroy when Jim Lefebvre tried him as a semi-regular closer. He had only one save after May. McElroy has shown that he does not have what it takes to be a major league closer, especially not the required bounce-back arm. However he is effective when used just on his good days.

	W	SV	ERA	IP	H	BB	SO	BPI	$
1992 Chicago NL	4	6	3.55	83	73	51	83	1.48	2
1993 Base Case	4	4	3.32	89	75	54	84	1.44	3

MEACHAM, RUSTY - Royals - TR - Age 25

Meacham emerged from a crowded Royals bullpen to become their best setup man. He throws a lot of pitches well and should return to a similar role in 1993.

	W	SV	ERA	IP	H	BB	SO	BPI	$
1992 Kansas City AL	10	2	2.74	101	88	21	64	1.07	12
1993 Base Case	7	1	3.43	70	68	17	44	1.21	6

MELENDEZ, JOSE - Red Sox - TR - Age 27

Melendez started the season beautifully in a setup role but fizzled in a brief stint in the rotation. He seems more suited to go as hard as he can for two or three innings. Without Myers, the hard-throwing Melendez will be a key member of a save committee.

	W	SV	ERA	IP	H	BB	SO	BPI	$
1992 San Diego NL	6	0	2.92	89	82	20	82	1.14	4
1993 Base Case	6	5	3.02	83	76	20	66	1.16	10

MENENDEZ, TONY - Reds - TR - Age 28

A nine-year farmhand with White Sox and Rangers, his best year was 1989 at Birmingham. The low ERA etc. with the Reds was just a fluke.

	W	SV	ERA	IP	H	BB	SO	BPI	$
1992 Nashville AAA	3	1	4.05	106	98	47	92	1.37	
1992 Cincinnati NL	1	0	1.93	4	1	0	5	0.21	-
1993 Base Case	1	0	3.74	32	27	11	19	1.20	

MERCKER, KENT - Braves - TL - Age 25

Can't be a closer if he continues to walk too many batters. He's a good setup man who will pick up some cheap wins and saves, but his other numbers won't help and may hurt. If he gets traded to another team, pay attention since he could get a shot at the closer job.

	W	SV	ERA	IP	H	BB	SO	BPI	$
1992 Atlanta NL	3	6	3.42	68	51	35	49	1.26	5
1993 Base Case	3	6	3.40	67	51	34	50	1.28	6

MESA, JOSE - Indians - TR - Age 26

Mesa began the '92 season in the Orioles rotation but was very erratic. The Orioles were forced to trade Mesa because he was out of options, and he couldn't clear waivers with his 93-mph fastball and a hard slider. The Indians made some minor adjustments to Mesa's pitching mechanics, but he's still not as consistent as they would like.

	W	SV	ERA	IP	H	BB	SO	BPI	$
1992 Two Teams AL	7	0	4.59	161	169	70	62	1.49	-
1993 Base Case	9	0	4.94	151	165	70	66	1.56	-

MILACKI, BOB - Orioles - TR - Age 28

Milacki has never regained his 1989 form. He is still a candidate for the rotation and pitching coach Dick Bosman is working with him to stop being such a nitpicker.

	W	SV	ERA	IP	H	BB	SO	BPI	$
1992 Baltimore AL	6	1	5.84	116	140	44	51	1.59	-
1992 Rochester AAA	7	0	4.57	61	57	21	35	1.28	
1993 Base Case	7	0	4.85	141	145	56	55	1.43	-

MILCHIN, MIKE - Cardinals - TL - Age 25

A second round pick and a 1988 Olympian. Bombed at Louisville in 1992.

MILITELLO, SAM - Yankees- TR - Age 23

The Sporting News rated him the top prospect in the minors. Baseball America named him the No.1 prospect in the International League. In the minors, he just toyed with the opposition, compiling a 34-8 record and a 1.44 ERA without a dominating fastball. Militello, throws four pitches for strikes. He hides the ball well, behind whirling elbows and knees. One negative is that hitters will make progress handling Militello, faster than he will make progress handling them. He was dominant from his first appearance.

	W	SV	ERA	IP	H	BB	SO	BPI	$
1992 Columbus AAA	12	0	2.29	141	105	48	152	1.09	
1992 New York AL	3	0	3.45	60	43	32	42	1.25	1
1993 Base Case	12	0	3.43	192	156	102	144	1.34	9

MILLER, KURT - Rangers - TL - Age 20

Miller put together a solid season at A and AA to retain his status as the Rangers' best pitching prospect. Because of his age, it is unlikely that he will reach the majors in 1993. He has a great arm and good presence on the mound. He complained of a tired arm in late 1991 but did not have that problem in 1992.

	W	SV	ERA	IP	H	BB	SO	BPI	$
1992 Tulsa AA	7	0	3.68	88	82	35	73	1.33	
1992 Charlotte A	5	0	2.39	75	51	29	58	1.07	

MILLER, PAUL - Pirates - TR - Age 27

After five years in the minor leagues, the hard-throwing Miller finally made the Pirates. However, a pulled rib muscle and tender shoulder caused him to go back and eventually cut short his season.

	W	SV	ERA	IP	H	BB	SO	BPI	$
1992 Buffalo AAA	2	0	3.90	32	38	16	18	1.69	
1992 Pittsburgh NL	1	0	2.38	11	11	1	5	1.06	-
1993 Base Case	1	0	3.29	22	24	7	10	1.43	-

MILLS, ALAN - Orioles - TR - Age 26

Mills' success was a surprise to some, especially the Yankees who traded him to the O's. Mills is a hard thrower who was very effective in middle and long relief, and in a few games as a starter. Manager Johnny Oates had enough confidence in Mills to start him against Toronto in the stretch drive, and Mills did not disappoint. However, he did experience some rough outings as a starter, and will lose value if pushed into a starting role.

	W	SV	ERA	IP	H	BB	SO	BPI	$
1992 Baltimore AL	10	2	2.61	103	78	54	60	1.28	9
1993 Base Case	6	1	3.18	68	55	36	40	1.35	4

MINOR, BLAS - Pirates - TR - Age 27

Though he led Class AAA Buffalo and the Pirates' farm system with 18 saves last season, Pittsburgh didn't give the impression he was in their plans. He appeared in only one game while spending nearly two weeks with the major league club in late July and early August and didn't get a September callup.

	W	SV	ERA	IP	H	BB	SO	BPI	$
1992 Buffalo AAA	5	18	2.43	96.0	72	26	60	1.02	
1992 Pittsburgh NL	0	0	4.50	2.0	3	0	0	1.50	-
1993 Base Case	0	0	5.18	16	21	6	10	1.68	-

MINUTELLI, GINO - Reds - TL - Age 28

A promising prospect in 1990-1991, Minutelli regressed last year. Compare ERA's at AAA Nashville: in 1991 is was 1.90 and then last year it was 4.27.

MIRANDA, ANGEL - Brewers - TL - Age 23

A dark-horse candidate for Brewer saves. Don't be scared off by his unimpressive showing at Triple-A Denver; Milwaukee used him as a starter there solely to give him innings and experience; besides, everyone gets pounded in Denver. The Brewers have no solid lefthanded relievers at the major league level, so there's a job open.

MLICKI, DAVE - Indians - TR - Age 24

Solid starter at AA and a good long-term prospect. Look for him in 1994.

	W	SV	ERA	IP	H	BB	SO	BPI	$
1992 Canton AA	11	0	3.60	172	143	80	146	1.29	
1992 Cleveland AL	0	0	4.98	21	23	16	16	1.80	-

MOELLER, DENNIS - Pirates - TL - Age 25

Moeller's been around a long time for his age -- over 700 IP as a professional. He followed up a good 1991 season with a good start at Omaha in 1992 and got his first big league promotion where he was positively awful. He can't hurt you much -- if he pitches poorly he'll go back to the minors.

	W	SV	ERA	IP	H	BB	SO	BPI	$
1992 Omaha AAA	8	2	2.46	120	121	34	56	1.28	
1992 Kansas City AL	0	0	7.00	18	24	11	6	1.94	-
1993 Base Case	0	0	5.08	40	44	21	22	1.61	-

MONTELEONE, RICH - Yankees - TR - Age 30

A basic fastball-slider-changeup pitcher, Monteleone is not overpowering. He needs to think all the time and move the ball around to be effective, which is exactly what he did in 1992

	W	SV	ERA	IP	H	BB	SO	BPI	$
1992 New York AL	7	0	3.30	92	82	27	62	1.18	6
1993 Base Case	5	0	3.67	72	66	23	47	1.24	3

MONTGOMERY, JEFF - Royals - TR - Age 31

Montgomery is one of the league's top closers. It took him a while to get where he is, first getting a part-time closer role in 1989, then gradually upping the ante every year to his career high 39 saves last year. He's at his peak, though, and won't come cheap. His strikeout-to-walk ratio is falling as he relies more on breaking pitches, but he's still very effective and will put up good numbers for a few more years.

	W	SV	ERA	IP	H	BB	SO	BPI	$
1992 Kansas City AL	1	39	2.18	82	61	27	69	1.06	35
1993 Base Case	2	36	2.61	84	70	28	73	1.16	36

MOORE, MIKE - Tigers - TR - Age 33
In the middle of Moore's worst slump of 1992, Dave Duncan gave me his opinion that Moore wasn't pitching much worse than expected. "His rhythm is a little off. It's like dancing. That's all. Nothing's wrong, and he'll be good other times, really does the same thing every time he goes out there. Sometimes the results are very good and sometimes not so good. He's doing what we expect." I think he'll do better in 1993.

	W	SV	ERA	IP	H	BB	SO	BPI	$
1992 Oakland AL	17	0	4.12	223	229	103	117	1.49	3
1993 Base Case	15	0	3.59	213	202	99	126	1.42	6

MORGAN, MIKE - Cubs - TR - Age 33
Morgan has never shaken the bum rap he acquired when he was rushed to the majors a week after high school graduation. Morgan has quietly become a top starting pitcher. His ERA's are 2.53, 3.75, 2.78, and 2.55 over the past four years. Take away a poor start, and Morgan's ERA would have been 2.14. Twenty-five of his final 29 games were quality starts.

	W	SV	ERA	IP	H	BB	SO	BPI	$
1992 Chicago NL	16	0	2.55	240	203	79	123	1.18	18
1993 Base Case	16	0	3.03	238	209	72	126	1.18	19

MORRIS, JACK - Blue Jays - TR - Age 37
Morris has just about completed the transition from full power pitcher to mostly finesse. He is enjoying a "second career" comparable to the great veterans like Tom Seaver, maybe a step below Seaver, but the same idea.

	W	SV	ERA	IP	H	BB	SO	BPI	$
1992 Toronto AL	21	0	4.04	240	222	80	132	1.25	12
1993 Base Case	18	0	3.71	241	222	80	148	1.25	13

MORTON, KEVIN - Red Sox - TL - Age 24
Good enough to get 15 starts with the Red Sox in 1991, Morton regressed in 1992. His Pawtucket ERA was 5.45 last year, compared to 3.49 the year before.

MOYER, JAMIE - Tigers - TL - Age 30
In 1992 Moyer had a good minor league season, 10 wins and a 2.86 ERA for AAA Toledo. But his last three years in the majors were pretty awful. Even if he comes up, I wouldn't want him.

MULHOLLAND, TERRY - Phillies - TL - Age 30
A chronic knee problem bothered him all season but he still led the club with 229 innings and has 29 wins the last two seasons.

	W	SV	ERA	IP	H	BB	SO	BPI	$
1992 Philadelphia NL	13	0	3.81	229	227	46	125	1.19	7
1993 Base Case	14	0	3.65	222	224	44	127	121	10

MUNOZ, MIKE - Tigers - TL - Age 27
Two things make Munoz interesting. He's a lefty and he got two saves last year. Sparky Anderson told me Munoz would never be an ace reliever, but he could get ten saves in a year in situations where the last out is a lefty hitter. For a dollar or three he is worth the risk.

	W	SV	ERA	IP	H	BB	SO	BPI	$
1992 Detroit AL	1	2	3.00	48	44	25	23	1.44	1
1993 Base Case	1	2	3.03	40	36	20	19	1.40	1

MUNOZ, ROBERTO - Yankees - TR - Age 25

Fine prospect with a solid year at AAA Albany, but the Yankees have so many good arms at AAA already, that Munoz won't likely appear before September and won't be valuable until 1994.

MURPHY, ROB - Astros - TL - Age 32

Made squad after coming to spring training with a minor league contract. Has lost some zip on his fastball. Should stick around for another year or two, but has essentially no value.

	W	SV	ERA	IP	H	BB	SO	BPI	$
1992 Houston NL	3	0	4.04	55	56	21	42	1.38	-
1993 Base Case	2	2	3.85	52	53	18	40	1.36	0

MUSSETT, JOSE - Angels - TL - Age 24

Mussett was a poor outfielder until '90 when he became a pitcher. He throws smoke and was very impressive last year in A-ball striking out an average of almost 1.5 batters per inning with good control.

	W	SV	ERA	IP	H	BB	SO	BPI	$
1992 Quad City A	8	6	2.39	72	41	25	104	0.92	

MUSSINA, MIKE - Orioles - TR - Age 24

Mussina produced a spectacular first full season. In fact, he improved throughout the year, going 4-0, 1.64 during the last four weeks. The only worry is whether the strain of 241 IP in 1992 will affect Mussina in 1993. On the upside, pitching coach Dick Bosman told me Mussina still has some learning to do, on how to work a hitter and how to work through a lineup the second and third time -- so he could actually improve.

	W	SV	ERA	IP	H	BB	SO	BPI	$
1992 Baltimore AL	18	0	2.54	241	212	48	130	1.08	26
1993 Base Case	18	0	2.70	180	159	38	104	1.09	24

MUTIS, JEFF - Indians - TL - Age 26

Mutis is a finesse-type lefty who has failed in several trials with the Indians. He also struggled in AAA in '92, and may become a career minor leaguer any day now.

	W	SV	ERA	IP	H	BB	SO	BPI	$
1992 Col. Sp. AAA	9	0	5.08	145	177	57	77	1.61	-
1993 Base Case	0	0	5.50	21	26	8	9	1.61	-

MYERS, JIMMY - Giants - TR - Age 23

Big season at Shreveport in 1991 with a 2.48 ERA got Myers to AAA Phoenix this year, but he stumbled, and then he couldn't even find himself again back at Shreveport. Needs more time.

MYERS, RANDY - Cubs - TL - Age 30

Myers disappointed Padre management with an awful first half. After the All-Star break, however, Myers re-established himself as an All-Star, with 23 saves and an ERA of 2.82. For the Rotisserian, Myers is a good risk, wherever he is in 1993.

	W	SV	ERA	IP	H	BB	SO	BPI	$
1992 San Diego NL	3	38	4.29	80	84	34	66	1.48	28
1993 Base Case	4	30	3.42	100	90	46	81	1.36	23

NABHOLZ, CHRIS - Expos - TL - Age 26

Good young lefty with curve and sinking fastball, should be a consistent starter for many years.

	W	SV	ERA	IP	H	BB	SO	BPI	$
1992 Montreal NL	11	0	3.32	195	176	74	130	1.28	6
1993 Base Case	10	0	3.30	177	159	63	112	1.25	8

NAGY, CHARLES - Indians - TR - Age 25

In '92, Nagy established himself as one of the top pitchers in baseball. Now he depends on Cleveland fielding a good team behind him. If the Tribe contends, he can win 18-20.

	W	SV	ERA	IP	H	BB	SO	BPI	$
1992 Cleveland AL	17	0	2.96	252	245	57	169	1.20	19
1993 Base Case	14	0	3.43	231	234	62	146	1.28	13

NAVARRO, JAIME - Brewers - TR - Age 26

Navarro finally harnessed his control in 1992; working from behind in the count had always hurt him before. If you need a comparison, think Chris Bosio -- big, strong but not overpowering, good command of three pitches. A plus: Navarro lacks Bosio's hot temper.

	W	SV	ERA	IP	H	BB	SO	BPI	$
1992 Milwaukee AL	17	0	3.33	246	224	64	100	1.17	18
1993 Base Case	16	0	3.43	238	223	65	109	1.21	17

NEAGLE, DENNY - Pirates -TL - Age 24

He came to the Pirates from the Twins in the controversial John Smiley trade last March and struggled as a starter early in the season. Moved to the bullpen for good in June, Neagle seemed to blossom. He threw harder and with more confidence. He won 20 games in the minor leagues in 1990 and was considered one of the Twins' top prospects.

	W	SV	ERA	IP	H	BB	SO	BPI	$
1992 Pittsburgh NL	4	2	4.48	86	81	43	77	1.44	-
1993 Base Case	8	0	4.00	164	145	65	90	1.28	3

NEIDLINGER, JIM - Dodgers - TR - Age 28

Pitched very well for the Dodgers (3.28 ERA) in 12 starts in 1990, but hasn't been invited back, even though his performance at AAA Albuquerque has been consistent for three years. He has good control and deserves another chance in 1993.

	W	SV	ERA	IP	H	BB	SO	BPI	$
1992 Albuquerque AAA	8	0	4.39	146	153	45	81	1.36	
1993 Base Case	1	0	3.56	45	50	10	13	1.33	1

NELSON, GENE - Athletics - TR - Age 32

Great setup man two years ago. Lost his rhythm.

	W	SV	ERA	IP	H	BB	SO	BPI	$
1992 Oakland AL	3	0	6.45	52	68	22	23	1.74	-
1993 Base Case	2	0	4.00	53	58	21	21	1.48	-

NELSON, JEFF - Mariners - TR - Age 26

Ineffective as a starting pitcher throughout his career, Nelson was moved to stopper while at Single-A in 1990. He recorded six saves that year, and 19 more in 1991 at AA and AAA, and then had a great winter ball performance. In 1992 Nelson struggled, like all other Mariners relievers, but found his groove and posted a 2.35 ERA over his last 30 innings, with five saves. Nelson will help set up Norm Charlton in 1993 and likely get a few saves himself in the process.

	W	SV	ERA	IP	H	BB	SO	BPI	$
1992 Seattle AL	1	6	3.44	81	71	44	46	1.42	4
1993 Base Case	1	10	3.03	72	65	37	44	1.41	8

NEN, ROB - Rangers - TR - Age 24

Top prospect, but has been held back by repeated arm miseries. Posted a 2.16 ERA at AA Tulsa.

NEWLIN, JIM - Mariners - TR - Age 26
Has posted two strong performances at AA Jacksonville but hasn't passed the test at Triple-A yet.

NEWMAN, ALAN - Twins - TL - Age 23
Followed a good year at AA Orlando in 1991 with a bad year in 1992.

NEZELEK, ANDY - Braves - TR - Age 27
Good year in relief at AA Greenville. Longshot candidate for a save or two in 1993.

NICHOLS, ROD - Indians - TR - Age 28
Keeps experimenting with different deliveries and different pitches, as if he were age 19. Getting nowhere.

	W	SV	ERA	IP	H	BB	SO	BPI	$
1992 Colorado Springs AAA	3	0	5.67	54	65	16	35	1.50	
1992 Cleveland AL	4	0	4.53	105	114	31	56	1.38	-
1993 Base Case	4	0	4.24	125	134	32	68	1.32	-

NIED, DAVE - Rockies - TR - Age 24
Nied filled the Braves needs with a couple of great spot starts down the stretch when the big three (Glavine, Smoltz, and Avery) were faltering. Nied is ready to pitch (and win) in the big leagues (note his great strikeout to walk ratio - 3.6 to 1), but he doesn't have the most favorable ballpark or the best team.

	W	SV	ERA	IP	H	BB	SO	BPI	$
1992 Richmond AAA	14	0	2.84	168	144	44	159	1.12	
1992 Atlanta NL	3	0	1.17	23	10	5	19	0.65	2
1993 Base Case	12	0	3.67	176	156	57	101	1.21	9

NIELSEN, JERRY - Angels - TL - Age 26
The save ace at AA Albany in 1992, and he didn't do badly at AAA Columbus, either (1.80 ERA). Has a good shot to do some setup and middle work with Cadaret and Guetterman gone.

	W	SV	ERA	IP	H	BB	SO	BPI	$
1992 Albany AA	3	11	1.19	53	38	15	59	1.00	
1992 Columbus AAA	0	1	1.80	5	2	2	5	0.80	
1992 New York AL	1	0	4.58	19	17	18	12	1.78	-
1993 Base Case	1	1	4.10	22	20	10	14	1.36	1

NUNEZ, EDWIN - Brewers - TR - Age 29
Had lots of opportunity in '92, and didn't do the job. The Rangers were in the race, and Nunez posted a 6.00 ERA in his first 16 appearances. He gained weight during the season which contributed to knee problems. Still throws hard, but will have a tough time finding a role in '93. Nunez had surgery in October. Some major league team may take a chance on him, but you shouldn't.

	W	SV	ERA	IP	H	BB	SO	BPI	$
1992 Texas AL	1	3	4.85	59	63	22	49	1.43	-
1993 Base Case	1	2	4.55	45	48	18	40	1.45	-

O'DONOGHUE, JOHN - Orioles - TL - Age 23

O'Donoghue is a smooth lefty who relies on a good curve ball. He may need more AAA-ball, but he could be in Camden Yards in mid-season. Most observers were shocked when O'Donoghue wasn't drafted.

	W	SV	ERA	IP	H	BB	SO	BPI	$
1992 Hagerstown AA	7	0	2.24	112	77	40	86	1.05	
1992 Rochester AAA	5	0	3.23	70	60	19	47	1.13	
1993 Base Case	3	0	4.25	55	56	22	34	1.42	-

OGEA, CHAD - Indians - TR - Age 22

Ogea is a young and talented Indians prospect who had an outstanding year in Class A and AA ball. He relies on slow stuff, so he may have difficulty in getting hitters out at higher levels.

	W	SV	ERA	IP	H	BB	SO	BPI	$
1992 Kinston A	13	0	3.50	139	135	29	123	1.18	
1992 Canton AA	6	0	2.20	49	39	12	40	1.04	

OJEDA, BOB - Indians - TL - Age 35

Ojeda was offered to the pennant contenders in September and there were no takers. That should tell you something about where baseball's best minds think Ojeda's career is headed. Still, he's an experienced lefty with a good changeup. In Dodger Stadium I like him for 1993.

	W	SV	ERA	IP	H	BB	SO	BPI	$
1992 Los Angeles NL	6	0	3.63	166	169	81	94	1.50	-
1993 Base Case	9	0	3.87	171	171	72	99	1.43	1

OLIN, STEVE - Indians - TR - Age 27

Although Olin racked up 29 saves, he is not a dominant closer because he has difficulty getting left handed hitters out. The lefties hit him for .324 in '92 and .330 in '91.

	W	SV	ERA	IP	H	BB	SO	BPI	$
1992 Cleveland AL	8	29	2.34	88	80	27	47	1.21	29
1993 Base Case	6	20	2.99	75	72	24	44	1.29	21

OLIVARES, OMAR - Cardinals - TR - Age 25

Shows ability to be the kind of pitcher that wins 15 games a year. Great talent, but needs to listen to his coaches more and doesn't always keep the sinker down in the strike zone. His potential is much higher than what we saw in 1992.

	W	SV	ERA	IP	H	BB	SO	BPI	$
1992 St. Louis NL	9	0	3.84	197	189	63	124	1.28	2
1993 Base Case	13	0	3.65	185	176	62	115	1.29	6

OLIVERAS, FRANCISCO - Giants - TR - Age 30

Crafty righty with good control and a nice mix of NL-style hard junk (slider, cut fastball).

	W	SV	ERA	IP	H	BB	SO	BPI	$
1992 San Francisco NL	0	0	3.63	44	41	10	17	1.14	-
1993 Base Case	2	1	3.74	67	60	17	33	1.14	3

OLSEN, STEVE - White Sox - TR - Age 23

One of an impressive group of young pitchers headed toward the White Sox, he was only slightly less effective in Double-A than in A ball, where he was 17-3 over 1 1/2 seasons.

	W	SV	ERA	IP	H	BB	SO	BPI	$
1992 Sarasota A	11	0	1.94	88	68	32	85	1.14	
1992 Birmingham AA	6	0	3.03	77	68	29	46	1.26	

OLSON, GREGG - Orioles - TR - Age 26
Olson was much more effective in '92 because Manager Johnny Oates used him more strategically; and secondly, he added a new sinker pitch. Olson usually has a short slump when he blows a few saves.

	W	SV	ERA	IP	H	BB	SO	BPI	$
1992 Baltimore AL	1	36	2.05	61	46	24	58	1.14	31
1993 Base Case	2	33	2.57	65	54	25	61	1.23	30

OQUIST, MIKE - Orioles - TR - Age 24
Oquist is an average prospect with the standard fastball, slides, changeup. He will need to prove himself further at Rochester to make the majors.

	W	SV	ERA	IP	H	BB	SO	BPI	$
1992 Rochester AAA	10	0	4.11	153	164	45	111	1.37	

OROSCO, JESSE - Brewers - TL - Age 35
Yet another reason why you should force your kid to throw left-handed. Orosco's throwing arm is the sole reason Milwaukee considered resigning this free agent. Since he's finding it difficult to get even lefties out anymore (.273 last year), Orosco will not play a significant role in 1993, for the Brewers or for anyone else.

	W	SV	ERA	IP	H	BB	SO	BPI	$
1992 Milwaukee AL	3	1	3.23	39	33	13	40	1.18	2
1993 Base Case	3	1	3.82	49	47	16	46	1.29	1

OSBORNE, DONOVAN - Cardinals - TL - Age 23
Had a hot-and-cold season in 1992 after making the jump from Class AA. Osborne told me that he definitely noticed hitters adjusting to him in midsummer; he made some adjustments of his own and finished strong in 1992. He has the stuff to be a big winner.

	W	SV	ERA	IP	H	BB	SO	BPI	$
1992 St. Louis NL	11	0	3.77	179	193	38	104	1.29	3
1993 Base Case	13	0	3.57	166	183	38	99	1.34	5

OSTEEN, GAVIN - Athletics - TL - Age 23
Has put in two good years at AA Huntsville but will need some AAA success before reaching Oakland.

	W	SV	ERA	IP	H	BB	SO	BPI	$
1992 Tacoma AAA	0	0	10.05	14	21	13	7	2.37	
1992 Huntsville AA	5	0	3.61	102	106	27	56	1.29	

OSUNA, AL - Astros - TL - Age 27
Astros' leader in saves as a rookie in 1991 was a disappointment in his sophomore campaign. Had difficulty getting ahead of the hitters and his wildness kept him in constant trouble. Smart pitcher with a strong arm, has a good chance to come back, and should be the team's top lefthander in the bullpen.

	W	SV	ERA	IP	H	BB	SO	BPI	$
1992 Houston NL	6	0	4.23	61	52	38	37	1.46	-
1993 Base Case	6	5	3.94	68	54	40	49	1.38	3

OTTO, DAVE - Indians - TL - Age 28
After showing some promise in late '91, Otto was given the opportunity to succeed as a starter in '92, but he failed miserably. It may have been his last opportunity as a starter.

	W	SV	ERA	IP	H	BB	SO	BPI	$
1992 Col. Sp. AAA	3	0	2.83	45	35	10	11	1.01	
1992 Cleveland AL	5	0	7.06	80	110	33	32	1.78	-
1993 Base Case	3	0	5.48	77	87	27	32	1.47	-

PAINTER, LANCE - Rockies - TL - Age 25
Good prospect with hard fastball. Has a shot at the Rockies rotation. Until he shows some major league success, though, regard him with caution. Had 10 wins and 3.53 ERA for AA Wichita last year.

PALACIOS, VINCE - Pirates - TR - Age 29
Once considered a potential star, rotator cuff surgeries in 1988 and 1989 have derailed his career. Shoulder problems again bothered him in 1992 and forced him to miss the final three months of the season.

	W	SV	ERA	IP	H	BB	SO	BPI	$
1992 Pittsburgh NL	3	0	4.25	53	56	27	33	1.57	-
1993 Base Case	4	1	3.94	54	50	26	39	1.41	-

PALL, DONN - White Sox - TR - Age 31
Journeyman reliever with a decent forkball. Without access to saves, he has little value.

	W	SV	ERA	IP	H	BB	SO	BPI	$
1992 Chicago AL	5	1	4.93	73	79	27	27	1.45	-
1993 Base Case	6	1	3.77	72	69	23	31	1.28	3

PARKER, CLAY - Mariners - TR - Age 30
Pitched well in 1989-1990 for the Yankees and Tigers, but now just hanging around.

	W	SV	ERA	IP	H	BB	SO	BPI	$
1992 Seattle AL	0	0	7.56	33	47	11	20	1.74	-
1993 Base Case	0	0	5.67	56	64	22	32	1.54	-

PARRETT, JEFF - Athletics - TR - Age 31
Classic Oakland revival story: good pitcher with sound arm and past success finds self again.

	W	SV	ERA	IP	H	BB	SO	BPI	$
1992 Oakland AL	9	0	3.02	98	81	42	78	1.25	6
1993 Base Case	6	0	3.49	63	58	28	48	1.38	2

PATTERSON, BOB - Pirates - TL - Age 33
He has become one of the National League's better lefthanded setup relievers over the past three seasons. He had an outstanding season in 1992 before giving up a pair of three-run homers and a grand slam in a stretch over a nine-day span in early September. His release was just a salary move.

	W	SV	ERA	IP	H	BB	SO	BPI	$
1992 Pittsburgh NL	6	9	2.92	64	59	23	43	1.27	10
1993 Base Case	4	6	3.38	64	61	20	48	1.26	7

PATTERSON, KEN - White Sox - TL - Age 28
Journeyman reliever with a good fastball and not much else. Won't get saves.

	W	SV	ERA	IP	H	BB	SO	BPI	$
1992 Chicago NL	2	0	3.89	41	41	27	23	1.63	-
1993 Base Case	3	0	3.67	59	52	36	31	1.49	-

PAVLAS, DAVE - Cubs - TR - Age 30
Tall righty becoming a career minor leaguer.

	W	SV	ERA	IP	H	BB	SO	BPI	$
1992 Iowa AAA	3	0	3.38	37	43	8	34	1.37	

PAVLIK, ROGER - Rangers - TR - Age 25

Pavlik proved that he was healthy again in 1992. After a very rocky start when he was used irregularly by the Rangers, he settled down and pitched well down the stretch, with a 3.18 ERA in his last 8 starts. His control remains a problem; with improvement in that area, he should be ready for a full season in the majors.

	W	SV	ERA	IP	H	BB	SO	BPI	$
1992 Texas AL	4	0	4.21	62	66	34	45	1.61	-
1992 Oklahoma City AAA	7	0	2.98	118	90	51	104	1.19	
1993 Base Case	3	0	4.30	57	57	33	46	1.58	-

PENA, ALEJANDRO - Pirates - TR - Age 33

For several years, Pena has produced one big hot streak each season, usually in the second half. Between the inevitable injuries in 1993 he might produce half a dozen saves in one good month.

	W	SV	ERA	IP	H	BB	SO	BPI	$
1992 Atlanta NL	1	15	4.07	42	40	13	34	1.26	10
1993 Base Case	4	6	3.25	67	62	19	52	1.21	6

PENA, JIM - Giants - TL - Age 28

His presence in the major leagues in 1992 was more a statement of SF's needs than Pena's merit.

	W	SV	ERA	IP	H	BB	SO	BPI	$
1992 Phoenix AAA	7	1	4.15	39	45	20	27	1.67	
1992 San Francisco NL	1	0	3.48	44	49	20	32	1.57	-
1993 Base Case	1	0	3.69	51	57	24	36	1.60	-

PENNINGTON, BRAD - Orioles - TL - Age 23

Comparisons to Mitch Williams are well-founded. In his first three pro seasons, Pennington had 324 Ks and 264 walks in 237 IP. The 24-year-old has a 96 MPH fastball and "settled down" in 1992, with "just" 33 walks in 39 AAA innings.

	W	SV	ERA	IP	H	BB	SO	BPI	$
1992 Hagerstown AA	1	7	2.54	28	20	17	32	1.32	
1992 Rochester AAA	1	5	2.08	39	12	33	56	1.15	
1993 Base Case	1	1	3.88	28	19	20	30	1.39	1

PERCIVAL, TROY - Angels - TR - Age 23

A catcher converted into a closer. Outstanding fastball. With Bryan Harvey gone, the Angels will be looking for relief help. Percival overcame a sore shoulder to have an impressive autumn performance in Arizona.

	W	SV	ERA	IP	H	BB	SO	BPI	$
1992 Palm Sp. A	1	2	5.06	11	6	8	16	1.31	
1992 Midland AA	3	5	2.37	19	18	11	21	1.53	
1993 Base Case	1	1	3.70	25	23	10	19	1.28	1

PEREZ, MELIDO - Yankees - TR - Age 27

Likes to throw the fastball for strike one. Once he gets ahead in the count, he just keeps throwing forkballs until the batter is out. In his prime now.

	W	SV	ERA	IP	H	BB	SO	BPI	$
1992 New York AL	13	0	2.87	247	212	93	218	1.23	17
1993 Base Case	12	0	2.95	201	171	71	182	1.20	18

PEREZ, MIKE - Cardinals - TR - Age 28
Taken off the roster and given up on after the 1991 season, Perez was one of baseball's most effective middle relievers last year. Set a major-league record for most appearances in a season (77) without a save. He saved 41 games, which was then the minor-league record in the Midwest League in 1987.

	W	SV	ERA	IP	H	BB	SO	BPI	$
1992 St. Louis NL	9	0	1.84	93	70	32	46	1.10	10
1993 Base Case	5	0	2.70	61	47	22	27	1.13	5

PEREZ, PASCUAL - Yankees - TR - Age 35
In September 1991 Perez was just recovering from shoulder surgery and had put together a few classic Perez outings when the season ended. The shoulder got plenty of rest in 1992.

	W	SV	ERA	IP	H	BB	SO	BPI	$
1992 New York AL			(did not play)						
1993 Base Case	9	0	3.40	180	150	55	120	1.14	10

PEREZ, YORKIS - Unsigned - TL - Age 25
Former Braves prospect and winter ball star. Worth a farm system pick if he returns.

PERSCHKE, GREG - White Sox - TR - Age 25
Showed definite improvement in his second year at Vancouver; deserves a good look in spring training.

	W	SV	ERA	IP	H	BB	SO	BPI	$
1992 Vancouver AAA	12	0	3.76	165	159	44	82	1.23	

PETERSON, ADAM - Padres - TR - Age 27
Had a good minor league record in the White Sox farm system and got a shot with the Padres in 1991, but he's only got mediocre stuff and is past the prospect stage.

	W	SV	ERA	IP	H	BB	SO	BPI	$
1992 Las Vegas AAA	6	0	3.75	100	99	37	67	1.35	

PETKOVSEK, MARK - Pirates - TR - Age 27
Surfaced with the Rangers in 1991 and made progress at AAA in 1992; still just an in-depth backup.

	W	SV	ERA	IP	H	BB	SO	BPI	$
1992 Buffalo AAA	8	1	3.53	150	150	44	49	1.29	

PIATT, DOUG - Expos - TR - Age 27
Pitched well in 34 IP in 1991, but just didn't fit their plans in 1992. Could appear any time and get one save.

	W	SV	ERA	IP	H	BB	SO	BPI	$
1992 Harrisburg AA	5	7	3.45	62	55	32	65	1.39	
1992 Indianapolis AAA	0	3	4.22	10	13	3	6	1.50	

PICHARDO, HIPOLITO - Royals - TR - Age 23
Reminds you of Pascual Perez: lanky, eccentric. Build and delivery are very similar. Pichardo probably has the third starting spot nailed down; could be a real steal for a couple of bucks.

	W	SV	ERA	IP	H	BB	SO	BPI	$
1992 Memphis AA	0	0	0.64	14	13	1	10	1.00	
1992 Kansas City AL	9	0	3.95	143	148	49	59	1.37	3
1993 Base Case	9	0	3.88	177	180	53	86	1.33	3

PIERCE, ED - Royals - TL - Age 24

One of the Royals' better prospects, Pierce jumped from AA to the majors for two games. He shows good poise. Probably won't begin the year in KC, but is certain to see major league action later in the summer.

	W	SV	ERA	IP	H	BB	SO	BPI	$
1992 Memphis AA	10	0	3.81	153.2	159	51	131	1.37	
1992 Kansas City AL	0	0	3.38	5.3	9	4	3	2.44	-
1993 Base Case	2	0	3.86	33	36	10	18	1.39	0

PLESAC, DAN - Cubs - TL - Age 31

He'll never be a dominant closer again, and he can't be a starter, because he has only two pitches. Has seen both success (1992) and failure (1991) in the middle relief role, with no clear indication as to what lies ahead. Risky but interesting.

	W	SV	ERA	IP	H	BB	SO	BPI	$
1992 Milwaukee AL	5	1	2.96	79	64	35	54	1.25	5
1993 Base Case	4	1	3.48	80	72	34	54	1.32	2

PLUNK, ERIC - Blue Jays - TR - Age 29

Following a poor '91, Plunk got it back together as a middle reliever and occasional closer with the Indians, with good velocity. The nine wins were a nice surprise, but can't be expected again.

	W	SV	ERA	IP	H	BB	SO	BPI	$
1992 Cleveland AL	9	4	3.64	72	61	38	50	1.38	5
1993 Base Case	5	2	4.15	93	93	51	74	1.55	-

PLYMPTON, JEFF - Red Sox - TR - Age 27

Looked like a longshot closer candidate in 1991 but made no progress in 1992.

	W	SV	ERA	IP	H	BB	SO	BPI	$
1992 Pawtucket AAA	6	1	3.43	81	78	34	57	1.38	

POOLE, JIM - Orioles - TL - Age 26

After an outstanding '91 season, '92 was almost a total loss for Poole as he developed shoulder problems spending almost the entire season recovering in the minors.

	W	SV	ERA	IP	H	BB	SO	BPI	$
1992 Rochester AAA	1	10	5.31	42	40	18	30	1.37	
1992 Baltimore AL	0	0	0.00	3	3	1	3	1.20	-
1993 Base Case	1	1	3.03	39	36	17	24	1.35	1

PORTUGAL, MARK - Astros - TR - Age 30

Dean of Astros' staff had promising season interrupted in July by surgery to remove bone chips. Came back to make two relief appearances and a strong start at the end of the season. Should be ready in 1993.

	W	SV	ERA	IP	H	BB	SO	BPI	$
1992 Houston NL	6	0	2.66	101	76	41	62	1.15	6
1993 Base Case	7	0	3.79	111	98	41	75	1.25	3

POWELL, DENNIS - Mariners - TL - Age 29

Last year was his best since 1987 and it really wasn't all that good. He was outstanding in the minors.

	W	SV	ERA	IP	H	BB	SO	BPI	$
1992 Seattle AL	4	0	4.58	57	49	29	35	1.37	0
1993 Base Case	2	0	4.43	49	46	22	30	1.39	-

POWELL, ROSS - Reds - TL - Age 25
Promising lefty. Needs better control.

	W	SV	ERA	IP	H	BB	SO	BPI	$
1992 Chattanooga AA	4	1	1.26	57	43	18	56	1.06	
1992 Nashville AAA	4	0	3.38	93	89	42	84	1.40	

POWER, TED - Indians - TR - Age 38
Middle relief and the right handed set-up man in Cleveland. He was effective in these roles for the Indians, and if he can duplicate his '92 record, he can be a valuable pitcher. A crafty righty.

	W	SV	ERA	IP	H	BB	SO	BPI	$
1992 Cleveland AL	3	6	2.54	99	88	35	51	1.25	10
1993 Base Case	4	4	3.04	95	88	32	50	1.27	8

PUGH, TIM - Reds - TR - Age 26
A 6th round pick in June 1989, Pugh has quickly moved into the Reds plans for 1993. Pugh led Nashville in wins and impressed in his September stint with the Reds.

	W	SV	ERA	IP	H	BB	SO	BPI	$
1992 Cincinnati NL	4	0	2.58	45	47	13	18	1.32	0
1993 Base Case	8	0	3.22	104	104	36	53	1.35	3

QUANTRILL, PAUL - Red Sox - TR - Age 24
Quantrill presents one opportunity for 1993. Write this on a scrap of paper, and drop it somewhere conspicuous on draft day: "Paul Quantrill - 2.19 ERA." Maybe someone will draft him.

	W	SV	ERA	IP	H	BB	SO	BPI	$
1992 Pawtucket AAA	6	0	4.46	119	143	20	56	1.29	
1992 Boston AL	2	1	2.19	49	55	15	24	1.42	1
1993 Base Case	2	1	4.03	87	101	20	34	1.39	0

QUIRICO, RAFAEL - Yankees - TL - Age 23
Good starter in low minors, still a couple years away.

RACZKA, MIKE - Athletics - TL - Age 30
Had a good year at Tacoma in 1992 (3.51 ERA) but just a journeyman lefty reliever.

	W	SV	ERA	IP	H	BB	SO	BPI	$
1992 Oakland AL	0	0	8.53	6	8	5	2	2.05	-
1993 Base Case	0	0	5.30	21	22	14	12	1.67	-

RADINSKY, SCOTT - White Sox - TL - Age 25
Good candidate for the closer job, although he was disappointing late in 1992. Will likely share the saves with Roberto Hernandez in a left/right tandem.

	W	SV	ERA	IP	H	BB	SO	BPI	$
1992 Chicago AL	3	15	2.73	59	54	34	48	1.48	12
1993 Base Case	4	19	2.87	63	57	28	46	1.34	18

RAPP, PAT - Marlins -TR - Age 25
Could have been in the Giants rotation if he wasn't drafted. Likely to be a starter for Florida from day one.

	W	SV	ERA	IP	H	BB	SO	BPI	$
1992 Phoenix AAA	7	3	3.05	121	115	40	79	1.28	
1992 San Francisco NL	0	0	7.20	10	8	6	3	1.40	-
1993 Base Case	5	0	4.22	94	95	30	55	1.33	1

RASMUSSEN, DENNIS - Royals - TL - Age 33
One of the most valuable pitchers in any stat league in September 1992 -- but hardly anyone had the courage to grab him. Those who did were richly rewarded. The lesson is: when it looks hopeless anyway, try something desperate. I do not think Rasmussen can do it again in 1993. No way.

	W	SV	ERA	IP	H	BB	SO	BPI	$
1992 Kansas City AL	4	0	1.43	37	25	6	12	0.82	5
1992 Chicago NL	0	0	10.80	5	7	2	0	1.80	-
1993 Base Case	6	0	3.80	92	89	27	40	1.26	3

REARDON, JEFF - Braves - TR - Age 37
Reardon isn't the fearsome fireballer he once was; he mixes his pitches more now, but is much more hittable. And he's had a sore back for years. For the price of 20 saves, get someone else in 1993.

	W	SV	ERA	IP	H	BB	SO	BPI	$
1992 Boston AL	2	27	4.25	42	53	7	32	1.42	19
1992 Atlanta NL	3	3	1.15	15	14	2	7	1.02	3
1993 Base Case	4	24	3.29	70	63	17	49	1.14	20

REED, RICK - Royals - TR - Age 28
Reed washed out of the Pirates system during spring training 1992 but now has an outside shot at a starter's job in 1993. He's got good control, so he won't kill you.

	W	SV	ERA	IP	H	BB	SO	BPI	$
1992 Omaha AAA	5	1	4.35	62	67	12	35	1.27	
1992 Kansas City AL	3	0	3.68	100	105	20	49	1.25	3
1993 Base Case	4	0	3.56	89	91	24	58	1.29	1

REED, STEVE - Rockies - TR - Age 27
Before last season, he had only 21 saves in two seasons above A ball. Then in '92, he set the minor league season record. Exceptional control. Could share saves with Darren Holmes.

	W	SV	ERA	IP	H	BB	SO	BPI	$
1992 Shreveport AA	1	23	0.62	29	18	0	33	0.62	
1992 Phoenix AAA	0	20	3.48	31	27	10	30	1.19	
1992 San Francisco NL	1	0	2.30	15	13	3	11	1.02	0
1992 Base Case	2	2	2.99	44	43	15	33	1.32	2

REMLINGER, MIKE - Mariners - TL - Age 27
Remlinger was a throw-in the Kevin Mitchell trade. After struggling for the most of the season at triple-A, he was demoted to double-A. He shaped up after his demotion, and a return to the show is likely.

	W	SV	ERA	IP	H	BB	SO	BPI	$
1992 Calgary AAA	1	0	6.65	70	97	48	24	2.06	
1992 Jacksonville AA	1	0	3.46	26	25	11	21	1.38	

RENFROE, LADDIE - Cubs - TR - Age 30
Long-time prospect, past his prime. Best year was 1989 at AA Charlotte.

	W	SV	ERA	IP	H	BB	SO	BPI	$
1992 Iowa AAA	3	6	4.74	100	115	40	55	1.54	

REVENIG, TODD - Athletics - TR - Age 23

The newest version of "the heir to Eckersley" -- and a very credible candidate.

	W	SV	ERA	IP	H	BB	SO	BPI	$
1992 Huntsville AA	1	33	1.70	63	32	11	49	0.68	
1992 Oakland AL	0	0	0.00	2	2	0	1	1.00	-
1993 Base Case	1	2	3.16	23	18	9	17	1.19	2

REYNOLDS, SHANE - Astros - TR - Age 25

Third round pick out of the U of Texas in 1989 has shown improvement every year but has given up more than a hit per inning at every level. Hit hard in all five starts with the Astros in 1992.

	W	SV	ERA	IP	H	BB	SO	BPI	$
1992 Tucson AAA	9	1	3.68	142	156	34	106	1.34	
1992 Houston NL	1	0	7.11	25	42	6	10	1.89	-
1993 Base Case	1	0	4.73	26	40	6	11	1.76	-

REYNOSO, ARMANDO - Rockies - TR - Age 26

Reynoso didn't pitch professionally in the States until he was 24. He's been remarkably consistent at AAA and in the majors. Has won 20 games in the Mexican League.

	W	SV	ERA	IP	H	BB	SO	BPI	$
1992 Richmond AAA	12	0	2.66	169	156	52	108	1.23	
1992 Atlanta NL	1	1	4.70	7	11	2	2	1.70	-
1993 Base Case	8	0	4.66	150	161	59	65	1.40	-

RHODES, ARTHUR - Orioles - TL - Age 23

Rhodes has some scouts talking about Vida Blue and Ron Guidry, while other scouts say that he has some weaknesses such as not having complete control of his breaking ball, and his fastball has no movement. He had some outstanding starts in '92, especially one in a pressure-filled must-win situation against Toronto late in the season. Based on his experience, the outlook for '93 is a much better record. He has the tools to go 20-7 in a year or two.

	W	SV	ERA	IP	H	BB	SO	BPI	$
1992 Rochester AAA	6	0	3.72	102	84	46	115	1.28	
1992 Baltimore AL	7	0	3.63	94	87	38	77	1.33	3
1993 Base Case	12	0	3.88	188	170	75	128	1.30	9

RICE, PAT - Mariners - TR - Age 29

Got a shot with the Mariners in 1991 but now fading rapidly.

RIGHETTI, DAVE - Giants - TL - Age 34

His 1992 season was ruined by a disastrous attempt to become a starter again. As a lefty short reliever he still has value; but in a rotation he will kill you.

	W	SV	ERA	IP	H	BB	SO	BPI	$
1992 San Francisco NL	2	3	5.06	78	79	36	47	1.47	-
1993 Base Case	2	5	3.71	73	69	29	47	1.34	4

RIJO, JOSE - Reds - TR - Age 27

Another excellent year for Juan Marichal's son in law. His stats are amazing considering he pitched the entire year with a tender elbow that limited his pitch selection. Can you believe Rijo has never won more than 15 games? That will change in 1993. Should win a Cy Young Award if healthy.

	W	SV	ERA	IP	H	BB	SO	BPI	$
1992 Cincinnati NL	15	0	2.56	211	185	44	171	1.09	19
1993 Base Case	17	0	2.42	210	173	49	166	1.06	28

RISLEY, BILL - Expos - TR - Age 25

He comes by the nickname "Wild Bill" quite naturally. He has a live fastball but his problem is throwing strikes. He continued to work on his control in the Florida Instructional League.

	W	SV	ERA	IP	H	BB	SO	BPI	$
1992 Indianapolis AAA	5	0	6.40	96	105	47	64	1.58	
1992 Montreal NL	1	0	1.80	5	4	1	2	1.00	-
1993 Base Case	1	0	4.33	22	21	11	14	1.50	-

RITCHIE, WALLY - Phillies - TL - Age 27

Can be a safe lefty short reliever if his manager uses him wisely. Has a very good changeup.

	W	SV	ERA	IP	H	BB	SO	BPI	$
1992 Philadelphia NL	2	1	3.00	39	44	17	19	1.56	-
1993 Base Case	2	1	2.81	51	53	20	26	1.43	1

RITZ, KEVIN - Rockies - TR - Age 27

Once the Tigers' most exciting young arm. Likely to be a starter for Colorado and will pile up lots of bad innings if they let him. Has had a sore elbow.

	W	SV	ERA	IP	H	BB	SO	BPI	$
1992 Detroit AL	2	0	5.60	80	88	44	57	1.64	-
1993 Base Case	7	0	4.12	133	136	58	84	1.46	-

RIVERA, BEN - Phillies - TR - Age 24

Acquired from Atlanta in a minor deal, the big, hard-throwing Dominican righthander blossomed into a one of Philadelphia's more pleasant surprises with 14 starts in which opposing hitters batted .211 against him.

	W	SV	ERA	IP	H	BB	SO	BPI	$
1992 Philadelphia NL	7	0	3.07	117	99	45	77	1.23	4
1993 Base Case	9	0	3.24	144	126	57	92	1.27	8

ROBINSON, DON - Phillies - TR - Age 35

How many pitchers get waived when they have stats like Robinson did for the California? Yet the Angels knew what they were doing.

	W	SV	ERA	IP	H	BB	SO	BPI	$
1992 California AL	1	0	2.20	16	19	3	9	1.35	-
1992 Philadelphia NL	1	0	6.18	43	49	4	17	1.21	-
1993. Base Case	2	0	4.74	50	55	14	22	1.38	-

ROBINSON, JEFF D - Cubs - TR - Age 32

Once a top setup man with a great forkball; now just hanging on.

	W	SV	ERA	IP	H	BB	SO	BPI	$
1992 Chicago NL	4	1	3.00	78	76	40	46	1.49	-
1993 Base Case	3	2	3.86	73	69	37	51	1.46	-

ROBINSON, JEFF M - Pirates - TR - Age 31

Top starter for the Tigers in 1988. Major league GM's and Rotisserians alike keep wishing he would come back, but he never does. Not a factor for 1993.

	W	SV	ERA	IP	H	BB	SO	BPI	$
1992 Pittsburgh NL	3	0	4.46	36	33	15	14	1.32	-
1992 Texas AL	4	0	5.72	45	50	21	18	1.55	-

ROBINSON, RON - Brewers - TR - Age 31
Missed almost all of 1992 with a reoccurrence of the arm trouble that kept him on the DL for all of 1991 after his first start. He won't likely come back, and if he does, you don't want him.

	W	SV	ERA	IP	H	BB	SO	BPI	$
1992 Milwaukee AL	1	0	5.86	35	51	14	12	1.84	-
1993 Base Case	1	0	5.72	31	44	12	11	1.79	-

RODRIGUEZ, FRANK - Red Sox - TR - Age 20
Boston's No. 2 pick out of high school in '90, he played his first pro season as a SS. He throws very hard. His future was clouded by a statutory rape charge during the winter.

	W	SV	ERA	IP	H	BB	SO	BPI	$
1992 Lynchburg A	12	0	3.09	149	125	65	129	1.31	

RODRIGUEZ, RICH - Padres - TL - Age 30
Rodriguez is a respectable bullpen lefty who has produced consistent numbers (but no saves) for the Padres for several seasons. He figures to continue in a similar role in 1993.

	W	SV	ERA	IP	H	BB	SO	BPI	$
1992 San Diego NL	6	0	2.37	91	77	29	64	1.16	6
1993 Base Case	4	2	2.99	81	68	33	52	1.24	5

RODRIGUEZ, ROSARIO - Pirates - TL - Age 23
Former top prospect with Reds and Bucs; missed almost all of 1992.

ROESLER, MIKE - Royals - TR - Age 29
Major leaguer in 1989-1990; just hanging on in 1992.

ROGERS, KENNY - Rangers - TL - Age 28
The '92 numbers hide a bad season. Successful in '90 as a setup man, Rangers made him a starter in '91 and disaster followed. After the Russell trade he failed as closer.

	W	SV	ERA	IP	H	BB	SO	BPI	$
1992 Texas AL	3	6	3.09	78	80	26	70	1.35	5
1993 Projection	6	6	3.30	88	92	28	73	1.36	
1993 Base Case	6	5	3.97	88	93	39	69	1.49	2

ROGERS, KEVIN - Giants - TL - Age 24
A late-blooming control pitcher. This season will tell whether he can elevate his game beyond the AA level.

	W	SV	ERA	IP	H	BB	SO	BPI	$
1992 Shreveport AA	8	0	2.58	101	87	29	110	1.15	
1992 Phoenix AAA	3	0	4.00	70	63	22	62	1.21	
1992 SanFrancisco NL	0	0	4.24	34	37	13	26	1.47	-
1993 Base Case	0	0	4.14	55	55	19	41	1.35	-

ROJAS, MEL - Expos - TR - Age 26
Expos' manager Felipe Alou can't be accused of favoring his nephew. Rojas is an outstanding talent. After a brief stint in the minors to start 1992, Rojas came back to the majors and became John Wetteland's top setup man. He has a live arm and is durable. Says uncle: "Rojas can get saves against any team."

	W	SV	ERA	IP	H	BB	SO	BPI	$
1992 Indianapolis AAA	2	0	5.40	8	10	3	7	1.63	
1992 Montreal NL	7	10	1.43	100	71	34	70	1.04	20
1993 Base Case	6	8	2.49	80	59	25	58	1.05	15

ROPER, JOHN - Reds - TR - Age 21

Missed time last year after hurting his back in an auto accident, but later pitched effectively. Hard thrower.

	W	SV	ERA	IP	H	BB	SO	BPI	$
1992 Chattanooga AA	10	0	4.03	121	115	36	98	1.25	

ROSENBERG, STEVE - Mets - TL - Age 28

Just one of many ex-White Sox acquired after Jeff Torborg's hiring. Got hurt and missed whole season.

ROSENTHAL, WAYNE - Rangers - TR - Age 28

Relies on location and deception, and has not pitched well in two stints in the majors.

	W	SV	ERA	IP	H	BB	SO	BPI	$
1992 Texas AL	0	0	7.71	4	7	2	1	1.93	-
1992 Okla. City AAA	1	11	5.69	62	72	29	54	1.61	
1993 Base Case	0	0	5.54	32	34	16	25	1.58	-

RUFFIN, BRUCE - Brewers - TL - Age 29

Pure, unadulterated cannon fodder. Friends don't let friends draft Ruffin.

	W	SV	ERA	IP	H	BB	SO	BPI	$
1992 Milwaukee AL	1	0	6.67	58	66	41	45	1.84	-
1993 Base Case	0	0	4.88	38	41	18	20	1.53	-

RUFFIN, JOHNNY - White Sox - TR - Age 21

Very good year at "A" Sarasota in 1991, but stumbled at AA Birmingham in 1992.

ROSSELLI, JOEY - Giants - TL - Age 21

The best pitcher in the best A-ball league. Was DL'd briefly with a sore shoulder last year.

	W	SV	ERA	IP	H	BB	SO	BPI	$
1992 San Jose A	11	0	2.41	150	145	46	111	1.27	

RUSKIN, SCOTT - Reds - TL - Age 29

A horrible first half destroyed Ruskin's stats, but he pitched well in a setup role in the second half. Relies on a curveball and is dead if he is not getting it over. The departure of Norm Charlton enhances his value.

	W	SV	ERA	IP	H	BB	SO	BPI	$
1992 Cincinnati NL	4	0	5.03	53	56	20	43	1.42	-
1993 Base Case	4	2	3.95	57	54	24	42	1.37	1

RUSSELL, JEFF - Athletics - TR - Age 31

Russell led the league in blown saves. His overall numbers, however, were fine, and he has saved at least 30 games in each season in which he has been the closer (except 1990 when he was injured). The projected statistics below assume that he will be the primary closer for the team that signs him.

	W	SV	ERA	IP	H	BB	SO	BPI	$
1992 Two Teams AL	4	30	1.63	66	55	25	48	1.21	28
1993 Base Case	5	25	2.66	68	58	23	46	1.19	26

RYAN, KEN - Red Sox - TR - Age 24

Good possibility for a shot at the closer's role, but completely unproven.

	W	SV	ERA	IP	H	BB	SO	BPI	$
1992 New Britain AA	1	22	1.95	50	44	24	51	1.34	
1992 Pawtucket AAA	2	7	2.08	8	6	4	6	1.15	
1992 Boston AL	0	1	6.43	7	4	5	5	1.29	-
1993 Base Case	1	10	3.50	22	21	14	20	1.59	6

RYAN, NOLAN - Rangers - TR - Age 46
Ryan did better than his 1992 stats would indicate. He was victimized by six blown saves, and he suffered through a number of bad-weather starts. He is not just hanging on at an advanced age. Although he may be limited to only 20 starts or so in 1993, he is capable of helping you and the Rangers.

	W	SV	ERA	IP	H	BB	SO	BPI	$
1992 Texas AL	5	0	3.72	157	138	69	157	1.32	4
1993 Base Case	8	0	3.37	164	124	71	172	1.19	11

SABERHAGEN, BRET - Mets - TR - Age 28
Forget the bunk about the odd/even jinx. If you look behind the full year stats over his career, you quickly see that Saberhagen is just a streaky pitcher. For half a season, he may be so good that no hitter can even get a sniff off him. The rest of the time, he's just an average pitcher. Some years Saberhagen has a long hot streak, and some years he doesn't. You just have to pay to roll the dice. For 1993? I think he's due.

	W	SV	ERA	IP	H	BB	SO	BPI	$
1992 New York NL	3	0	3.50	97	84	27	81	1.14	2
1993 Base Case	14	0	3.21	190	162	48	137	1.10	16

SALKELD, ROGER - Mariners - TR - Age 22
Missed all of 1992. May miss all of 1993. If you want a top minor leaguer, pick a center fielder.

SAMPEN, BILL - Expos - TR - Age 30
The best that can be said of Bill Sampen is that he throws strikes. Sampen lacks an outstanding pitch; his stuff is mediocre. He'll probably win a bullpen job with the Royals in 1993.

	W	SV	ERA	IP	H	BB	SO	BPI	$
1992 Indianapolis AAA	1	0	6.00	3	5	3	4	2.67	
1992 Montreal NL	1	0	3.13	63	62	29	23	1.44	
1992 Kansas City AL	0	0	3.66	19	21	3	14	1.22	-
1993 Base Case	4	0	3.57	83	84	35	42	1.44	0

SANCHEZ, ALEX - Royals -TR - Age 26
Long-time Blue Jays prospect. Probably peaked in 1989.

	W	SV	ERA	IP	H	BB	SO	BPI	$
1992 Baseball Cy A	6	0	3.43	78.2	61	41	42	1.30	

SANDERSON, SCOTT - Yankees - TR - Age 36
Because he can no longer throw the fastball by anyone, Sanderson must have pinpoint control to be effective. Last year he didn't always have it, obviously. Has already had his big comeback year.

	W	SV	ERA	IP	H	BB	SO	BPI	$
1992 New York AL	12	0	4.93	193	220	64	104	1.47	0
1993 Base Case	13	0	4.53	192	202	48	108	1.31	2

SANFORD, MO - Rockies - TR - Age 26
On the verge of breaking through to the majors in 1991, Sanford regressed in 1992, surrendering 22 homers in 122 IP at AAA Nashville. Sanford is the most overpowering pitcher in the organization, averaging 10 K's/9 IP in his minor league career. An obvious talent, but still very raw.

	W	SV	ERA	IP	H	BB	SO	BPI	$
1992 Chattanooga AA	4	0	1.35	26	14	6	28	0.76	
1992 Nashville AAA	8	0	5.68	122	128	65	129	1.58	
1993 Base Case	6	0	4.16	158	121	88	133	1.32	1

SATRE, JASON - Reds - TR - Age 22
Big year at A-ball in 1991; hasn't made much progress since.

	W	SV	ERA	IP	H	BB	SO	BPI	$
1992 Chattanooga AA	3	0	5.43	58	56	26	36	1.41	

SAUVEUR, RICH - Royals - TL - Age 29
Keeps surfacing, but will never amount to anything.

	W	SV	ERA	IP	H	BB	SO	BPI	$
1992 Kansas City AL	0	0	4.40	14	15	8	7	1.60	-

SCANLAN, BOB - Cubs - TR - Age 26
Acquired from the Phillies along with Chuck McElroy for Mitch Williams, he may turn out to be the gem in the deal. Scanlan was a starter for most of his minor league career, but after the Cubs promoted him from AAA last year, he was used mostly in relief and earned his first professional save. Last year he was solely a relief pitcher and was a closer when the season ended. Jim Lefebvre told me Scanlan was his choice to pitch in critical situaions where a strikeout is needed; that recommendation is close to saying he's your top reliever.

	W	SV	ERA	IP	H	BB	SO	BPI	$
1992 Chicago NL	3	14	2.89	87	76	30	42	1.21	14
1993 Base Case	4	10	3.50	93	91	33	40	1.33	9

SCHEID, RICH - Astros - TL - Age 28
Veteran minor league pitcher obtained in a trade with the White Sox for Eric Yelding made one unimpressive start and six relief appearances for the Astros in September. Has no established credentials that would suggest he is a prospect.

	W	SV	ERA	IP	H	BB	SO	BPI	$
1992 Tucson AAA	3	1	2.63	92	78	51	58	1.40	
1992 Houston NL	0	0	6.00	12	14	6	8	1.67	-
1993 Base Case	0	0	4.06	28	31	14	18	1.58	-

SCHILLING, CURT - Astros - TR - Age 26
No pitcher in baseball came farther in 1992. Buried in the Houston Astros bullpen, he was acquired early in the season by Philadelphia and over the second half, there was no better pitcher in the league than Schilling, who completed 10 of his 26 starts and held opposing hitters to a .201 average.

	W	SV	ERA	IP	H	BB	SO	BPI	$
1992 Philadelphia NL	14	2	2.35	226	165	59	147	0.99	26
1993 Base Case	14	0	2.51	169	132	51	114	1.08	21

SCHMIDT, DAVE - Mariners - TR - Age 35
Got 13 saves in 1990, but really has nothing left.

	W	SV	ERA	IP	H	BB	SO	BPI	$
1992 Seattle AL	0	0	18.90	3	7	3	1	3.00	-

SCHOOLER, MIKE - Mariners - TR - Age 30
Had 33 saves in 1989 followed by 30 in 1990, but never fully recovered from injuries during the 1991 season. Schooler converted only 13 of 18 save chances and allowed 17 of 40 inherited runners to score. He yielded seven home runs, including three grand slams despite limited pitching time. His days as a closer appear to be numbered, especially with the arrival of Norm Charlton.

	W	SV	ERA	IP	H	BB	SO	BPI	$
1992 Seattle AL	2	13	4.70	51	55	24	33	1.53	7
1993 Base Case	2	8	3.96	41	40	16	30	1.39	5

SCHOUREK, PETE - Mets - TL - Age 23
Talented pitcher, still learning. Big upside potential for 1993. Good curveball.

	W	SV	ERA	IP	H	BB	SO	BPI	$
1992 New York NL	6	0	3.64	136	137	44	60	1.33	-
1993 Base Case	10	0	3.71	187	181	68	100	1.34	2

SCOTT, TIM - Padres - TR - Age 26
Padres' pitching coach Mike Rourke said Scott has "great stuff" and labeled him a candidate for the closer committee in San Diego. Scott had 15 saves at Vegas and was named to the AAA All-Star game. He was not particularly effective in his 38-inning call-up to San Diego although he did strike out 30.

	W	SV	ERA	IP	H	BB	SO	BPI	$
1992 Las Vegas AAA	1	15	2.25	28	20	3	28	0.82	
1992 San Diego NL	4	0	5.26	38	39	21	30	1.58	-
1993 Base Case	3	2	4.08	36	36	15	30	1.40	1

SCUDDER, SCOTT - Indians - TR - Age 25
Scudder has carried the "great potential" label for the past four years. He had a rough first half in '92, but appeared to have turned things around with some good starts in mid-season. He then came down with a pulled muscle in his upper arm, and effectiveness eluded him. Scudder is a very high risk.

	W	SV	ERA	IP	H	BB	SO	BPI	$
1992 Cleveland AL	6	0	5.28	109	134	55	66	1.73	-
1993 Base Case	5	0	5.01	91	100	48	50	1.63	-

SEANEZ, RUDY - Rockies - TR - Age 24
Great velocity. Sore back. Seanez was a Rule Five pick by the Dodgers and had a tremendous winter ball performance 1991-92, then went on the DL with a bad back. Even when he was most dominant, Seanez walked a lot of people. The disciplined hitters in the NL are quite different from the free swingers in the Caribbean leagues. Summary: high risk, unlikely payoff; but intriguing for $1.

SEARCY, STEVE - Phillies - TL - Age 28
Once a top Detroit prospect, Searcy has been horrible in every major league trial. It's getting late.

	W	SV	ERA	IP	H	BB	SO	BPI	$
1992 Albuquerque AAA	3	0	6.48	58	79	31	40	1.90	
1993 Base Case	1	0	5.38	39	43	24	25	1.72	-

SEGURA, JOSE - Reds - TR - Age 30
Has appeared in 22 games with the Cubs and Giants, 1988-1991. Just about finished.

	W	SV	ERA	IP	H	BB	SO	BPI	$
1992 Nashville AAA	1	1	3.98	31	33	18	16	1.63	

SELE, AARON - Red Sox - TR - Age 22
Boston's No. 1 pick in '91, out of Washington State U. Not overpowering, but throws four pitches for strikes. Baseball America rated him the fifth-best prospect in the Carolina League, just ahead of teammate Frank Rodriguez. Sele's Eastern League ERA was hurt by one ten-run game.

	W	SV	ERA	IP	H	BB	SO	BPI	$
1992 Lynchburg A	13	0	2.91	127	104	46	112	1.18	
1992 New Britain AA	2	0	6.27	33	43	15	29	1.76	

SEMINARA, FRANK - Padres - TR - Age 25

Seminara is a genuine prospect. His minor league numbers are more than adequate, especially because they were assembled in notorious hitters' parks.

	W	SV	ERA	IP	H	BB	SO	BPI	$
1992 Las Vegas AAA	6	0	4.13	81	92	33	48	1.54	
1992 San Diego NL	9	0	3.68	100	98	46	61	1.44	
1993 Base Case	6	0	3.79	94	98	40	58	1.47	-

SERVICE, SCOTT- Reds - TR - Age 25

Long-time Phillies prospect, still has potential. Looks like a good pitcher (big).

	W	SV	ERA	IP	H	BB	SO	BPI	$
1992 Indianapolis AAA	2	2	0.74	24	12	9	25	0.96	
1992 Nashville AAA	6	4	2.29	70	54	35	87	1.26	
1992 Montreal NL	0	0	14.14	7	15	5	11	2.86	-
1993 Base Case	0	0	3.86	14	13	6	12	1.33	-

SHAW, CEDRIC - Rangers - TL - Age 25

In his third season at Tulsa, Shaw pitched his way to prospect status with the Rangers. He was less successful upon being promoted to AAA, and needs a year or two before he's ready for the majors.

	W	SV	ERA	IP	H	BB	SO	BPI	$
1992 Okla. City AAA	2	0	5.59	56	58	31	25	1.58	
1992 Tulsa AA	6	0	3.75	70	64	18	49	1.16	

SHAW, CURTIS - Athletics - TL - Age 23

A top reliever at the University of Kansas, Shaw has been used as a starter in the A's system, making good progress at low A and high A in 1991-1992. His key is being able to spot the fastball. If you were writing fiction about a ballplayer, you couldn't come up with a better hometown: Bartlesville, Oklahoma.

	W	SV	ERA	IP	H	BB	SO	BPI	$
1992 Tulsa AA	6	0	3.75	69	64	18	49	1.34	
1992 Oklahoma City AAA	2	0	5.59	56	58	31	25	1.58	

SHAW, JEFF - Indians - TR - Age 26

Shaw is struggling, and may need more AAA-ball to become an effective pitcher. He's a very high risk.

	W	SV	ERA	IP	H	BB	SO	BPI	$
1992 Col. Sp. AAA	10	0	4.76	155	174	45	84	1.41	
1992 Cleveland AL	0	0	8.22	8	7	4	3	1.44	-
1993 Base Case	0	0	4.21	35	34	14	15	1.38	-

SHEPHERD, KEITH - Phillies - TR - Age 25

Never pitched above AA before joining the Phillies in 1992, but held his own. Had ERA's of 2.14 at AA Birmingham and 2.78 at AA Reading before the callup.

	W	SV	ERA	IP	H	BB	SO	BPI	$
1992 Philadelphia NL	1	2	3.27	22.0	19	6	10	1.14	0
1993 Base Case	1	2	3.38	26	23	7	11	1.16	1

SHERRILL, TIM - Cardinals - TL - Age 27

Very successful reliever at Louisville, but hasn't made any real progress in three years.

	W	SV	ERA	IP	H	BB	SO	BPI	$
1992 Louisville AAA	7	1	3.90	62	61	22	28	1.33	

SHIFFLETT, STEVE - Royals - TR - Age 27
Steady progress up the KC farm ladder. Passable reliever can have value setting up Montgomery.

	W	SV	ERA	IP	H	BB	SO	BPI	$
1992 Omaha AAA	3	14	1.65	43	30	15	19	1.03	
1992 Kansas City AL	1	0	2.60	52	55	17	25	1.38	1
1993 Base Case	0	1	3.17	55	56	20	26	1.39	1

SHINALL, ZAK - Dodgers - TR - Age 24
Shinnall led Dodger farmhands and the PCL with 13 wins yet he did not make a single start all season. He is solely a middle relief candidate.

	W	SV	ERA	IP	H	BB	SO	BPI	$
1992 Albuquerque AAA	13	6	3.29	82	91	37	46	1.56	

SIMON, RICHIE - Astros - TR - Age 27
Seven year Astros farmhand, has had good success at AA (20 Saves and 2.18 ERA in 1991) but can't seem to advance further.

	W	SV	ERA	IP	H	BB	SO	BPI	$
1992 Tucson AAA	0	1	5.03	19	26	11	12	1.92	
1992 Jackson AA	3	4	3.88	48	40	25	30	1.35	

SIMONS, DOUG - Expos - TL - Age 26
Drafted by the mets under Rule Five, from the Twins in 1990 and kept him on the major league roster throughout the 1991 season, though he clearly was overmatched. Then traded to Montreal. Despite the poor big league numbers, he is still a propsect.

	W	SV	ERA	IP	H	BB	SO	BPI	$
1992 Expos NL	0	0	23.63	5	15	2	6	3.19	-
1992 Indianapolis AAA	11	0	3.08	120	114	25	66	1.16	
1993 Base Case	2	0	3.68	83	77	30	54	1.29	1

SLOCUMB, HEATHCLIFF - Cubs - TR - Age 26
Keeps producing well at Iowa and then getting hammered in Chicago.

	W	SV	ERA	IP	H	BB	SO	BPI	$
1992 Iowa AAA	0	7	2.59	41	36	16	47	1.25	
1992 Chicago NL	0	1	6.50	36	52	21	27	2.03	-
1993 Base Case	1	1	5.08	54	63	29	35	1.70	-

SLUSARSKI, JOE - Athletics - TR - Age 26
Major talent held back by injuries. Slusarski is exactly the kind of pitcher who can come out of nowhere suddenly: high velocity, good movement fastball; not much of a repertoire, and never been healthy long enough to compile any numbers.

	W	SV	ERA	IP	H	BB	SO	BPI	$
1992 Oakland AL	5	0	5.45	76	85	27	38	1.47	-
1993 Base Case	4	0	4.61	76	79	28	41	1.41	-

SMALL, AARON - Blue Jays - TR - Age 20
Had an outstanding season in the Arizona Fall league. Don't let the name fool you, he's 6-foot-5.

SMILEY, JOHN - Reds - TL - Age 28
Smiley had a rough first month in the American League, then settled down to pitch some outstanding ball. Was arguably the league's best SP in August-September. He's one of those pitchers who can pitch effectively anywhere.

	W	SV	ERA	IP	H	BB	SO	BPI	$
1992 Minnesota AL	16	0	3.21	241	205	65	163	1.12	20
1993 Base Case	17	0	3.11	227	206	56	149	1.15	22

SMITH, BRYN - Cardinals - TR - Age 37

He suffered an elbow injury in his first start, underwent surgery, and didn't return until September. He worked in relief upon his return and was adequate. His age and damaged arm make his future cloudy, but he has good control and a smart approach. In St. Louis he should be OK, elsewhere could be dangerous.

	W	SV	ERA	IP	H	BB	SO	BPI	$
1992 Louisville AAA	1	0	1.80	10	6	2	2	0.80	
1992 St. Louis NL	4	0	4.64	21	20	5	9	1.17	0
1993 Base Case	8	0	3.73	97	91	22	45	1.17	4

SMITH, DAVE - Cubs - TR - Age 38

He was injured for almost all of last season and looks about through. Even when he was last healthy, the velocity was about gone.

	W	SV	ERA	IP	H	BB	SO	BPI	$
1992 Chicago NL	0	0	2.51	14	15	4	3	1.33	-
1993 Base Case	0	1	4.38	25	28	11	9	1.56	-

SMITH, DAN - Rangers - TL - Age 23

Smith followed a horrendous (4-17, 5.52 ERA) 1991 season at AAA with a fine AA season in 1992, renewing hope in the former #1 pick. In a brief stint with the parent club this season, Smith had significant trouble with righthanded hitters (.347 BA). He must still prove himself at the AAA level to earn more than a September callup.

	W	SV	ERA	IP	H	BB	SO	BPI	$
1992 Texas AL	0	0	5.02	14	18	8	5	1.81	-
1992 Tulsa AA	11	0	2.52	146	110	34	122	0.99	
1993 Base Case	0	0	3.70	55	58	20	41	1.41	-

SMITH, LEE - Cardinals - TR - Age 36

Has saved 40 games in a row the past two seasons, and is still the most-feared reliever in the NL. But he can't possibly get any better. He already came up with a new pitch (the forkball, in 1991).

	W	SV	ERA	IP	H	BB	SO	BPI	$
1992 St. Louis NL	4	43	3.12	75	62	26	60	1.17	39
1993 Base Case	5	30	2.83	74	64	23	62	1.19	28

SMITH, PETE - Braves - TR - Age 27

Smith rebounded from career threatening injuries that limited him to 189 IP over the previous two years. He had phenomenal success replacing injured Mike Bielecki in the rotation in 1992 -- he was the Braves most effective starter for a while, going 7-0 in 11 starts. He's no prospect, but is still only 27 despite spending part of each of the last six years in the majors. He'll fight Bielecki for the fifth spot in the rotation.

	W	SV	ERA	IP	H	BB	SO	BPI	$
1992 Richmond AAA	7	0	2.14	109	75	24	93	0.91	
1992 Atlanta NL	7	0	2.05	79	63	28	43	1.15	
1993 Base Case	6	0	3.09	82	72	29	46	1.24	4

SMITH, WILLIE - Indians - TR - Age 25

Looks like Lee Smith and pitches like Lee Smith; just hasn't been so successful. The Yankees' attempt to convert Smith into a starter was a failure and set back his career.

	W	SV	ERA	IP	H	BB	SO	BPI	$
1992 Canton AA	1	0	4.68	32	33	14	28	1.46	
1992 Colorado Springs AAA	3	1	4.75	41	39	25	30	1.56	

SMITH, ZANE - Pirates - TL - Age 32

Shoulder tendinitis limited him to only four appearances in the second half of the season and kept him off the Pirates' post-season roster. Though the injury was not considered serious, he also had elbow surgery in 1988. The two injuries make him at least a bit of a question mark now. Major talent when healthy.

	W	SV	ERA	IP	H	BB	SO	BPI	$
1992 Pittsburgh NL	8	0	3.06	141	138	19	56	1.11	8
1993 Base Case	10	0	3.18	152	154	20	72	1.14	11

SMOLTZ, JOHN - Braves - TR - Age 25

Every day he looks more like the ace of the staff, giving the Braves consistent deep starts with a chance to win every game. He would have won 20 games with reasonable relief pitching and run support. Smoltz led the NL in strikeouts. This is the starting pitcher to get from the Braves deep staff.

	W	SV	ERA	IP	H	BB	SO	BPI	$
1992 Atlanta NL	15	0	2.85	246	206	80	215	1.16	17
1993 Base Case	16	0	3.01	234	202	74	182	1.18	19

SOPER, MIKE - Indians - TR - Age 26

In 1991, Soper pitched for AA Kinston and led the minors with 41 saves. 1992 was an adjustment year, with Soper pitching well but not dominating. Needs more AAA-ball experience.

	W	SV	ERA	IP	H	BB	SO	BPI	$
1992 Canton AA	3	19	3.02	48	37	17	43	1.13	
1992 Col. Sp. AAA	0	1	6.06	16	26	6	16	1.96	

SPRINGER, RUSS - Angels - TR - Age 24

The Yankees were looking at Springer as a future closer, someone who could help their middle relief corps now. Springer has a live, bounce-back type of arm and a 93 MPH fastball.

	W	SV	ERA	IP	H	BB	SO	BPI	$
1992 New York AL	0	0	6.19	16	18	10	12	1.75	-
1993 Base Case	2	3	3.60	70	68	28	60	1.37	2

STANFORD, LARRY - Yankees - TR - Age 25

Big year at Albany (AA) in 1991: 24 saves with a 1.89 ERA. But still learning. Not to be confused with Don Stanford, the 27-year-old righty who also pitched at Albany in 1991 and Columbus in 1992.

	W	SV	ERA	IP	H	BB	SO	BPI	$
1992 Columbus AAA	3	0	4.01	82	81	26	54	1.30	

STANTON, MIKE - Braves - TL - Age 25

Stanton is in the same predicament as Mercker; both have good enough stuff but aren't going to get a chance at many saves as long as the other is around. Stanton's chances are slightly better for emerging with a part-time closer job since he has better control and he does better when he comes in to throw hard for just one inning. After mid August Stanton was just about unhittable and unscored upon.

	W	SV	ERA	IP	H	BB	SO	BPI	$
1992 Atlanta NL	5	8	4.10	63	59	20	44	1.24	6
1993 Base Case	5	10	3.20	70	61	20	48	1.17	10

ST. CLAIRE, RANDY - Braves - TR - Age 32

Had some good years with the Expos in the late 1980's, but now far past his prime.

	W	SV	ERA	IP	H	BB	SO	BPI	$
1992 Atlanta NL	0	0	5.87	15	17	8	44	1.63	-
1993 Base Case	0	0	5.01	24	26	10	18	1.52	-

STEWART, DAVE - Blue Jays - TR - Age 36

After a very bad start, Stewart settled down and helped his team in the stretch. He had a 3.27 ERA in the second half of 1992.

	W	SV	ERA	IP	H	BB	SO	BPI	$
1992 Oakland AL	12	0	3.66	199	175	79	130	1.27	9
1993 Base Case	14	0	3.56	205	187	85	132	1.33	11

STIEB, DAVE - White Sox - TR - Age 35

With a bad back and a sore arm, Stieb hasn't had a good year since 1990. At this point he isn't even among the better speculations among staring pitchers. One good attribute is: if he pitches badly, he will most likely stop pitching entirely.

	W	SV	ERA	IP	H	BB	SO	BPI	$
1992 Toronto AL	4	0	5.04	96	98	43	45	1.46	-
1993 Base Case	4	0	3.89	69	66	29	33	1.37	0

STOTTLEMYRE, TODD - Blue Jays - TR - Age 27

With his 90+ MPH velocity and good movement on his fastball, and two decent breaking pitches, Stottlemyre's lack of success is a mystery. He told me it's just a matter of consistency, practice and confidence. For a low price, you could do a lot worse in 1993.

	W	SV	ERA	IP	H	BB	SO	BPI	$
1992 Toronto AL	12	0	4.50	174	175	63	98	1.37	2
1993 Base Case	14	0	3.89	192	180	64	106	1.27	8

SUTCLIFFE, RICK - Orioles - TR - Age 36

Sutcliffe deserves credit for coming back from two injury-plagued seasons to steady a young staff and taking the pressure off the kids. Sutcliffe is much better in real life than in Rotisserie; his innings will help the Orioles get through the season, but they won't help you.

	W	SV	ERA	IP	H	BB	SO	BPI	$
1992 Baltimore AL	16	0	4.47	237	251	74	109	1.37	4
1993 Base Case	9	0	4.54	173	180	63	83	1.41	-

SWAN, RUSS - Mariners - TL - Age 29

He had good success as a middle reliever in 1991 was awful as a starter at the beginning of 1992. When returned to relief, he regained his effectiveness. He converted nine of 11 save opportunites and allowed only 11 of 44 inherited runners to score. He is particualrly effective against lefthanded batters.

	W	SV	ERA	IP	H	BB	SO	BPI	$
1992 Seattle AL	3	9	4.74	104	104	45	45	1.43	4
1993 Base Case	4	6	4.27	83	87	34	37	1.45	2

SWIFT, BILL - Giants - TR - Age 31

Performed magnificently as a starter untii his arm became tired. Also pitched great in relief. His role will depend on who manages the Giants in 1993. Whatever the role, he'll be valuable.

	W	SV	ERA	IP	H	BB	SO	BPI	$
1992 San Francisco NL	10	1	2.08	164	144	43	77	1.14	15
1993 Base Case	6	8	2.89	131	118	34	67	1.16	15

SWINDELL, GREG - Astros - TL - Age 28

Swindell performed as expected, and could have easily been 17-5 with better run support and relief pitching. Swindell features a full assortment of pitches and outstanding control. The definition of a rotation anchor.

	W	SV	ERA	IP	H	BB	SO	BPI	$
1992 Cincinnati NL	12	0	2.70	213	210	41	138	1.17	14
1993 Base Case	15	0	2.99	215	214	36	144	1.16	18

SWINGEL, PAUL - Angels - TR - Age 26

Hard thrower but wild. Watch the K/BB ratio at Triple-A to see whether he improves.

	W	SV	ERA	IP	H	BB	SO	BPI	$
1992 Midland AA	8	0	4.75	150	158	51	104	1.396	

TANANA, FRANK - Mets - TL - Age 39

The best use for Tanana is during September, when you need lots of lucky innings to get your ERA and ratio down and you have nothing to lose. In April you don't want Tanana, which is why he's always available in September.

	W	SV	ERA	IP	H	BB	SO	BPI	$
1992 Detroit AL	13	0	4.39	186	188	90	91	1.49	0
1993 Base Case	12	0	4.14	198	197	82	96	1.41	1

TAPANI, KEVIN - Twins - TR - Age 29

Tapani had a few rough outings in '92 ballooning his ERA, but the low number of walks keeps his ratio down. Tapani is a very good Rotisserie pitcher.

	W	SV	ERA	IP	H	BB	SO	BPI	$
1992 Minnesota AL	16	0	3.97	220	226	48	138	1.24	10
1993 Base Case	15	0	3.37	227	223	45	135	1.18	18

TAYLOR, BRIEN - Yankees -TL - Age 21

Has the ability to be the first 100 MPH thrower since Nolan Ryan, but it's still way too early to translate that velocity into major league success. Showed last season why he was the first player taken in the 1991 draft, why he got such a high bonus and why his baseball cards already are as hot as his fastball.

	W	SV	ERA	IP	H	BB	SO	BPI	$
1992 Ft.Lauderdale A	6	0	2.57	161	121	66	187	1.16	

TAYLOR, SCOTT - Red Sox - TL - Age 25

Taylor's numbers make you yawn. But, try this one: In four minor league seasons he fanned 327 batters in 269 innings. Closer stuff.

	W	SV	ERA	IP	H	BB	SO	BPI	$
1992 Boston AL	1	0	4.91	14	13	4	7	1.16	-
1993 Base Case	4	0	4.63	58	63	24	34	1.50	-

TAYLOR, WADE - Yankees - TR - Age 27

Something of a flash in 1991, Taylor was set back by a sore arm in 1992.

	W	SV	ERA	IP	H	BB	SO	BPI	$
1992 Tampa R	0	0	1.50	6	5	1	9	1.00	
1992 Ft. Lauderdale A	0	0	0.00	4	1	1	1	0.50	
1992 Columbus AAA	0	0	3.00	3	2	4	2	2.00	

TELFORD, ANTHONY - Orioles - TR - Age 27
Telford is a curveballing righthander who is fighting for a major league job. He should have done better at Rochester to get another shot. At age 27, he may be out of chances.

	W	SV	ERA	IP	H	BB	SO	BPI	$
1992 Rochester AAA	12	0	4.18	181	183	64	129	1.37	

TERRELL, WALT - Tigers - TR - Age 34
The former starter is now a mop up guy and as risky a pick as you can make. Stay away.

	W	SV	ERA	IP	H	BB	SO	BPI	$
1992 Detroit AL	7	0	5.20	136	163	48	61	1.54	-
1993 Base Case	9	0	4.69	165	200	58	67	1.56	-

TERRY, SCOTT - Cardinals - TR - Age 33
Elbow surgery caused Terry to miss the entire 1992 season and might end his career.

TEWKSBURY, BOB - Cardinals - TR - Age 32
No pitcher in the majors gets more out of less talent. He wins by throwing strikes, changing speeds and hitting spots to perfection. He walked only an incredible 0.77 batters per nine innings last season. Not only does he paint corner but he's good on the canvas, too, with his artwork appearing in Sports Illustrated.

	W	SV	ERA	IP	H	BB	SO	BPI	$
1992 St. Louis NL	16	0	2.16	233	217	20	91	1.32	26
1993 Base Case	14	0	2.89	209	205	28	82	1.11	20

THIGPEN, BOBBY - White Sox - TR - Age 29
We've seen this before; look at the decline of Dan Plesac, once a premier closer, now just a decent middle reliever. Thigpen's fall has been from greater heights, but it just serves to illustrate that saves come mainly because the manager gives you the ball -- not because you're a great pitcher. Thigpen has always had a tendency to get hit hard; before, the Sox didn't have alternatives. Now there are at least two competitors, meaning Thigpen will never have the job to himself again.

	W	SV	ERA	IP	H	BB	SO	BPI	$
1992 Chicago AL	1	22	4.75	55	58	33	45	1.65	12
1993 Base Case	3	10	3.76	57	55	25	41	1.39	9

THOMAS, LARRY - White Sox - TL - Age 23
You have to love those guys who get midseason promotions. Thomas made it all the way up to Vancouver before the minor league season ended. Not overpowering, but good at moving the ball around, pitching inside, and changing speeds.

	W	SV	ERA	IP	H	BB	SO	BPI	$
1992 Sarasota A	5	0	1.62	55	44	7	50	0.92	
1992 Birmingham AA	8	0	1.94	120	102	30	72	1.10	

THOMAS, MIKE - Indians - TL - Age 23
Had a big year in the NY-Penn League in 1991 and then 20 saves in the SAL in 1991. Moving up slowly but steadily.

	W	SV	ERA	IP	H	BB	SO	BPI	$
1992 Rockford A	5	2	3.58	113	98	51	108	1.31	
1993 Base Case									

TIMLIN, MIKE - Blue Jays - TR - Age 27
Just your basic 90-MPH fastball. Timlin could reach a higher level quickly, if he just came up with a good

breaking pitch, or even a decent changeup.

	W	SV	ERA	IP	H	BB	SO	BPI	$
1992 Toronto AL	0	1	4.12	43	45	20	35	1.49	-
1993 Base Case	4	2	3.59	78	74	36	62	1.40	2

TOMLIN, RANDY - Pirates - TL - Age 26
He set a career high in victories in 1992 but was very inconsistent. He went through stretches where he was unbeatable and others where he was awful. The lack of consistency is a big reason why he has started just one game in the three National League Championship Series for the Pirates.

	W	SV	ERA	IP	H	BB	SO	BPI	$
1992 Pittsburgh NL	14	0	3.41	208	226	42	90	1.28	7
1993 Base Case	11	0	3.24	193	201	45	94	1.27	9

TORRES, SALOMON - Giants -TR - Age 21
Started last season 6-2, then lost his last eight decisions. Caution: He threw 210 innings at age 19 in '91.

	W	SV	ERA	IP	H	BB	SO	BPI	$
1992 Shreveport AA	6	0	4.21	162	167	34	151	1.24	

TRLICEK, RICK - Blue Jays - TR - Age 23
Potential closer, had 16 saves and a 2.41 ERA at AA Knoxville in 1991.

	W	SV	ERA	IP	H	BB	SO	BPI	$
1992 Syracuse AAA	1	1	4.36	43	37	31	35	1.57	
1992 Toronto AL	0	0	10.80	1	2	2	1	2.40	-
1993 Base Case	0	0	4.37	19	18	9	13	1.44	-

TROMBLEY, MIKE - Twins - TR - Age 25
Trombley has posted outstanding records with low ERA's and ratios everywhere he's pitched. The number of strikeouts per inning, and the strikeout/walk ratios are also very impressive. As far as rookie pitchers go, Trombley is a lower risk than others because of his impressive record and because he's pitching for a contender where he just won't pitch if he's not effective.

	W	SV	ERA	IP	H	BB	SO	BPI	$
1992 Portland AAA	10	0	3.65	165	149	58	138	1.25	
1992 Minnesota AL	3	0	3.30	46	43	17	38	1.29	1
1993 Base Case	8	0	3.63	103	96	37	78	1.29	4

TSAMIS, GEORGE - Twins - TL - Age 25
Tsamis is a lefty prospect who spent the past two years at AAA Portland trying to earn a Twins' roster spot. He posted high ratios in the two AAA years with poor K/BB and K/IP ratios. Tsamis is a high risk, and it's best to let someone else have him.

	W	SV	ERA	IP	H	BB	SO	BPI	$
1992 Portland AAA	10	0	3.66	165	195	51	71	1.49	

TURNER, MATT - Astros - TR - Age 26
Former Braves farmhand, still young enough to get some major league relief work; low value.

	W	SV	ERA	IP	H	BB	SO	BPI	$
1992 Tucson AAA	2	14	3.51	100	93	40	84	1.33	

VALDEZ, EFRAIN - Brewers - TL - Age 26
Has been let go by the Indians and Blue Jays, and did nothing in 1992 to lengthen his career.

	W	SV	ERA	IP	H	BB	SO	BPI	$
1992 Denver AAA	1	0	5.43	68	76	22	43	1.44	

VALDEZ, RAFAEL - Padres - TR - Age 24

Former shortstop, had two good years as a pitcher in A and AA leagues, and pitched for San Diego briefly in 1990. Missed almost all of 1991 due to injury. Not a factor for 1993.

	W	SV	ERA	IP	H	BB	SO	BPI	$
1992 Spokane A	1	0	4.15	34	41	19	34	1.76	
1992 Las Vegas AAA	2	0	6.14	14	19	7	12	1.85	

VALDEZ, SERGIO - Expos - TR - Age 27

Right back where he started his nondescript career with the Expos in 1986. Has always had a live arm. Shows good control in minors but it disappears in the majors against disciplined hitters.

	W	SV	ERA	IP	H	BB	SO	BPI	$
1992 Indianapolis AAA	4	0	3.75	62	59	13	41	1.16	
1992 Montreal NL	0	0	2.41	37	25	12	32	0.99	1
1993 Base Case	0	0	3.60	36	26	12	30	1.03	1

VALERA, JULIO - Mets - TR - Age 24

Acquired in the Dick Schofield deal with the Mets, Valera proved to be a steady pitcher with a fine live arm and was one of the bright spots for the Angels in an otherwise dismal 1992. He's got the stuff to be very effective, and he's been pitching against major leaguers since was age 15 in winter ball.

	W	SV	ERA	IP	H	BB	SO	BPI	$
1992 California AL	8	0	3.73	188	188	64	113	1.34	5
1993 Base Case	11	0	3.61	181	182	66	103	1.37	6

VAN POPPEL, TODD - Athletics - TR - Age 21

Another prime example of why you should pick hitters (preferably shortstops and center fielders) for your long-term prospects. Developed tendinitis in June and will miss about a year.

	W	SV	ERA	IP	H	BB	SO	BPI	$
1992 Tacoma AAA	4	0	3.97	45	44	35	29	1.76	

VASQUEZ, JULIAN - Angels - TR - Age 24

Vasquez was sent to the Angels by the Mets to complete the Dick Schofield trade. He was one of the best Mets relief prospects, and was outstanding at AA Binghamton. With Bryan Harvey gone, Vasquez could make the Angels bullpen at mid-season and get some saves.

	W	SV	ERA	IP	H	BB	SO	BPI	$
1992 Binghamton AA	2	17	1.35	27	17	7	24	0.89	
1992 Tidewater AAA	1	6	5.56	23	22	8	22	1.30	

VIOLA, FRANK - Red Sox - TL - Age 32

He can still pitch, and 238 innings pitched suggest his arm is sound. Be wary of lefties at Fenway Park.

	W	SV	ERA	IP	H	BB	SO	BPI	$
1992 Boston	13	0	3.44	238	214	89	121	1.27	12
1993 Base Case	13	0	3.65	231	230	76	123	1.32	10

VITKO, JOSEPH - Mets - TR - Age 23

Got 11 wins with a 2.24 ERA in high A-ball in 1991, after an 8-1 season with a 2.49 ERA in low A-ball in 1990.

	W	SV	ERA	IP	H	BB	SO	BPI	$
1992 Binghamton AA	12	0	3.49	165	163	53	90	1.31	
1992 New York NL	0	0	13.50	4	12	1	6	2.79	-
1993 Base Case	0	0	4.62	10	11	3	8	1.42	-

WAGNER, HECTOR - Royals - TR - Age 24
Almost made the team out of spring training 1991. Missed all of 1992 with shoulder surgery.

WAGNER, PAUL - Pirates - TR - Age 25
Never a highly-touted prospect, he showed much promise in a cameo appearance in 1992. He showed a live arm with a 95-mph fastball and was not intimidated by major league hitters. Though primarily a starter, he can also pitch out of the bullpen.

	W	SV	ERA	IP	H	BB	SO	BPI	$
1992 Carolina AA	6	0	3.03	122	104	47	101	1.24	
1992 Buffal AAA	3	0	5.49	39	51	14	19	1.67	
1992 Pittsburgh NL	2	0	0.69	13	9	5	5	1.08	0
1993 Base Case	2	0	3.50	14	14	5	6	1.31	0

WAINHOUSE, DAVE - Expos - TR - Age 25
Ex-Canadian Olympic team, Wainhouse is now Montreal's closer-in-training. He could appear and get a save or two in 1993 but won't displace John Wetteland, or even Mel Rojas.

	W	SV	ERA	IP	H	BB	SO	BPI	$
1992 Indianapolis AAA	5	21	4.11	46	48	24	37	1.56	
1993 Base Case	1	1	3.90	30	26	15	25	1.37	1

WAKEFIELD, TIM - Pirates - TR - Age 26
The rookie knuckleballer was one of the most remarkable stories of the 1992 season. In 1989, he was converted to pitching after flopping as a power-hitting first base prospect. Wakefield has extremely good control of the knuckleball and that is the key as hitters can't wait out walks.

	W	SV	ERA	IP	H	BB	SO	BPI	$
1992 Buffalo AAA	10	0	3.06	135	122	51	71	1.28	
1992 Pittsburgh NL	8	0	2.15	92	76	35	51	1.21	7
1993 Base Case	11	0	3.15	126	110	48	69	1.26	8

WALK, BOB - Pirates - TR - Age 36
Quietly, he has been one of the game's most consistent pitchers in recent years. In fact, he has put together six straight winning seasons. Always taken for granted and prone to groin pulls, Walk puts up solid numbers year after year.

	W	SV	ERA	IP	H	BB	SO	BPI	$
1992 Pittsburgh NL	10	2	3.20	135	132	43	60	1.30	6
1993 Base Case	7	1	3.72	133	129	42	62	1.29	3

WALKER, MIKE - Tigers - TR - Age 26
Got nine wins, 11 saves, and a 2.79 ERA at AA Canton in 1991, but struggled in AAA.

	W	SV	ERA	IP	H	BB	SO	BPI	$
1992 Toledo AAA	2	4	5.83	78	102	44	44	1.87	
1993 Base Case	0	0	5.89	28	35	14	14	1.73	-

WALKER, MIKE - Mariners - TR - Age 28
Started three games for the Seattle in 1992, but he's not a prospect. Hasn't had a good year since 1988.

WALL, DONNIE - Astros - TR - Age 25
Led the Astro minor league system in strikeouts in 1992. Has not been considered a top prospect. Should pitch at the AAA level in 1993 and a solid year could give him a shot at the majors.

	W	SV	ERA	IP	H	BB	SO	BPI	$
1992 Osceola A	3	0	2.63	41	37	8	30	1.10	
1992 Jackson AA	9	0	3.54	114	114	26	99	1.23	
1992 Tucson AAA	0	0	1.13	8	11	1	2	1.50	

WALTON, BRUCE - Athletics - TR - Age 30

Got 20 saves with a 1.35 ERA for AAA Tacoma in 1991, but has looked bad in two trials with Oakland.

	W	SV	ERA	IP	H	BB	SO	BPI	$
1992 Oakland AL	0	0	9.90	10.0	17	3	7	2.00	-
1993 Base Case	0	0	4.95	36	44	11	22	1.51	-

WAPNIK, STEVE - White Sox - TR - Age 27

Former Blue Jays prospect, has appeared with the Tigers and White Sox in 1990-1991 with mixed results. Not a big factor for 1993.

	W	SV	ERA	IP	H	BB	SO	BPI	$
1992 Vancouver AAA	4	1	4.42	71	75	48	59	1.73	

WARD, DUANE - Blue Jays - TR - Age 28

Ward has been stuck behind Tom Henke for five years. Most of Ward's saves have come in April-May, when Henke had slumps or injuries. For years it has been a standard sucker ploy to draft Ward in April, and then trade him on May 15 when he looked like an ace reliever. This year will be the year to keep him.

	W	SV	ERA	IP	H	BB	SO	BPI	$
1992 Toronto AL	7	12	1.95	101	76	39	103	1.13	19
1993 Base Case	6	20	2.46	102	76	34	114	1.08	28

WARING, JIM - Astros - TR - Age 23

Got a midseason promotion from low A to high A. Outstanding control.

	W	SV	ERA	IP	H	BB	SO	BPI	$
1992 Bulington A	11	0	2.21	122	100	19	104	0.97	
1992 Asheville A	1	0	0.45	20	11	4	20	0.75	

WASSENAAR, ROB - Twins - TR - Age 27

Has produced well at every minor league level, but doesn't figure prominently in the Twins' plans.

	W	SV	ERA	IP	H	BB	SO	BPI	$
1992 Portland AAA	6	5	3.50	90	96	33	60	1.43	

WATSON, ALLEN - Cardinals - TL - Age 22

One year after being a first-round draft pick, Watson climbed two rungs to Class AAA in 1992. He was voted the 10th-best prospect in the Class AA Southern League and the seventh-best prospect in the Class A Florida State League in a poll of league managers by Baseball America.

	W	SV	ERA	IP	H	BB	SO	BPI	$
1992 St. Petersburg A	5	0	1.91	90	81	18	80	1.10	
1992 Arkansas AA	8	0	2.15	96	77	23	93	1.04	
1992 Louisville AAA	1	0	1.46	12	8	5	9	1.08	

WAYNE, GARY - Twins - TL - Age 30

Wayne is a lefty setup man for Rick Aguilera and a situational pitcher frequently brought in to get a lefty batter out. He can give you some safe stats, but he doesn't pitch many innings.

	W	SV	ERA	IP	H	BB	SO	BPI	$
1992 Minnesota AL	3	0	2.63	48	46	19	29	1.35	1
1993 Base Case	3	0	2.91	43	41	17	26	1.34	2

WEATHERS, DAVE - Marlins - TR - Age 23

Good prospect with a live arm. Will get a chance to start for Florida. Best year was 1991 at AA Knoxville: 10 wins with a 2.45 ERA

	W	SV	ERA	IP	H	BB	SO	BPI	$
1992 Syracuse AAA	1	0	4.66	48	48	21	30	1.43	
1992 Toronto AL	0	0	8.10	3	5	2	3	2.10	-
1993 Base Case	8	0	3.94	158	160	61	90	1.39	1

WEGMAN, BILL - Brewers - TR - Age 30

Had his second consecutive injury-free season, making the Brewers' decision to give him a four-year contract look brilliant, at least for now. His arm problems (traceable to 15 complete games in A-ball as a 20-year-old) mean that he will never blow hitters away, but intelligence and control (1.9 BB per nine) are enough to sustain Wegman's success. Beware the injury history, however; few pitchers bounce back from 260-inning workloads these days.

	W	SV	ERA	IP	H	BB	SO	BPI	$
1992 Milwaukee	13	0	3.20	261	251	55	127	1.17	18
1993 Base Case	14	0	3.31	229	214	48	110	1.14	20

WELCH, BOB - Athletics - TR - Age 36

Still has good zip on the fastball, and uses the curve and forkball more every year. Welch is a smart veteran making the necessary adjustments and can remain productive for at least a couple more years.

	W	SV	ERA	IP	H	BB	SO	BPI	$
1992 Oakland	11	0	3.27	123	114	43	47	1.27	7
1993 Base Case	12	0	3.69	158	153	62	67	1.36	6

WELLS, DAVID - Blue Jays - TL - Age 29

Wells has good stuff but is notoriously out of shape. If he ever gets himself into top condition and gets a full-time starter's role, he can still be valuable.

	W	SV	ERA	IP	H	BB	SO	BPI	$
1992 Toronto AL	7	2	5.40	120	138	36	62	1.45	-
1993 Base Case	9	1	3.95	148	148	41	77	1.28	5

WENDELL, TURK - Cubs - TR - Age 25

Noted for his strange behavior, Wendell had a big minor league season in the Braves system in 1991, and then added a fine winter in the Puerto Rican league. Held back by injuries.

	W	SV	ERA	IP	H	BB	SO	BPI	$
1992 Iowa AAA	2	0	1.44	25	17	15	12	1.28	

WERTZ, BILL - Indians - TR - Age 26

Wertz is an older prospect who will not get to Cleveland unless the Tribe's excellent bullpen falls apart.

	W	SV	ERA	IP	H	BB	SO	BPI	$
1992 Canton AA	8	8	1.20	97	75	30	67	1.08	

WEST, DAVID - Phillies - TL - Age 28

Once regarded as a top prospect with great expectations, West has been struggling for years. He's very risky as a Rotisserie pitcher especially if he starts regularly.

	W	SV	ERA	IP	H	BB	SO	BPI	$
1992 Portland AAA	7	0	4.44	103	88	65	87	1.48	
1992 Minnesota AL	1	0	6.99	28	32	20	19	1.83	-
1993 Base Case	2	0	4.52	51	52	24	36	1.48	-

WESTON, MICKEY - Phillies - TR - Age 32
Produced ERA's of 2.23, 2.09, and 1.98 in three years of Triple-A competition 1988-1990, but failed in repeated trials with Orioles and Blue Jays. Now just a faded prospect.

	W	SV	ERA	IP	H	BB	SO	BPI	$
1992 Philadelphia NL	0	0	12.27	3	7	1	0	2.18	-

WETTELAND, JOHN - Expos - TR - Age 26
Felipe Alou told me in June 1992 that Wetteland would become a premier closer as soon as he began using fewer pitches per batter -- just so he would have enough left to go again the next day. Has always had a good arm and good stuff, but is now maturing both physically and mentally.

	W	SV	ERA	IP	H	BB	SO	BPI	$
1992 Montreal NL	4	37	2.92	83	64	36	99	1.20	34
1993 Base Case	3	36	2.73	59	45	27	70	1.21	31

WHISENANT, MATT - Phillies - TL - Age 23
This 21-year old may be the hardest thrower in the Philadelphia organization. If his control continues to improve will move up in the farm system rapidly.

	W	SV	ERA	IP	H	BB	SO	BPI	$
1992 Spartanburg A	11	0	3.23	150	117	85	151	1.34	

WHITE, GABE - Expos -TL - Age 21
Led the Class A Midwest League with 187 innings and 176 strikeouts in 1992. Has a live fastball, good mechanics and an outstanding mental approach. Montreal's first-round pick in '90.

	W	SV	ERA	IP	H	BB	SO	BPI	$
1992 Rockford A	14	0	2.84	187	148	61	176	1.12	

WHITEHURST, WALLY - Padres - TR - Age 28
A direct worker who doesn't like to waste pitches, Whitehurst always wanted to be a started, but failed in this role as soon as the Mets planted him firmly in the rotation. Now just a journeyman curveballer with good control.

	W	SV	ERA	IP	H	BB	SO	BPI	$
1992 New York NL	3	0	3.62	97	99	33	70	1.36	-
1993 Base Case	5	0	4.03	110	115	30	75	1.31	0

WHITESIDE, MATT - Rangers - TR - Age 25
His four saves for the Rangers capped a meteoric rise from obscurity through the minors in 1992. Whiteside was 33-for-33 in save situations at Tulsa, Oklahoma City and Texas. Despite this success, he is regarded as being better suited to the setup role than the closer role. With the Rangers, he allowed only 2 of 18 inherited runners to score.

	W	SV	ERA	IP	H	BB	SO	BPI	$
1992 Texas AL	1	4	1.93	28	26	11	13	1.32	3
1992 Okla. City AAA	1	8	0.79	11	7	3	13	0.91	
1992 Tulsa AA	0	21	2.41	34	31	3	30	0.98	
1993 Base Case	1	5	3.04	68	66	22	34	1.29	5

WICKANDER, KEVIN - Indians - TL - Age 28
Wickander is a lefty situational pitcher often brought in to face one lefty batter. He doesn't give you much.

	W	SV	ERA	IP	H	BB	SO	BPI	$
1992 Colo. Sp. AAA	0	2	1.64	11	4	6	18	0.91	
1992 Cleveland AL	2	1	3.07	41	39	28	38	1.63	-
1993 Base Case	2	2	3.44	55	56	28	34	1.53	-

WICKMAN, BOB - Yankees - TR - Age 24
Just one of the benefits from the Steve Sax trade. Working on a changeup to go with his 90-mph fastball and slider.

	W	SV	ERA	IP	H	BB	SO	BPI	$
1992 Columbus AAA	12	0	2.92	157	131	55	108	1.18	
1992 New York AL	6	0	4.11	50	51	20	21	1.41	0
1993 Base Case	5	0	3.82	92	93	36	45	1.40	0

WILKINS, DEAN - Expos - TR - Age 26
A second round pick in 1986, Wilkins quickly became a top minor league reliever but failed (7.84 ERA) in three trials with the Cubs and Astros.

WILLIAMS, BRIAN - Astros - TR - Age 24
1990 compensation draft pick for Kevin Bass has apparently made it to the majors to stay in second full season. Missed last four starts in 1992 after spraining his ankle as a pinch runner. Started the season at AAA Tucson after disappointing spring training when he couldn't control his breaking pitches. Made steady improvement in 1992. Should be in the rotation in 1993.

	W	SV	ERA	IP	H	BB	SO	BPI	$
1992 Tucson AAA	6	0	4.50	70	78	26	58	1.49	
1992 Houston NL	7	0	3.92	96	92	42	54	1.39	-
1993 Base Case	7	0	4.13	159	166	59	99	1.41	-

WILLIAMS, MIKE - Phillies - TR - Age 24
When injuries crippled the Phils' starting rotation in 1992, he was brought up and held his own. A late-round draft pick in 1991, he is only player drafted by Lee Thomas regime to appear in the majors.

	W	SV	ERA	IP	H	BB	SO	BPI	$
1992 Scranton AAA	9	0	2.43	92	84	30	59	1.24	
1992 Philadelphia NL	1	0	5.34	28	29	7	5	1.26	-
1993 Base Case	4	0	4.14	60	60	16	20	1.27	1

WILLIAMS, MITCH - Phillies - TL - Age 28
The Wild Thing managed 29 saves in 1992 but also blew 10 other save opportunities and had another high ERA as his career-long control problems (64 walks in 81 innings) continued to plague him.

	W	SV	ERA	IP	H	BB	SO	BPI	$
1992 Philadelphia NL	5	29	3.78	81	69	64	74	1.64	20
1993 Base Case	6	25	3.64	83	66	61	78	1.53	18

WILLIAMS, TODD - Dodgers - TR - Age 22
A submarine-style reliever, Williams was voted the Dodgers' minor league pitcher of the year. One look at his ratio raises concern, however. Williams will get a shot to save games at the AAA level in 1993.

	W	SV	ERA	IP	H	BB	SO	BPI	$
1992 San Antonio AA	7	13	3.48	44	47	23	35	1.59	

WILLIAMSON, MARK - Orioles - TR - Age 33
Williamson had elbow surgery early in the season and spent rehab time in the minors. Williamson can be a very effective reliever if he still has his fastball, but without it, he's like batting practice.

	W	SV	ERA	IP	H	BB	SO	BPI	$
1992 Hagerstown AA	0	0	4.91	15	13	2	8	1.02	
1992 Rochester AAA	0	2	0.00	4	2	0	1	0.50	
1992 Baltimore AL	0	1	0.96	19	16	10	14	1.39	0
1993 Base Case	2	1	3.37	47	48	20	32	1.44	0

WILLIS, CARL - Twins - TR - Age 32

Although he had a couple rough outings, Willis was a very effective middle reliever for the second consecutive year. His good control keeps his ratio down.

	W	SV	ERA	IP	H	BB	SO	BPI	$
1992 Minnesota AL	7	1	2.72	79	73	11	45	1.06	8
1993 Base Case	5	1	2.89	84	85	14	48	1.18	7

WILSON, STEVE - Dodgers - TL - Age 28

With good movement on the fastball, Wilson can be a highly effective lefty versus lefty situational reliever. But he hasn't had that good movement since he first came to the Dodgers in 1991.

	W	SV	ERA	IP	H	BB	SO	BPI	$
1992 Los Angeles NL	2	0	4.19	66	74	29	54	1.55	-
1993 Base Case	1	1	3.75	46	47	16	33	1.38	-

WILSON, TREVOR - Giants - TL - Age 26

Among established starters who haven't yet produced much Rotisserie value, Wilson is one of the better picks to break into the positive range in 1993. Has a good fastball and is learning to keep it down in the strike zone.

	W	SV	ERA	IP	H	BB	SO	BPI	$
1992 San Francisco NL	8	0	4.21	154	152	64	88	1.40	-
1993 Base Case	12	0	3.69	164	153	64	102	1.33	4

WITT, BOBBY - Athletics - TR - Age 28

The change of scenery means many will be tempted to play Russian roulette once again. This time, however, there may be only three bullets in the gun. He's gone to the best pitcher's park in the game, under the supervision of a superior pitching coach, pitching in front of a much better defense than he had in Texas. Nevertheless, he's still Bobby Witt. Under no circumstances is Witt anything more than a flyer for your last starter spot -- and if you can't drop healthy pitchers, maybe not even that. Just for fun, we isolated his Oakland stats below.

	W	SV	ERA	IP	H	BB	SO	BPI	$
1992 Texas AL	9	0	4.46	161	152	95	100	1.53	-
1992 Oakland AL	1	0	3.41	31	31	19	25	1.60	-
1992 Totals	10	0	4.29	193	183	114	125	1.54	-
1993 Base Case	6	0	3.90	145	142	79	104	1.52	-

WITT, MIKE - Yankees - TR - Age 32

Had elbow surgery in July 1991 to reconstruct a ligament. Pitched some rehab innings in the GCL. If the Yankees hadn't given up Dave Winfield to get him, they probably would have given up on Witt by now.

	W	SV	ERA	IP	H	BB	SO	BPI	$
1992 Yankees R	1	0	0.00	12	7	2	13	0.75	

WOHLERS, MARK - Braves - TR - Age 23

Braves fans are waiting for this strikeout wunderkind to get a full-time shot at the closer role. He may finally get that chance this year. Since 1990, 36% of the outs Wohlers has recorded have been strikeouts. He hasn't had good command of his blazing fastball yet in the majors. Once he does, Wohlers will challenge Rob Dibble for the title of fastest gun in the west.

	W	SV	ERA	IP	H	BB	SO	BPI	$
1992 Richmond AAA	0	9	3.93	34	32	17	33	1.43	
1992 Atlanta NL	1	4	2.55	35	28	14	17	1.19	3
1993 Base Case	2	15	2.69	36	29	16	19	1.26	14

WOODSON, KERRY - Mariners - TR - Age 23

He missed much of last season due to injuries. Anyone who makes it to the majors at his young age has to be good. In 1990, he was 8-6 with a 3.03 ERA at single-A. The next year he was only 4-6 but kept his ERA at 3.06 while moving up a level. Despite the two quality seasons as a starter, the Mariners moved him to relief last year. He continued to excel and should be a major league pitcher in 1993 or 1994.

	W	SV	ERA	IP	H	BB	SO	BPI	$
1992 Seattle AL	0	0	3.29	13	12	11	6	1.68	-
1993 Base Case	0	0	3.68	38	39	23	23	1.64	-

WORRELL, TIM - Padres - TR - Age - 25

Like his older brother Todd, this Worrell can be overpowering at times, as evidenced by a AAA no-hitter in his last start. He has been on the fast track, rising from A ball to AAA in the space of one and a half seasons. Look for him to get a few September starts.

	W	SV	ERA	IP	H	BB	SO	BPI	$
1992 Wichita AA	8	0	2.86	126	115	32	109	1.17	
1992 Las Vegas AAA	4	0	4.26	63	61	19	32	1.27	

WORRELL, TODD - Dodgers - TR - Age 33

Worrell knows he can perform at a very high level, and wants to be a closer. During spring training 1992, he told me was already back to 99% of his old peak form. Throws 90 MPH with one strikeout per inning; only problem is: Dodgers have never given anyone 30 saves in a season. Worrell has a clear shot at the LA franchise record.

	W	SV	ERA	IP	H	BB	SO	BPI	$
1992 St. Louis NL	5	3	2.11	64	45	25	64	1.09	7
1993 Base Case	3	20	2.43	59	42	25	54	1.14	20

YORK, MIKE - Pirates - TR - Age 28

Veteran farmhand in the Pittsburgh organization, was traded to Cleveland for Mitch Webster, then released by Indians and passed through Padres organization. Most noted for his 1990 callup and clutch start in the heat of the NL East race. You never know when it may happen again.

	W	SV	ERA	IP	H	BB	SO	BPI	$
1992 Las Vegas AAA	5	0	4.79	88	96	55	54	1.71	
1992 Buffalo AAA	4	0	3.06	32	31	20	20	1.58	

YOUNG, ANTHONY - Mets - TR - Age 27

The desperate, though well-intentioned conversion to closer looked good for about a month, but the wheels sure came off in September. It got to the point where he was blowing a save more often than not. The problem is simply that Young does not have a resilient arm and cannot pitch game after game. He was out there with no gas in the tank. In setup work he might be OK, but not closer duty.

	W	SV	ERA	IP	H	BB	SO	BPI	$
1992 New York NL	2	15	4.17	121	134	31	64	1.37	9
1993 Base Case	2	5	3.73	82	85	21	39	1.29	3

YOUNG, CLIFF - Angels - TL - Age 28

He has become part of the landscape at Edmonton. Best year was 1990. Got 28 major league appearances in 1990-1991, with fair results.

	W	SV	ERA	IP	H	BB	SO	BPI	$
1992 Edmonton AAA	10	0	5.59	143	174	42	104	1.50	

YOUNG, CURT - Yankees - TL - Age 32
In five starts for New York, Young was 3-0 with a 2.53 ERA, so of course they dropped him from the rotation. Actually, he was sidelined with a hamstring injury, found the rotation too crowded when he returned, and pitched badly in relief work. Decent comeback candidate for 1993.

	W	SV	ERA	IP	H	BB	SO	BPI	$
1992 Two Teams	4	0	3.99	68	80	17	20	1.43	0
1993 Base Case	6	0	4.11	69	70	24	24	1.36	1

YOUNG, MATT - Red Sox - TL - Age 34
Young is among the worst Rotisserie values in the major leagues. Lefties in Fenway must be very sharp, which Young isn't.

	W	SV	ERA	IP	H	BB	SO	BPI	$
1992 Boston AL	0	0	4.58	70	69	42	57	1.57	-
1993 Base Case	1	0	3.95	77	76	45	64	1.56	-

YOUNG, PETE - Expos - TR - Age 25
The stocky reliever has made a quick ascent through the Expos' farm system. He could become a useable pitcher, but it's doubtful he will ever be the closer type.

	W	SV	ERA	IP	H	BB	SO	BPI	$
1992 Indianapolis AAA	6	7	3.51	49	53	21	34	1.51	
1992 Montreal NL	0	0	3.98	20	18	9	11	1.33	-
1993 Base Case	1	0	3.93	34	36	16	22	1.51	-

ZAPPELLI, MARK - Angels - TR - Age 26
Had another good year at Midland, but always runs into trouble when he rises to Edmonton.

	W	SV	ERA	IP	H	BB	SO	BPI	$
1992 Midland AA	7	1	3.19	98	104	19	59	1.25	

ZAVARAS, CLINT - Mariners - TR - Age 26
Just after making it to the major leagues, he was DL'd for a full year in 1990. Comeback is going poorly.

	W	SV	ERA	IP	H	BB	SO	BPI	$
1992 Calgary AAA	1	0	13.17	13	24	12	5	2.72	
1992 Jacksonville AA	3	0	5.28	109	108	67	88	1.60	

ZURN, RICKY - Brewers - TR - Age 24
Large, hard thrower. Had a fine year at Peoria in 1991 but failed to make progress in 1992. Time is moving faster than Zurn now.

	W	SV	ERA	IP	H	BB	SO	BPI	$
1992 Beloit A	2	0	5.60	27.1	35	12	22	1.73	

John Benson
Wilton, Connecticut

Dear Reader:

Like me, do you follow baseball year round? That job will be especially difficult during 1993. We will be seeing more changes in major league rosters, and more news affecting player performance, than at any time in the past 30 years -- maybe more than ever!

The N.L. Expansion Draft created 50 new major league roster spots, and took players from both leagues to fill them, creating 50 vacancies in other franchises.

Almost 200 free agents went looking for new jobs. Some are still looking.

The *Benson Baseball Monthly* (formerly *Winning Rotisserie Baseball*) is the only publication that tells you all the implications of every player move, and lots more: player valuation and scouting methods, draft and auction strategies, roster management techniques , and league rules and scorekeeping. We have exclusive quotes and interviews from players, coaches, managers, and GM's, plus insightful analysis and predictions from dozens of top writers; the B.B. Monthly gives you a comprehensive vision of the future. Throughout the winter and spring and all year, we update you with all the expected changes in player performance for 1993. We watch every team closely always looking for affected players who don't get full coverage in the conventional baseball media. We have at least one writer covering every team, year round.

In addition to covering the news like no other publication, we'll be coming out with updated forecast stats periodically, as players change roles, get injured, demoted, or promoted. Every winter we have suggestions for new rules, and letters and essays from our own readers -- all the latest thinking for serious fans and pick-your-player contestants.

If you want to enjoy baseball news year round and stay ahead of the competition, get on board now. The monthly is 25 to 40 pages every month, and comes with an unconditional 100% money-back guarantee and 30-day return privilege on any issue. See the back page of this book for prices and how to order.

Best wishes for a happy and successful season. And please keep in touch, even if you're not buying anything. I read all my mail; although I don't have time to answer everyone, your thoughts are always appreciated.

Sincerely,

John B.

DIAMOND LIBRARY ORDER FORM

Title:	Quantity	Price	Total
The Rotisserie Baseball Annual 1993, by John Benson The biggest, most serious, most in-depth preview of the coming season available February 25, 1993	_____	$ 22.95	_____
Rotissserie Baseball A to Z, by John Benson Your complete player guide and who's who for 1993 available January 15, 1993	_____	15.95	_____
Rotisserie Baseball - Playing for Fun, by John Benson and Randall Baron All the essentials of getting organized and playing smart available January 15, 1993	_____	12.95	_____
Rotisserie Baseball - Playing for Blood, by John Benson and Randall Baron All the serious stuff: valuation, auction economics, roster management available February 25, 1993	_____	12.95	_____

Back issues of the **Rotisserie Baseball Annual:**

	Quantity	Price	Total
1989 First Edition, just 500 copies printed, limit one per customer	(1)	40.00	_____
1990, 1991, or 1992 -- each	_____	22.95	_____

John Benson's 1993 **Winning Rotisserie Draft Software** for IBM and compatibles
Two programs in one: player valuation module for any size league, any player
population, any dollar amounts PLUS draft manager program.

	Quantity	Price	Total
Comes with 50-page user manual. Specify disk size _____	_____	49.95	_____

John Benson's **Baseball Monthly** -- exclusive news, quotes, interviews,
latest developments in player valuation and performance forecasting,
periodic review and update of entire player population. Letters, opinions.

			Total
Sample issue $7 -- Six months $35 -- One year $59 -- Two years $99 (Canada add 10%)			_____
Shipping: $3 per book, $2 per software disk (Canada $5 per book, $4 per disk)			_____
		Order Total	_____

Call toll free, 24 hours/day **1-800-292-6338** for Mastercard and Visa orders
For customer service, questions or Canadian orders, call **203-834-0812**
Or write: Diamond Library, Wilton Center, P.O. Box 7302, Wilton, CT 06897

Please print your name _____ Address _____

City _____ State _____ Zip _____ Phone _____

Mastercard/Visa # _____ - _____ - _____ - _____ Exp _____ Signature _____

Please make check or M.O. payable to Diamond Library -- U.S. funds drawn on U.S. banks only, please